Perspectives on Career Transitioning of Students with Attention Deficit Hyperactivity Disorder (ADHD)

Boitumelo M. Diale
Sol Plaatje University, Kimberley, South Africa

Chiedu Eseadi
University of Johannesburg, South Africa

Published in the United States of America by
IGI Global Scientific Publishing
701 East Chocolate Avenue
Hershey, PA, 17033, USA
Tel: 717-533-8845
Fax: 717-533-8661
E-mail: cust@igi-global.com
Website: https://www.igi-global.com

Copyright © 2025 by IGI Global Scientific Publishing. All rights reserved. No part of this publication may be reproduced, stored or distributed in any form or by any means, electronic or mechanical, including photocopying, without written permission from the publisher.
Product or company names used in this set are for identification purposes only. Inclusion of the names of the products or companies does not indicate a claim of ownership by IGI Global Scientific Publishing of the trademark or registered trademark.

Library of Congress Cataloging-in-Publication Data

CIP PENDING

ISBN13: 9798369326350
EISBN13: 9798369326367

Vice President of Editorial: Melissa Wagner
Managing Editor of Acquisitions: Mikaela Felty
Managing Editor of Book Development: Jocelynn Hessler
Production Manager: Mike Brehm
Cover Design: Phillip Shickler

British Cataloguing in Publication Data
A Cataloguing in Publication record for this book is available from the British Library.

All work contributed to this book is new, previously-unpublished material.
The views expressed in this book are those of the authors, but not necessarily of the publisher.
This book contains information sourced from authentic and highly regarded references, with reasonable efforts made to ensure the reliability of the data and information presented. The authors, editors, and publisher believe the information in this book to be accurate and true as of the date of publication. Every effort has been made to trace and credit the copyright holders of all materials included. However, the authors, editors, and publisher cannot assume responsibility for the validity of all materials or the consequences of their use. Should any copyright material be found unacknowledged, please inform the publisher so that corrections may be made in future reprints.

Table of Contents

Preface v

Acknowledgement xii

Introduction xiii

Chapter 1
Inclusive School Teachers' Perspectives on Career Transition of Students With ADHD 1

Chapter 2
School Counselors' Perspectives on Theories and Techniques for Career Transition Counseling of Students With ADHD 39

Chapter 3
Teachers' Perspectives on the Effectiveness of Educational and Public Policies and Legislation in Promoting Career Transition of Students With ADHD 77

Chapter 4
Counselors' and Teachers' Perspectives on Psychological Interventions for Students With ADHD During Career Transitioning 113

Chapter 5
Educational Psychologists' Perspectives on Practice Guidelines for Students With ADHD During Career Transitioning 161

Chapter 6
Perspectives on School Support Services for Students With ADHD: Student Survey 197

Chapter 7
Perspectives on Assessment Tools for Evaluating Students With ADHD During Career Transitioning: Student Survey 243

Chapter 8
Exploring Career Counseling Models and Services for Students With ADHD:
Counselors' Perspectives 283

Chapter 9
Examining Barriers to Career Transition of Students With ADHD: Teachers
and Parents' Perspectives 327

Chapter 10
Determining Solutions to Challenges in the Career Transition of Students
With ADHD: Teachers' and Parents' Perspectives 363

About the Authors 405

Index 407

Preface

INTRODUCTION

As we engage with the intricate and shifting landscape of education and career development, it has become increasingly evident that students with Attention-Deficit/Hyperactivity Disorder (ADHD) face various challenges that can significantly affect their transition from school to the workforce. Complex barriers, misunderstood needs, and a lack of appropriate support systems often mark the journey for these individuals. ADHD is a neurodevelopmental disorder identified by symptoms of inattention, impulsivity, and hyperactivity, which have been connected to occupational preferences and work performance (Verheul et al., 2016a), as well as challenges in learning and academic performance (Mulholland, 2016). According to Weissenberger et al. (2017), ADHD can be seen as a lifelong neurodevelopmental disorder that is identified by its noticeable behavioral characteristics. According to Nadeau (2005), there is a growing recognition of ADHD as a common disorder that can have a substantial impact on workplace performance. Despite this awareness, many career counseling professionals lack the necessary training to guide individuals with ADHD in selecting careers or job positions that are well-suited to their individual strengths, weaknesses, ADHD traits, and co-occurring conditions. As noted by Samosh et al. (2024), individuals with ADHD are at an increased risk of being unemployed, underemployed, and experiencing poverty relative to their peers. In a longitudinal study comprising 7,905 individuals with ADHD, it was shown that an increase of one standard deviation in the polygenic risk score for ADHD correlates with a 32% rise in the probability of self-employment, alongside a 5% decline in yearly earnings; self-employment was responsible for 59% of the negative association observed between the polygenic risk score for ADHD and earnings (Patel et al., 2019). In accordance with a developmental psychopathology approach, ADHD is recognized as a condition that arises from the dynamic relationship between individuals and their environments (Lasky et al., 2016). In a previous study by Martin (2014), ADHD was found to significantly contribute to the variance in several academic adversities, such as failure to complete school assignments, suspensions, expulsions, transitions between schools, and repeating grades. The study further indicated that ADHD maintains a unique role in students' academic adversity, independent of numerous personal and contextual covariates.

Bordoff (2017) emphasized the difficulties associated with diagnosing and treating ADHD in students, attributing these challenges to the lack of reliable childhood histories, the constraints of neuropsychological assessment tools, and the possibility of individuals feigning the condition to gain benefits such as psychostimulants and academic accommodations. Norwalk et al. (2008) found a significant correlation between elevated ADHD symptoms and diminished levels of career decision-making self-efficacy, academic adjustment, study skills, and grade point average. Weyandt and DuPaul (2008) revealed that students with ADHD are at an increased risk for both academic and psychological difficulties when compared to the general student population, and the misuse of prescription stimulants is a challenge on various campuses. Thus, the issues faced by students with ADHD when preparing to enter the labor market are not solely academic; they are also closely linked to psychological, social, and environmental contexts. The available research on career transition for these students often lacks the depth and specificity needed to truly support their unique circumstances. This book intends to address this gap by providing a comprehensive analysis of perspectives on theories, strategies, policy matters, interventions, practice guidelines, and institutional support systems that are vital for ensuring a successful and smooth transition into the workforce for students with ADHD. One of the foremost issues faced by students with ADHD is the imperative to identify and utilize their strengths while managing their weaknesses. This entails an in-depth self-assessment and the careful selection of career paths that resonate with their interests and competencies. For instance, individuals prone to distraction may achieve success in careers that are particularly engaging, which can help lessen the influence of their distractibility. Also, some individuals with ADHD may find greater success in positions that involve physical movement, as this can serve to direct their energy and improve their focus. According to Antshel (2018), anecdotal reports from individuals with ADHD who pursue entrepreneurial activities indicate that their condition can provide significant benefits in their business efforts. This suggests that the traits and symptoms associated with ADHD may enhance rather than obstruct their entrepreneurial success.

This book project, "Perspectives on Career Transitioning of Students with Attention-Deficit/Hyperactivity Disorder", is a rigorously researched work aimed at addressing identified issues and providing a transformative resource for school counselors, educational psychologists, schoolteachers, parents, policymakers, researchers, and most importantly, the students themselves. This publication emerges from a research project conducted under the Global Excellence and Stature (GES) 4.0 Postdoctoral Research Fellowship. The subject of career transition for students with ADHD has gained significant attention in recent years as teachers, parents, school counselors, educational psychologists, researchers, and policymakers continue to seek ways to effectively support this student group. ADHD presents concerns which can affect a student's career transition. Nevertheless, students with ADHD often showcase creativity, resilience, and a distinctive viewpoint that can be beneficial in various professional fields. In fact, certain characteristics of ADHD, especially hyperactivity, can be advantageous, as they are associated with a greater tendency towards self-employment (Verheul et al., 2016b). Their transition from school to employment, however, is often hindered by numerous potential barriers, including social, emotional, academic, and systemic challenges. Achieving successful career transitions for students with ADHD necessitates collaborative efforts from all parties involved in their education and career transition. This book aims to explore these intricacies, providing insights from diverse perspectives and emphasizing potential strategies to promote the career transition of these students.

It has been shown that ADHD results in considerable direct and indirect costs that affect nations across the globe (Maia et al., 2015). Ornoy and Spivak (2019) indicated that the estimated treatment cost for an individual with ADHD, attributed to factors such as reduced educational achievement, increased criminal activity, involvement in vehicular accidents, and higher rates of substance abuse, amounted to 289,969 USD. In contrast, the estimated cost for optimal treatment was 41,667 USD. The benefit-cost ratio was calculated at 7.02, and even when considering a treatment success rate of only 50%, the ratio remained substantial at 3.51. Also, several countries have implemented different practices and policy frameworks to enhance inclusive education systems for students with special educational needs, including those with ADHD (*see* Mezzanotte, 2020). The educational and policy landscapes are pivotal in facilitating the transition for students with ADHD. While it is a policy requirement for schools to provide reasonable accommodations for students with ADHD, the quality and accessibility of these accommodations can vary greatly. This inconsistency may result in uncertainty and increased stress for these students during their career transition. Therefore, the involvement of schools, teachers, parents and policymakers is essential in this regard. Teachers' understanding of how ADHD affects students' career paths reveals the urgent need for early intervention and sustained support. ADHD impacts not just the learners but also their families and the educational setting from an early stage (Maree & Warnock, 2023). Promoting an understanding of the critical role of parental perception in shaping career transition decisions and the necessity for holistic interventions to address the enduring consequences of ADHD on career transition decisions is crucial. According to Majko (2017), students with ADHD are often misjudged by most teachers and parents, who may interpret their symptoms as intentional behaviors.

Existing frameworks designed to assist students with ADHD often prove insufficient in various crucial dimensions, thereby worsening the obstacles these students experience during their transition from school to the workforce. The prevailing understanding and perceptions surrounding career transition for students with ADHD also seem to be insufficient. This lack of insight impedes the creation of effective strategies and resources that cater to the specific career transition needs of these individuals. Furthermore, students with ADHD are most often stigmatized within the educational system. According to the findings of Thompson and Lefler (2015), stigma was related to the behaviors characteristic of ADHD but not to the diagnostic label. This stigma can follow them from elementary school through college and into their adult lives, making it challenging for them to feel included and appreciated. Bell et al. (2010) revealed that teachers with special education certification reported elevated ratings reflecting significant stigma perceptions. Nevertheless, the study found no correlation between years of teaching experience and stigma scores. Furthermore, the compulsion to medicate in order to adhere to societal expectations can result in harmful outcomes for students with ADHD, including emotional flatness and physical side effects (Madden, 2024), which can significantly impact their overall health and career prospects. Students with ADHD frequently encounter barriers in making career decisions, primarily due to issues related to sustained attention and effective planning. Although career counseling services exist, they may not always be sufficiently tailored to meet the transition needs of these individuals. For instance, students with ADHD could greatly benefit from career counseling approaches that incorporate visual tools and structured frameworks to enhance their focus during the decision-making process. Unfortunately, such resources are not consistently available, and many students may also struggle with the self-advocacy skills required to successfully manage their career transition. Students with ADHD also encounter obstacles in formulating long-term career goals, largely stemming from their difficulties with planning and organization. Career counselors can play a pivotal role by segmenting these students' long-term goals into smaller, attainable objectives, yet this assistance is not consistently available. Moreover, the lack of organizational resources, such as calendars and binders, can further impede their capacity to navigate career transition. The primary strategies for treatment involve psychostimulant medication, coaching, and educational accommodations (Weyandt & DuPaul, 2008). Shaw (2021) reported that while individuals with ADHD did engage in masking specific symptoms, their reactions to stigma were predominantly focused on self-acceptance. This included forming friendships with other neurodivergent individuals and adopting a positive perspective on ADHD. The institutional support available to students with ADHD, valid assessment tools, practice guidelines, and therapeutic interventions are often inadequate or poorly implemented. Consequently, students with ADHD do not obtain the required support for a smooth transition into their future careers.

This book project includes perspectives from schoolteachers, school counselors, educational psychologists, and parents who are directly involved in supporting students with ADHD as well as students themselves. The diverse viewpoints presented aim to create a well-rounded understanding of the complexities surrounding career transition for these students. The book examines not only the theoretical aspects of career transition but also interventions and support systems that can impact the career transition outcomes of students with ADHD. By presenting a diverse array of perspectives, this book seeks to empower teachers, counselors, educational psychologists, parents, and policymakers to make informed decisions that promote the successful career transition of students with ADHD. Structured into ten chapters, the book focuses on specific dimensions of career transitioning, showcasing the challenges and opportunities faced by students with ADHD during this crucial period. The policy and practical implications of the findings from this book project cannot be overemphasized. To improve the support systems for Nigerian students with ADHD, policymakers can implement a range of strategies that address the educational, social, and health needs of these students during their career transition. A policy should be tailored to establish public campaigns that support neurodiversity to alter social attitudes and lessen the stigma surrounding ADHD in Nigeria. These campaigns should involve educational efforts and awareness initiatives designed to enhance understanding and promote acceptance and career transition of individuals with ADHD. There is a necessity to designate funds for the support of disability and advocacy organizations that facilitate career transition planning and counseling, as well as other critical services for individuals with ADHD. Developing and implementing national frameworks for ADHD is essential, as they can serve as an evidence-based blueprint for clinical and educational practices, research, and policy execution. These frameworks should encompass collaborative care models that involve diverse school-based professionals and transition teams. There is also a need to intensify efforts to promote effective collaboration among schools, parents, transition service providers, and various stakeholders in the Nigerian school system. This should involve regular communication with parents, the active participation of school counselors or psychologists, and transition service providers to provide comprehensive career transition support for students with ADHD. It is important to equip teachers, early-career counselors and parents with the necessary training and resources to effectively assist students with ADHD as they navigate their career transition. This support should encompass workshops focused on behavioral management, organizational skills development, and techniques for reducing distractions while fostering positive behavior. Finally, it is crucial to provide schoolteachers, educational psychologists, parents, and school counselors with clear guidelines for responsive caregiving, service delivery, and advocacy aimed at enhancing career transition for students with ADHD

Organization of the Book

The book is organised into ten chapters, and its visualization is shown in Figure 1. The organization of the book is as follows:

Chapter 1 examines the perspectives of inclusive schoolteachers on the career transitions of students with ADHD. The chapter delves into the insights of inclusive schoolteachers who have firsthand experience working with students with ADHD.

Chapter 2 discusses theories and techniques for career transition counseling as perceived by school counselors. Here, we examine the perspectives on theories and techniques that school counselors use in career transition counseling.

Chapter 3 examines the effectiveness of educational policies and legislation as perceived by teachers. This chapter assesses the impact of educational policies and legislation on the career transition of students with ADHD from the perspective of teachers. It evaluates how current policies support or hinder the career transition of these students.

Chapter 4 explores psychological interventions for students with ADHD from the perspectives of school counselors and teachers. This chapter explores various interventions that school counselors and teachers use to support students with ADHD. It discusses the efficacy of various interventions within the context of career transition of students with ADHD.

Chapter 5 focuses on practice guidelines from the viewpoint of educational psychologists. This was considered necessary given that educational psychologists can provide useful insight into the practice guidelines for supporting students with ADHD in their career transition.

Chapter 6 assesses school support services based on student surveys. Here, we analyze the perceptions of students with ADHD regarding the support services provided by their schools. This chapter highlights what students find most helpful and what gaps exist in current support systems.

Chapter 7 focuses on the assessment tools used to support students with ADHD during their career transition. It discusses the perceived effectiveness of these tools using student surveys.

Chapter 8 investigates the perceived effectiveness of various career counseling models and services from the perspective of school counselors.

Chapter 9 addresses barriers to career transition as perceived by both teachers and parents.

Chapter 10 investigates solutions to the challenges identified through teachers' and parents' perspectives. It synthesizes the participants' insights to offer practical recommendations for schools, teachers, counselors, and families to support students with ADHD in their career transition.

Figure 1. Visualization of the book chapters

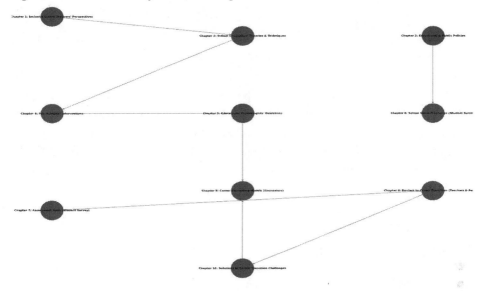

Boitumelo Molebogeng Diale
Sol Plaatje University, South Africa

Chiedu Eseadi
University of Johannesburg, South Africa

Acknowledgement

The authors express their sincere appreciation to the reviewers for their essential contributions, which have significantly enhanced the quality, coherence, and presentation of each chapter in this book. Additionally, the authors would like to recognize Dr. Batholomew Nwefuru, Dr. Faith Olanike Mesagan, and Dr. Chika O. Ujah for their invaluable expertise, insights, and guidance during the course of this book project.

Boitumelo Molebogeng Diale
Sol Plaatje University, South Africa

Chiedu Eseadi
University of Johannesburg, South Africa

Introduction

This research book project was developed as an aspect of a larger research project, "Perspectives on Career Transitioning of Students with Neurodiversity," and executed through the Global Excellence and Stature (GES) 4.0 Postdoctoral Research Fellowship awarded to Dr C Eseadi, with the mentoring and collaboration of Prof. BM Diale. This book is crafted to serve as a significant resource for school counselors, educational psychologists, schools, parents, researchers, transition specialists, special educators, and organizations dedicated to supporting students with ADHD in their career transition journey.

The publication titled "Perspectives on Career Transitioning of Students with ADHD" represents a significant and timely addition to the discourse surrounding career transition within inclusive education settings. The transition from school to the world of work is a critical goal for all students; however, for those with ADHD, this shift frequently necessitates additional support and understanding of their transition needs. This book consolidates a variety of viewpoints on navigating this transition, providing perspectives of students with ADHD, their teachers, counselors, educational psychologists, and their parents who support them in their career transition. Through various research methodologies, the authors provided an in-depth examination of the variables influencing perspectives concerning the career transition of students with ADHD. This book is an essential resource for teachers, counselors, educational psychologists, parents, and policymakers dedicated to promoting an inclusive society where every individual is afforded the chance to thrive. It serves as a clarion call for collective action to ensure that students with ADHD receive not only academic support but also the empowerment needed to realize their full potential in their careers and beyond.

Boitumelo Molebogeng Diale
Sol Plaatje University, South Africa

Chiedu Eseadi
University of Johannesburg, South Africa

Chapter 1
Inclusive School Teachers' Perspectives on Career Transition of Students With ADHD

ABSTRACT

The study investigates the perspectives of inclusive schoolteachers regarding the career transition of students with attention deficit hyperactivity disorder (ADHD) in Enugu State, Nigeria. Utilizing a survey research design, the research collected data from 38 inclusive schoolteachers through a questionnaire. The findings revealed that teachers hold moderately positive perspectives on the career transition of students with ADHD, with no significant differences based on gender, teaching experience, or school location. The study's major contribution lies in highlighting the uniformity of teachers' perspectives across various sociodemographic variables, suggesting that these factors do not significantly influence their views on supporting the career transition of these students. This insight is crucial for developing inclusive school practices and policies that support career transition for students with ADHD.

BACKGROUND

Attention-deficit/hyperactivity disorder (ADHD) is a neurodevelopmental disorder that influences an individual's ability to maintain focus, manage impulses, and regulate activity levels. This condition typically presents in childhood but can extend into adulthood, with symptoms that differ in intensity across individuals (Leahy, 2018; Hagan, 2019). Those with ADHD often face challenges related to inattention, hyperactivity, and impulsivity (Cleveland Clinic, 2023; Mayo Clinic Staff,

2019). Inattention may lead to difficulties in concentrating, following directions, and completing tasks, as well as a propensity to become easily distracted, struggle with listening, and frequently misplace belongings. Hyperactivity is characterized by excessive and often inappropriate physical activity, resulting in behaviors such as constant fidgeting, restlessness, an inability to remain still, and a persistent need for movement. Impulsivity is defined by actions taken without consideration of the consequences, which may include interrupting others, blurting out answers, or engaging in risky behaviors without adequate thought (American Psychiatric Association, 2013; National Institute of Mental Health, 2024). ADHD is divided into three main categories: the predominantly inattentive type, which is primarily associated with inattention; the predominantly hyperactive/impulsive type, which is characterized by hyperactivity and impulsivity; and the combined type, which features a combination of symptoms from both categories (American Psychiatric Association, 2013; Mayo Clinic Staff, 2019; National Institute of Mental Health, 2024). Evaluating inclusive schoolteachers' viewpoints regarding students with ADHD can allow for the identification of their potential strengths and weaknesses in guiding these students toward suitable career options (Ronson, 2021). In inclusive educational settings, teachers exhibit a range of viewpoints, attitudes, and beliefs concerning the career transitions of students with ADHD. The evaluation of these viewpoints can take into account various factors, such as gender differences, the length of teaching experience, and the school's geographical context. Prior professional or personal interactions with individuals, family members, or students with ADHD (Klopfer et al., 2019), as well as values (Sunko et al., 2021), stigma, societal biases, and negative perceptions (Bell et al., 2011), along with the level of knowledge and comprehension of ADHD, are significant factors that can influence teachers' perspectives towards the inclusion of these students in their classrooms. Mohammed et al. (2023) indicated that a heightened negative perception of ADHD among the teachers may stem from their increased awareness of the challenges associated with the condition. The study further posits that enhancing teachers' recognition of ADHD and equipping them with knowledge of alternative, effective, and non-physical strategies for managing student behavior could significantly improve the educational experiences of affected students. Aquilina's (2017) study demonstrated that teachers' beliefs about the likelihood of students achieving considerable academic improvement through instructional support were significantly influenced by the nature of the disability. In terms of their own willingness to provide instructional support to students with disabilities, teacher evaluations did not reveal significant differences across various disabilities. Additionally, when questioned about whether students were failing academically due to insufficient effort, teachers' reports remained consistent. In contrast, when asked if they thought students had agency over their academic success, the ratings varied significantly according to the type of disability. According to Ewe (2019), students with ADHD often perceive their relationship with teachers as less intimate than that of their non-ADHD peers, a view that is corroborated by teachers' own observations. As a result, teachers frequently encounter lower levels of emotional engagement, decreased collaboration, and heightened conflicts with students with ADHD compared to their interactions with other students. This rejection from teachers can serve as a critical risk factor, leading not only to academic adversities but also to social isolation and rejection from peers, which can result in diminished self-esteem and feelings of loneliness.

It is crucial to recognize that teachers are often shaped by the beliefs they have cultivated throughout their lives and their continuous experiences within the classroom (Massé et al., 2022). Metzger et al. (2020) reported that teachers tend to assess students with ADHD as performing below their grade level, while they are less inclined to recognize these students as exceeding grade-level performance, irrespective of their actual capabilities as evidenced by subject-specific assessments. Oronoz (2011) identified several challenges faced by teachers in relation to ADHD, including difficulties in defining the condition, managing it within the classroom environment, determining the appropriate protocol for diagnosing students and experiencing insufficient parental engagement. The study also revealed a lack of consensus among teachers regarding ADHD as an actual disease and the associated treatment alternatives. The findings from Sciutto et al. (2016) demonstrated a positive correlation between the length of teaching experience and prior interactions with students with ADHD and teachers' knowledge of the disorder. It further uncovered potential differences in how male and female teachers perceive students with ADHD, which contrasts with the majority of existing literature that focuses on the gender of the students rather than that of the teachers (Coles et al., 2010; Gershon & Gershon, 2002; Abikoff et al., 2002; Isaksson et al., 2020). Nonetheless, DuPaul et al., (2020) found that the gender of the teacher did not significantly influence perceptions of students with ADHD, while years of experience were deemed significant across all evaluated dimensions. Genetic factors were observed to have a more significant effect on boys whom female teachers instructed compared to those taught by male teachers, while the opposite was noted for girls (De Zeeuw et al., 2015). Despite the fact that ADHD is affecting approximately 7.6% to 8.7% of the school-age population (Adewuya & Famuyiwa, 2007; Ambuabunos et al., 2011), several teachers in Nigeria seems lack the essential knowledge and training required to effectively support students exhibiting ADHD symptoms in mainstream schools (Ojionuka, 2007; Mohammed et al., 2023). Insufficient understanding on the part of schoolteachers can foster negative sentiments towards these students, which may impede their career transition. This research highlights the substantial influence of factors such as experience, age, and qualifications on schoolteachers' perspectives of students with ADHD during career transition.

Teachers' perceptions, ability to anticipate favorable results, and attitudes towards students with ADHD can have a substantial impact on the students' overall assessments of their academic and professional capacities (Krtek et al., 2022). Given the multitude of factors that can shape differing viewpoints, it is vital to understand teachers' perspectives to effectively tackle the challenge of establishing an appropriate professional pathway for students with ADHD (Onyishi, 2022; Wilson et al., 2023; Youssef et al., 2015). Teachers in developing nations, such as Nigeria, may possess distinct perspectives on the career transition of students with ADHD within inclusive school settings. Inclusive schoolteachers acknowledge the difficulties in assisting students with disabilities to attain career transition success (Eseadi & Diale, 2024). Analyzing teachers' perspectives will aid in identifying areas that require improvement for them to be able to support students with ADHD during career transitioning. For inclusion to be realized, it is essential for inclusive schoolteachers to adopt a viewpoint that recognizes students with ADHD as fully capable of managing their learning within an inclusive environment (Baluyot, 2024). In Nigeria, there is a rising concern about the educational system's capacity to adequately address the transition needs of students with ADHD because many teachers are not equipped with the appropriate training, resources, or institutional support to effectively guide these students (Angwaomaodoko, 2023; Garuba, 2003; Ogba et al., 2020). This inadequacy may result in unfavorable career outcomes for many students with ADHD, further contributing to their marginalization in the employment sector. Most teachers do possess critical insights about career transition strategies and the difficulties faced by students with ADHD, but prior studies have overlooked their viewpoints. A thorough understanding of how these teachers perceive their role in the career transition of students with ADHD is essential; otherwise, initiatives aimed at enhancing career transition outcomes for students with ADHD may lack coherence and effectiveness. The objective of this study, therefore, is to examine the perspectives of teachers in Nigerian inclusive schools, with the goal of understanding how these perspectives influence the career transitions of students with ADHD.

Research Objectives

1. To ascertain the general perspectives of inclusive schoolteachers on the career transition of students with ADHD.
2. To determine whether male and female inclusive schoolteachers differ in their perspectives on the career transition of students with ADHD.
3. To ascertain whether work experience influences inclusive schoolteachers' perception of the career transition of students with ADHD.
4. To determine whether rural and urban inclusive schoolteachers differ in their perspectives on the career transition of students with ADHD.

Research Questions

1. What are the general perspectives of inclusive schoolteachers on the career transition of students with ADHD?
2. Do male and female inclusive schoolteachers significantly differ in their perspectives on the career transition of students with ADHD?
3. Does work experience influence inclusive schoolteachers' perspectives on the career transition of students with ADHD?
4. Are there significant differences between rural and urban inclusive schoolteachers in their perspectives on the career transition of students with ADHD?

Theoretical Framework

The Social Cognitive Career Theory (SCCT) by Lent et al. (1994; 2002) offers a theoretical framework for analyzing the perspectives of inclusive schoolteachers and their impact on the career transitions of students with ADHD. According to Brown and Lent (2023), the SCCT framework comprises interrelated models, each incorporating a shared set of social cognitive variables, characteristics of other individuals, and contextual factors within its foundational assumptions. These models assume that beliefs in self-efficacy and expectations regarding outcomes serve as fundamental motivators for various dimensions of educational and vocational behavior. Consequently, they act as psychological precursors influencing the interests individuals cultivate, the career aspirations they pursue, the decisions they make, the persistence they exhibit in their choices, the quality of their performance, and the satisfaction they derive from their academic and professional experiences (Lent et al., 1994; Wang, et al., 2022). The SCCT is grounded in Bandura's Social Cognitive Theory (Nabavi & Bijandi, 2012), highlighting the interplay between individual characteristics, such as ADHD, and environmental influences, including teacher attitudes, which are pivotal in shaping career development and transitions. Bandura's theory offers a conceptual structure for comprehending, forecasting, and modifying human behavior (Drucker, 2012). The SCCT aims to explore the influences of culture, gender, genetic predispositions, social environments, and unforeseen life events that may interact with and potentially overshadow the impact of career-related decisions (Aliero & Aliero, 2023). SCCT suggests that contextual factors might enhance task-specific self-efficacy, outcome expectations, and career goals (Lent et al., 1994). Teachers are pivotal personalities in the learning environments of students, and their views have an essential function in influencing students' career transition (see Figure 1). According to Meoli et al. (2020), SCCT focuses on the process by which an individual forms professional interests and ultimately chooses a career decision. Within the scope of this research, SCCT is particularly significant in elucidating how teachers' perspectives, as influential figures in school settings, directly affect the self-efficacy, career interests, and expectations of students with ADHD—factors that are essential for successful career transitions. The fundamental assertion drawn from the theory is that environmental factors, particularly teacher attitudes, are crucial in shaping students' self-efficacy and career-related behaviors. SCCT suggests that teachers' perceptions can either facilitate or obstruct the development of positive career self-efficacy in students with ADHD, thereby affecting their capacity to manage career transitions effectively. Teachers who maintain affirmative views about students with ADHD are more likely to foster supportive learning environments, consequently bolstering the students' confidence in their professional success. SCCT also serves as a valuable theory for examining how gender may function as a contextual variable influencing teachers' perception of students with ADHD. The theory recognizes that personal attributes, including gender, can interact with environmental factors to shape career-related outcomes. Thus, gender may affect how teachers perceive and respond to students with ADHD, thereby impacting the support provided during career transitions. SCCT further highlights the influence of prior experiences on an individual's self-efficacy and behavior. Experienced inclusive schoolteachers are likely to have cultivated more effective strategies for aiding students with ADHD, which may foster a more optimistic view regarding their potential for career transitions. In contrast, less experienced schoolteachers might lack confidence in their capacity to support these students, leading to a more negative outlook. Drawing from the theory, we argue that it emphasizes the significance of contextual factors in influencing the accessibility of resources and the mindsets of individuals in those settings. As a result, inclusive schoolteachers in rural areas may encounter unique challenges and possess different viewpoints than their urban peers, shaped by the socio-economic and educational circumstances of their institutions. Thus, SCCT can provide insight into how differences in gender, teaching experience and contextual variations may affect teachers' perceptions of students with ADHD as they navigate their career transition in inclusive school settings.

Figure 1. Framework of the study

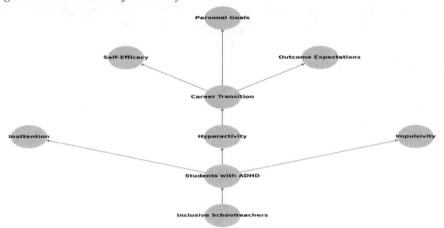

METHODOLOGY

Ethics Statement

Ethical approval for this study was obtained from the relevant institutional review boards. First, it received approval from the Research Ethics Committee of the Faculty of Education, University of Nigeria. It also received additional ethical approval from the Faculty of Education Research Ethics Committee at the University of Johannesburg, South Africa (Sem 2-2020-057). Informed consent was secured from participants. We assured confidentiality and clarified participants' right to withdraw from the study at any given time.

Research Design and Approach

This study used a survey research design by adopting a quantitative research approach. Bhattacherjee (2012) characterizes survey research as a design that employs standardized questionnaires or interviews to systematically gather data regarding individuals' preferences, thoughts, and behaviors. Akman (2023) emphasized that this design is particularly effective for gaining insights into the characteristics, interests, opinions, or beliefs of a specific group. The size of the survey sample is crucial in this context. Ponto (2015) noted that survey research can incorporate quantitative methods (such as questionnaires with numerical ratings), qualitative methods (such as open-ended questions), or a combination of both (known as mixed methods). Our study utilizes a quantitative research approach to examine inclusive schoolteachers' perspectives on the career transition of students with ADHD.

Research Paradigm

This study is grounded in the positivist research paradigm. Proponents of positivism assert that there exists a singular reality that can be quantified and comprehended through quantitative methodologies (Abbadia, 2022). Jansen (2023) pointed out that the foundation of positivism lies in the conviction that knowledge is derived from objective observations and measurements. Our research has embraced the positivist research paradigm, which helps to establish explanatory connections or causal relationships that ultimately facilitate the prediction and management of the phenomena under examination (Park et al., 2020). The selection of methods aligns with the particular goals and questions posed by the study.

Study Area

This research was conducted in Enugu State, located in Southeast Nigeria. Enugu State is situated in the eastern region of Nigeria, bordered to the south by Abia State and Imo State, to the east by Ebonyi State, to the north-east by Benue State, to the north-west by Kogi State, and to the west by Anambra State (Amalu et al., 2018). The capital city of the state is Enugu.

Population and Sampling

The study involves inclusive schoolteachers from public secondary schools. A total of 38 inclusive schoolteachers were selected using purposive and convenience sampling techniques. Purposive sampling and convenience sampling are classified as nonprobability sampling techniques utilized by researchers to select a sample of subjects or units from a given population (Etikan et al., 2016). A purposive sample is characterized by specific traits that are pertinent to the objectives of the study (Andrade, 2021). In contrast, the convenience sampling method involves gathering data from a readily accessible and available group of individuals (Simkus, 2023). This technique offers several advantages, such as cost-effectiveness, reduced time requirements, and ease of implementation (Golzar et al., 2022). Given the nature and objectives of the research topic, a combination of Purposive Sampling and Convenience Sampling techniques was employed to enhance the reliability of the results. Teachers who met certain criteria (from public secondary schools) and were available for participation were carefully chosen. A total of 19 male teachers and

19 female teachers were chosen. There were 12 male and 12 female teachers from rural schools, whereas there were 7 male and 7 female teachers from urban schools. The participants' mean age was 41.13±6.00.

Data Collection

The data was gathered through the use of a questionnaire. The researchers received assistance from two postgraduate students to complete the data collection process. The Inclusive School Teachers' Perspectives on Career Transition and ADHD Questionnaire (ISTPCQ), which was used for data collection, is an 18-item scale, ranging from Strongly disagree (1) to Strongly Agree (5), which measures teachers' awareness and beliefs in supporting career transitioning of students with ADHD. High scores signify positive perceptions. Some examples of item statements in the questionnaire are: 'I am aware of the career transition needs of students with ADHD', I feel that students with ADHD are given equal opportunities in career-related activities at school', and 'I think that students with ADHD have the potential to excel in various career paths.' The ISTPCQ has an internal consistency reliability of 0.68 Cronbach's alpha in the current study.

Data Analysis

Statistical analysis was conducted using Jeffreys' Amazing Statistics Program software (JASP), version 0.18.3. JASP represents a significant advancement in statistical software. This program is a free, multi-platform, open-source statistics package (Gangemi et al., 2024) that encompasses both fundamental and sophisticated statistical methodologies. JASP has several innovative features in its user interface; results are displayed instantly as users modify their selections, the output is visually appealing and minimalist, adhering to the principle of progressive disclosure, and analyses can be subjected to peer review without the necessity of a syntax (Love et al., 2019). The study further adopts descriptive statistics to summarize the sociodemographic data, while ANOVA was used to analyze the research questions at a .05 significance level. ANOVA is a statistical method employed to assess the variances among the means of various groups (Henson, 2015; Stoker et al., 2020). This technique is utilized in numerous situations to ascertain whether there are significant differences between the means of distinct groups.

FINDINGS

Table 1. Mean analysis of perspectives of inclusive schoolteachers on the career transition of students with ADHD

Questionnaire	Mean	SE of Mean	95% CI Upper Lower	SD	CV	Skewness	SE of Skewness
ISTPCQ	3.061	.061	3.187 2.944	.379	.124	.091	.383

In Table 1, the total mean score reflecting the perspectives of inclusive schoolteachers is 3.061. The confidence interval spans from 2.944 to 3.187. The standard error is .061, which is relatively small, suggesting that the sample mean serves as a dependable estimate of the population mean. The standard deviation (SD) is .379. The coefficient of variation (CV) stands at .124, which is considered low. The skewness value is .091, suggesting that the distribution of perspectives is nearly symmetrical. These results imply that inclusive schoolteachers generally maintain moderately positive perspectives regarding the career transition of students with ADHD, as evidenced by the mean score being slightly above the midpoint of the scale. The narrow confidence interval and low standard deviation indicate that these perspectives are consistently shared among the surveyed teachers. The low coefficient of variation and skewness further reinforces the uniformity and symmetry of the responses. In Figure 2, the mean distribution of the teachers' perspectives is further illustrated using a distribution plot.

Figure 2. Distribution plot of perspectives of inclusive schoolteachers

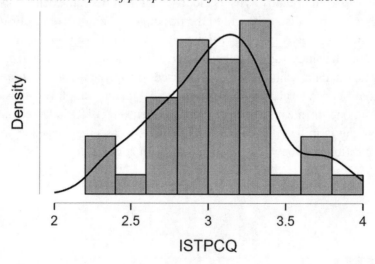

Table 2. Mean analysis of perspectives of inclusive schoolteachers on the career transition of students with ADHD by sociodemographic variables

Gender	Experience	Location	N	Mean	SD	SE	Coefficient of variation
Female	Early career teachers	Rural school	3	2.98	.51	.296	.172
		Urban school	4	3.14	.22	.108	.069
	Experienced teachers	Rural school	9	3.14	.39	.129	.123
		Urban school	3	3.04	.13	.074	.042
Male	Early career teachers	Rural school	6	3.18	.45	.183	.141
		Urban school	5	2.91	.49	.217	.167
	Experienced teachers	Rural school	6	3.03	.45	.182	.148
		Urban school	2	2.83	.24	.167	.083

Table 2 indicates the mean analysis of teachers' perspectives towards the career transition of students with ADHD by gender, work experience and school location. Table 2 presents the mean analysis of perspectives of inclusive schoolteachers on the career transition of students with ADHD, categorized by gender, teaching experience, and school location. Early-career female teachers in rural schools had a mean perspective score of 2.98 (SD=.51), while those in urban schools had a mean score of 3.14 (SD=.22). Experienced female teachers in rural schools had a mean score of 3.14 (SD=.387), while those in urban schools had a mean score of 3.04 (SD=.13). Early-career male teachers in rural schools had a mean perspective score of 3.18 (SD=.45), while those in urban schools had a mean score of 2.91 (SD=.49). Experienced male teachers in rural schools had a mean score of 3.03 (SD=.45), and those in urban schools had a mean score of 2.83 (SD=.24).

Table 3. Analysis of variance for perspectives of inclusive schoolteachers on the career transition of students with ADHD by gender, work experience and school location

Cases	Sum of Squares	df	Mean Square	F	p
Gender	2.028	1	2.028	.310	.58
Experience	.343	1	.343	.053	.82
Location	2.827	1	2.827	.432	.52
Gender Experience	1.433	1	1.433	.219	.64
Gender Location	5.072	1	5.072	.776	.39
Experience Location	.831	1	.831	.127	.72
Gender Experience Location	2.157	1	2.157	.330	.57
Residuals	196.125	30	6.538		

Table 3 shows the analysis of variance (ANOVA) results for gender, work experience and school location differences. The results showed that there was no significant difference between male and female teachers in their perspectives on the career transition of students with ADHD, $F(1,30)=.310$, $p=.58$. It was also shown that there was no significant influence of work experience on teachers' perspectives on the career transition of students with ADHD, $F(1,30)=.053$, $p=.82$. Furthermore, there was no significant difference in perspectives between rural and urban teachers regarding the career transition of students with ADHD, $F(1,30)=.432$, $p=.52$.

DISCUSSION

This study aimed to explore how variables, including the teacher's gender, location, and years of experience, may shape their perspectives on the career transition of students with ADHD. The study found that there was no significant difference between male and female teachers in their perspectives on the career transition of students with ADHD. This is consistent with De Zeeuw et al. (2015) who indicated that teachers possess well-informed perspectives regarding general childhood behavior for both boys and girls, enabling them to more accurately evaluate normative behaviors associated with specific ages and genders. Rollins (2005) indicated that teachers exhibit a consistent understanding of children's behavior, regardless of the children's socioeconomic status, gender, or ethnicity. On the other hand, Lawrence et al. (2017) observed that both gender and cultural background significantly influence teachers' perceptions of students with ADHD. According to Schultz and Evans (2012), women and younger teachers generally provide more severe ratings on average than their male and older colleagues. Most existing studies have concentrated on how the gender of students with ADHD impacts teachers' perceptions of inattentiveness, hyperactivity, or oppositional behaviors, and how these perceptions influence teachers' evaluations of children's challenges and their referral recommendations (Gaub & Carlson, 1997; Abikoff et al., 2002; Gershon, 2005; Bauermeister et al., 2007; Groenewald et al., 2009; Coles et al., 2010). Therefore, there is a need for more research to explore how the gender of teachers might affect their perspectives on students with ADHD during the career transition process.

Our study further revealed that there was no significant influence of work experience on teachers' perspectives on the career transition of students with ADHD. Ronson's (2021) study showed that teachers who have accumulated more years of experience and have instructed a larger number of students with ADHD demonstrated increased confidence and improved their teaching strategies. Results from Gehrman (2013) identified significant differences among teachers based on their years of teaching experience, specifically between those who have taught for 20 years or less and those who have taught for 21 years or more. Vereb and DiPerna (2004) found that there were positive associations between teachers' comprehension of ADHD, their years of experience working with ADHD students, and their training. A study by Girio and Owens (2009) indicates that the level of experience among teachers was a significant predictor of acceptability, with those possessing greater experience showing attitudes of acceptability. Furthermore, Ojionuka (2016) revealed that the educational qualifications and teaching experience of teachers did not correlate with an improvement in their overall knowledge of ADHD. Although these observations may hold validity, our study does not support the notion that the duration of teaching experience significantly influences teachers' perspectives on the career transitions of students with ADHD. The research by Frigerio et al. (2014) presents that the perceptions of Italian teachers regarding the disorder were mixed, and there was no significant relationship between their teaching experience and their knowledge or perceptions of ADHD. The provision of specialized information regarding ADHD had a limited effect on shaping their perceptions. Further analysis regarding the influence of teachers' years of experience revealed a positive correlation with their knowledge of ADHD (Sciutto et al., 2000), not necessarily their perception of the career transition of students with ADHD.

In this research, no notable differences were found in the perspectives of rural and urban inclusive schoolteachers concerning the career transition of students with ADHD. Our study is consistent with the conclusions drawn by Faizan et al. (2021), which indicated that there were no notable differences in knowledge, practices, and attitudes regarding ADHD among various groups, including schoolteachers from urban and rural areas, male and female teachers, as well as those from public and private institutions. While there may exist underlying disparities in the training levels, exposure, and opportunities available to teachers, a study examining the ADHD support training program revealed that urban teachers exhibited a higher overall knowledge level prior to the training (Jongh & Wium, 2021). When provided with comparable conditions and opportunities, geographical location may not serve as an impediment. Location did not significantly affect teachers' perceptions regarding the support for students; the majority maintained a positive attitude towards these students (Mulholland et al., 2023). Robinson (2017) revealed that in the UK, parents and teachers are more inclined to connect behavioral difficulties and their influence on social acceptance in their perspectives of children and students with ADHD. Whereas US parents and teachers seemed to focus more on the implications of ADHD for academic achievement. This observation highlights a cultural difference in perceptions of ADHD, which may have yielded different results. The study did not explore whether the outcomes would vary based on whether participants were from rural or urban areas.

The result of this study also noted that inclusive schoolteachers generally maintain moderately positive perspectives regarding the career transition of students with ADHD. Ojok and Wormnaes (2012) revealed a modestly favorable attitude of teachers towards educating students with ADHD in an inclusive classroom. The analysis conducted from the perspectives of teachers revealed that teachers who exhibit favorable behaviors towards these students diagnosed with ADHD are generally more knowledgeable, confident, and experienced in training related to managing ADHD-related attitudes (Moon, 2016). Similarly, Toma (2010) found that their study participants demonstrated a positive disposition towards ADHD. The study further indicated that the highest educational qualifications of teachers, their years of experience in mainstream settings, their experience with teaching children diagnosed with ADHD, and the frequency of their participation in educational activities were linked to the scores on knowledge and attitudes. Labrinopoulou (2022) revealed that a positive and moderate relationship was found between the number of years of teaching and the belief that general education teachers cannot effectively meet the special needs of children. The findings of Labrinopoulou (2022) generally suggest that the majority of participants (preschool teachers) hold either positive or neutral attitudes towards students with ADHD in their classrooms. Other studies (Chiner & Cardona, 2013; Ojok & Wormnaes, 2012; Esteen, 2019) also suggests that when teachers hold a positive discernment of the part they play in the lives of students with ADHD, as well as considering their personal, work-life experiences and knowledge, it significantly boosts their rapport and their effectiveness in accommodating the interest of students with ADHD.

Syed and Hussein (2010) highlighted that teachers' understanding and awareness of ADHD significantly improved following their participation in targeted ADHD training. When teachers engage in workshops and seminars, their attitudes towards inclusive education tend to improve positively. This change may be attributed to the knowledge and awareness gained through these experiences, as it is plausible that their attitudes were previously neutral or even negative. However, the post-training analysis in another study showed no statistically significant differences in knowledge acquisition following the training (Jongh & Wium, 2021). One possible explanation is that before the training, the teachers possessed substantial knowledge regarding ADHD and had developed effective strategies to address its associated challenges. Sluiter et al. (2019) revealed that the attitudes of teachers are often shaped more by their personal encounters than by professional and scientific literature. Meanwhile, Memisevic and Hodzic (2011) opined that fifty per cent of teachers support the concept of inclusion. While this suggests a degree of optimism, the teachers involved in the research also highlighted a significant shortfall in the support necessary to adequately tackle the challenges associated with inclusion. On the other hand, some studies (Rakap & Kaczmarek, 2010; Boyle et al., 2013) revealed that a significant proportion of teachers had unfavorable views regarding the integration of students who have disabilities into mainstream school settings. Clarke (2014) also opined that teachers typically hold a negative perception of students diagnosed with ADHD. Other research indicated a lack of adequate knowledge and moderately tolerant attitudes among teachers concerning ADHD (Dessie et al., 2021). This skepticism can be attributed to a lack of understanding and the anticipated stress that may arise from managing students with ADHD in a conventional classroom. Study shows many teachers express that they have not received sufficient training to effectively support and instruct children with ADHD (Martinussen et al., 2011). It is also crucial to emphasize that policies have been implemented to address the needs of these teachers and safeguard the interests of students diagnosed with ADHD. At the international level, Article 29 of the United Nations Convention on the Rights of the Child (UNCRC) aims to eliminate all forms of marginalization affecting children (The United Nations Convention on the Rights of the Child, 1989). However, many young individuals, particularly those with ADHD, continue to experience marginalization within the educational system (Franklyn & Dharan, 2021). Article 29 of UNCRC stipulates that a child's education should foster the development of their mind, body, and talents to their fullest potential. African and regional legislations have attempted to address the concerns of these students, as reflected in the African Union Agenda 2063 and Nigeria's National Development Plan. Our findings contribute to the realization of the African Union Agenda of 2063 and the National Development Plan in a certain way. The African Union Agenda 2063 is designed to achieve its vision of inclusive and sustainable development (African Union, 2015). The National Development Plan succeeds the Economic Recovery and Growth Plan (Anam et al., 2024). This Plan is structured around four strategic objectives: to create a robust foundation for a diversified economy; to invest in essential physical, financial, scientific, and innovative infrastructure; to establish a solid framework that enhances capacities for security and good governance; and to foster a vibrant, educated, and healthy population (Federal Ministry of Finance, Budget and National Planning, 2021). While many of these objectives have yet to be realized, the nation remains optimistic. Our study promotes inclusivity in the educational setting to ensure that teachers in their schools positively view all students with ADHD.

Our finding suggests a shared understanding among teachers regarding the career transition of students with ADHD. The shared perspective can contribute to the promotion of an inclusive education environment. One significant factor that can promote this is the implementation of teacher training programs that incorporate career transition modules concerning students with disabilities. A study by Hossennia et al. (2020) indicated that teachers possess a commendable understanding of ADHD and attributed it to educational interventions that have notably enhanced their knowledge, attitudes, and approaches to managing students with ADHD. However, teachers need further interactive experiences and practical classroom training to fully understand the importance of inclusion and the methods for creating an inclusive learning environment (Leyser et al., 2011; Hossennia et al., 2020; Elvia, 2022). The teacher is one of the key individuals who can facilitate the success of these students (Hapsari et al., 2020). Krtek et al. (2022) showed that the nature of the relationship between teachers and students with ADHD is correlated with the behaviors of these students, the teacher's ambivalent feelings, the teacher's understanding of ADHD, and their beliefs concerning the causes of ADHD behaviors, along with the teaching methods and approaches employed in the classroom. Similarly, data regarding teacher expectations indicated that special education teachers tended to lower expectations for students more frequently than their general education counterparts. Nevertheless, general education teachers also acknowledged a reduction in expectations for students with ADHD when compared to those who are typically developing (Hustus et al., 2020).

Given the increasing prevalence of students with ADHD, it is essential for teachers to undergo specialized and advanced training focused on recognizing the signs and symptoms of ADHD in order to effectively apply targeted teaching strategies to promote career transition (Guerra et al., 2017). Evidence from the prior study suggests that a significant number of teachers lacked access to any preparation curriculum addressing the needs of students with ADHD in their teacher training programs. ADHD-focused teacher training programs can significantly enhance teachers' understanding of ADHD, foster a supportive classroom atmosphere, and develop strategies to manage challenging behaviors (Ward et al., 2022), thereby leading to a more positive approach towards these students. When teachers participate in similar training initiatives, it can facilitate a collective positive attitude towards aiding students with ADHD in their career transition process. However, there remains a necessity for continuous professional development programs for teachers to recognize and address the unique career transition needs of these students within inclusive classrooms. Limitations of this study include its small sample size and geographic location. The research was conducted in Enugu state, Nigeria, which represents a location populated by the Igbos. The perspective of teachers may differ in other regions. A larger number of participants would have been better. With a larger number and more geographical settings, future researchers can deduce a better understanding of teachers' perspectives on the career transition of students with ADHD. An important limitation of this study was that the study focused only on gender, teaching experience, or school location to decipher the perspectives of inclusive schoolteachers on the career transition of students with ADHD. In subsequent studies, researchers can discuss other factors such as age, level of education, and race. It is crucial to initiate training programs that can improve teachers' abilities to effectively manage the career transition needs of students with ADHD in inclusive classrooms. Future studies may examine how the perspectives of inclusive schoolteachers influence the career decisions of students with ADHD, adopting a broader participant base that encompasses other regions of Nigeria.

CONCLUSIONS

This research sheds light on the perspectives of inclusive schoolteachers regarding the career transition of students with ADHD. A key aspect of this study is its examination of how various sociodemographic factors, including gender, work experience, and school location, shape teachers' opinions on this issue. The study concludes that inclusive schoolteachers generally maintain moderately positive perspectives towards the career transition of students with ADHD. The study indicated a consistency in the teachers' perspectives across gender, work experience, or school location. This uniformity suggests that policies and practices concerning career transition for students with ADHD could benefit from a standardized approach rather than one tailored to specific teacher demographics. While the moderately positive perspectives reflect a supportive stance, there remains an opportunity for improvement in training and resources to better equip teachers in assisting students with ADHD. Future research could explore how teachers' perspectives change over time and the implications of these changes on the career transition of students with ADHD. Qualitative methods could be employed to gain a deeper understanding of teachers' experiences in supporting these students during their career transition. There is a need for training programs aimed at enhancing teachers' capabilities in facilitating career transitions for students with ADHD. Furthermore, expanding this research to encompass a wider geographic area beyond Enugu State, Nigeria, could help ascertain whether these findings are applicable in diverse cultural and educational contexts.

REFERENCES

Abbadia, J. (2022, October 3). Research Paradigm: An Introduction with Examples. *Mind the Graph Blog.* https://mindthegraph.com/blog/research-paradigm/

Abikoff, H. B., Jensen, P. S., Arnold, L. L. E., Hoza, B., Hechtman, L., Pollack, S., Martin, D., Alvir, J., March, J. S., Hinshaw, S., Vitiello, B., Newcorn, J., Greiner, A., Cantwell, D. P., Conners, C. K., Elliott, G., Greenhill, L. L., Kraemer, H., Pelham, W. E.Jr, & Wigal, T. (2002). Observed Classroom Behavior of Children with ADHD: Relationship to Gender and Comorbidity. *Journal of Abnormal Child Psychology*, 30(4), 349–359. DOI: 10.1023/A:1015713807297 PMID: 12109488

Adewuya, A. O., & Famuyiwa, O. O. (2007). Attention deficit hyperactivity disorder among Nigerian primary school children: Prevalence and co-morbid conditions. *European Child & Adolescent Psychiatry*, 16(1), 10–15. DOI: 10.1007/s00787-006-0569-9 PMID: 17136303

African Union. (2015, September). *Agenda 2063 The Africa We Want.* https://au.int/sites/default/files/documents/33126-doc-framework_document_book.pdf

Akman, S. (2023, July 03). *What is survey design: Definition, methods & good examples.* https://forms.app/en/blog/survey-design

Aliero, B. U., & Aliero, H. S. (2023). A Study of Perception of Secondary School Students on the Impact of School Counselors in Career Choice: A case study of Yauri Local Government Area of Kebbi State. *African Journal of Humanities and Contemporary Education Research*, 10(1), 259–275.

Amalu, T., Otop, O. O., Oko, U., & Oko-Isu, P. E. (2018). Spatial Distribution and Patronage of Ecotourism Attractions in Enugu State, Nigeria. *Sustainable Geoscience and Geotourism*, 2, 1–15. . DOI: 10.18052/www.scipress.com/SGG.2.1

Ambuabunos, E. A., Ofevwe, E. G., & Ibadin, M. O. (2011). Community survey of attention-deficit/hyperactivity disorder among primary school pupils in Benin City, Nigeria. *Annals of African Medicine*, 10(2), 91–96. DOI: 10.4103/1596-3519.82065 PMID: 21691013

American Psychiatric Association. (2013). *Diagnostic and statistical manual of mental disorders* (5th ed.)., DOI: 10.1176/appi.books.9780890425596

Anam, B. E., Ijim, U. A., Ironbar, V. E., Otu, A. P., Duke, O. O., & Achuk Eba, M.-B. (2024). Economic recovery and growth plan, economic sustainability plan and national development plan (2021-2025): The Nigerian experience under President Muhammadu Buhari. *Cogent Social Sciences*, 10(1), 2289600. DOI: 10.1080/23311886.2023.2289600

Andrade, C. (2021). The Inconvenient Truth About Convenience and Purposive Samples. *Indian Journal of Psychological Medicine*, 43(1), 86–88. DOI: 10.1177/0253717620977000 PMID: 34349313

Angwaomaodoko, E. A. (2023). The challenges and opportunities of inclusive education in Nigeria. *Traektoriâ Nauki*, 9(7), 1001–1009. DOI: 10.22178/pos.94-1

Aquilina, A. (2017). Is Teacher Stigma Associated with the Delivery of Instructional Supports to Students with Disabilities? (Master's Thesis, University of Alberta). DOI: 10.7939/R37941782

Baluyot, L. (2024). Inclusive Classrooms and ADHD: Exploring Collaborative Practices and Academic Achievement. *International Multidisciplinary Journal of Research for Innovation, Sustainability, and Excellence*, 1(5), 333–340.

Bauermeister, J. J., Shrout, P. E., Chávez, L., Rubio-Stipec, M., Ramírez, R., Padilla, L., Anderson, A., García, P., & Canino, G. (2007). ADHD and gender: Are risks and sequela of ADHD the same for boys and girls? *Journal of Child Psychology and Psychiatry, and Allied Disciplines*, 48(8), 831–839. DOI: 10.1111/j.1469-7610.2007.01750.x PMID: 17683455

Bell, L., Long, S., Garvan, C., & Bussing, R. (2011). The impact of teacher credentials on ADHD Stigma Perceptions. *Psychology in the Schools*, 48(2), 184–197. DOI: 10.1002/pits.20536

Bhattacherjee, A. (2012). *Social science research: Principles, methods, and practices* (2nd ed.). Anol Bhattacherjee.

Boyle, C., Topping, K., & Jindal-Snape, D. (2013). Teachers' attitudes towards inclusion in high schools. *Teachers and Teaching*, 19(5), 527–542. DOI: 10.1080/13540602.2013.827361

Brown, S. D., & Lent, R. W. (2023). Social cognitive career theory. In Walsh, W. B., Flores, L. Y., Hartung, P. J., & Leong, F. T. L. (Eds.), *Career psychology: Models, concepts, and counseling for meaningful employment* (pp. 37–57). American Psychological Association., DOI: 10.1037/0000339-003

Chiner, E., & Cardona, M. C. (2013). Inclusive education in Spain: How do skills, resources, and supports affect regular education teachers' perceptions of inclusion? *International Journal of Inclusive Education*, 17(5), 526–541. DOI: 10.1080/13603116.2012.689864

Clarke, T. (2014). Correlation between teachers' perceptions of students with Attention Deficit Hyperactivity Disorder and use of supportive instructional strategies [Capella University].

Cleveland Clinic. (2023, February 22). Attention-Deficit/Hyperactivity Disorder (ADHD). https://my.clevelandclinic.org/health/diseases/4784-attention-deficithyperactivity-disorder-adhd

Coles, E. K., Slavec, J., Bernstein, M., & Baroni, E. (2010). Exploring the Gender Gap in Referrals for Children With ADHD and Other Disruptive Behavior Disorders. *Journal of Attention Disorders*, 16(2), 101–108. DOI: 10.1177/1087054710381481 PMID: 20837979

de Jongh, M., & Wium, A.-M. (2021). Attention deficit hyperactivity disorder: Training outcomes for Grade R teachers in an urban and semi-rural context. *South African Journal of Childhood Education*, 11(1), 1–11. DOI: 10.4102/sajce.v11i1.894

De Zeeuw, E. L., van Beijsterveldt, C. E. M., Lubke, G. H., Glasner, T. J., & Boomsma, D. I. (2015). Childhood ODD and ADHD Behavior: The Effect of Classroom Sharing, Gender, Teacher Gender and Their Interactions. *Behavior Genetics*, 45(4), 394–408. DOI: 10.1007/s10519-015-9712-z PMID: 25711757

Dessie, M., Techane, M. A., Tesfaye, B., & Gebeyehu, D. A. (2021). Elementary school teachers knowledge and attitude towards attention deficit-hyperactivity disorder in Gondar, Ethiopia: A multi-institutional study. *Child and Adolescent Psychiatry and Mental Health*, 15(1), 16. DOI: 10.1186/s13034-021-00371-9 PMID: 33827642

Drucker, M. V. (2012). Attention deficit hyperactivity disorder and career ideation: An application of hope theory and social cognitive career theory. https://scholarworks.smith.edu/theses/905/

DuPaul, G. J., Fu, Q., Anastopoulos, A. D., Reid, R., & Power, T. J. (2020). ADHD Parent and Teacher Symptom Ratings: Differential Item Functioning across Gender, Age, Race, and Ethnicity. *Journal of Abnormal Child Psychology*, 48(5), 679–691. DOI: 10.1007/s10802-020-00618-7 PMID: 31938952

Elvia, B. (2022). *General Education Teachers' Knowledge on Attention Deficit Hyperactivity Disorder.* [Alliant International University].

Eseadi, C., & Diale, B. M. (2024). *Perspectives on Career Transitioning of Students with Hearing Impairments*. IGI Global., DOI: 10.4018/979-8-3693-2631-2

Esteen, B. A. (2019). *Exploring the Experiences of Middle School Teachers Supporting Learners with ADHD: A Qualitative Study*. [Northcentral University].

Etikan, I., Musa, S. A., & Alkassim, R. S. (2016). Comparison of Convenience Sampling and Purposive Sampling. *American Journal of Theoretical and Applied Statistics*, 5(1), 1–4. DOI: 10.11648/j.ajtas.20160501.11

Ewe, L. P. (2019). ADHD symptoms and the teacher–student relationship: A systematic literature review. *Emotional & Behavioural Difficulties*, 24(2), 136–155. DOI: 10.1080/13632752.2019.1597562

Faizan, M., Shah, S., Shah, S., Seema, S., & Naz, S. (2021). Knowledge, Attitudes, And Practices Of Primary School Teachers Towards Adhd Students. *Humanities & Social Sciences Reviews*, 9(3), 1258–1265. DOI: 10.18510/hssr.2021.93124

Federal Ministry of Finance, Budget and National Planning. (2021). *National Development Plan (NDP 2021 – 2025)*. https://nationalplanning.gov.ng/wp-content/uploads/2021/12/NDP-2021-2025_AA_FINAL_PRINTING.pdf

Franklyn, R., & Dharan, V. (2021). Teacher Awareness and Responsivity–Perspectives of students with ADHD. *International Journal of Student Voice*, 9(1), 1–25.

Frigerio, A., Montali, L., & Marzocchi, G. M. (2014). Italian Teachers' Knowledge and Perception of Attention Deficit Hyperactivity Disorder (ADHD). *International Journal of School & Educational Psychology*. https://www.tandfonline.com/doi/abs/10.1080/21683603.2013.878677

Gangemi, A., Fabio, R. A., Suriano, R., De Luca, R., Marra, A., Tomo, M., & Calabrò, R. S. (2024). Does Transcranial Direct Current Stimulation Affect Potential P300-Related Events in Vascular Dementia? Considerations from a Pilot Study. *Biomedicines*, 12(6), 1290. DOI: 10.3390/biomedicines12061290 PMID: 38927497

Garuba, A. (2003). Inclusive education in the 21st century: Challenges and opportunities for Nigeria. *Asia Pacific Disability Rehabilitation Journal*, 14(2), 191–200.

Gaub, M., & Carlson, C. L. (1997). Gender Differences in ADHD: A Meta-Analysis and Critical Review. *Journal of the American Academy of Child and Adolescent Psychiatry*, 36(8), 1036–1045. DOI: 10.1097/00004583-199708000-00011 PMID: 9256583

Gehrman, D. R. (2013). *General Education Teachers' Perceptions of Students with ADHD and Professional Development.* (Doctoral dissertation, University of Wisconsin--Stout).

Gershon, J. (2005). Gender Differences in ADHD. *The ADHD Report*, 10(4), 8–16. Advance online publication. DOI: 10.1521/adhd.10.4.8.22991

Gershon, J., & Gershon, J. (2002). A meta-analytic review of gender differences in ADHD. *Journal of Attention Disorders*, 5(3), 143–154. DOI: 10.1177/108705470200500302 PMID: 11911007

Girio, E. L., & Owens, J. S. (2009). Teacher Acceptability of Evidence-Based and Promising Treatments for Children with Attention-Deficit/Hyperactivity Disorder. *School Mental Health*, 1(1), 16–25. DOI: 10.1007/s12310-008-9001-6

Golzar, J., Noor, S., & Tajik, O. (2022). Convenience Sampling. *International Journal of Education & Language Studies*, 1(2), 72–77. DOI: 10.22034/ijels.2022.162981

Groenewald, C., Emond, A., & Sayal, K. (2009). Recognition and referral of girls with Attention Deficit Hyperactivity Disorder: Case vignette study. *Child: Care, Health and Development*, 35(6), 767–772. DOI: 10.1111/j.1365-2214.2009.00984.x PMID: 19531118

Guerra, F., Tiwari, A., Das, A., Cavazos Vela, J., & Sharma, M. (2017). Examining teachers' understanding of attention deficit hyperactivity disorder. *Journal of Research in Special Educational Needs*, 17(4), 247–256. DOI: 10.1111/1471-3802.12382

Hagan, S. (2019). The difference between child and adult attention-deficit/hyperactivity disorder. *Mental Health Matters*, 6(4), 12–14. DOI: 10.10520/EJC-18ef62b242

Hapsari, I. I., Iskandarsyah, A., Joefiani, P., & Siregar, J. R. (2020). Teacher and problem in student with ADHD in Indonesia: A case study. *The Qualitative Report*, 25(11), 4104–4126. DOI: 10.46743/2160-3715/2020.4381

Henson, R. N. (2015). Analysis of Variance (ANOVA). In *Brain Mapping* (pp. 477–481). Elsevier. DOI: 10.1016/B978-0-12-397025-1.00319-5

Hossennia, M., Mazaheri, M. A., & Heidari, Z. (2020). The Effect of An Educational Intervention on Teachers' Knowledge, Attitude, and Behavior regarding Attention Deficit Hyperactivity Disorder (ADHD). ResearchSquare. DOI: 10.21203/rs.3.rs-56749/v1

Hustus, C. L., Evans, S. W., Owens, J. S., Benson, K., Hetrick, A. A., Kipperman, K., & DuPaul, G. J. (2020). An evaluation of 504 and individualized education programs for high school students with attention deficit hyperactivity disorder. *School Psychology Review*, 49(3), 333–345. DOI: 10.1080/2372966X.2020.1777830

Isaksson, J., Ruchkin, V., & Lindblad, F. (2020). Unseen and Stressed? Gender Differences in Parent and Teacher Ratings of ADHD Symptoms and Associations With Perceived Stress in Children With ADHD. *Journal of Attention Disorders*, 24(11), 1565–1569. DOI: 10.1177/1087054716658381 PMID: 27401240

Jansen, D. (2023, June 15). Research Philosophy & Paradigms: Positivism, Interpretivism & Pragmatism. *Grad Coach*. https://gradcoach.com/research-philosophy/

Klopfer, K. M., Scott, K., Jenkins, J., & Ducharme, J. (2019). Effect of Preservice Classroom Management Training on Attitudes and Skills for Teaching Children With Emotional and Behavioral Problems: A Randomized Control Trial. *Teacher Education and Special Education*, 42(1), 49–66. DOI: 10.1177/0888406417735877

Krtek, A., Malinakova, K., Rudnicka, R. K., Pesoutova, M., Zovincova, V., Meier, Z., Tavel, P., & Trnka, R. (2022). Ambivalent bonds, positive and negative emotions, and expectations in teachers' perceptions of relationship with their students with ADHD. *International Journal of Qualitative Studies on Health and Well-being*, 17(1), 2088456. DOI: 10.1080/17482631.2022.2088456 PMID: 35711126

Labrinopoulou, M. (2022). The Views of Preschool Teachers on the Integration of Children with Attention Deficit Hyperactivity Disorder (ADHD) in Kindergarten. *OAlib*, 9(8), 8. Advance online publication. DOI: 10.4236/oalib.1109136

Lawrence, K., Estrada, R. D., & McCormick, J. (2017). Teachers' Experiences With and Perceptions of Students With Attention Deficit/hyperactivity Disorder. *Journal of Pediatric Nursing*, 36, 141–148. DOI: 10.1016/j.pedn.2017.06.010 PMID: 28888495

Leahy, L. G. (2018). Diagnosis and treatment of ADHD in children vs adults: What nurses should know. *Archives of Psychiatric Nursing*, 32(6), 890–895. DOI: 10.1016/j.apnu.2018.06.013 PMID: 30454634

Lent, R. W., Brown, S. D., & Hackett, G. (1994). Toward a unifying social cognitive theory of career and academic interest, choice, and performance. *Journal of Vocational Behavior*, 45(1), 79–122. DOI: 10.1006/jvbe.1994.1027

Lent, R. W., Brown, S. D., & Hackett, G. (2002). Social Cognitive Career Theory. In *Career Choice and Development* (4th ed., pp. 255–311). John Wiley & Sons.

Leyser, Y., Greenberger, L., Sharoni, V., & Vogel, G. (2011). Students with Disabilities In Teacher Education: Changes In Faculty Attitudes Toward Accommodations Over Ten Years. *International Journal of Special Education*, 26(1), 162–174.

Love, J., Selker, R., Marsman, M., Jamil, T., Dropmann, D., Verhagen, J., & Wagenmakers, E. J. (2019). JASP: Graphical statistical software for common statistical designs. *Journal of Statistical Software*, 88(2), 1–17. DOI: 10.18637/jss.v088.i02

Martinussen, R., Tannock, R., & Chaban, P. (2011). Teachers' Reported Use of Instructional and Behavior Management Practices for Students with Behavior Problems: Relationship to Role and Level of Training in ADHD. *Child and Youth Care Forum*, 40(3), 193–210. DOI: 10.1007/s10566-010-9130-6

Massé, L., Nadeau, M.-F., Gaudreau, N., Nadeau, S., Gauthier, C., & Lessard, A. (2022). Pre-service Teachers' Attitudes toward Students With Behavioral Difficulties: Associations With Individual and Education Program Characteristics. *Frontiers in Education*, 7, 846223. Advance online publication. DOI: 10.3389/feduc.2022.846223

Mayo Clinic Staff. (2019, June 25). Attention-deficit/hyperactivity disorder (ADHD) in children. https://www.mayoclinic.org/diseases-conditions/adhd/symptoms-causes/syc-20350889

Memisevic, H., & Hodzic, S. (2011). Teachers' attitudes towards inclusion of students with intellectual disability in Bosnia and Herzegovina. *International Journal of Inclusive Education*, 15(7), 699–710. DOI: 10.1080/13603110903184001

Meoli, A., Fini, R., Sobrero, M., & Wiklund, J. (2020). How entrepreneurial intentions influence entrepreneurial career choices: The moderating influence of social context. *Journal of Business Venturing*, 35(3), 105982. DOI: 10.1016/j.jbusvent.2019.105982

Metzger, A. N., & Hamilton, L. T. (2021). The stigma of ADHD: Teacher ratings of labeled students. *Sociological Perspectives*, 64(2), 258–279. DOI: 10.1177/0731121420937739

Mohammed, M., Bella-Awusah, T., Adedokun, B., Lagunju, I., & Ani, C. (2023). Effectiveness of a training programme on the knowledge and perception of Attention-Deficit Hyperactivity Disorder among primary school teachers in Kano, Nigeria. *International Journal of Mental Health*, 0(0), 1–15. DOI: 10.1080/00207411.2023.2253397

Mulholland, S., Cumming, T. M., & Lee, J. (2023). Accurately Assessing Teacher ADHD-Specific Attitudes Using the Scale for ADHD-Specific Attitudes. *Journal of Attention Disorders*, 27(5), 554–568. DOI: 10.1177/10870547231153938 PMID: 36843350

Nabavi, R. T., & Bijandi, M. S. (2012). Bandura's Social Learning Theory & Social Cognitive Learning Theory.https://www.researchgate.net/publication/267750204 _Bandura's_Social_Learning_Theory_Social_Cognitive_Learning_Theory National Institute of Mental Health (2024, September).Attention-Deficit/Hyperactivity Disorder. https://www.nimh.nih.gov/health/topics/attention-deficit-hyperactivity -disorder-adhd

Ogba, F. N., Ugodulunwa, C. A., & Igu, N. C. (2020). Assessment of Training Needs of Teachers and Administrators for Effective Inclusive Education Delivery in Secondary Schools in South East Nigeria. *The International Journal of Educational Leadership Preparation*, 15(1), 72–91.

Ojionuka, A. N. (2016). *Nigerian Educators' Attention Deficit Hyperactivity Disorder Knowledge and Classroom Behavior Management Practices*. [Doctoral Dissertation, Walden University]. https://scholarworks.waldenu.edu/dissertations/2224

Ojok, P., & Wormnaes, S. (2012). Inclusion of pupils with intellectual disabilities: Primary school teachers' attitudes and willingness in a rural area in Uganda. *International Journal of Inclusive Education*, 17(9), 1003–1021. DOI: 10.1080/13603116.2012.728251

Onyishi, C. N. (2022). Teachers' use of inclusive education practices for learners with neuro-developmental disorders in Enugu State, Nigeria. *Ikenga*, 23(3), 1–16. DOI: 10.53836/ijia/2022/23/3/003

Oronoz, H. J. (2011). *Teachers' Perspectives: An Understanding of ADHD in a predominantly Hispanic school district*. [The University of Texas at El Paso].

Park, Y. S., Konge, L., & Artino, A. R. (2020). The Positivism Paradigm of Research. *Philosophy of Science*, 95(5), 690–694. PMID: 31789841

Ponto, J. (2015). Understanding and Evaluating Survey Research. *Journal of the Advanced Practitioner in Oncology*, 6(2), 168–171. PMID: 26649250

Rakap, S., & Kaczmarek, L. (2010). Teachers' attitudes towards inclusion in Turkey. *European Journal of Special Needs Education*, 25(1), 59–75. DOI: 10.1080/08856250903450848

Robinson, M. (2017). *ADHD in the United States and the United Kingdom: A Comparison of Teacher and Parent Perspectives*. [Alliant International University].

Ronson, K. M. (2021). *Primary School Teachers' Knowledge of Attention-Deficit/ Hyperactivity Disorder*. [Notre Dame of Maryland University].

Schultz, B., & Evans, S. (2012). Sources of Bias in Teacher Ratings of Adolescents with ADHD. *Journal of Educational and Developmental Psychology*, 2(1), 151–162. DOI: 10.5539/jedp.v2n1p151

Sciutto, M. J., Frank, A. S. B., & Terjesen, M. D. (2000). *Teachers' knowledge and misperceptions of Attention-Deficit/Hyperactivity Disorder*. Westminster College Milestone School for Child Development. DOI: 10.1002/(SICI)1520-6807(200003)37:2<115::AID-PITS3>3.0.CO;2-5

Sciutto, M. J., Terjesen, M. D., Kučerová, A., Michalová, Z., Schmiedeler, S., Antonopoulou, K., Shaker, N. Z., Lee, J., Alkahtani, K., Drake, B., & Rossouw, J. (2016). Cross-national comparisons of teachers' knowledge and misconceptions of ADHD. *International Perspectives in Psychology : Research, Practice, Consultation*, 5(1), 34–50. DOI: 10.1037/ipp0000045

Simkus, J. (2023, July 31). *Convenience Sampling: Definition, Method and Examples*. https://www.simplypsychology.org/convenience-sampling.html

Sluiter, M. N., Wienen, A. W., Thoutenhoofd, E. D., Doornenbal, J. M., & Batstra, L. (2019). Teachers' role and attitudes concerning ADHD medication: A qualitative analysis. *Psychology in the Schools*, 56(8), 1259–1270. DOI: 10.1002/pits.22270

Stoker, P., Tian, G., & Kim, J. Y. (2020). Analysis of Variance (ANOVA). In *Basic Quantitative Research Methods for Urban Planners*. Routledge. DOI: 10.4324/9780429325021-11

Sunko, E., Kokic, I., & Vlah, N. (2021). Teachers' Inclusive Beliefs and Teaching Practices in Work with Students with some Inattentive Symptoms Associated with ADHD. *Proceedings of the Islamic Pedagogical Faculty in Zenica*, 19(19), 103–126. DOI: 10.51728/issn.2637-1480.2021.19.103

Syed, E. U., & Hussein, S. A.Ehsan Ullah SyedSajida Abdul Hussein. (2010). Increase in Teachers' Knowledge About ADHD After a Week-Long Training Program: A Pilot Study. *Journal of Attention Disorders*, 13(4), 420–423. DOI: 10.1177/1087054708329972 PMID: 19474460

The United Nations Convention on the Rights of the Child (UNCRC). (1989). *The United Nations Convention on the Rights of the Child (UNCRC)* (United Nations Treaty Series). https://www.cypcs.org.uk/rights/uncrc/articles/article-29/

Toma, M. (2010). Students With ADHD and their Teachers. An Investigation of the Relationship Between Teachers' characteristics, Teachers' knowledge And Teachers' attitudes In Primary School. *ICERI2010 Proceedings*, 202–211. 3rd International Conference of Education, Research and Innovation.

Vereb, R. L., & DiPerna, J. C. (2004). Teachers' Knowledge of ADHD, Treatments for ADHD, and Treatment Acceptability: An Initial Investigation. *School Psychology Review*, 33(3), 421–428. DOI: 10.1080/02796015.2004.12086259

Wang, D., Liu, X., & Deng, H. (2022). The perspectives of social cognitive career theory approach in current times. *Frontiers in Psychology*, 13, 1023994. DOI: 10.3389/fpsyg.2022.1023994 PMID: 36533045

Ward, R. J., Bristow, S. J., Kovshoff, H., Cortese, S., & Kreppner, J. (2022). The Effects of ADHD Teacher Training Programs on Teachers and Pupils: A Systematic Review and Meta-Analysis. *Journal of Attention Disorders*, 26(2), 225–244. DOI: 10.1177/1087054720972801 PMID: 33331193

Wilson, C., Green, C. N., Toye, M. K., & Ballantyne, C. (2023). Teachers' perceptions and practices towards inclusive education for children with ADHD in Scotland: A qualitative investigation. *International Journal of Disability Development and Education*, •••, 1–15.

Youssef, M. K., Hutchinson, G., & Youssef, F. F. (2015). Knowledge of and Attitudes Toward ADHD Among Teachers: Insights From a Caribbean Nation. *SAGE Open*, 5(1), 2158244014566761. DOI: 10.1177/2158244014566761

ADDITIONAL READINGS

Burke, J., & Loeber, R. (2010). Oppositional defiant disorder and the explanation of the comorbidity between behavioral disorders and depression. *Clinical Psychology : a Publication of the Division of Clinical Psychology of the American Psychological Association*, 17(4), 319–326. DOI: 10.1111/j.1468-2850.2010.01223.x

Cavanagh, M., Quinn, D., Duncan, D., Graham, T., & Balbuena, L. (2017). Oppositional defiant disorder is better conceptualized as a disorder of emotional regulation. *Journal of Attention Disorders*, 21(5), 381–389. DOI: 10.1177/1087054713520221 PMID: 24481934

Chen, W., Epstein, A., Toner, M., Murphy, N., Rudaizky, D., & Downs, J. (2023). Enabling successful life engagement in young people with ADHD: New components beyond adult models of recovery. *Disability and Rehabilitation*, 45(14), 2288–2300. DOI: 10.1080/09638288.2022.2087763 PMID: 35944517

DuPaul, G. J., Pinho, T. D., Pollack, B. L., Gormley, M. J., & Laracy, S. D. (2017). First-year college students with ADHD and/or LD: Differences in engagement, positive core self-evaluation, school preparation, and college expectations. *Journal of Learning Disabilities*, 50(3), 238–251. DOI: 10.1177/0022219415617164 PMID: 26712797

Eschenauer, R., & Chen-Hayes, S. F. (2005). The transformative individual school counseling model: An accountability model for urban school counselors. *Professional School Counseling*, •••, 244–248.

Hamilton, S. S., & Armando, J. (2008). Oppositional defiant disorder. *American Family Physician*, 78(7), 861–866. PMID: 18841736

Hawkley, L. C., & Cacioppo, J. T. (2010). Loneliness matters: A theoretical and empirical review of consequences and mechanisms. *Annals of Behavioral Medicine*, 40(2), 218–227. DOI: 10.1007/s12160-010-9210-8 PMID: 20652462

Heidbreder, R. (2015). ADHD symptomatology is best conceptualized as a spectrum: A dimensional versus unitary approach to diagnosis. *Attention Deficit and Hyperactivity Disorders*, 7(4), 249–269. DOI: 10.1007/s12402-015-0171-4 PMID: 25957598

Heinrich, L. M., & Gullone, E. (2006). The clinical significance of loneliness: A literature review. *Clinical Psychology Review*, 26(6), 695–718. DOI: 10.1016/j.cpr.2006.04.002 PMID: 16952717

Houghton, S., Roost, E., Carroll, A., & Brandtman, M. (2015). Loneliness in children and adolescents with and without attention-deficit/hyperactivity disorder. *Journal of Psychopathology and Behavioral Assessment*, 37(1), 27–37. DOI: 10.1007/s10862-014-9434-1

Laslo-Roth, R., Bareket-Bojmel, L., & Margalit, M. (2022). Loneliness experience during distance learning among college students with ADHD: The mediating role of perceived support and hope. *European Journal of Special Needs Education*, 37(2), 220–234. DOI: 10.1080/08856257.2020.1862339

Lebowitz, M. S. (2016). Stigmatization of ADHD: A developmental review. *Journal of Attention Disorders*, 20(3), 199–205. DOI: 10.1177/1087054712475211 PMID: 23407279

Martin, A. J. (2014). The role of ADHD in academic adversity: Disentangling ADHD effects from other personal and contextual factors. *School Psychology Quarterly*, 29(4), 395–408. DOI: 10.1037/spq0000069 PMID: 24820011

Rushton, S., Giallo, R., & Efron, D. (2020). ADHD and emotional engagement with school in the primary years: Investigating the role of student–teacher relationships. *The British Journal of Educational Psychology*, 90(S1), 193–209. DOI: 10.1111/bjep.12316 PMID: 31654412

Sonuga-Barke, E., & Harold, G. (2018). Conceptualizing and investigating the role of the environment in ADHD. In *Oxford Textbook of Attention Deficit Hyperactivity Disorder*. Oxford University Press.

Streeter, B., & Sadek, J. (2022). Developmental risk, adversity experiences and ADHD clinical profiles: A naturalistic exploratory study. *Brain Sciences*, 12(7), 919. DOI: 10.3390/brainsci12070919 PMID: 35884726

Thompson, A. C., & Lefler, E. K. (2016). ADHD stigma among college students. *Attention Deficit and Hyperactivity Disorders*, 8(1), 45–52. DOI: 10.1007/s12402-015-0179-9 PMID: 26135022

Wolf, L. E., & Wasserstein, J. (2001). Adults ADHD: Concluding thoughts. *Annals of the New York Academy of Sciences*, 931(1), 396–408. DOI: 10.1111/j.1749-6632.2001.tb05793.x PMID: 11462756

Zayats, T., & Neale, B. M. (2019). Recent advances in understanding of attention deficit hyperactivity disorder (ADHD): how genetics are shaping our conceptualization of this disorder. *F1000Research, 8*.DOI: 10.12688/f1000research.18959.2

KEY TERMS AND DEFINITIONS

Academic Adversity: refers to the various challenges and obstacles that students may encounter during their educational experiences, which can significantly obstruct their academic progress and personal development. These challenges can arise from a variety of factors, including learning difficulties, lack of resources, insufficient instructional support, socio-economic issues, and emotional or mental health challenges. The effects of academic adversity often result in poor academic performance, lowered self-esteem, and a lack of motivation, making it difficult for students to realize their full potential. External pressures such as family expectations, discrimination, or social stigma can further exacerbate these challenges, complicating the educational journey. To effectively overcome academic adversity, students must develop resilience and adaptability, supported by mentoring, counseling, and access to educational resources. Educational institutions play a critical role in addressing academic adversity by creating inclusive environments, implementing targeted intervention programs, and fostering a culture of empathy and support. The overarching objective is to empower students to navigate these challenges and achieve their educational and personal aspirations.

ASCA Model Program: An extensive framework for school counseling created by the American School Counselor Association (ASCA). It outlines a series of guidelines for the effective implementation and management of school counseling programs that aim to enhance student achievement, well-being, and readiness for future careers. The model is founded on three essential domains: academic, career, and social/emotional development. It promotes a data-driven strategy to identify and fulfill the needs of all students, ensuring fair access to counseling services. The ASCA Model is structured around four key components: foundation, management, delivery, and accountability. Counselors utilizing this model are dedicated to providing proactive, preventive, and developmental support, assisting students in overcoming academic challenges, exploring career opportunities, and developing crucial social and emotional skills. By following this model, school counselors can create organized programs that align with educational goals, support student success, and contribute to a positive school atmosphere. The ASCA Model highlights the significance of continuous improvement, collaboration, and the application of evidence-based practices.

Attention Deficit Hyperactivity Disorder (ADHD): A neurodevelopmental condition that is characterized by ongoing difficulties with attention, hyperactivity, and impulsivity, which can obstruct daily functioning and hinder personal development. Symptoms generally appear in childhood and may continue into later stages, such as adolescence and adulthood. Individuals diagnosed with ADHD may find it challenging to focus, often display disorganized behavior, and experience frequent forgetfulness. Hyperactivity and impulsivity can be evident through behaviors such as excessive fidgeting, talking, restlessness, or difficulty waiting for their turn. The disorder impacts various areas of life, including academic performance, social interactions, and work responsibilities, leading to challenges in educational contexts, professional environments, and personal relationships. The intensity and expression of symptoms can vary widely among individuals, with causes believed to stem from a combination of genetic, environmental, and neurological factors. A successful management strategy for ADHD entails a well-rounded plan that combines behavioral therapy, educational aid, and, if appropriate, medication to foster improved focus and decrease impulsivity.

Career Transition: Defined as the process of shifting from one job, role, or career path to another, often driven by personal goals, external circumstances, or new opportunities that present themselves. This change can be a voluntary decision, where individuals seek to follow new interests, or it may be involuntary, arising from job loss, organizational changes, or health-related issues. Such transitions often demand the acquisition of new skills, retraining, or adjustment to different work environments and responsibilities. While some individuals may navigate this transition with ease, others may encounter obstacles, including changes in identity, financial challenges, or the necessity to adapt to a new industry or professional culture. The effectiveness of career transitions frequently relies on self-awareness, meticulous planning, resilience, and the ability to leverage existing skills in unfamiliar contexts. This process calls for adaptability, an openness to change, and, at times, support from mentors, career coaches, or professional networks to successfully navigate the transition and find satisfaction in the new role.

Emotional Engagement: The degree of emotional involvement and connection that individuals experience with an activity, task, or relationship. It is the feelings of enthusiasm, interest, commitment, or passion that arise in response to specific situations or contexts. In both educational and professional environments, emotional engagement is important in shaping motivation, participation, and entire performance. Individuals who are emotionally engaged are more inclined to invest time and effort, demonstrate persistence, and derive satisfaction from their activities. This engagement is essential for promoting deep learning, creativity, and a sense of purpose. In contrast, insufficient emotional engagement can result in disinterest, diminished motivation, and disengagement. To enhance emotional engagement, it is important to create supportive environments, acknowledge achievements, and foster meaningful connections. Additionally, emotional engagement plays a significant role in interpersonal relationships, where empathy, trust, and mutual understanding enhance the bonds between individuals, leading to positive and fulfilling interactions.

Gender: Defined by the array of sociocultural and psychological characteristics linked to either maleness, femaleness, or non-binary. It further encompasses those expectations as well as norms that societies impose on individuals in respect of sex perception or assignment upon birth. While many cultures traditionally recognize two genders (male and female), growing awareness of gender diversity acknowledges non-binary, transgender, and gender-fluid identities. Gender identity relates to how individuals perceive themselves, while gender expression pertains to how they outwardly present their identity through behavior, appearance, and roles. Social constructs of gender can influence various aspects of life, including opportunities, social interactions, and power dynamics. Efforts towards gender inclusivity aim to challenge stereotypes, promote equality, and support the rights of all individuals to express their authentic selves without facing discrimination or prejudice.

Hyperactivity: Defined by an elevated degree of physical activity, restlessness, and impulsive actions that deviate from accepted social or situational standards. It is a primary symptom of ADHD but can also be present in various other behavioral disorders. Individuals exhibiting hyperactivity frequently demonstrate behaviors such as persistent fidgeting, an inability to remain seated, excessive verbalization, or interruptions during conversations. In children, hyperactivity may manifest as excessive running, challenges in participating in quiet activities, and a pronounced need for movement. For adults, it may present as a sensation of internal agitation or a compulsion to remain active. Hyperactivity can interfere with academic or occupational performance, complicating the ability to focus or complete tasks that necessitate prolonged attention. Effective management of hyperactivity typically includes structured activities, physical exercise, and methods to productively channel surplus energy, alongside behavioral strategies aimed at enhancing impulse control and attention management.

Inattentiveness: Characterized by an inability to maintain prolonged focus, difficulties in sustaining attention, and obstacles in organizing or completing tasks. While it is frequently associated with ADHD, it can also occur in individuals who do not have the disorder. Manifestations of inattentiveness may include tendencies to daydream, losing track of ongoing tasks, or overlooking important details in conversations or assignments. Individuals experiencing inattentiveness often face challenges with time management, forgetfulness, and organization, which can adversely affect their academic achievements, work efficiency, and daily functioning. This condition is commonly linked to struggles with prioritization, planning, and sustaining mental engagement in both routine and complex activities. Effective management of inattentiveness often involves implementing structured routines, utilizing visual aids, or practicing mindfulness techniques. It is essential to approach inattentiveness with empathy and support, as it can significantly impact an individual's self-esteem and motivation, especially in educational settings or social contexts where focus and attention are paramount.

Inclusive School: An educational establishment dedicated to offering equitable learning opportunities and fostering a supportive atmosphere for all students, irrespective of their backgrounds, abilities, or requirements. These institutions prioritize the cultivation of an inclusive culture that values diversity and encourages social integration. They adopt practices and policies designed to accommodate students with disabilities, learning challenges, and other marginalized groups, ensuring they receive the same high-quality education as their peers. This methodology includes the implementation of a flexible curriculum, differentiated instruction, and suitable support services tailored to address the varied needs of students. Furthermore, Inclusive Schools highlight the importance of collaboration among educators, parents, and specialists to promote comprehensive student development. The objective is to eliminate physical, social, and instructional barriers that hinder learning and participation, thereby fostering a sense of belonging and acceptance. By emphasizing inclusivity, these schools enable students to cultivate mutual respect, enhance empathy, and acquire skills essential for thriving in a diverse society.

An Inclusive Teacher: An educator who prioritizes the promotion of inclusivity in the classroom, ensuring that all students are recognized, respected, and supported throughout their learning experiences. These professionals are adept at identifying and tackling the needs of their students, including those with learning difficulties, and language barriers. They implement differentiated instruction, adaptive teaching techniques, and accessible learning resources to meet the diverse learning styles and abilities present in their classrooms. By fostering a safe, supportive, and engaging environment, inclusive teachers encourage participation and collaboration among all students. Their commitment goes beyond mere academic success to embrace the students' social and emotional growth, cultivating a sense of community and personal value in them. They are dedicated to continuous professional development, enhancing their ability to recognize and combat biases while adopting inclusive pedagogical approaches. The overarching goal is to empower every student to realize their potential and promote equity within the educational system.

Location: Denotes a particular site or geographical region where an entity exists, takes place, or is positioned. This can encompass tangible areas such as cities, neighborhoods, buildings, or landmarks, characterized by specific coordinates, boundaries, or identifiable features. The notion of location transcends simple geography, incorporating cultural, economic, and social aspects that contribute to a place's distinct identity. In various scenarios, location plays a crucial role in influencing individuals' experiences, access to resources, and available opportunities. For example, a location can affect access to education, employment opportunities, healthcare services, and social interactions. In the realm of digital environments, location may also pertain to virtual or online spaces where individuals engage or conduct activities. Regardless of being physical or virtual, location significantly influences community dynamics, human behavior, and connectivity. A thorough understanding of location is essential for grasping the environmental, cultural, and situational elements that shape people's lives, choices, and relationships within a specific context.

Loneliness: An emotional state characterized by feelings of isolation and disconnection, often experienced even in the company of others. It arises from the perception of a disparity between one's desired social interactions and the reality of their social connections. Various factors contribute to loneliness, including physical separation, significant life changes, challenges in relationships, and broader societal or cultural dynamics. It is important to note that loneliness is not solely a consequence of solitude; rather, it is closely linked to the perceived quality of one's relationships and the overall sense of belonging. This emotional condition may adversely impact both mental and physical well-being, potentially resulting in issues such as depression, anxiety, and compromised immune function. Furthermore, the stigma surrounding loneliness can prevent individuals from seeking the social support they need. To effectively combat loneliness, it is essential to create inclusive social settings, encourage open dialogue, and promote community involvement, thereby enabling individuals to cultivate and sustain meaningful relationships and a robust sense of connection.

Oppositional Behavior: Denotes a recurring pattern of defiance, resistance to authority, and negative interactions with others, often evident through arguing, disobedience, and hostility. This behavior is a significant characteristic of Oppositional Defiant Disorder (ODD) in children and adolescents, but it can also manifest in adults who encounter various stressors or conflicts. Those who display oppositional behavior may disregard rules, challenge authority, or intentionally irritate others. Such conduct can lead to strained relationships with parents, teachers, peers, or coworkers, and may result in disciplinary actions within structured environments like schools or workplaces. The origins of oppositional behavior can often be traced to environmental factors, unmet emotional needs, psychological conditions, or difficulties in managing frustration. Addressing this behavior effectively involves implementing consistent discipline, fostering empathetic communication, and utilizing positive reinforcement to promote cooperation. In cases of severe oppositional behavior, professional interventions such as behavioral therapy may be necessary to help individuals cultivate healthier coping mechanisms and improve their social interactions.

Societal Bias: Refers to the ingrained prejudices, stereotypes, and discriminatory attitudes that exist within a society, affecting how individuals perceive and interact with one another based on characteristics such as race, gender, religion, disability, social class, or sexual orientation. These biases can be both conscious and unconscious, often perpetuated by cultural norms, media representations, and institutional practices. The impact of societal biases results in unequal opportunities, reinforces existing social hierarchies, and contributes to systemic discrimination in various areas, including education, employment, healthcare, and the justice system. For example, biases present in educational contexts may influence teachers' expectations of their students or lead to the unfair treatment of certain demographics. To combat societal bias, it is essential to raise awareness, challenge stereotypes, and promote inclusivity and equity within social, economic, and political systems. Efforts to address these biases involve advocating for policy reforms, creating inclusive spaces, and fostering empathy and understanding among individuals to establish a just and equitable society.

Stigma: The negative beliefs, attitudes, and discriminatory behaviors that are directed toward individuals or groups based on particular characteristics, conditions, or circumstances. It originates from societal biases, stereotypes, and misconceptions, which lead to social disapproval and the exclusion of those who are stigmatized. This issue is often associated with mental health disorders, disabilities, racial or ethnic identities, gender, and socioeconomic factors. The consequences of stigma extend beyond marginalization, as it also perpetuates inequality, prejudice, and systemic barriers that hinder access to services and support. Addressing stigma requires the promotion of awareness, empathy, and inclusive practices, which together foster a culture of acceptance and challenge harmful stereotypes, ultimately creating equitable and supportive environments for all individuals, regardless of their unique differences or challenges.

School: A structured institution dedicated to the provision of formal education, where students engage in learning under the guidance of teachers across diverse academic subjects and skills. These institutions are vital for the progress of society, acting as venues for the dissemination of knowledge, values, and social competencies. The role of a school extends beyond academic instruction; it also aims to nurture the overall development of students, encompassing their cognitive, social, emotional, and physical dimensions. Schools function within defined curricula and educational policies that inform teaching strategies, learning outcomes, and assessment practices. They may take various forms, including early childhood centers, primary and secondary schools, and higher education establishments. The atmosphere within a school significantly influences students' experiences, aspirations, and the development of critical thinking, creativity, and social skills. A positive school atmosphere encourages inclusivity, equity, and a dedication to lifelong learning, equipping students with the necessary skills and knowledge to thrive in their personal and professional lives.

APPENDIX I: STUDY QUESTIONNAIRE

Table 4. The inclusive school teachers' perspectives on career transition and ADHD questionnaire (ISTPCQ)

No	Statements	SD	A	UD	D	SA
1	I feel confident in my ability to support students with ADHD in their career transitions.					
2	My school provides adequate resources for supporting students with ADHD in career transition planning.					
3	I feel that students with ADHD can successfully transition to a career with proper support.					
4	I have received sufficient training to assist students with ADHD during career transition.					
5	Collaboration with parents is essential for the successful career transition of students with ADHD.					
6	I am aware of the career transition needs of students with ADHD.					
7	My school has support programs in place for the career transition of students with ADHD.					
8	I regularly communicate with school counselors about the needs of students with ADHD.					
9	I feel that inclusive education impacts the career transition outcomes of students with ADHD.					
10	I feel that students with ADHD are given equal opportunities in career-related activities at school.					
11	I am comfortable discussing career options with students who have ADHD.					
12	My school encourages professional development focused on ADHD and career transitions.					
13	I find it challenging to address the career needs of students with ADHD due to time constraints.					
14	I think that students with ADHD have the potential to excel in various career paths.					
15	I am aware of external resources available to support students with ADHD in their careers.					
16	I feel that students with ADHD are well-prepared for the workforce upon graduation.					
17	I actively seek out strategies to improve career transition outcomes for students with ADHD.					
18	I think that students with ADHD need individualized career transition plans.					

SD=Strongly Disagree, D=Disagree, UD=Undecided, A=Agree, SA=Strongly Agree

APPENDIX II: ADDITIONAL STATISTICS

Table 5. Item-total statistics

No	Statements	Cronbach's Alpha if Item Deleted
1	I feel confident in my ability to support students with ADHD in their career transitions.	.670
2	My school provides adequate resources for supporting students with ADHD in career transition planning.	.689
3	I feel that students with ADHD can successfully transition to a career with proper support.	.700
4	I have received sufficient training to assist students with ADHD during career transition.	.652
5	Collaboration with parents is essential for the successful career transition of students with ADHD.	.644
6	I am aware of the career transition needs of students with ADHD.	.637
7	My school has support programs in place for the career transition of students with ADHD.	.646
8	I regularly communicate with school counselors about the needs of students with ADHD.	.668
9	I feel that inclusive education impacts the career transition outcomes of students with ADHD.	.670
10	I feel that students with ADHD are given equal opportunities in career-related activities at school.	.660
11	I am comfortable discussing career options with students who have ADHD.	.663
12	My school encourages professional development focused on ADHD and career transitions.	.690
13	I find it challenging to address the career needs of students with ADHD due to time constraints.	.658
14	I think that students with ADHD have the potential to excel in various career paths.	.707
15	I am aware of external resources available to support students with ADHD in their careers.	.678
16	I feel that students with ADHD are well-prepared for the workforce upon graduation.	.659
17	I actively seek out strategies to improve career transition outcomes for students with ADHD.	.648
18	I think that students with ADHD need individualized career transition plans.	.697

Table 6. Communalities (extraction method: principal component analysis)

No	Statements	Extraction
1	I feel confident in my ability to support students with ADHD in their career transitions.	.788
2	My school provides adequate resources for supporting students with ADHD in career transition planning.	.769
3	I feel that students with ADHD can successfully transition to a career with proper support.	.833
4	I have received sufficient training to assist students with ADHD during career transition.	.601
5	Collaboration with parents is essential for the successful career transition of students with ADHD.	.863
6	I am aware of the career transition needs of students with ADHD.	.801
7	My school has support programs in place for the career transition of students with ADHD.	.837
8	I regularly communicate with school counselors about the needs of students with ADHD.	.860
9	I feel that inclusive education impacts the career transition outcomes of students with ADHD.	.476
10	I feel that students with ADHD are given equal opportunities in career-related activities at school.	.723
11	I am comfortable discussing career options with students who have ADHD.	.681
12	My school encourages professional development focused on ADHD and career transitions.	.761
13	I find it challenging to address the career needs of students with ADHD due to time constraints.	.492
14	I think that students with ADHD have the potential to excel in various career paths.	.790
15	I am aware of external resources available to support students with ADHD in their careers.	.740
16	I feel that students with ADHD are well-prepared for the workforce upon graduation.	.683
17	I actively seek out strategies to improve career transition outcomes for students with ADHD.	.817
18	I think that students with ADHD need individualized career transition plans.	.810

Chapter 2
School Counselors' Perspectives on Theories and Techniques for Career Transition Counseling of Students With ADHD

ABSTRACT

The study examines how inclusive secondary school counselors perceive the use of career counseling theories and techniques in supporting students with ADHD during career transition. The study aimed to understand counselors' overall perspectives, examine gender differences, and evaluate the impact of professional experience and school location. This research used a survey research design and involved 20 counselors selected through purposive and convenience sampling techniques. The findings revealed that counselors had neutral to slightly positive perspectives on applying theories and techniques to facilitate the career transition of students with ADHD, with no significant differences based on gender, experience, or location. A major contribution of this study is the identification of a consensus among counselors concerning career counseling approaches for supporting the career transition of students with ADHD.

DOI: 10.4018/979-8-3693-2635-0.ch002

BACKGROUND

With the rising number of students with attention-deficit/hyperactivity disorder (ADHD) (*see* Abassi et al., 2023; Mohamed et al., 2023), it is crucial for school counselors to have a thorough understanding of the theories and techniques that are accessible to these students (Evert, 2009). Their perspectives on feasible theories and strategies can influence their support for students with ADHD in managing the challenges associated with career transition. Theories and therapeutic interventions such as rational emotive behavior therapy theory, contingency management, group counseling, and social cognitive career theory serve as a framework for counselors to help students develop valuable skills that will facilitate their career transition (Duong & St-Jean, 2024; Evert, 2009; Jensen & Cooper, 2002; Langberg et al., 2008; Webb & Myrick, 2003). According to Champ et al. (2021), research-driven treatment guidelines largely advocate for cognitive behavioral therapy, which builds upon cognitive behavioral theory. This methodology focuses on a deficit-based interpretation of ADHD and emphasizes the importance of symptom alleviation and cognitive self-regulation as primary goals of treatment. In spite of the significance of existing career counseling theories and techniques, inclusive education remains difficult to attain (Slee, 2018; Srivastava et al., 2017). Counselors can handle the difficulties posed by students with ADHD by embracing more inclusive styles in their theoretical orientation and practices (Hart & Kourkoutas, 2015; Eseadi & Diale, 2024). However, there is a lack of guidance available to them in this regard (Gibson, 2017). Some of the inclusive techniques encompass awareness and advocacy (Shillingford & Theodore, 2012). Furthermore, school counselors must educate themselves on the traits of students with ADHD as they are responsible for providing career support to these students (ADD Resource Center, 2017). In order to meet the unique demands of students with ADHD, Schwiebert et al. (1995) stated that school counselors should employ a multidisciplinary team approach and foster consistency and collaboration in their approach to meeting the requirements of students with ADHD. The role of school counselors also entails fostering the personal, social, academic, and career development of every student (Christian & Brown, 2018). Yaden et al. (1995) noted the unique position of school counselors in assisting students with ADHD, along with their teachers, parents, and peers. The authors highlighted two critical roles that school counselors fulfill for these students: the coordination of multidisciplinary services and the provision of counseling to these students and their significant others. Fitriyani et al. (2024) emphasized that counselors take part in assisting with special needs students to adjust to an inclusive school setting. Dumigan (2017) observed that counseling itself serves as a valuable intervention for enhancing self-awareness and coping mechanisms in students. The assessment services offered by school counselors also play a crucial role in shaping the career selection of students in senior secondary schools (Aliero & Aliero, 2023). However, a research study in Cameroon indicated that school counseling had minimal impact on students' educational and career decisions as well as psychological issues (Ilongo, 2015). Conversely, research by Blake (2020) suggested that school counselors possess the capacity to enhance students' social and academic outcomes.

Wingfield and Reese (2010) assert that school counseling constitutes a professional field, detailing the historical evolution of various school counseling models, such as vocational guidance, the mental health movement, and developmental guidance. They advocated for the advancement of school counselors into leadership positions and offered guidance for those counselors aspiring to achieve such status. Alharahsheh and Pius (2020) opined that the school counselors involved in the research conducted in the Northern Border Region of Saudi Arabia possess inadequate knowledge regarding ADHD. These shortcomings in knowledge directly limit their effectiveness in supporting students with ADHD. As a result, these students struggle to establish a career trajectory, facing numerous challenges associated with their disability. Most school counselors, regardless of their training background, appear to operate with incomplete or inaccurate knowledge concerning disabilities, leaving them ill-equipped to assist these students in navigating their unique challenges (Gibson, 2017). Meanwhile, in the United States, federal legislation mandates that all counselors working with children and adolescents, regardless of their employment in public school environments, must possess a thorough understanding of the identification and services available for individuals with disabilities (Tarver Behring & Spagna, 2004). Furthermore, it is the professional and ethical duty of all counselors to create conditions that enable every individual, including those with special educational needs, to reach their full potential (Tarver Behring & Spagna, 2004).

Martin (2017) indicated that school counselors have historically received training focused on individual models, which often results in a deficiency in the family systems perspective to counseling, which is crucial for delivering a holistic school counseling program to students. School counselors with extensive experience may be more adept at supporting students with ADHD as they possess a more profound understanding of the disorder's complexities (Faiz et al., 2021). Their ability to provide appropriate levels of structure enhances the support they offer (Dickson, 2022). With increased knowledge and experience, school counselors are more capable of delivering effective career guidance to students with ADHD compared to those with limited expertise (Branscome et al., 2014). It becomes crucial for less experienced counselors to engage in additional professional development opportunities to enhance their skills. The geographical location of school counselors may play a crucial role in shaping their perspectives on the theories and techniques utilized for career transition counseling of students with ADHD. This is important because students in rural areas often face fewer opportunities and have less access to career counseling services than their urban counterparts, which limits their engagement in career exploration activities that are typically regarded as essential for career transition. In rural regions, 14% of schools often lack a school counselor, in contrast to 6% in urban areas (Quintero & Gu, 2019). While urban school counselors encounter their own set of challenges, they are generally better equipped to assist students (Toby et al., 2016). Yılmaz (2019) showed that the alterations in counselors' perceptions are primarily linked to their levels of knowledge regarding inclusive educational practices. Research examining gender disparities revealed that girls are often underidentified and underdiagnosed due to variations in how the disorder manifests in boys compared to girls (Skogli et al., 2013). These gender differences may shape school counselors' views on the theories and methodologies employed for assisting students with ADHD in their career transition. Boys exhibiting the inattentive subtype of ADHD encounter more academic obstacles than girls, while girls tend to experience greater social difficulties (Kamal et al., 2021). Consequently, it may be imperative for counselors to adopt a gender-sensitive approach, recognizing that these disparities can influence students' career transition. In other words, transition counselors may need to implement techniques and theories that take gender differences into account to achieve the best possible outcomes for students with ADHD during career transition counseling.

Okere et al. (2016) revealed that Nigerian school counselors play a substantial role in enhancing the educational pursuits of students. They indicated that these counselors exert a positive impact on the advancement of students' educational activities. In Nigeria, school counselors also play a pertinent role in aiding students during their transition phases (Eseadi & Diale, 2024); however, there is a lack of understanding regarding their views on effective theories and techniques for career transition counseling specifically designed for these students. The distinct cognitive and behavioral traits associated with ADHD (van der Meer et al., 2017) can significantly influence career decisions. Therefore, it is imperative to investigate how school counselors perceive their responsibilities in assisting students with ADHD during this pivotal stage of their lives. The cultural landscape in Nigeria presents further challenges to school counselors (Eseadi & Ikechukwu-Ilomuanya, 2015; Olatunji et al., 2023; Song, 2024) in meeting the needs of students with ADHD during career transition counseling. The stigma associated with neurodivergent conditions, including ADHD (Olatunji et al., 2023), often obstructs candid conversations regarding career transition goals and the essential support mechanisms between school counselors and students with ADHD. Also, most school counselors may encounter difficulties in applying effective counseling methods due to insufficient training or resources tailored to students with ADHD (Ogba et al., 2020). Understanding Nigerian school counselors' perspectives can help reveal deficiencies in current practices and guide the creation of more effective counseling frameworks that are in harmony with the career transition needs of students with ADHD. To this end, this study aims to examine the perspectives of Nigerian inclusive school counselors concerning career counseling theories and techniques used to support the career transition of students with ADHD.

Research Objectives

1. To determine the overall mean perspective of inclusive secondary school counselors on the use of career counseling theories and techniques in supporting the career transition of students with ADHD.
2. To investigate gender differences in perspectives of inclusive secondary school counselors on the use of career counseling theories and techniques in supporting the career transition of students with ADHD.
3. To determine the extent to which inclusive secondary school counselors' perspectives on the use of career counseling theories and techniques in supporting career transition of students with ADHD vary due to years of professional experience.
4. To investigate whether rural and urban inclusive secondary school counselors exhibit contrasting perspectives on the use of career counseling theories and techniques in supporting career transition of students with ADHD.

Research Questions

1. What is the overall mean perspective of inclusive secondary school counselors on the use of career counseling theories and techniques in supporting the career transition of students with ADHD?
2. Are there gender differences in the perspectives of inclusive secondary school counselors on the use of career counseling theories and techniques in supporting the career transition of students with ADHD?
3. To what extent do inclusive secondary school counsellors vary in their perspectives on the use of career counseling theories and techniques in supporting career transition of students with ADHD due to years of professional experience?
4. Do rural and urban inclusive secondary school counselors exhibit contrasting perspectives on the use of career counseling theories and techniques in supporting career transition of students with ADHD?

Theoretical Framework

This research utilizes Rational Emotive Behavior Therapy (REBT) theory as its theoretical framework to examine the viewpoints of inclusive school counselors regarding the career transitions of students diagnosed with ADHD. Established by Albert Ellis in 1955, REBT theory is a cognitive-behavioral framework that emphasizes the identification and challenge of irrational beliefs, encouraging the adoption of rational and constructive thought patterns (Ellis, 2000; Obiweluozo et al., 2021; Rosner, 2011). According to the REBT theory, individuals with a high frustration tolerance are more likely to effectively pursue their objectives and attain success (Nelson, 1997; Oltean et al., 2017). Within the educational sphere, especially in inclusive environments, REBT offers practitioners tools to assist students in cultivating rational thinking and managing their emotions (Eseadi et al., 2023; Ogbuanya et al., 2018; Prout & Brown, 2007). The potential application of REBT theory and techniques in supporting students with ADHD has been illustrated by REBT clinicians (David, Silviu, & Cardos, 2020; Doyle & Terjesen, 2006; Doyle & Terjesen, 2020). However, in mainstream classrooms, inclusive school counselors frequently engage with students who present a range of needs, including those with ADHD, where counselors' bias concerning these students' career choices may obstruct the transition process. As a result, inclusive school counselors may possess varying opinions regarding the efficacy of school counseling theories and techniques in addressing the distinct needs of students with ADHD during career transitions. This study, therefore, explores school counselors' overall perspectives on the application of such theories and techniques, such as the REBT, in assisting students with ADHD during their career transition. School counselors' perceptions of counseling theories and techniques used in supporting the career transition of students with ADHD might differ based on their gender, which could influence how they apply such theories and techniques in practice. With respect to REBT theory and its associated techniques, there may exist a potential divergence in the ways that male and female school counselors perceive its efficacy in providing emotional and cognitive support to students diagnosed with ADHD, especially when it comes to addressing irrational beliefs. Counselors at different stages of their careers may have varying insights into the application of REBT theory and techniques for aiding students during their career transition. More experienced school counselors may possess a more nuanced understanding of how it effectively challenges irrational beliefs, thus employing REBT theory and techniques in a manner that better supports students' career transition. Furthermore, the challenges faced by inclusive school counselors in rural and urban contexts can shape their perspectives on the use of REBT for facilitating the career transition of students with ADHD. For example, rural school counselors may struggle with limited resources and access to REBT training, while urban school counselors may contend with larger student population and unique socio-economic challenges. The critical nature of addressing irrational beliefs cannot be overstated for inclusive school counselors who aim to deliver effective emotional and behavioral support to students with ADHD during career transition. Insights into inclusive school counselors' views on the applicability and effectiveness of counseling theories and techniques, such as REBT theory and techniques, can illuminate the success of career transition counseling strategies within inclusive education settings for students with ADHD (see Figure 1).

Figure 1. Study framework

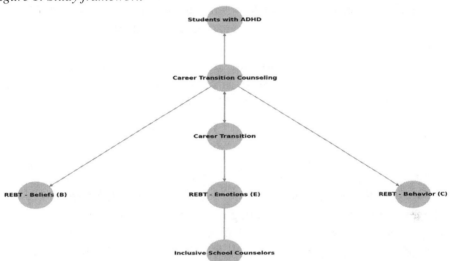

METHODOLOGY

Ethics Statement

Ethical approval for this study was obtained from the relevant institutional review boards. First, it received approval from the Research Ethics Committee of the Faculty of Education, University of Nigeria. It also received additional ethical approval from the Faculty of Education Research Ethics Committee at the University of Johannesburg, South Africa (Sem 2-2020-057). Informed consent was secured from participants. We assured confidentiality and clarified participants' right to withdraw from the study at any given time.

Research Design and Approach

This study employed a survey research design, utilizing a quantitative approach to gather data. Survey research has been extensively employed in the fields of educational research and evaluation (Pugh, 2021). Mills (2024) noted that survey research constitutes a specific category of research design wherein surveys serve as instruments for researchers to enhance their comprehension of individual or group opinions concerning a specific concept or topic of interest. In this study, we employed a quantitative research strategy through the use of questionnaires to collect responses from individuals. The utilization of survey research design is favored due to its distinctive characteristics, including an unbiased representation of the target population, standardization of measurements, and its ability to complement existing data from secondary sources (Owens, 2002). By utilizing a survey research design alongside a quantitative framework, this study facilitates an examination of school counselors' viewpoints on the theories and methods applied in career transition counseling for students diagnosed with ADHD.

Research Paradigm

This study is grounded in the positivist research paradigm. Paradigms can be understood as distinct perspectives through which the world is interpreted, serving as the foundational basis for conducting research. They encompass a collection of assumptions regarding the nature of reality, the process of knowledge creation, and the significance of what is worth learning (Davies & Fisher, 2020). The positivist paradigm posits that reality exists independently of human perception, asserting that it is not influenced by our sensory experiences and is governed by unchanging laws (Rehman & Alharthi, 2021). Our research has adopted the positivist paradigm, which emphasizes that positivism aligns with the philosophical approach of natural scientists who engage with observable realities in society, thereby facilitating the development of reliable generalizations (Alharahsheh & Pius, 2020).

Study Area

This research was conducted in Ebonyi State, located in Southeast Nigeria. Ebonyi State is situated approximately between the latitudes of 5° 40' and 6° 45' North of the Equator, as well as the longitudes of 7° 30' and 8° 30' East of the Greenwich meridian (Diagi, 2018).

Population and Sampling

The study involves inclusive secondary school counselors in public secondary schools. A total of 20 inclusive secondary school counselors were selected using purposive and convenience sampling techniques. The mean age of these participants was 38.50±6.54. Purposive and convenience sampling techniques are classified as non-random sampling methods, also known as Non-Probability Sampling Methods (Alvi, 2016). In non-probability sampling, the likelihood of each element in the population being selected for the sample is unknown, which can be advantageous for qualitative research (Van Haute, 2021). Purposive sampling involves the selection of samples based on the judgment or specific purpose of the researcher, making the representation inherently subjective (Barreiro & Albandoz, 2001). Conversely, convenience sampling involves gathering data from individuals who are readily available and willing to participate in the study, thus prioritizing accessibility for the researcher (Andrade, 2021; Scholtz, 2021). Utilizing both purposive and convenience sampling techniques facilitates the achievement of the objectives of this study. Counselors who meet specific criteria, such as secondary school counselors, were deliberately selected based on their availability for participation.

Data Collection

The data was collected using a questionnaire. The researchers received help from two postgraduate students to complete the data collection process. The questionnaire used for data collection is called the Inclusive School Counselors' Perspectives on Theories and Techniques Relevant to Career Transition and ADHD Questionnaire (ISCPTCTQ). It is a 20-item scale, with response options ranging from Not at All (1) to Very Great Extent (5). This scale measures counselors' knowledge and the extent of the use of career counseling theories and techniques in career transition counseling services provided to students with ADHD. Higher scores indicate more knowledge and adequate use of counseling theories and techniques. An example of an item statement in the questionnaire includes: "To what extent are you familiar with the use of career counseling theories for students with ADHD?" The ISCPTCTQ has good internal consistency reliability, with a Cronbach's alpha of 0.69 in the present research.

Data Analysis

Statistical analysis was conducted using Jeffreys' Amazing Statistics Program software (JASP), version 0.18.3. JASP is an innovative information and communication technology tool developed by a team of researchers at the University of Amsterdam. It facilitates Bayesian analyses for both students and practitioners (Agawin, 2020). The methodology proposed by the JASP Team is based on the premise that a general law, such as the null hypothesis, possesses a positive point mass. This allows practitioners to assess the extent to which the data supports or contradicts this hypothesis, with recent enhancements available through the open-source software (Ly et al., 2020). JASP serves as a complimentary, open-source option that provides straightforward and user-friendly outputs, making it particularly suitable for students who are in the process of mastering statistical concepts in psychology (Bartlett, 2017). Statistics plays a crucial role in the quantitative methodology of acquiring knowledge (Ramachandran & Tsokos, 2015). It encompasses scientific techniques for the collection, organization, summarization, presentation, and analysis of data, in addition to facilitating the formulation of valid conclusions and informed decisions based on such analyses. Furthermore, the term statistics can also refer to the data itself (Jambu, 1991a, 1991b). The two main categories involved in summarizing and analyzing data are known as descriptive and inferential statistics (Nick, 2007). Descriptive statistics were used to analyse the sociodemographic data, while inferential statistics (t-tests) were used to analyse the research questions at a .05 significance level.

FINDINGS

Table 1. Mean perspective of inclusive secondary school counselors on the use of career counseling theories and techniques in supporting the career transition of students with ADHD

Group	Category	N	Mean	SD	SE	Coefficient of variation
Gender	Male Counselors	8	2.78	.15	.053	.054
	Female Counselors	12	2.86	.21	.060	.073
Professional Experience	Early Career School Counselors	12	2.82	.20	.058	.071
	Experienced School Counselors	8	2.84	.18	.063	.063
School Location	Rural School Counselors	10	2.88	.25	.078	.086
	Urban School Counselors	10	2.78	.09	.027	.031
Mean Perspective		30	2.83	.19	.042	.066

Table 1 shows that male counselors had a mean perspective score of 2.78 (SD=.15) while female counselors had a mean perspective score of 2.86 (SD=.21). Early career school counselors had a mean score of 2.82 (SD=.20) while experienced school counselors had a mean score of 2.84 (SD = 0.18). Rural school counselors reported a mean score of 2.88 (SD = 0.25), while urban school counselors had a mean score of 2.78 (SD=.09). The overall mean perspective of 2.83 suggests that counselors have a neutral to slightly positive perspective regarding the use of career counseling theories and techniques in supporting students with ADHD during career transition. Figures 2-4 further elucidates these mean perspectives of the inclusive secondary school counselors on the use of career counseling theories and techniques in supporting the career transition of students with ADHD.

Figure 2. Mean perspectives of inclusive school counselors by gender

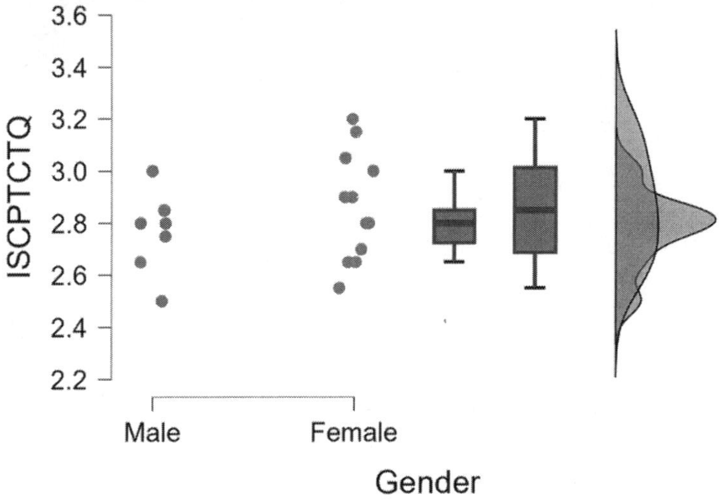

Figure 3. Mean perspectives of inclusive school counselors by professional experience

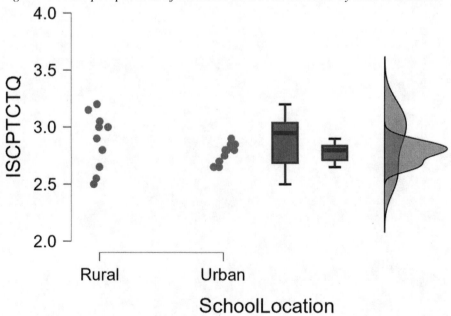

Figure 4. Mean perspectives of inclusive school counselors by school location

Table 2. T-test analysis on perspectives of inclusive secondary school counselors on the use of career counseling theories and techniques in supporting the career transition of students with ADHD by gender, professional experience and school location

Group	t	df	P	Mean Difference	SE Difference	95% CI
Gender	-1.024	18	.319	-.087	.085	-.267, .092
Professional Experience	-.309	18	.761	-.027	.088	-.211, .157
School Location	1.273	18	.219	.105	.082	-.068, .278

The t-test result in Table 2 shows that there are no significant gender differences in the perspectives of inclusive secondary school counselors on the use of career counseling theories and techniques in supporting the career transition of students with ADHD, $t(18)=-1.024, p=.319$. The mean difference is -0.087 (SE = 0.085), with a 95% confidence interval ranging from -0.267 to 0.092. For professional experience, the t-test result is $t(18)=-0.309, p=.761$ and the mean difference is -0.027 (SE = 0.088), with a 95% confidence interval from -0.211 to 0.157. This suggests no significant difference in the perspectives of inclusive secondary school counselors on the use of career counseling theories and techniques in supporting the career transition of students with ADHD based on years of professional experience. The analysis for school location shows the t-test result as $t(18)=1.273, p=.219$, and the mean difference is 0.105 (SE = 0.082), with a 95% confidence interval from -0.068 to 0.278. This result indicates no significant difference in perspectives between rural and urban counselors on the use of career counseling theories and techniques in supporting the career transition of students with ADHD.

DISCUSSION

This study examined the perspectives of Nigerian inclusive school counselors on the theories and techniques related to the career transition processes for students with ADHD. The findings revealed that inclusive secondary school counselors generally have similar perspectives on the use of career counseling theories and techniques for supporting students with ADHD during their career transition, regardless of gender, professional experience, or school location. The lack of significant differences across these categories implies a consensus concerning the relevance of the approaches to career counseling for students with ADHD during career transition among the school counselors surveyed. Pugh (2021) revealed no significant differences in the attitudes and opinions of secondary school counselors working in schools recognized by the American School Counselor Association (ASCA) model program compared to those in non-recognized ASCA model program schools; both groups shared a perspective of inclusion for their students. In our study, there was a higher representation of female school counselors compared to their male colleagues, and the results suggest that counselors generally hold a neutral to slightly positive view regarding the application of career counseling theories and techniques to assist students with ADHD during their career transition. Pugh (2021) indicated that the field of school counseling is predominantly occupied by females. In Pugh's (2021) study, the majority of respondents, who were school counselors, were females.

Our findings also revealed that the geographical setting of a school, whether urban or rural, does not appear to influence the perceptions of school counselors regarding the career transition of students with ADHD. In a prior study, schools designated as Recognized ASCA Model Program (RAMP) viewed school counselors as primarily responsible for counseling students with disciplinary issues, offering teachers strategies for improved study hall management, and interpreting student records more frequently than their non-RAMP school counterparts (Mullen et al., 2019). Moreover, ADHD is a widespread comorbid concern among children in rural areas characterized by low socioeconomic status, where mental health services are often insufficient (Wofford & Ohrt, 2018). While our study revealed that rural and urban counselors shared similar perspectives on the relevance of career counseling theories and techniques to support the career transitions of students diagnosed with ADHD, a previous study by Morgan et al. (2014) found that urban counselors felt more prepared than their rural counterparts in delivering career development programs that incorporated technology, whereas rural and suburban counselors believed they were nearly equal in competency to their peers.

Our result demonstrated that there is no significant disparity in the perspectives of inclusive secondary school counselors concerning the relevance of career counseling theories and techniques to support the career transitions of students with ADHD, regardless of their years of experience in the field. According to Azeem's et al. (2021) findings, a significant number of school psychologists recognized the benefits of utilizing REBT for students with ADHD, especially concerning screening, diagnosis, and intervention methods. These professionals expressed the opinion that a variety of treatment approaches could effectively decrease hyperactivity and enhance both social and cognitive abilities among these students. In general, we feel that professionals with greater years of experience are more likely to offer effective support to students with ADHD. Similarly, those professionals who have encountered these students in their professional practice were more likely to have relevant insights derived from their past experiences. Counselors with extensive experience could be better equipped to understand evidence-based interventions, which are essential for supporting students dealing with ADHD (Dimmitt et al., 2007). McMahon et al. (2009) observed that professional school counselors, particularly those who are older and possess more experience and tenure in their schools, reported higher levels of leadership practices compared to their younger and less experienced counterparts. However, counselors often receive insufficient training regarding disabilities within their educational programs (Gibson, 2017). In many institutions, there is a notable absence of training programs for school counselors (Gordon, 2002). Oral and Karakurt (2020) revealed that counselors exhibited a moderate level of knowledge and awareness regarding ADHD. The study demonstrated that counselors who had received prior training on ADHD achieved significantly higher scores compared to those who had not undergone such training (Oral & Karakurt, 2020). The study further indicated that a majority of counselors expressed a need for additional education on this subject. As a result, it is crucial for all school counselors to recognize the importance of ongoing supervision and to leverage their professional status as advocates for their field (Mecadon-Mann, 2023).

Our research has confirmed that school counselors possess a favorable attitude towards the implementation of diverse career theories and techniques for the counseling of students with ADHD during career transition. No matter what the theoretical perspective adopted, familiarity with counseling theories is vital for the accurate assessment and conceptualization of a client's case (Crawford & Studer, 2015). Counselors are uniquely qualified to offer individual and group counseling, fostering a nurturing and supportive atmosphere for those with ADHD, their significant adults, and their peers (Yaden et al., 1995). Stewart (2006) noted that group counseling could prove to be an effective treatment modality for school counselors aiming to support the emotional well-being of students with ADHD. School counselors are strategically positioned to work alongside school and community stakeholders in order to mitigate and respond to the difficulties faced by students who exhibit one or more behavioral disorders (Grothaus, 2013). The counselor is equipped with training that enables them to play dual roles as a coordinator and consultant, working alongside teachers and various educational professionals (Lavin, 1991). Therapist-coach evaluations and client evaluations are examples of the techniques adopted by school counselors; therapist-coach evaluations were indicative of task completion, in contrast to client evaluations, which did not demonstrate this predictive ability (Prevatt et al., 2017). Interpersonal group therapy contributes positively to self-esteem, psychosocial competence, and emotional maturity and should be considered a treatment option for students experiencing ADHD (Shaikh, 2018). Webb and Myrick (2003) posited that it is important for students with ADHD to be exposed to group counseling interventions for them to realize that the pathway to success involves the ability to regulate their thoughts, feelings, and actions. Furthermore, it is essential that counselors receive training in behavioral interventions that are devoid of side effects in the management of ADHD. School counselors have expressed feelings of inadequacy in their preparedness to assist students with disabilities (Cimsir & Carney, 2017). To effectively support students, school leaders should first enhance the utilization of school professionals by reallocating tasks that are less critical to school career transition service delivery to other staff members. They should adopt an integrated model of school services to make the most of the training that school professionals possess (Lambie et al., 2019; Zabek et al., 2023).

Our research advances the objectives of the African Union Agenda 2063, with a focus on promoting inclusivity and reducing inequality (African Union, 2015). The African Union Agenda emphasizes the importance of creating an environment where individuals, irrespective of their backgrounds or abilities, have equitable access to quality education within their communities (The Pan-African Parliament, 2020). The Pan-African Parliament (2020) highlights that inclusive education plays a crucial role in dismantling barriers and cultivating a culture of respect, understanding, and acceptance, ultimately contributing to an educated and prosperous Africa. Nigeria has undertaken various development planning strategies to achieve its national development objectives. Among these initiatives are the National Development Plan (Igbozuruike et al., 2022), the National Policy on Inclusive Education, and the National Policy on Special Needs Education (Federal Ministry of Education, 2015, 2023). The fourth objective of Nigeria's National Development Plan (NDP-2021-2025) aims to cultivate an educated and healthy populace, thereby promoting inclusivity (Federal Ministry of Budget and Economic Planning, 2021). Furthermore, the National Policy on Inclusive Education seeks to involve key stakeholders, enhance awareness, develop capacity, and improve service delivery to ensure that education is standardized and accessible for all individuals, irrespective of age, nationality, ethnicity, gender, or disability (Federal Ministry of Education, 2023). There are several potential constraints regarding the results obtained in the present study. The study involved a participant sample of a few school counselors, thereby limiting the extent to which the findings can be generalized. The research took place in a designated area of Ebonyi State, Nigeria, thereby restricting the potential for incorporating other regions that have diverse contexts and social dynamics, which could result in different findings regarding the same issue. The study also employed purposive and convenience sampling methods. Findings derived from such sampling techniques may only be generalized to the specific (sub) population from which the sample was taken rather than the entire population, which may not adequately represent the diversity of school counselors. Future research should be improved by incorporating larger sample sizes and investigating regional variations alongside robust comparisons between urban and rural school counselors. Abikwi (2010) advocated for the establishment of more counseling units within Nigerian school settings in accordance with the guidelines set forth in the National Policy on Education. This initiative can help to alleviate many challenges encountered by students with ADHD during their career transition. In future research, it is crucial to explore the specific theories and methodologies that school counselors consider most advantageous for career transition counseling. This exploration should include an assessment of whether counselors employ established models or modify them to better accommodate the unique career transition needs of students with ADHD.

CONCLUSIONS

The study demonstrates that counselors typically maintain a neutral to mildly positive view regarding the application of career counseling theories and techniques for supporting students with ADHD during career transition. No substantial differences exist in their views when considering factors such as gender, years of experience, or the setting in which counselors operate, whether rural or urban. These findings suggest a shared understanding among counselors in their methods for assisting students with ADHD, which could help shape the development of counselor education training and future practices. Policymakers can leverage these findings to formulate policies that provide all school counselors with equal access to resources and training, thus ensuring that students with ADHD receive equitable career counseling services. Schools can enhance their resource distribution, given that counselor perspectives show minimal variation across sociodemographic lines. To strengthen the validity of our findings, future research should include a larger and more diverse array of counselors from various regions and educational contexts. Furthermore, it is essential for future research to explore how the application of these theories and techniques by counselors directly influences the career transition outcomes of students with ADHD.

REFERENCES

Abbasi, L. N., Mazzawi, T., Abasi, L., Haj Ali, S., Alqudah, A., & Al-Taiar, H. (2023). The Prevalence and Associated Factors of Attention Deficit Hyperactivity Disorder Among Primary School Children in Amman, Jordan. *Cureus*, 15(4), e37856. DOI: 10.7759/cureus.37856 PMID: 37214023

Abikwi, M. I. (2010). Attention Deficit Hyperactivity Disorder Intervention: Strategies & Counselling Tips for Primary School Teachers. *Edo Journal of Counselling*, 2(2), 214–227. DOI: 10.4314/ejc.v2i2.60861

ADD Resource Center. (2017, October 23). *Strategies for ADHD: How Counselors Help Today's Students Succeed*.https://www.addrc.org/strategies-for-adhd-how-counselors-help-todays-students-succeed/

African Union. (2015, January). *Agenda 2063: The Africa We Want.* African Union. https://au.int/en/agenda2063/overview

Agawin, M. (2020). Perceived Ease of Use, Perceived Usefulness, and Attitude towards Jeffrey's Amazing Statistics Program (JASP) among Students of a Private Higher Educational Institution in Region IV-A. LPU-Laguna. *Journal of Multidisciplinary Research*, 4(1), 10–23.

Alharahsheh, H. H., & Pius, A. (2020). A Review of key paradigms: Positivism VS interpretivism. *Global Academic Journal of Humanities and Social Sciences*, 2(3), 39–43. DOI: 10.36348/gajhss.2020.v02i03.001

Aliero, B. U., & Aliero, H. S. (2023). A Study of Perception of Secondary School Students on the Impact of School Counselors in Career Choice: A case study of Yauri Local Government Area of Kebbi State. *African Journal of Humanities and Contemporary Education Research*, 10(1), 1.

Alvi, M. H. (2016). A Manual for Selecting Sampling Techniques in Research. *Munich Personal RePEc Archive,* Paper No. 70218. https://mpra.ub.uni-muenchen.de/70218/

Andrade, C. (2021). The Inconvenient Truth About Convenience and Purposive Samples. *Indian Journal of Psychological Medicine*, 43(1), 86–88. DOI: 10.1177/0253717620977000 PMID: 34349313

Azeem, A., Faiz, Z., Siddique, M., Ali, M. S., & Warraich, W. (2021). School psychologists' perspectives about effectiveness of behavior therapy for children with attention deficit hyperactivity disorder in Pakistan. *Humanities & Social Sciences Reviews*, 9(3), 1142–1155. DOI: 10.18510/hssr.2021.93113

Barreiro, P. L., & Albandoz, J. P. (2001). Population and Sampling techniques. *Management Mathematics for European Schools*, 1, 1–18.

Bartlett, J. E. (2017, June). *An Introduction to JASP: A Free and User-Friendly Statistics Package*. OSF Storage, https://osf.io/7x8hj/

Blake, M. K. (2020). Other Duties as Assigned: The Ambiguous Role of the High School Counselor. *Sociology of Education*, 93(4), 315–330. DOI: 10.1177/0038040720932563

Branscome, J., Cunningham, T., Kelley, H., & Brown, C. (2014). *ADHD: Implications for School Counselors*. https://files.eric.ed.gov/fulltext/EJ1084428.pdf

Champ, R. E., Adamou, M., & Tolchard, B. (2021). The impact of psychological theory on the treatment of Attention Deficit Hyperactivity Disorder (ADHD) in adults: A scoping review. *PLoS One*, 16(12), e0261247. DOI: 10.1371/journal.pone.0261247 PMID: 34932573

Christian, D., & Brown, C. (2018). Recommendations for the Role and Responsibilities of School-Based Mental Health Counselors. *Journal of School-Based Counseling Policy and Evaluation*, 1(1), 26–39. DOI: 10.25774/nmfk-y245

Cimsir, E., & Carney, J. V. (2017). School counsellor training, attitudes, and perceptions of preparedness to provide services to students with disabilities in inclusive schools in Turkey. *European Journal of Special Needs Education*, 32(3), 346–361. DOI: 10.1080/08856257.2016.1240340

Crawford, C., & Studer, J. R. (2015). Applying Counseling Theories During the Clinical Experiences. In *A Guide to Practicum and Internship for School Counselors-in-Training* (2nd ed.). Routledge.

David, D. O., Silviu, M. A., & Cardos, R. A. (2020). *Applications of Rational-Emotive and Cognitive-Behavior Technologies with Children and Adolescents. Rational-Emotive and Cognitive-Behavioral Approaches to Child and Adolescent Mental Health: Theory, Practice, Research, Applications*. Springer US.

Davies, C., & Fisher, M. (2020). Understanding research paradigms. *JARNA*, 21(3), 21–25. DOI: 10.3316/informit.160174725752074

Diagi, B. (2018). Analysis of rainfall trend and variability in Ebonyi state, South Eastern Nigeria. *Environmental and Earth Sciences Research Journal*, 5(3), 53–57. DOI: 10.18280/eesrj.050301

Dickson, H. (2022, April 1). *Tailoring Career Development Practices for Clients with ADHD*. https://www.ncda.org/aws/NCDA/pt/sd/news_article/430859/_PARENT/CC_layout_details/false

Dimmitt, C., Carey, J. C., & Hatch, T. (2007). *Evidence-Based School Counseling: Making a Difference With Data-Driven Practices*. Corwin Press.

Doyle, K. A., & Terjesen, M. D. (2006). Rational-emotive behavior therapy and attention deficit hyperactivity disorder. In *Rational emotive behavioral approaches to childhood disorders: Theory, practice and research* (pp. 281–309). Springer US. DOI: 10.1007/0-387-26375-6_10

Doyle, K. A., & Terjesen, M. D. (2020). *Rational-Emotive and Cognitive-Behavioral Treatment for Attention-Deficit/Hyperactivity Disorder Among Youth. Rational-Emotive and Cognitive-Behavioral Approaches to Child and Adolescent Mental Health: Theory, Practice, Research, Applications*. Springer US.

Dumigan, K. (2017). The Effects of Individual Counseling on Students with Disciplinary Issues. *Counselor Education Capstone. 34*. http://digitalcommons.brockport.edu/edc_capstone/34

Duong, C. D., & St-Jean, É. (2024). Social cognitive career theory and higher education students' entrepreneurial intention: The role of perceived educational support and perceived entrepreneurial opportunity. *Journal of Entrepreneurship. Management and Innovation*, 20(1), 86–102. DOI: 10.7341/20242015

Ellis, A. (2000). Can rational emotive behavior therapy (REBT) be effectively used with people who have devout beliefs in God and religion? *Professional Psychology, Research and Practice*, 31(1), 29–33. DOI: 10.1037/0735-7028.31.1.29

Eseadi, C., & Diale, B. M. (2024). *Perspectives on Career Transitioning of Students with Hearing Impairments*. IGI Global., DOI: 10.4018/979-8-3693-2631-2

Eseadi, C., Diale, B. M., Oloidi, F. J., Amanambu, O. V., & Umeano, B. C. (2023). School engagement of undergraduate history students: Effect of REBT intervention. *Journal of Rational-Emotive & Cognitive-Behavior Therapy*, 41(1), 209–221. DOI: 10.1007/s10942-022-00463-1

Eseadi, C., & Ikechukwu-Ilomuanya, A. B. (2015). Cultural sensitivity in counselling: A panacea for cultural revival in Nigeria. *Journal of Counselling and Communication*, 1(5), 114–132.

Evert, B. (2009). *Attention Deficit Hyperactivity Disorder (ADHD) in the schools: Alternative interventions for school counselors*.

Faiz, Z., Azeem, A., Siddique, M., & Warraich, W. (2021). A Comparative Study between Online and Traditional Counseling for Students with Attention Deficit Hyperactivity Disorder (ADHD): School Psychologists Perspective in the Obsequies of Pandemic COVID-19. *Linguistica Antverpiensia*, 2021, 5763–5777.

Federal Ministry of Budget and Economic Planning. (2021). National Development Plan (NDP) 2021-2025. Volume 1. Abuja: FMBEP. https://nationalplanning.gov.ng/wp-content/uploads/2021/12/NDP-2021-2025_AA_FINAL_PRINTING.pdf

Federal Ministry of Education. (2015). National Policy on Special Needs Education in Nigeria. Abuja: FME. https://planipolis.iiep.unesco.org/sites/default/files/ressources/nigeria_special_needs_policy.pdf

Federal Ministry of Education. (2023). National Policy on Inclusive Education. Abuja: FME.https://planipolis.iiep.unesco.org/sites/default/files/ressources/INCLUSIVE-EDUCATION- POLICY.pdf

Fitriyani, F., Sari, A. F., & Sari, E. N. (2024). The Role of Counselors for Special Needs Children with Attention Hyperactivity Disorder in Inclusion Schools. *ALACRITY : Journal of Education*, 496–501. DOI: 10.52121/alacrity.v4i2.394

Gibson, S. (2017). *Counseling College Students with Attention-Deficit/Hyperactivity Disorder (ADHD): A Consensual Qualitative Research (CQR) Study Examining the Experiences of College Counselors*. https://etd.ohiolink.edu/acprod/odb_etd/etd/r/1501/10?clear=10&p10_accession_num=ohiou1502293771734809

Gordon, T. R. (2002). Comprehensive School Health and Comprehensive Guidance and Counselling Programs: A Call for Collaboration. *Canadian Journal of Counselling and Psychotherapy*, 36(1), 1. https://cjc-rcc.ucalgary.ca/article/view/58684

Grothaus, T. (2013). School Counselors Serving Students with Disruptive Behavior Disorders. *Professional School Counseling*, 16(4), 2156759X150160404. DOI: 10.1177/2156759X150160404

Hart, A., & Kourkoutas, E. (2015). *Innovative Practice and Interventions for Children and Adolescents with Psychosocial Difficulties and Disabilities*. Cambridge Scholars Publishing.

Igbozuruike, I., Clancy, A., & O., O. (2022). Education and Nigeria's Developmental Plans. In *Emerging Educational Issues in Nigeria* (pp. 67-82). Ibadan, Nigeria: Constellation Publishers.

Ilongo, F. N. (2015). Students' perception of the role of school counselling. *Journal for Journal for Studies in Humanities and Social Sciences*, 4(1 & 2).

Jambu, M. (1991a). Statistical Data Elaboration. In Jambu, M. (Ed.), *Exploratory and Multivariate Data Analysis* (pp. 19–25). Academic Press., DOI: 10.1016/B978-0-08-092367-3.50006-X

Jambu, M. (1991b). *Statistics—An overview.* https://www.sciencedirect.com/topics/mathematics/statistics

Kamal, M., Al-Shibli, S., Shahbal, S., & Yadav, S. K. (2021). Impact of attention deficit hyperactivity disorder and gender differences on academic and social difficulties among adolescents in Qatari Schools. *Qatar Medical Journal*, 1(1), 11. DOI: 10.5339/qmj.2021.11 PMID: 33777722

Lambie, G. W., Stickl Haugen, J., Borland, J. R., & Campbell, L. O. (2019). Who Took" Counseling" out of the Role of Professional School Counselors in the United States? *Journal of School-Based Counseling Policy and Evaluation*, 1(3), 51–61. DOI: 10.25774/7kjb-bt85

Langberg, J. M., Epstein, J. N., & Graham, A. J. (2008). Organizational-skills interventions in the treatment of ADHD. *Expert Review of Neurotherapeutics*, 8(10), 1549–1561. DOI: 10.1586/14737175.8.10.1549 PMID: 18928347

Lavin, P. (1991). The counselor as consultant-coordinator for children with attention deficit hyperactivity disorder. *Elementary School Guidance & Counseling*, 26(2), 115–120.

Ly, A., Stefan, A., van Doorn, J., Dablander, F., van den Bergh, D., Sarafoglou, A., Kucharský, Š., Derks, K., Gronau, Q. F., Raj, A., Boehm, U., van Kesteren, E.-J., Hinne, M., Matzke, D., Marsman, M., & Wagenmakers, E. J. (2020). The Bayesian methodology of Sir Harold Jeffreys as a practical alternative to the p value hypothesis test. *Computational Brain & Behavior*, 3(2), 153–161. DOI: 10.1007/s42113-019-00070-x

Martin, D. M. (2017). School counselors' perceptions of family systems perspectives. *The Family Journal (Alexandria, Va.)*, 25(3), 271–277. DOI: 10.1177/1066480717711109

McMahon, H. G., Mason, E. C. M., & Paisley, P. O. (2009). School Counselor Educators as Educational Leaders Promoting Systemic Change. *Professional School Counseling, 13*(2), 2156759X0901300207. DOI: 10.1177/2156759X0901300207

Mecadon-Mann, M., & Tuttle, M. (2023). School Counselor Professional Identity in Relation to Post-master's Supervision. *Professional School Counseling*, 27(1), 2156759X221143932. Advance online publication. DOI: 10.1177/2156759X221143932

Mills, J. G. (2024, March 16). Survey Research Design, A Simple Introduction. https://www.supersurvey.com/Research

Mohamed, G. M., Al-Deen, Z. N., & Alanee, A. H. (2023). Prevalence of Attention Deficit Hyperactivity Disorder among Primary School Students in Tikrit City, Iraq 2023. *The Medical Journal of Tikrit University*, 29(2), 29–35. DOI: 10.25130/mjotu.29.1.5

Morgan, L. W., Greenwaldt, M. E., & Gosselin, K. P. (2014). School Counselors' Perceptions of Competency in Career Counseling. *The Professional Counselor*, 4(5), 481–496. DOI: 10.15241/lwm.4.5.481

Mullen, P. R., Chae, N., & Backer, A. (2019). Comparison of School Characteristics Among RAMP and Non-RAMP Schools. *The Professional Counselor*, 9(2), 156–170. DOI: 10.15241/prm.9.2.156

Nelson, J. M. (1997). Applications of rational emotive behavior therapy in the school setting. Graduate Research Papers. 1267. https://scholarworks.uni.edu/grp/1267

Nick, T. G. (2007). Descriptive Statistics. In Ambrosius, W. T. (Ed.), *Topics in Biostatistics* (pp. 33–52). Humana Press., DOI: 10.1007/978-1-59745-530-5_3

Obiweluozo, P. E., Dike, I. C., Ogba, F. N., Elom, C. O., Orabueze, F. O., Okoye-Ugwu, S., Ani, C. K., Onu, A. O., Ukaogo, V., Obayi, L. N., Abonyi, S. E., Onu, J., Omenma, Z. O., Okoro, I. D., Eze, A., Igu, N. C., Onuigbo, L. N., Umeano, E. C., & Onyishi, C. N. (2021). Stress in teachers of children with neuro-developmental disorders: Effect of blended rational emotive behavioral therapy. *Science Progress*, 104(4), 00368504211050278. DOI: 10.1177/00368504211050278 PMID: 34783626

Obiweluozo, P. E., Dike, I. C., Ogba, F. N., Elom, C. O., Orabueze, F. O., Okoye-Ugwu, S., Ani, C. K. C., Onu, A. O., Ukaogo, V., Obayi, L. N., Abonyi, S. E., Onu, J., Omenma, Z. O., Okoro, I. D., Eze, A., Igu, N. C. N., Onuigbo, L. N., Umeano, E. C., & Onyishi, C. N. (2021). Stress in teachers of children with neuro-developmental disorders: Effect of blended rational emotive behavioral therapy. *Science Progress*, 104(4), 00368504211050278. DOI: 10.1177/00368504211050278 PMID: 34783626

Ogba, F. N., Ugodulunwa, C. A., & Igu, N. C. (2020). Assessment of Training Needs of Teachers and Administrators for Effective Inclusive Education Delivery in Secondary Schools in South East Nigeria. *The International Journal of Educational Leadership Preparation*, 15(1), 72–91.

Ogbuanya, T. C., Eseadi, C., Orji, C. T., Anyanwu, J. I., Ede, M. O., & Bakare, J. (2018). Effect of rational emotive behavior therapy on negative career thoughts of students in technical colleges in Nigeria. *Psychological Reports*, 121(2), 356–374. DOI: 10.1177/0033294117724449 PMID: 28776484

Okere, A. U., Onyechi, K. C. N., Eseadi, C., Onuorah, A., Ncheke, C. D., Ogbuabor, S. E., & Ogidi, C. I. (2016). Influence of Counsellors in the Promotion of Educational Activities of Pupils in Primary Schools in Anambra State, Nigeria. *European Journal of Soil Science*, 53(1), 6–16.

Olatunji, G., Faturoti, O., Jaiyeoba, B., Toluwabori, A. V., Adefusi, T., Olaniyi, P., Aderinto, N., & Abdulbasit, M. O. (2023). Navigating unique challenges and advancing equitable care for children with ADHD in Africa: A review. *Annals of Medicine and Surgery (London)*, 85(10), 4939–4946. DOI: 10.1097/MS9.0000000000001179 PMID: 37811061

Oltean, H.-R., Hyland, P., Vallières, F., & David, D. O. (2017). An Empirical Assessment of REBT Models of Psychopathology and Psychological Health in the Prediction of Anxiety and Depression Symptoms. *Behavioural and Cognitive Psychotherapy*, 45(6), 600–615. DOI: 10.1017/S1352465817000133 PMID: 28347384

Oral, M., & Karakurt, N. (2020). Knowledge and Awareness of Guidance Counselors About Attention Deficit and Hyperactivity Disorder and Specific Learning Disability/Psikolojik Danisman ve Rehber Ogretmenlerin Dikkat Eksikligi ve Hiperaktivite Bozuklugu ve Ozgul Ogrenme Guclugu Hakkindaki Bilgi ve Farkindalik Duzeyleri. *Çocuk ve Gençlik Ruh Sağlığı Dergisi*, 27(1), 20–27. DOI: 10.4274/tjcamh.galenos.2019.98752

Owens, L. K. (2002, January). Introduction to survey research design. In *SRL Fall 2002 Seminar Series* (Vol. 1).

Prevatt, F., Smith, S. M., Diers, S., Marshall, D., Coleman, J., Valler, E., & Miller, N. (2017). ADHD Coaching With College Students: Exploring the Processes Involved in Motivation and Goal Completion. *Journal of College Student Psychotherapy*, 31(2), 93–111. DOI: 10.1080/87568225.2016.1240597

Prout, H. T., & Brown, D. T. (2007). *Counseling and Psychotherapy with Children and Adolescents: Theory and Practice for School and Clinical Settings*. John Wiley and Sons.

Pugh, C. D. L. (2021). Opinions, Attitudes, and Self-Efficacy of Secondary School Counselors in RAMP and non-RAMP Designated Schools and their Work with Students with Disabilities. (Doctoral dissertation, The University of Mississippi).

Quintero, D., & Gu, Y. (2019, July 3). *Rural schools need career counselors, too.* Brookings. https://www.brookings.edu/articles/rural-schools-need-career-counselors-too/

Ramachandran, K. M., & Tsokos, C. P. (2015). Descriptive Statistics. In Ramachandran, K. M., & Tsokos, C. P. (Eds.), *Mathematical Statistics with Applications in R* (2nd ed., pp. 1–52). Academic Press., DOI: 10.1016/B978-0-12-417113-8.00001-1

Rehman, A. A., & Alharthi, K. (2016). An introduction to research paradigms. *International Journal of Educational Investigations*, 3(8), 51–59.

Rosner, R. (2011). Albert Ellis' rational-emotive behavior therapy. *Adolescent Psychiatry (Hilversum, Netherlands)*, 1(1), 82–87. DOI: 10.2174/2210676611101010082

Scholtz, S. E. (2021). Sacrifice is a step beyond convenience: A review of convenience sampling in psychological research in Africa. *SA Journal of Industrial Psychology*, 47(1), 1–12. DOI: 10.4102/sajip.v47i0.1837

Schwiebert, V. L., Sealander, K. A., & Tollerud, T. R. (1995). attention-deficit hyperactivity disorder: An overview for school counselors. *Elementary School Guidance & Counseling*, 29(4), 249–259.

Shaikh, A. (2018). Group Therapy for Improving Self-Esteem and Social Functioning of College Students With ADHD. *Journal of College Student Psychotherapy*, 32(3), 220–241. DOI: 10.1080/87568225.2017.1388755

Shillingford-Butler, M. A., & Theodore, L. (2012). Students Diagnosed with Attention Deficit Hyperactivity Disorder: Collaborative Strategies for School Counselors. *Professional School Counseling*, 16(2_suppl), 2156759X12016002S05. DOI: 10.1177/2156759X12016002S05

Skogli, E. W., Teicher, M. H., Andersen, P. N., Hovik, K. T., & Øie, M. (2013). ADHD in girls and boys – gender differences in co-existing symptoms and executive function measures. *BMC Psychiatry*, 13(1), 298. DOI: 10.1186/1471-244X-13-298 PMID: 24206839

Slee, R. (2018). Defining the scope of inclusive education. *Ministerio De Educación*. https://repositorio.minedu.gob.pe/handle/20.500.12799/5977

Song, S. (2024). The Role of Cultural Factors in Attention Deficit Hyperactivity Disorder (ADHD) Diagnosis in Children in Nigeria. *Studies in Psychological Science*, 2(1), 40–47. DOI: 10.56397/SPS.2024.03.05

Srivastava, M., de Boer, A. A., & Pijl, S. J. (2017). Preparing for the inclusive classroom: Changing teachers' attitudes and knowledge. *Teacher Development*, 21(4), 561–579. DOI: 10.1080/13664530.2017.1279681

Stewart, T. I. (2006). *Supporting Children with Attention-Deficit/Hyperactivity Disorder: Using Group Counseling to Help Increase Understanding and Self-Concept.* (Master of Science in Education, SUNY Brockport). http://hdl.handle.net/20.500.12648/4698

Tarver Behring, S., & Spagna, M. (2004). Counseling With Exceptional Children. *Focus on Exceptional Children*, 36(8), 1–12. DOI: 10.17161/fec.v36i8.6806

The Pan-African Parliament. (2020, June 6). *Breaking down barriers to inclusive education*. Pan-African Parliament. https://pap.au.int/en/news/press-releases/2024-06-26/breaking-down-barriers-inclusive-education

Toby, J. M., Neale-McFall, C. W., & Owens, E. W. (2016). A Review of Rural and Urban School Counseling: Exploring Implications for Successful Post-Secondary Student Outcomes. *Journal of the Pennsylvania Counseling Association*, 15, 1–8.

van der Meer, J. M., Lappenschaar, M. G., Hartman, C. A., Greven, C. U., Buitelaar, J. K., & Rommelse, N. N. (2017). Homogeneous combinations of ASD–ADHD traits and their cognitive and behavioral correlates in a population-based sample. *Journal of Attention Disorders*, 21(9), 753–763. DOI: 10.1177/1087054714533194 PMID: 24819924

Van Haute, E. (2021). Sampling Techniques. Sample Types and Sample Size. In *Research Methods in the Social Sciences: An A-Z of key concepts*. Oxford University Press., DOI: 10.1093/hepl/9780198850298.003.0057

Webb, L. D., & Myrick, R. D. (2003). A Group Counseling Intervention for Children with Attention Deficit Hyperactivity Disorder. *Professional School Counseling*, 7(2), 108–115.

Wingfield, R. J., & Reese, R. F. (2010). Counselors as Leaders in Schools. *Florida Journal of Educational Administration & Policy*, 4(1), 114–130.

Wofford, J. R., & Ohrt, J. H. (2018). An Integrated Approach to Counseling Children Diagnosed With ADHD, ODD, and Chronic Stressors. *The Family Journal (Alexandria, Va.)*, 26(1), 105–109. DOI: 10.1177/1066480718756594

Yaden, J., Privette, G., & Keller, J. (1995). The Role of the Counselor with Attention Deficit Disorder Students in Middle Schools. https://files.eric.ed.gov/fulltext/ED392002.pdf

Zabek, F., Lyons, M. D., Alwani, N., Taylor, J. V., Brown-Meredith, E., Cruz, M. A., & Southall, V. H. (2023). Roles and Functions of School Mental Health Professionals Within Comprehensive School Mental Health Systems. *School Mental Health*, 15(1), 1–18. DOI: 10.1007/s12310-022-09535-0 PMID: 35911088

ADDITIONAL READINGS

Akos, P., Bastian, K. C., Domina, T., & de Luna, L. M. M. (2019). Recognized ASCA Model Program (RAMP) and student outcomes in elementary and middle schools. *Professional School Counseling, 22*(1), 2156759X19869933.

American School Counselor Association. (2003). The ASCA national model: A framework for school counseling programs. *Professional School Counseling*, •••, 165–168.

Belser, C. T., Shillingford, M., & Joe, J. R. (2016). The ASCA model and a multi-tiered system of supports: A framework to support students of color with problem behavior. *The Professional Counselor*, 6(3), 251–262. DOI: 10.15241/cb.6.3.251

Eseadi, C., Anyanwu, J. I., Ogbuabor, S. E., & Ikechukwu-Ilomuanya, A. B. (2016). Effects of cognitive restructuring intervention program of rational-emotive behavior therapy on adverse childhood stress in Nigeria. *Journal of Rational-Emotive & Cognitive-Behavior Therapy*, 34(1), 51–72. DOI: 10.1007/s10942-015-0229-4

Hart, K. C., Fabiano, G. A., Evans, S. W., Manos, M. J., Hannah, J. N., & Vujnovic, R. K. (2017). Elementary and middle school teachers' self-reported use of positive behavioral supports for children with ADHD: A national survey. *Journal of Emotional and Behavioral Disorders*, 25(4), 246–256. DOI: 10.1177/1063426616681980

Jensen, C. M., Amdisen, B. L., Jørgensen, K. J., & Arnfred, S. M. (2016). Cognitive behavioural therapy for ADHD in adults: Systematic review and meta-analyses. *Attention Deficit and Hyperactivity Disorders*, 8(1), 3–11. DOI: 10.1007/s12402-016-0188-3 PMID: 26801998

Jobson, M. C. (2020). Emotional maturity among adolescents and its importance. *Indian Journal of Mental Health*, 7(1), 35–41. DOI: 10.30877/IJMH.7.1.2020.35-41

Jogsan, Y. A. (2013). Emotional maturity and adjustment in ADHD children. *Journal of Psychology & Psychotherapy*, 3(2), 1–4. DOI: 10.4172/2161-0487.1000114

Martinussen, R., Tannock, R., & Chaban, P. (2011, June). Teachers' reported use of instructional and behavior management practices for students with behavior problems: Relationship to role and level of training in ADHD. [). Springer US.]. *Child and Youth Care Forum*, 40(3), 193–210. DOI: 10.1007/s10566-010-9130-6

Messina, I., Calvo, V., Masaro, C., Ghedin, S., & Marogna, C. (2021). Interpersonal emotion regulation: From research to group therapy. *Frontiers in Psychology*, 12, 636919. DOI: 10.3389/fpsyg.2021.636919 PMID: 33859593

Onuigbo, L. N., Eseadi, C., Ebifa, S., Ugwu, U. C., Onyishi, C. N., & Oyeoku, E. K. (2019). Effect of rational emotive behavior therapy program on depressive symptoms among university students with blindness in Nigeria. *Journal of Rational-Emotive & Cognitive-Behavior Therapy*, 37(1), 17–38. DOI: 10.1007/s10942-018-0297-3

Pfiffner, L. J., Mikami, A. Y., Huang-Pollock, C., Easterlin, B., Zalecki, C., & McBurnett, K. (2007). A randomized, controlled trial of integrated home-school behavioral treatment for ADHD, predominantly inattentive type. *Journal of the American Academy of Child and Adolescent Psychiatry*, 46(8), 1041–1050. DOI: 10.1097/chi.0b013e318064675f PMID: 17667482

Pyne, J. R. (2011). Comprehensive School Counseling Programs, Job Satisfaction, and the ASCA National Model. *Professional School Counseling*, 15(2), 2156759X1101500202. Advance online publication. DOI: 10.1177/2156759X1101500202

Sharma, B. (2012). Adjustment and emotional maturity among first year college students. *Pakistan Journal of Social and Clinical Psychology*, 9(3), 32–37.

Sunko, E., Batarelo Kokić, I., & Vlah, N. (2021). Teachers' inclusive beliefs and teaching practices in work with students with some inattentive symptoms associated with ADHD. *Zbornik radova Islamskog pedagoškog fakulteta u Zenici*, 19(19), 103-126.

KEY TERMS AND DEFINITIONS

Behavioral Support: Refers to a collection of strategies and interventions aimed at assisting individuals in managing and improving their behavior, especially in educational, therapeutic, or social contexts. This approach prioritizes the identification of the underlying factors contributing to challenging behaviors and encourages the adoption of positive alternatives through structured guidance and reinforcement. Behavioral support may include personalized plans, such as Behavior Intervention Plans (BIPs), which delineate specific goals, triggers, and strategies for addressing disruptive or maladaptive behaviors. Common methods employed in this process include positive reinforcement, the establishment of clear expectations, consistent routines, and social-emotional learning, all of which contribute to the development of self-regulation, communication, and social skills. Effective behavioral support necessitates collaboration among educators, counselors, therapists, and families to establish a cohesive and supportive environment that promotes growth and positive change. The overarching goal is to empower individuals to adopt healthier behaviors, enhance their well-being, and improve their social and academic experiences, ultimately allowing them to succeed in various contexts.

Career Transition Counseling: A process designed to assist individuals in navigating the complexities of changing or advancing their careers. This form of counseling is particularly beneficial for those facing career changes due to factors such as job loss, retirement, emerging interests, or shifts in personal circumstances. Career transition counselors evaluate clients' skills, interests, values, and experiences to pinpoint appropriate career paths and develop tailored transition strategies. They provide support in various areas, including goal setting, job search techniques, networking; resume development, and interview preparation. Additionally, counselors address the emotional challenges that may arise during transitions, such as stress management, uncertainty, and the potential loss of professional identity. Through comprehensive guidance and practical resources, career transition counseling seeks to enhance clients' confidence, improve their adaptability, and facilitate the pursuit of rewarding new career opportunities. The overarching aim is to empower individuals to attain success and fulfillment in their changing professional journeys.

Cognitive Behavioral Therapy (CBT): A well-established, evidence-based psychological approach that centers on recognizing and altering negative thought processes and behaviors. It is founded on the understanding that thoughts, emotions, and behaviors are interconnected, and that modifying negative or distorted thinking can result in beneficial changes in feelings and actions. CBT aids individuals in identifying cognitive distortions, such as dichotomous thinking or catastrophizing, and encourages the development of more realistic and balanced perspectives. The therapy involves the formulation of specific, measurable goals and the acquisition of practical skills to tackle issues like anxiety, depression, phobias, or stress. Techniques frequently utilized in CBT include cognitive restructuring, exposure therapy, and relaxation exercises. Therapists engage in a collaborative process with clients to challenge unhelpful beliefs and foster healthier coping strategies. By empowering individuals to take charge of their thoughts and reactions, CBT enhances emotional resilience and contributes to long-term improvements in mental health and well-being.

Counselors: Qualified professionals dedicated to offering guidance, support, and advice to individuals or groups encountering personal, emotional, social, or psychological difficulties. They assist clients in examining their feelings, thoughts, and behaviors, collaborating to formulate coping strategies and solutions. With expertise in active listening, empathy, and effective communication, counselors foster a secure, non-judgmental environment where clients can freely express themselves. Depending on their specialization, counselors may tackle a variety of issues, including relationship problems, mental health challenges, grief, academic pressures, career choices, or life transitions. They utilize diverse therapeutic methods, such as person-centered therapy, cognitive-behavioral therapy, and solution-focused brief therapy, tailored to the specific needs and objectives of their clients. The primary goal of a counselor is to empower clients to comprehend and navigate their challenges, enhance their self-awareness, and improve their overall well-being, thereby facilitating healthier and more satisfying lives.

Disability: A range of physical, mental, intellectual, or sensory impairments that significantly hinder an individual's capacity to engage in daily activities, fully participate in society, or interact with their surroundings. These impairments may be present from birth or acquired later in life, and they can vary in intensity, impacting mobility, communication, cognitive functions, or sensory abilities. It is essential to understand that disabilities are not merely defined by an individual's challenges but also by the societal and environmental obstacles that impede their complete participation and inclusion. The understanding of disability has progressed from a strictly medical perspective, which emphasizes deficits, to a social model that highlights the significance of accessibility, inclusion, and rights. Acknowledging the unique strengths and viewpoints of individuals with disabilities, initiatives are undertaken to foster supportive environments, enact inclusive policies, and offer reasonable accommodation. Disability advocacy seeks to advance equality, respect, and dignity, ensuring that all individuals, irrespective of their abilities, have the opportunity to lead fulfilling and independent lives.

Emotional Maturity: Refers to the capacity to comprehend, manage, and articulate one's emotions in a balanced and constructive manner, particularly in difficult circumstances. This quality encompasses self-awareness, empathy, and the ability to regulate one's feelings, allowing for thoughtful decision-making instead of impulsive reactions. Individuals who exhibit emotional maturity show resilience, take responsibility for their actions, and manage stress and adversity with poise. They are adept at recognizing and valuing the emotions of others, which promotes healthy relationships and effective communication. Furthermore, emotional maturity entails a readiness to learn from experiences, accept constructive criticism, and pursue personal and interpersonal growth. The journey toward developing emotional maturity is gradual and often necessitates self-reflection, emotional intelligence, and ongoing learning. It is essential for personal well-being, social interactions, and professional achievement, equipping individuals to face life's challenges with patience, adaptability, and a constructive outlook.

Frustration Tolerance: Defined as an individual's ability to cope with and withstand challenging circumstances, setbacks, or unmet expectations without succumbing to feelings of being overwhelmed or reacting in an impulsive manner. This vital emotional competency allows individuals to maintain their composure and tranquility when confronted with obstacles, delays, or difficulties. Those who possess a high level of frustration tolerance can exhibit patience, engage in rational thinking, and devise constructive solutions when faced with unforeseen challenges. Conversely, individuals with low frustration tolerance may experience heightened feelings of irritation, anger, or helplessness, potentially leading to negative behaviors such as emotional outbursts, resignation, or avoidance. Enhancing frustration tolerance requires the development of effective coping mechanisms, including deep breathing techniques, problem-solving skills, and the reframing of negative thoughts. Additionally, it involves gradually facing challenging situations to bolster resilience. This skill is essential for personal development, as it improves problem-solving capabilities, emotional regulation, and adaptability across various life domains.

Gender-Sensitive Approach: Focuses on identifying and addressing the unique needs, experiences, and challenges that individuals face in relation to their gender. This viewpoint acknowledges that societal conventions, expectations, and power structures can affect individuals in varying ways depending on their gender identity. In practice, this approach strives to establish inclusive environments that uphold principles of equality, respect, and fairness. It involves a thorough consideration of gender-related barriers, biases, and stereotypes in diverse scenarios, such as education and workplaces. The approach prioritizes equitable opportunities and treatment for all individuals, ensuring that harmful stereotypes and gender-based discrimination are not perpetuated. The ultimate aim is to nurture environments that are supportive, inclusive, and responsive to the varied experiences and needs of individuals across the gender spectrum.

Inclusive School Counselors: Dedicated professionals who emphasize equity and diversity in their efforts to assist students within educational environments. They strive to cultivate a setting where every student, irrespective of their background, abilities, or circumstances, is recognized, respected, and supported. These counselors are attuned to the distinct challenges encountered by marginalized or underrepresented populations, including students with disabilities, those from varied cultural or socio-economic backgrounds, and individuals facing social or emotional challenges. They partner with other stakeholders to create strategies that eliminate obstacles to learning and foster inclusivity. By advocating for equitable policies, inclusive practices, and culturally sensitive interventions, inclusive school counselors ensure that all students are given access to resources and support services to thrive academically, socially, and emotionally. Their commitment lies in nurturing a sense of belonging and developing initiatives that promote the overall well-being of every student.

Interpersonal Group Therapy (IPT-G): A therapeutic method aimed at enhancing individuals' relationships and communication dynamics within a group framework. This approach is predicated on the understanding that psychological distress frequently arises from challenges in interpersonal relationships and social interactions. Within IPT-G, participants delve into their emotions, behaviors, and interactions with others in a nurturing group atmosphere. The therapist guides discussions that enable members to identify and confront patterns of conflict, social withdrawal, role changes, and unresolved grief. The group setting provides participants with the opportunity to gain insights into their own behaviors, receive constructive feedback, and discover new ways to engage with others. The primary objective of IPT-G is to improve individuals' social competencies, emotional expression, and ability to cultivate healthier, more satisfying relationships. Addressing interpersonal challenges allows group members to improve their emotional regulation, self-awareness, and resilience, which in turn contributes to better mental health.

Irrational Beliefs: Inflexible, unrealistic, and self-sabotaging notions or assumptions that individuals maintain regarding themselves, others, or the world at large. Such beliefs frequently result in negative emotional states, maladaptive behaviors, and a skewed understanding of reality. These beliefs are often marked by demands, such as "I must achieve perfection" or "People ought to treat me with respect," and typically include absolutes like "always," "never," or "must." Consequently, they can lead to feelings of frustration, anxiety, depression, or anger when expectations are not met. For instance, the belief that failure is intolerable may incite a profound fear of making errors and result in avoidance behaviors. Identifying and disputing irrational beliefs is a fundamental aspect of Rational Emotive Behavior Therapy (REBT) and various cognitive-behavioral methods. By substituting irrational beliefs with more adaptable and rational thoughts, individuals can cultivate healthier emotional responses and enhance their capacity to navigate life's challenges in a more balanced manner.

Neurodivergent Conditions: Refers to the diverse variations in brain function and development that result in unique cognitive processes, learning styles, and interactions with the environment. This concept encompasses a variety of neurological differences, including Autism Spectrum Disorder, ADHD, dyslexia, dyspraxia, and other neurodivergent conditions. Neurodivergence challenges the traditional understanding of "normal" brain function, asserting that these differences should not be viewed as deficits but as alternative ways of experiencing and processing information. Individuals with neurodivergent conditions may struggle in conventional settings due to rigid standards, uniform teaching methods, and societal expectations. However, with the appropriate support, accommodations, and inclusive practices, neurodivergent individuals can excel and utilize their distinctive strengths. Promoting neurodiversity cultivates acceptance, understanding, and appreciation for diverse cognitive experiences, leading to more inclusive environments in education, workplaces, and society as a whole. The focus transitions from "fixing" differences to embracing and valuing them as vital aspects of human diversity.

Rational Emotive Behavior Therapy (REBT): A kind of cognitive-behavioral intervention created by psychologist Albert Ellis. This therapeutic approach centers on recognizing and disputing irrational beliefs that can lead to emotional and behavioral issues. Participants in REBT often cling to rigid and unrealistic beliefs about themselves, others, or the world around them, which may result in negative feelings such as anxiety, anger, or depression. These irrational beliefs are commonly articulated through "must," "should," or "ought" statements, such as "I must be flawless" or "Others should always treat me with fairness." The aim of REBT is to guide individuals in replacing these irrational beliefs with more rational, flexible, and realistic perspectives. Through cognitive restructuring, clients learn to alter negative thinking patterns and foster healthier emotional responses and behaviors. REBT highlights that while individuals may not be able to control every external event, they can influence their interpretations and reactions, leading to enhanced emotional health and improved problem-solving capabilities.

Recognized ASCA Model Program (RAMP): A prestigious designation conferred by the American School Counselor Association (ASCA) to school counseling programs that exemplify outstanding alignment with the ASCA National Model framework. Schools that achieve RAMP designation have developed a comprehensive, data-driven counseling program that prioritizes enhancing student outcomes in academic performance, career development, and social-emotional well-being. The ASCA Model highlights critical program components such as foundation, management, delivery, and accountability to ensure both consistency and effectiveness. RAMP schools illustrate that their programs are proactive, developmental, and designed to cater to the diverse needs of all students. The recognition process requires a meticulous application that demonstrates how the school counseling program adheres to ASCA standards, including goal setting, program planning, implementation, and results evaluation. Earning RAMP status signifies that a school's counseling program is evidence-based, focused on students, and committed to continuous improvement and professional growth.

School Counselors: Dedicated professionals within educational institutions who assist students in their academic, career, personal, and social growth. Their main responsibility is to guide students through the various challenges encountered in the school environment, including academic stress, peer interactions, emotional struggles, and career development. They offer both individual and group counseling sessions aimed at fostering positive mental health, boosting self-esteem, and addressing behavioral concerns. Collaborating closely with teachers, parents, and school administrators, school counselors strive to create supportive educational settings and devise strategies to enhance student performance and overall well-being. Additionally, they play a vital role in assisting students with educational transitions, exploring career options, and making informed decisions. Utilizing a range of tools, such as assessments and career planning resources, they help students establish realistic goals and prepare for their future endeavors. Through their proactive interventions and preventive initiatives, school counselors significantly contribute to the comprehensive development of students and promote an inclusive and supportive school culture.

Therapeutic Interventions: A set of organized strategies and techniques employed by mental health professionals to tackle psychological, emotional, or behavioral difficulties faced by individuals. The primary objective of these interventions is to facilitate healing, improve coping mechanisms, and enhance overall well-being. Various methodologies, including talk therapy, art therapy, play therapy, and mindfulness practices, may be utilized, each customized to address the unique needs of the individual. The choice of intervention is generally informed by a comprehensive assessment of the individual's challenges, aspirations, and context. These interventions can take place in individual, group, or family settings and may address a wide array of issues, including anxiety, depression, trauma, and relationship problems. By fostering a secure and supportive atmosphere, therapeutic interventions allow individuals to examine their thoughts, emotions, and behaviors, cultivate healthier coping strategies, and pursue personal development. The overarching aim is to empower individuals to surmount their challenges and improve their quality of life.

APPENDIX I: STUDY QUESTIONNAIRE

Table 3. Inclusive school counselors' perspectives on theories and techniques relevant to career transition and ADHD questionnaire (ISCPTCTQ)

No	Statements	NAA	SE	ME	GE	VGE
1	To what extent are you familiar with the use of career counseling theories for students with ADHD?					
2	To what extent do you use the Trait and Factor Theory in your counseling sessions with ADHD students?					
3	To what extent do you incorporate the Social Cognitive Career Theory in your career counseling sessions with students who have ADHD?					
4	To what extent do you apply the Person-Environment Fit Theory in career counseling for students with ADHD?					
5	To what extent do you apply counseling techniques to understand the unique career challenges faced by students with ADHD?					
6	To what extent do you use career development theories in your counseling practice with students who have ADHD?					
7	To what extent do you apply Cognitive Information Processing Theory in your career counseling?					
8	To what extent do you use narrative approaches in career counseling with students who have ADHD?					
9	To what extent do you focus on using counseling techniques to promote the career transition outcomes of students with ADHD during counseling sessions?					
10	To what extent do you employ motivational interviewing techniques in your counseling sessions with students who have ADHD?					
11	To what extent do you assess the executive functioning skills of students with ADHD during career counseling?					
12	To what extent do you integrate technology-based tools in career counseling with students who have ADHD?					
13	How well do you tailor your counseling strategies to accommodate the learning styles of students with ADHD?					
14	To what extent do you use goal-setting strategies in your counseling sessions?					
15	To what extent do you collaborate with teachers and parents in the career counseling process for students with ADHD?					
16	To what extent are you familiar with new techniques in counseling students with ADHD?					
17	To what extent do you evaluate the impact of your counseling interventions with students who have ADHD?					
18	To what extent do you adapt techniques from other disciplines in providing services related to ADHD and career counseling?					
19	How well do you understand the impact of ADHD on career decision-making processes and career transition during counseling sessions?					
20	To what extent do you feel confident in your ability to adapt transition theories in counseling students with ADHD?					

NAA=Not at All, SE=Small Extent, ME=Moderate Extent, GE=Great Extent, VGE=Very Great Extent

APPENDIX II: ADDITIONAL STATISTICS

Table 4. Item-total statistics

No	Statements	Cronbach's Alpha if Item Deleted
1	To what extent are you familiar with the use of career counseling theories for students with ADHD?	.720
2	To what extent do you use the Trait and Factor Theory in your counseling sessions with ADHD students?	.707
3	To what extent do you incorporate the Social Cognitive Career Theory in your career counseling sessions with students who have ADHD?	.711
4	To what extent do you apply the Person-Environment Fit Theory in career counseling for students with ADHD?	.701
5	To what extent do you apply counseling techniques to understand the unique career challenges faced by students with ADHD?	.692
6	To what extent do you use career development theories in your counseling practice with students who have ADHD?	.680
7	To what extent do you apply Cognitive Information Processing Theory in your career counseling?	.665
8	To what extent do you use narrative approaches in career counseling with students who have ADHD?	.642
9	To what extent do you focus on using counseling techniques to promote the career transition outcomes of students with ADHD during counseling sessions?	.694
10	To what extent do you employ motivational interviewing techniques in your counseling sessions with students who have ADHD?	.687
11	To what extent do you assess the executive functioning skills of students with ADHD during career counseling?	.675
12	To what extent do you integrate technology-based tools in career counseling with students who have ADHD?	.657
13	How well do you tailor your counseling strategies to accommodate the learning styles of students with ADHD?	.629
14	To what extent do you use goal-setting strategies in your counseling sessions?	.664
15	To what extent do you collaborate with teachers and parents in the career counseling process for students with ADHD?	.720
16	To what extent are you familiar with new techniques in counseling students with ADHD?	.674
17	To what extent do you evaluate the impact of your counseling interventions with students who have ADHD?	.712
18	To what extent do you adapt techniques from other disciplines in providing services related to ADHD and career counseling?	.648
19	How well do you understand the impact of ADHD on career decision-making processes and career transition during counseling sessions?	.737
20	To what extent do you feel confident in your ability to adapt transition theories in counseling students with ADHD?	.686

Table 5. Communalities (extraction method: principal component analysis)

No	Statements	Extraction
1	To what extent are you familiar with the use of career counseling theories for students with ADHD?	.887
2	To what extent do you use the Trait and Factor Theory in your counseling sessions with ADHD students?	.855
3	To what extent do you incorporate the Social Cognitive Career Theory in your career counseling sessions with students who have ADHD?	.912
4	To what extent do you apply the Person-Environment Fit Theory in career counseling for students with ADHD?	.903
5	To what extent do you apply counseling techniques to understand the unique career challenges faced by students with ADHD?	.727
6	To what extent do you use career development theories in your counseling practice with students who have ADHD?	.912
7	To what extent do you apply Cognitive Information Processing Theory in your career counseling?	.870
8	To what extent do you use narrative approaches in career counseling with students who have ADHD?	.931
9	To what extent do you focus on using counseling techniques to promote the career transition outcomes of students with ADHD during counseling sessions?	.871
10	To what extent do you employ motivational interviewing techniques in your counseling sessions with students who have ADHD?	.762
11	To what extent do you assess the executive functioning skills of students with ADHD during career counseling?	.851
12	To what extent do you integrate technology-based tools in career counseling with students who have ADHD?	.937
13	How well do you tailor your counseling strategies to accommodate the learning styles of students with ADHD?	.861
14	To what extent do you use goal-setting strategies in your counseling sessions?	.916
15	To what extent do you collaborate with teachers and parents in the career counseling process for students with ADHD?	.834
16	To what extent are you familiar with new techniques in counseling students with ADHD?	.736
17	To what extent do you evaluate the impact of your counseling interventions with students who have ADHD?	.937
18	To what extent do you adapt techniques from other disciplines in providing services related to ADHD and career counseling?	.883
19	How well do you understand the impact of ADHD on career decision-making processes and career transition during counseling sessions?	.805
20	To what extent do you feel confident in your ability to adapt transition theories in counseling students with ADHD?	.654

Chapter 3
Teachers' Perspectives on the Effectiveness of Educational and Public Policies and Legislation in Promoting Career Transition of Students With ADHD

ABSTRACT

This study investigated the perspectives of inclusive secondary school teachers regarding the effectiveness of educational and public policies in facilitating the career transition of students with ADHD. A survey design was employed, involving 45 teachers who responded to a 16-item questionnaire to share their perspectives. The results indicate that teachers have a moderate view of the effectiveness of these policies educational and public policies in facilitating the career transition of students with ADHD. No significant differences were observed based on gender, teaching experience, or school location of the teachers. This finding urges policymakers to consider more proactive policy initiatives to effectively support the career transition of students with ADHD.

DOI: 10.4018/979-8-3693-2635-0.ch003

BACKGROUND

It is imperative to comprehend the diverse perspectives surrounding educational and public policies and the nature of such policies, as this is crucial for enhancing positive career transition outcomes for students with attention-deficit/hyperactivity disorder (ADHD). Gaining insight into the efficacy of educational and public policies can be instrumental in facilitating policy changes at both school and societal levels. A holistic policy support system is essential to ensure the success of educational and public policies and legislation in facilitating the career transition of students with ADHD. Although our interest is to ascertain whether teachers have differing opinions about the efficacy of educational and public policies in relation to career transition, it is important to acknowledge the work of Milsom (2002) who observed that legislative actions have significantly influenced the educational experiences of students with disabilities. The inclusive education policy for students with disabilities in mainstream educational environments has received international support through legislation and has been bolstered by research over the past years (Alkhateeb et al., 2016). Inclusive education can help reduce inequality by providing equitable educational opportunities for all learners (Slee, 2018). The objective is to ensure that every learner has access to meaningful and high-quality educational experiences within their local community alongside their peers (Watkins, 2017). This situation necessitates a more critical examination of the recent inclusive education policies and the attitudes of teachers towards them.

In the United States, there exist some laws that facilitate special assistance for those with ADHD within educational settings. Section 504 of the Vocational Rehabilitation Act of 1973 serves as a civil rights statute, prohibiting discrimination in federally funded programs and, under specific conditions, obligating school districts to provide necessary accommodations for students with ADHD (Shaughnessy & Waggoner, 2015). This law applies to any citizen of the United States who has a disability (Holmes, 2006). The Americans with Disabilities Act (ADA) of 1990 further enhanced the protections established by Section 504. The Americans with Disabilities Act (ADA) mandates that postsecondary institutions provide equal access to services for these students (Gibson, 2017). Both the Rehabilitation Act and the ADA emerged from the dedicated efforts of numerous advocates, organizations, and supporters who strived to secure improved access and equity for individuals with disabilities across various sectors, including employment (Office of Disability Employment Policy, 2023). Another federal law, the Individuals with Disabilities Education Act (IDEA), stipulates that eligible students must be granted access to special education and related services tailored to their individual educational requirements. In addition, the United States implemented the 'No Child Left Behind Act' in 2002 (Klein, 2015). Mertler (2010) indicated that this legislation has significantly intensified the pressure on teachers, potentially to an unquantifiable extent. The author noted that key findings suggest teachers perceive the No Child Left Behind Act as detrimental to their instructional and curricular practices, contributing to increased stress associated with enhancing student performance. Consequently, this law has compelled teachers to alter their classroom focus. Conversely, Murnane and Papay (2010) reported that teachers largely endorse the foundational principles of the No Child Left Behind Act, particularly the notion that schools must be accountable for effectively educating all children. However, they express concern that certain incentives established by the law have led to unintended consequences that diminish the quality of education for some students, particularly those who do not have ADHD.

True inclusivity must ensure that the needs of every student are recognized and addressed. In 2015, the United States government enacted the 'Every Student Succeeds Act,' which superseded the 'No Child Left Behind Act' (Hess & Eden, 2021; Klein, 2016). This new legislation outlines frameworks for accountability plans, goals, and systems, along with provisions aimed at supporting low-performing schools and students with special needs, among other initiatives. Xie (2023) stated that the enactment of the Act and the subsequent implementation of related policies seldom demonstrate a clear strategy for attaining educational equity. This is particularly evident in their failure to adequately support and foster teachers' interest, which is essential for advancing students' overall development in the context of long-term educational objectives. Conversely, Zinskie and Rea (2016) highlight that the Act has the potential to strengthen teachers' abilities to assist students and schools that are at risk of underachievement. Thus far, this development has proven beneficial in the United States. Should Nigeria consider adopting a similar approach within its educational framework, and can it yield substantial advantages for schools, the workforce, and the overall economy?

Historically, Nigeria has enacted legislation aimed at safeguarding students with disabilities, which includes those with ADHD (Adeosun et al., 2013), and which bears some resemblance to the previously mentioned US policies and legislations. The National Policy on Education in Nigeria established a framework for special needs education, along with implementation guidelines that reflect best practices from around the world (National Educational Research and Development Council, 2013). This framework is designed to support Individualized Education Programs and includes recognition of ADHD. The Federal Ministry of Education is tasked with the coordination of national activities aimed at meeting the educational needs of students with disabilities (Razaq-Shuaib, 2019). In December 2018, the President of the Federal Republic of Nigeria enacted the Discrimination against Persons with Disability Prohibition Act 2018 (Amucheazi & Nwankwo, 2020). Furthermore, section 42 of the Constitution of the Federal Republic of Nigeria (1999) ensures the right to freedom from discrimination, while Article 26 of the Universal Declaration of

Human Rights (1948) affirms that every individual is entitled to an education. The Child Rights Act (CRA) (2003) also serves as a legal framework that ensures the protection of children's rights throughout Nigeria. Notably, Abia State is among the Nigerian states that embraced the CRA as state legislation in 2006 (Partners West Africa Nigeria, 2024). This legislation underscores the significance of inclusive education as a fundamental right within the country (Nwosu et al. 2015).

The Discrimination Against Persons with Disabilities (Prohibition) Act 2019 represents a significant advancement in Nigeria's legislative framework, dedicated to safeguarding the rights and dignity of individuals with disabilities (Federal Republic of Nigeria, 2019). According to this Act, a person with a disability is entitled to participate in the workforce on an equal basis with others. This encompasses the entitlement to pursue opportunities for earning a livelihood through work that is freely selected or accepted within an accessible labor market and work environment. This Act aims to eliminate all forms of discrimination, encompassing areas such as employment, education, healthcare, and public services, by ensuring equal treatment and opportunities for individuals with disabilities. It advocates for inclusion through the provision of accessibility accommodations, reasonable adjustments, and equal participation in both the public and private sectors. Furthermore, the Act delineates specific rights and protections, including the right to live independently, access information, and engage in political, cultural, and social activities. The Act guarantees equal opportunities in employment by obligating employers to make reasonable accommodations and cultivate an inclusive workforce. In the educational sector, it promotes inclusive practices by ensuring that educational materials and support services are accessible to students with disabilities, which helps to lower dropout rates and encourage social inclusion. The Act is in alignment with international human rights standards, notably the United Nations Convention on the Rights of Persons with Disabilities (UNCRPD) (United Nations, 2006) and acknowledges the social and economic advantages of inclusive policies. Nevertheless, its implementation encounters obstacles such as insufficient awareness, limited resources, barriers to accessibility, and ongoing societal stigma (Atoyebi, 2024).

While existing policies, such as the National Policy on Special Needs Education in Nigeria (Federal Ministry of Education, 2015) and the National Policy on Inclusive Education (Federal Ministry of Education, 2023), aim to provide inclusive education support for students with special needs, they raise concerns about their effectiveness in meeting the career transition needs of students with ADHD. In addition, not minding that the existing policies appear to be aligned with global standards, there is a disconnect between their implementation and monitoring across states of the federation. As a result, the country has not sufficiently addressed the career transition needs of the students that these policies are designed to assist. Moreover, there is a lack of empirical evidence regarding the effectiveness of these policies in aiding career transition for students with ADHD in Abia and other states in Nigeria. Secondary school teachers, who are pivotal in the implementation of these policies, frequently encounter challenges that may impact the successful career transition of students with ADHD. The core issue revolves around assessing how inclusive secondary school teachers perceive the effectiveness of these policies and whether they sufficiently cater to the distinct needs of students with ADHD during career transition. This knowledge gap raises significant concerns about the capacity of the current educational and public policy frameworks to provide equitable career prospects for Nigerian inclusive secondary school students with ADHD. Consequently, it is essential to investigate the views of inclusive secondary school teachers concerning the existing policies. In this context, the present study aims to evaluate the perspectives of inclusive secondary schoolteachers regarding the effectiveness of educational and public policies in facilitating the career transitions of students with ADHD in Abia State, Nigeria.

Research Objectives

1. To ascertain inclusive secondary teachers' overall mean perspective on the effectiveness of educational and public policies and legislation in promoting the career transition of students with ADHD.
2. To determine the extent to which teachers' perspectives on the effectiveness of educational and public policies and legislation in promoting the career transition of students with ADHD differ by gender.
3. To ascertain the extent to which perspectives of inclusive secondary school teachers differ on the effectiveness of educational and public policies and legislation in promoting the career transition of students with ADHD based on years of teaching experience.
4. To ascertain whether inclusive secondary school teachers differ significantly in their perspectives on the effectiveness of educational and public policies and legislation in promoting the career transition of students with ADHD by school location.

Research Questions

1. What is the inclusive secondary teachers' mean perspective on the effectiveness of educational and public policies and legislation in promoting the career transition of students with ADHD?
2. To what extent do teachers' perspectives on the effectiveness of educational and public policies and legislation in promoting the career transition of students with ADHD differ by gender?

3. To what extent do the perspectives of inclusive secondary school teachers differ on the effectiveness of educational and public policies and legislation in promoting the career transition of students with ADHD based on years of teaching experience?
4. Do inclusive secondary school teachers differ significantly in their perspectives on the effectiveness of educational and public policies and legislation in promoting the career transition of students with ADHD by school location?

Theoretical Framework

The social model of disability serves as a relevant theoretical framework that empowers students with ADHD and other disabilities to actively enhance their inclusion and participation within society (Pfeifer et al., 2021). This model emerged prominently through the joint efforts of the Union of the Physically Impaired against Segregation and influential scholars in disability studies (Twardowski, 2022). Disability scholars contributed to the understanding of the social model, which asserts that impairments do not inherently lead to disability unless societal structures and expectations impose restrictions on individuals (Pfeifer et al., 2020; 2021). Within the context of inclusive education, this model highlights the necessity of transforming societal attitudes, practices, and policies to better support and accommodate students with disabilities, including those with ADHD. In examining the perspectives of inclusive secondary teachers regarding the effectiveness of educational and public policies in facilitating the career transition of students with ADHD, the social model's focus on eliminating societal barriers is particularly pertinent. This model highlights that students with ADHD can succeed in settings where policies actively work to remove institutional obstacles and foster inclusion. The viewpoints of teachers are essential in assessing the extent to which these laws and policies aid the career transition of students with ADHD (see Figure 1). Their feedback will be instrumental in evaluating whether existing legislation aligns with the social model's principles, which empower students with ADHD to advocate for themselves and ensure that societal frameworks do not impede their career trajectories (Coles, 2001). In assessing the potential differences in teachers' perceptions of the effectiveness of policies and legislation based on gender, the social model's emphasis on varied experiences and contexts is significant. Gender may affect how male and female teachers interpret the influence of these policies, possibly uncovering discrepancies in their understanding and execution of inclusivity. The social model's ability to adapt and evolve (Sang et al., 2022) ensures its applicability across different demographic groups, making it an effective tool for analyzing gender-specific differences in teacher viewpoints. Evaluating the variations in teachers' viewpoints according to their years of teaching experience also relates to the critique of static societal expectations within the social model. Teachers with greater experience may have observed the evolution or stagnation of policies over time, thus providing valuable insights into the current policies' effectiveness. The social model emphasizes that barriers to inclusion are developed over time, which aids in comprehending how experience can influence teachers' perspectives. Those with longer teaching careers might identify more discrepancies between policy and practice, whereas newer teachers may interpret these policies with a more hopeful outlook, highlighting the impact of experience on the perception of policy effectiveness. The inquiry into whether teachers' viewpoints differ based on the geographical context of their schools corresponds with the social model's premise that environmental and societal elements significantly impact the understanding of disability. Teachers operating in urban settings may encounter different obstacles than those in rural institutions when it comes to executing policies and supporting career transitions for students with ADHD. The social model prioritizes societal structures over individual deficits, thereby emphasizing the need to consider differences that arise from location. Policies that are successful in urban areas may necessitate adaptations to effectively tackle the specific challenges faced in rural schools, where both resources and societal attitudes towards disabilities can differ markedly. Aligning the viewpoints of teachers with the foundational principles of this social model of disability allows the study to offer a nuanced understanding of how educational and public policies can be enhanced to support career transition for students with ADHD.

Figure 1. Study framework

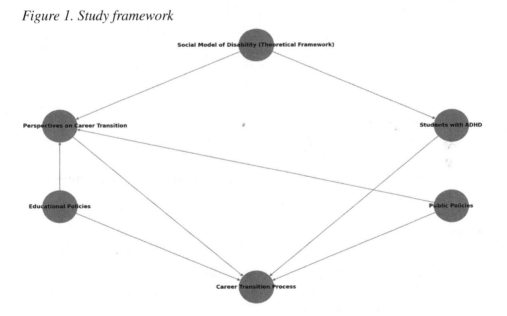

METHODOLOGY

Ethics Statement

Ethical approval for this study was obtained from the relevant institutional review boards. First, it received approval from the Research Ethics Committee of the Faculty of Education, University of Nigeria, Nigeria. It also received additional ethical approval from the Faculty of Education Research Ethics Committee at the University of Johannesburg, South Africa (Sem 2-2020-057). Informed consent was secured from participants. We assured confidentiality and clarified participants' right to withdraw from the study at any given time.

Research Design and Approach

The research design serves as a crucial framework for conducting a study and selecting an appropriate research methodology, as it dictates the means by which pertinent information will be gathered (Sileyew, 2019). This study used a survey research design. The study adopted a quantitative research approach. Survey studies involve posing questions to individuals regarding their behaviors, attitudes, and opinions. Additionally, the study indicates that some surveys focus solely on describing respondents' self-reported thoughts and actions, while others seek to identify correlations between the respondents' characteristics and their expressed behaviors and opinions (Marczyk et al., 2005). Survey research can be executed through various methods, including mail, telephone, in-person interviews, or digital platforms, and may target specific populations (Gürbüz, 2017). According to Watson (2014), surveys represent the primary research designs utilized in quantitative research. This type of research aims to collect data through measurement, analyze it for patterns and relationships, and validate the measurements obtained (Watson, 2014). Quantitative researchers employ numerical data and large sample sizes to test theoretical propositions (Sobh & Perry, 2006). Through the application of a survey research design and a quantitative framework, this study aims to analyze teachers' perspectives on how effective educational and public policies and legislation are in promoting the career transitions of students with ADHD.

Research Paradigm

Essentially, a paradigm signifies a researcher's interpretation of the nature of existence, which is beyond the realm of "logical" argumentation, as each paradigm is considered "rational" within its own established framework (Sobh & Perry, 2006). This study is grounded in the positivist research paradigm. The positivistic research paradigm, a term introduced two centuries ago, asserts that knowledge can only be deemed true if it is derived through the scientific method; consequently, it involves empirical approaches where data is collected through experimentation and observation, yielding supporting evidence (McGregor & Murnane, 2010). Our research has adopted the positivist paradigm, which underscores that Positivism is universally applicable in organizational contexts and, despite its alleged neutrality, may simply investigate events or occurrences influenced by the researcher (Aliyu et al., 2014).

Study Area

This research was conducted in Abia State in Southeast Nigeria. Abia State constitutes one of the five states within the southeastern geopolitical zone of Nigeria (Chukwuonye et al., 2013). The state is organized into seventeen administrative divisions known as Local Government Authorities. Geographically, Abia State is bordered by Imo State to the west, Ebonyi and Enugu States to the north, Cross River and Akwa Ibom States to the east, and Rivers State to the south (Oteh & Nwachukwu, 2014).

Population and Sampling

In the process of designing a study, the choice of sampling method for selecting research participants is a significant decision that involves numerous considerations, given the multitude of potential sampling techniques and participant selection options (Magnone & Yezierski, 2024). The study involves inclusive schoolteachers from public secondary schools. A total of 45 inclusive secondary schoolteachers were selected using purposive and convenience sampling techniques. Participants' mean age was 41.78 ± 7.77 years. Convenience and purposive sampling are classified as non-probability sampling methods, where the selection of participants is based on the ease of access for the researcher. Often, respondents are chosen simply because they are available at the right time and place (Acharya et al., 2013). The purposive sampling approach is particularly advantageous when the aim is to explore a specific cultural area with knowledgeable individuals and can also be utilized alongside quantitative research methods (Tongco, 2007). Convenience sampling focuses on elements of the population that are readily accessible to the researcher and includes a variety of advanced systematic sampling techniques (Leiner, 2014). Employing both purposive and convenience sampling methods aids in achieving the study's objectives.

Data Collection

The data was collected using a questionnaire. The researchers received help from two postgraduate students to complete the data collection process. The questionnaire used for data collection is called the Teachers' Perspectives on the Effectiveness of Educational and Public Policies and Legislation in Promoting Career Transition of Students with ADHD Questionnaire (TPEEPPCLQ). It is a 16-item scale, with response options ranging from Not at All (1) to Very Great Extent (5). This scale measures teachers' attitudes and understanding of educational and public policies and legislation for promoting the career transition of students with ADHD. Higher scores indicate a great extent. Some examples of item statements in the questionnaire include: "To what extent do you think current public policies are supporting career transitions of students with ADHD?", and "To what extent do you think current policies align with the career transition needs of students with ADHD?" The ISCPTCTQ has a good internal consistency reliability, with a Cronbach's alpha of 0.74 in the present research.

Data Analysis

Statistical analysis was conducted using Jeffreys' Amazing Statistics Program software (JASP), version 0.18.3. Descriptive statistics was used to summarize the sociodemographic data, while analysis of variance was used to analyze the research questions at a .05 significance level. JASP is crafted to be user-friendly, featuring an accessible interface and robust graphical capabilities, which significantly enhances its usage in both academic and research contexts (McBride & Garcés Manzanera, 2024). One of the most significant aspects of JASP is its no-cost access for users while providing a variety of functionalities, all through a graphical user interface (Han & Dawson, 2020). Additionally, JASP is a cross-platform, open-source software solution that allows users to conduct hypothesis tests for common statistical challenges (Wagenmakers et al., 2018). Given the various advantages offered by JASP, we chose to adopt it for data analysis in our study.

FINDINGS

The first research question focused on the overall mean perspective of inclusive secondary teachers on the effectiveness of educational and public policies and legislation in promoting the career transition of students with ADHD. Table 1 revealed the mean perspective score of 2.024, with a standard error of 0.052 and a 95% confidence interval of approximately 2.128. The standard deviation is 0.919, indicating some variability in responses. The skewness of 0.731 suggests a slight positive skew in the distribution of responses.

Table 1. Mean perspective of teachers on the effectiveness of educational and public policies and legislation in promoting the career transition of students with ADHD

	Mean	Std. Error of Mean	95% Confidence Interval Mean	Std. Deviation	Coefficient of variation	Skewness
TPEEPPCLQ	2.024	0.052	2.128. 1.919	0.347	.171	.731

Figure 2. Boxplot on mean perspectives of teachers on the effectiveness of educational and public policies and legislation in promoting the career transition of students with ADHD

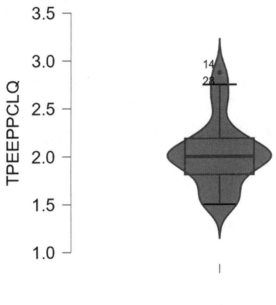

Figure 2 represents the distribution of teachers' mean perspectives, showing the central tendency and variability.

Table 2. Independent samples T-Test for teachers' perspectives on the effectiveness of educational and public policies and legislation in promoting the career transition of students with ADHD by gender

	T	df	P	Mean Difference	SE Difference	95% CI Lower Upper
Gender	-1.846	43	.07	-.190	.103	-.397, .018

The second research question investigates whether teachers' perspectives on the effectiveness of educational and public policies and legislation in promoting the career transition of students with ADHD differ by gender. Table 2 shows the results of an independent samples t-test, showing a t-value of -1.846 with a p-value of .07, indicating that the difference in perspectives by gender is not statistically significant at .05 level. Table 3 shows descriptives by gender, with male teachers having a mean score of 1.91 and female teachers having a mean score of 2.10. Although female teachers have a slightly higher mean score, the difference is not statistically significant.

Table 3. Descriptives by gender for teachers' perspectives on the effectiveness of educational and public policies and legislation in promoting the career transition of students with ADHD

	Group	N	Mean	SD	SE	Coefficient of variation
Gender	Male teachers	18	1.91	.29	.068	.152
	Female teachers	27	2.10	.37	.070	.174

Figure 3. Bar plot on teachers' perspectives on the effectiveness of educational and public policies and legislation in promoting the career transition of students with ADHD by gender

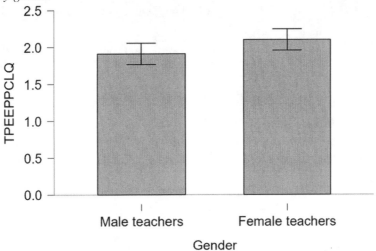

Figure 3 illustrates the mean perspectives of male and female teachers, reinforcing the slight but not significant difference.

Table 4. Independent samples T-Test for teachers' perspectives on the effectiveness of educational and public policies and legislation in promoting the career transition of students with ADHD by teaching experience

	t	Df	P	Mean Difference	SE Difference	95%CI Lower Upper
Teaching Experience	.554	43	.58	.060	.109	-.159, .280

The third research question examines differences in the perspectives of teachers on the effectiveness of educational and public policies and legislation in promoting the career transition of students with ADHD based on years of teaching experience. Table 4 shows the t-test results for this comparison, with a t-value of .554 and a p-value of .58, indicating no significant difference based on teaching experience. While Table 5 indicates the descriptives for early career teachers, showing a mean score of 2.06, the absence of significant mean difference suggests that experience level does not substantially affect teachers' perspectives.

Table 5. Descriptives by professional experience for teachers' perspectives on the effectiveness of educational and public policies and legislation in promoting the career transition of students with ADHD

	Group	N	Mean	SD	SE	Coefficient of variation
Professional Experience	Early career teachers	16	2.06	.36	.089	.172
	Experienced teachers	29	2.00	.35	.064	.173

Figure 4. Bar plot on teachers' perspectives on the effectiveness of educational and public policies and legislation in promoting the career transition of students with ADHD by teaching experience

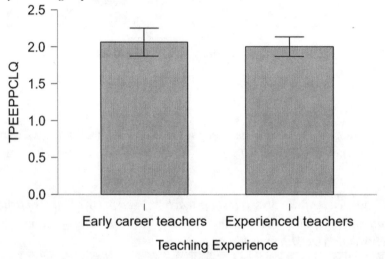

Figure 4 displays the perspectives by teaching experience, supporting the finding of no significant difference.

Table 6. Independent samples T-Test for teachers' perspectives on the effectiveness of educational and public policies and legislation in promoting the career transition of students with ADHD by school location

	t	df	P	Mean Difference	SE Difference	95%CI Lower Upper
School Location	-.070	43	.95	-.007	.105	-.218, .204

The fourth research question explores whether teachers' perspectives on the effectiveness of educational and public policies and legislation in promoting the career transition of students with ADHD differ by school location. Table 6 shows the t-test results, with a t-value of -.070 and a p-value of .95, indicating no significant difference in perspectives between rural and urban inclusive secondary school teachers. Table 7 reveals the descriptives by school location, with rural teachers having a mean score of 2.02 and urban teachers having a mean score of 2.03, further supporting the lack of significant difference.

Table 7. Descriptives by professional experience for teachers' perspectives on the effectiveness of educational and public policies and legislation in promoting the career transition of students with ADHD

	Group	N	Mean	SD	SE	Coefficient of variation
School Location	Rural schoolteachers	22	2.02	.37	.078	.182
	Urban schoolteachers	23	2.03	.34	.070	.165

Figure 5. Bar plot on teachers' perspectives on the effectiveness of educational and public policies and legislation in promoting the career transition of students with ADHD by school location

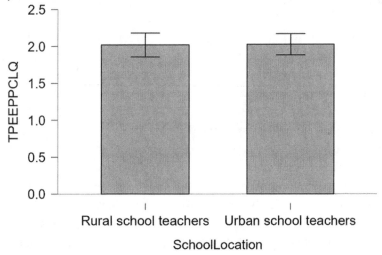

Figure 5 shows the perspectives by school location, consistent with the statistical results indicating no significant difference.

DISCUSSION

This study examined the perspective of teachers on the effectiveness of educational and public policies in promoting the career transition of students with ADHD. The study indicates a moderately positive perspective of Nigerian inclusive schoolteachers on the effectiveness of policies and legislation in supporting career transitions for students with ADHD. The research by Avramidis et al. (2000) demonstrated that teachers who have engaged in inclusive programs tend to exhibit favorable attitudes. In the research conducted by Almotairi (2013), it was revealed that among the teachers who held negative views towards inclusion, their criticisms primarily stemmed from the belief that, although inclusion might offer some social advantages, these advantages were insufficient to warrant the potential jeopardization of the academic performance of mainstream students. Conversely, Alghazo and Naggar Gaad (2004) reported a neutral stance towards the inclusion of individuals with disabilities in regular school settings. Findings from Lindner et al. (2023) revealed that schoolteachers often maintain neutral or ambivalent attitudes regarding inclusive education for students with ADHD. The study further suggests that the notion of inclusion is still influenced by the type of disability a student has, leading many regular schoolteachers to be less supportive of the inclusion of all students within the framework of inclusive education. For other teachers, policies advocating for inclusion present challenges due to the complexities associated with various disabilities. Dissenting voices advocate for special education schools, overlooking its potential drawbacks, such as the public perception of a child as having a problem, the exclusion of the child from mainstream education and their peers, being seen as inadequate by society, and the lowered expectations from teachers regarding these students (Mahapatra, 2007). These concerns are among the reasons why advocates of inclusive education and policies supporting inclusion argue that students with special education needs stand to gain significant benefits from inclusion. Crook and McDowall (2024) highlighted their professional achievements, noting that they succeeded both "in spite of" and "because of" their ADHD, utilizing the feed-forward interview technique grounded in positive psychology. Embracing this viewpoint may prompt policymakers to implement a strength-oriented approach in formulating career transition policies tailored for students with ADHD. It can be posited that the benefits of inclusion may surpass its disadvantages, one of which is the encouragement and support that these students can receive from their peers.

Furthermore, the study indicates that the difference in perspectives by gender and school location is not statistically significant as regards the effectiveness of educational and public policies. The policies regarding inclusion implied that students with ADHD should be educated within mainstream school environments (Braude & Dwarika, 2020). Eseadi and Diale (2024) reported that teachers in inclusive schools fully supported the principles of inclusive education and highlighted the necessity for enhanced funding policies designed to meet the financial obligations of inclusive secondary schools to support students with disabilities in achieving successful career transitions. The authors underscored the importance of developing targeted educational and public policies regarding career transitions, which should prioritize collaboration among agencies, accessibility to employment, and equity to facilitate career transitions for individuals with disabilities. In terms of gender and school type, Almotairi (2013) found that teachers from mainstream institutions are more favorable towards inclusion policies compared to their counterparts in special schools, and male teachers demonstrated more supportive attitudes compared to female teachers. According to the findings of Alghazo and Naggar Gaad (2004), there were no significant variations in teachers' attitudes towards the inclusion of students with disabilities based on gender; however, years of experience played a role in this context as teachers with more years of experience exhibited more favorable attitudes toward the inclusion of students with disabilities compared to their less experienced counterparts. According to Greenway and Rees Edwards (2020), both teachers and teaching assistants (TAs) demonstrated sufficient knowledge, with TAs exhibiting a greater understanding and more favorable attitudes towards ADHD compared to their teacher counterparts. Furthermore, there is a tendency for teachers to focus on high-achieving students, often overlooking the potential challenges faced by those who may be struggling with disabilities. This is why effective policies are important to ensure that teachers receive appropriate training to meet educational standards and cater to the needs of all students. In supporting this view, Zentall and Javorsky (2007) indicated that the introduction of comprehensive programs resulted in improved teacher attitudes and confidence regarding the education of students with ADHD, along with a greater self-reported ability to make necessary adjustments. Similarly, the authors pointed out that the successful implementation of inclusive education policies is vital for improving teaching effectiveness and enhancing student learning outcomes.

CONCLUSION

This study indicates a fairly consistent perspective among teachers about how effective current policies and legislation are in supporting the career transition of students with ADHD. The study suggests that the existing educational and public policies may not adequately meet the career transition needs of these students, as reflected in the moderate overall perspectives of teachers. This points to a possible gap in how these policies are implemented or understood by teachers, which could affect the career transition outcomes of students with ADHD. The absence of significant mean differences in perspectives across various demographic factors suggests that the perceived effectiveness of these policies remains stable, regardless of the teachers' backgrounds or school settings. Future research should delve into the specific aspects of educational and public policies that teachers find ineffective and pinpoint areas that could be improved. Future studies could offer deeper insight into the challenges teachers face when applying these policies and the support they require to boost their effectiveness. It would also be beneficial for future research to gather perspectives from other stakeholders, such as students, parents, and policymakers, to gain a more holistic view of the policy landscape and its effects on the career transition of students with ADHD. Future studies could also evaluate the impact of policy changes on the career transition of students with ADHD to provide valuable data to guide future policy development.

REFERENCES

Acharya, A., Prakash, A., Saxena, P., & Nigam, A. (2013). Sampling: Why and How of it? Anita S Acharya, Anupam Prakash, Pikee Saxena, Aruna Nigam. *Indian Journal of Medical Specilaities*. DOI: 10.7713/ijms.2013.0032

Adeosun, I., Ogun, O., Fatiregun, O., & Adeyemo, S. (2013). Attitude of Nigerian primary school teachers to children with attention deficit hyperactivity disorder. *European Psychiatry*, 28, 1. DOI: 10.1016/S0924-9338(13)76428-9

Alghazo, E. M., & El Naggar Gaad, E. (2004). General Education Teachers in the United Arab Emirates and Their Acceptance of the Inclusion of Students with Disabilities. *British Journal of Special Education*, 31(2), 94–99. DOI: 10.1111/j.0952-3383.2004.00335.x

Aliyu, A. A., Bello, M. U., Kasim, R., & Martin, D. (2014). Positivist and Non-Positivist Paradigm in Social Science Research: Conflicting Paradigms or Perfect Partners? *Journal of Management and Sustainability*, 4(3), 79. DOI: 10.5539/jms.v4n3p79

Alkhateeb, J. M., Hadidi, M. S., & Alkhateeb, A. J. (2016). Inclusion of children with developmental disabilities in Arab countries: A review of the research literature from 1990 to 2014. *Research in Developmental Disabilities*, 49–50, 60–75. DOI: 10.1016/j.ridd.2015.11.005 PMID: 26672678

Almotairi, M. (2013). *Investigating Kuwaiti teachers' and head teachers' attitudes towards inclusion* (Doctoral dissertation, University of Birmingham).

Amucheazi, C., & Nwankwo, C. M. (2020). Accessibility to infrastructure and disability rights in Nigeria: An analysis of the potential of the discrimination against persons with disability (prohibition) act 2018. *Commonwealth Law Bulletin*, 46(4), 689–710. DOI: 10.1080/03050718.2020.1781674

Atoyebi, O. M. (2024, July 22). An Appraisal of the Discrimination Against Persons with Disabilities (Prohibition) Act 2019. https://omaplex.com.ng/an-appraisal-of-the-discrimination-against-persons-with-disabilities-prohibition-act-2019/#post-3499-footnote-ref-1

Avramidis, E., Bayliss, P., & Burden, R. (2000). A Survey into Mainstream Teachers' Attitudes Towards the Inclusion of Children with Special Educational Needs in the Ordinary School in one Local Education Authority. *Educational Psychology*, 20(2), 191–211. DOI: 10.1080/713663717

Braude, S., & Dwarika, V. (2020). Teachers' experiences of supporting learners with attention-deficit hyperactivity disorder: Lessons for professional development of teachers. *South African Journal of Childhood Education*, 10(1), 1–10. DOI: 10.4102/sajce.v10i1.843

Buder, S., & Perry, R. (2021, April 12). *The Social Model of Disability Explained*. https://www.thesocialcreatures.org/thecreaturetimes/the-social-model-of-disability

Child's Right Act. (2003). https://placng.org/lawsofnigeria/laws/C50.pdf

Chukwuonye, I. I., Chuku, A., Okpechi, I. G., Onyeonoro, U. U., Madukwe, O. O., Okafor, G. O. C., & Ogah, O. S. (2013). Socioeconomic status and obesity in Abia State, South East Nigeria. *Diabetes, Metabolic Syndrome and Obesity*, 6, 371–378. DOI: 10.2147/DMSO.S44426 PMID: 24204167

Coles, J. (2001). The Social Model of Disability: What does it mean for practice in services for people with learning difficulties? *Disability & Society*, 16(4), 501–510. DOI: 10.1080/09687590120059504

Constitution of the Federal Republic of Nigeria. (Act No. 24). (1999). https://nigeriarights.gov.ng/files/constitution.pdf

Crook, T., & McDowall, A. (2024). Paradoxical career strengths and successes of ADHD adults: An evolving narrative. *Journal of Work-Applied Management*, 16(1), 112–126. DOI: 10.1108/JWAM-05-2023-0048

Eseadi, C., & Diale, B. M. (2024). Exploring Inclusive Schoolteachers' Policy Perspectives on Career Transitioning of Students with Hearing Impairments. In *Perspectives on Career Transitioning of Students with Hearing Impairments* (pp. 55–78). IGI Global., DOI: 10.4018/979-8-3693-2631-2.ch003

Federal Ministry of Education. (2015). National Policy on Special Needs Education in Nigeria. Abuja: FME. https://planipolis.iiep.unesco.org/sites/default/files/ressources/nigeria_special_needs_policy.pdf

Federal Ministry of Education. (2023). National Policy on Inclusive Education. Abuja: FME.https://planipolis.iiep.unesco.org/sites/default/files/ressources/INCLUSIVE-EDUCATION- POLICY.pdf

Federal Republic of Nigeria. (2019). Discrimination Against Persons with Disabilities (Prohibition) Act 2019. https://archive.gazettes.africa/archive/ng/2019/ng-government-gazette-supplement-dated-2019-01-21-no-10.pdf

Gibson, S. (2017). *Counseling College Students with Attention-Deficit/Hyperactivity Disorder (ADHD): A Consensual Qualitative Research (CQR) Study Examining the Experiences of College Counselors.*

Greenway, C. W., & Rees Edwards, A. (2020). Knowledge and attitudes towards attention-deficit hyperactivity disorder (ADHD): A comparison of teachers and teaching assistants. *Australian Journal of Learning Difficulties*, 25(1), 31–49. DOI: 10.1080/19404158.2019.1709875

Gürbüz, S. (2017). Survey as a quantitative research method. www.researchgate.net/profile/Salih-Guerbuez/publication/321874371_Survey_as_a_Quantitative_Research_Method/links/5b1533890f7e9b4981099e38/Survey-as-a-Quantitative-Research-Method.pdf

Han, H., & Dawson, K. J. (2020). *JASP (Software)*. OSF. https://doi.org/DOI: 10.31234/osf.io/67dcb

Hess, F. M., & Eden, M. (2021). *The Every Student Succeeds Act (ESSA): What It Means for Schools, Systems, and States*. Harvard Education Press.

Klein, A. (2015, April 11). No Child Left Behind: An Overview. *Education Week*. https://www.edweek.org/policy-politics/no-child-left-behind-an-overview/2015/04

Klein, A. (2016, March 31). The Every Student Succeeds Act: An ESSA Overview. *Education Week*. https://www.edweek.org/policy-politics/the-every-student-succeeds-act-an-essa-overview/2016/03

Leiner, D. J. (2014, January 13). Convenience Samples from Online Respondent Pools: A case study of the SoSci Panel. *Studies in Communication Media*, 5(4), 367–396. DOI: 10.5771/2192-4007-2016-4-367

Lindner, K.-T., Schwab, S., Emara, M., & Avramidis, E. (2023). Do teachers favor the inclusion of all students? A systematic review of primary schoolteachers' attitudes towards inclusive education. *European Journal of Special Needs Education*, 38(6), 766–787. DOI: 10.1080/08856257.2023.2172894

Magnone, K. Q., & Yezierski, E. J. (2024). Beyond Convenience: A Case and Method for Purposive Sampling in Chemistry Teacher Professional Development Research. *Journal of Chemical Education*, 101(3), 718–726. DOI: 10.1021/acs.jchemed.3c00217

Mahapatra, K. S. A. B. C. (2007). Emerging Trends. In *Inclusive Education*. Sarup & Sons.

Marczyk, G. R., DeMatteo, D., & Festinger, D. (2005). *Essentials of research design and methodology*. John Wiley & Sons.

McBride, S., & Garcés Manzanera, A. (2024). Exploring JASP as a data analysis tool in L2 research: A snapshot. *TEISEL.Tecnologías Para La Investigación En Segundas Lenguas*, 3. Advance online publication. DOI: 10.1344/teisel.v3.45189

McGregor, S. L. T., & Murnane, J. A. (2010). Paradigm, methodology and method: Intellectual integrity in consumer scholarship. *International Journal of Consumer Studies*, 34(4), 419–427. DOI: 10.1111/j.1470-6431.2010.00883.x

Mertler, C. A. (2010). Teachers' Perceptions of the Influence of No Child Left Behind On Classroom Practices. *Current Issues in Education (Tempe, Ariz.)*, 13(3), 3. https://cie.asu.edu/ojs/index.php/cieatasu/article/view/392

Milsom, A. S. (2002). Students with disabilities: School counselor involvement and preparation. *Professional School Counseling*, 5(5), 331–339.

Murnane, R. J., & Papay, J. P. (2010). Teachers' Views on No Child Left Behind: Support for the Principles, Concerns about the Practices. *The Journal of Economic Perspectives*, 24(3), 151–166. DOI: 10.1257/jep.24.3.151

National Educational Research and Development Council. (2013). National Policy on Education, 6th ed. Lagos, Nigeria: NERDC Press. https://educatetolead.wordpress.com/wp-content/uploads/2016/02/national-education-policy-2013.pdf

Nwosu, E. N., Akaneme, I. N., Eseadi, C., Arinola, A., Abah, J. I., & Asogwa, D. E. (2015). Counseling Needs of Parents for Increased Awareness of Child's Rights Acts in Nigeria. *Buletin Teknologi Tanaman*, 12, 249–253.

Office of Disability Employment Policy. (2023, July 26). Examining 50 Years of the Rehabilitation Act of 1973 – Section 504 [Blog Website]. *U.S Department of Labor Blog*. https://blog.dol.gov/2023/07/26/examining-50-years-of-the-rehabilitation-act-of-1973-section-504

Oteh, O. U., & Nwachukwu, I. N. (2014). Effect of Commercialization on productive capacity among cassava producing households In Ikwuano Local Government Area of Abia State, Nigeria. *Scientific Papers. Series Management, Economic, Engineering in Agriculture and Rural Development*, 14(3).

Partners West Africa Nigeria. (2024). Child Rights Act Tracker. *Partners West Africa Nigeria*. https://www.partnersnigeria.org/childs-rights-law-tracker/

Pfeifer, M. A., Reiter, E. M., Cordero, J. J., & Stanton, J. D. (2021). Inside and Out: Factors That Support and Hinder the Self-Advocacy of Undergraduates with ADHD and/or Specific Learning Disabilities in STEM. *CBE Life Sciences Education*, 20(2), ar17. DOI: 10.1187/cbe.20-06-0107 PMID: 33769838

Pfeifer, M. A., Reiter, E. M., Hendrickson, M., & Stanton, J. D. (2020). Speaking up: A model of self-advocacy for STEM undergraduates with ADHD and/or specific learning disabilities. *International Journal of STEM Education*, 7(1), 33. DOI: 10.1186/s40594-020-00233-4

Razaq-Shuaib, B. (2019, September 24). *Making inclusive education for special needs work in Nigeria -5*. https://www.linkedin.com/pulse/making-inclusive-education-special-needs-work-nigeria-razaq-shuaib-5e

Sang, K., Calvard, T., & Remnant, J. (2022). Disability and Academic Careers: Using the Social Relational Model to Reveal the Role of Human Resource Management Practices in Creating Disability. *Work, Employment and Society*, 36(4), 722–740. DOI: 10.1177/0950017021993737

Shaughnessy, M. F., & Waggoner, C. R. (2015). The Educational Implications of ADHD: Teachers and Principals Thoughts Concerning Students with ADHD. *Creative Education*, 6(2), 2. Advance online publication. DOI: 10.4236/ce.2015.62020

Sileyew, K. J. (2019). Research Design and Methodology. In *Cyberspace*. IntechOpen., DOI: 10.5772/intechopen.85731

Slee, R. (2018). Defining the scope of inclusive education. *MINISTERIO DE EDUCACIÓN*. https://repositorio.minedu.gob.pe/handle/20.500.12799/5977

Tongco, M. D. C. (2007). Purposive Sampling as a Tool for Informant Selection. *Ethnobotany Research and Applications*, 5, 147. DOI: 10.17348/era.5.0.147-158

Twardowski, A. (2022). Cultural Model of Disability – Origins, Assumptions, Advantages. *Kultura i Edukacja*, 136(2), 48–61. DOI: 10.15804/kie.2022.02.03

United Nations. (2006). Convention on the Rights of Persons with Disabilities. *Treaty Series, 2515*, 3.https://www.ohchr.org/en/instruments-mechanisms/instruments/convention-rights-persons-disabilities

Wagenmakers, E.-J., Love, J., Marsman, M., Jamil, T., Ly, A., Verhagen, J., Selker, R., Gronau, Q. F., Dropmann, D., Boutin, B., Meerhoff, F., Knight, P., Raj, A., van Kesteren, E.-J., van Doorn, J., Šmíra, M., Epskamp, S., Etz, A., Matzke, D., & Morey, R. D. (2018). Bayesian inference for psychology. Part II: Example applications with JASP. *Psychonomic Bulletin & Review*, 25(1), 58–76. DOI: 10.3758/s13423-017-1323-7 PMID: 28685272

Watkins, A. (2017). Inclusive Education and European Educational Policy. In *Oxford Research Encyclopedia of Education*. https://oxfordre.com/education/display/10.1093/acrefore/9780190264093.001.0001/acrefore-9780190264093-e-153

Watson, R. (2014). *Quantitative research. Nursing Standard*. [University of Hull, Hull, England.]. https://hull-repository.worktribe.com/preview/374667/Nursing%20Standfard%20Quantitative%20research.pdf

Xie, N. (2023). The Negative Impact of ESSA on Educational Equity: A Teacher Accountability Perspective. *Lecture Notes in Education Psychology and Public Media*, 11(1), 135–144. DOI: 10.54254/2753-7048/11/20230731

Zentall, S. S., & Javorsky, J. (2007). Professional Development for Teachers of Students with ADHD and Characteristics of ADHD. *Behavioral Disorders*, 32(2), 78–93. DOI: 10.1177/019874290703200202

Zinskie, C. D., & Rea, D. (2016). The Every Student Succeeds Act (ESSA): What It Means for Educators of Students at Risk. *National Youth-At-Risk Journal*, 2(1). Advance online publication. DOI: 10.20429/nyarj.2016.020101

ADDITIONAL READINGS

Abidi, J., & Sharma, D. (2014). Poverty, disability, and employment: Global perspectives from the National Centre for Promotion of Employment for Disabled People. *Career Development and Transition for Exceptional Individuals*, 37(1), 60–68. DOI: 10.1177/2165143413520180

Barnes, C. (2019). Understanding the social model of disability: Past, present and future. In *Routledge handbook of disability studies* (pp. 14–31). Routledge. DOI: 10.4324/9780429430817-2

Becker, K., Banaschewski, T., Brandeis, D., Dose, C., Hautmann, C., Holtmann, M., Jans, T., Jendreizik, L., Jenkner, C., John, K., Ketter, J., Millenet, S., Pauli-Pott, U., Renner, T., Romanos, M., Treier, A.-K., von Wirth, E., Wermter, A.-K., & Döpfner, M. (2020). Individualised stepwise adaptive treatment for 3–6-year-old preschool children impaired by attention-deficit/hyperactivity disorder (ESCApreschool): Study protocol of an adaptive intervention study including two randomised controlled trials within the consortium ESCAlife. *Trials*, 21(1), 1–19. DOI: 10.1186/s13063-019-3872-8 PMID: 31918739

Bergey, M., Chiri, G., Freeman, N. L., & Mackie, T. I. (2022). Mapping mental health inequalities: The intersecting effects of gender, race, class, and ethnicity on ADHD diagnosis. *Sociology of Health & Illness*, 44(3), 604–623. DOI: 10.1111/1467-9566.13443 PMID: 35147240

Birchwood, J., & Daley, D. (2012). Brief report: The impact of attention deficit hyperactivity disorder (ADHD) symptoms on academic performance in an adolescent community sample. *Journal of Adolescence*, 35(1), 225–231. DOI: 10.1016/j.adolescence.2010.08.011 PMID: 20880572

Carr-Fanning, K. (2020). The right to dignity or disorder? The case for attention deficit hyperactivity diversity. *Studies in Arts and Humanities*, 6(1), 14–30. DOI: 10.18193/sah.v6i1.192

Daley, D., & Birchwood, J. (2010). ADHD and academic performance: Why does ADHD impact on academic performance and what can be done to support ADHD children in the classroom? *Child: Care, Health and Development*, 36(4), 455–464. DOI: 10.1111/j.1365-2214.2009.01046.x PMID: 20074251

Ek, U., Westerlund, J., Holmberg, K., & Fernell, E. (2011). Academic performance of adolescents with ADHD and other behavioural and learning problems—A population-based longitudinal study. *Acta Paediatrica (Oslo, Norway)*, 100(3), 402–406. DOI: 10.1111/j.1651-2227.2010.02048.x PMID: 21054512

Eseadi, C. (2023). Enhancing Educational and Career Prospects: A Comprehensive Analysis of Institutional Support for Students with Specific Learning Disabilities. *International Journal of Research in Counseling and Education*, 7(1), 1–7. DOI: 10.24036/00628za0002

Fabiano, G. A., Naylor, J., Pelham, W. E.Jr, Gnagy, E. M., Burrows-MacLean, L., Coles, E., Chacko, A., Wymbs, B. T., Walker, K. S., Wymbs, F., Garefino, A., Mazzant, J. R., Sastry, A. L., Tresco, K. E., Waschbusch, D. A., Massetti, G. M., & Waxmonsky, J. (2022). Special Education for Children with ADHD: Services Received and a Comparison to Children with ADHD in General Education. *School Mental Health*, 14(4), 818–830. DOI: 10.1007/s12310-022-09514-5

Hennessey, M. L., Rumrill, P. D., Fitzgerald, S., & Roessler, R. (2008). Disadvantagement-related correlates of career optimism among college and university students with disabilities. *Work (Reading, Mass.)*, 30(4), 483–492. PMID: 18725711

Kendall, J., & Hatton, D. (2002). Racism as a source of health disparity in families with children with attention deficit hyperactivity disorder. *Advances in Nursing Science*, 25(2), 22–39. DOI: 10.1097/00012272-200212000-00003 PMID: 12484639

Kistler, R. (2022). Trouble Sitting Still Disorder: ADHD Through the Social Model of Disability. *WWU Honors College Senior Projects*. 587. https://cedar.wwu.edu/wwu_honors/587

Manago, B., Davis, J. L., & Goar, C. (2017). Discourse in action: Parents' use of medical and social models to resist disability stigma. *Social Science & Medicine*, 184, 169–177. DOI: 10.1016/j.socscimed.2017.05.015 PMID: 28550803

Mezzanotte, C. (2020). *Policy approaches and practices for the inclusion of students with attention-deficit hyperactivity disorder (ADHD)*. OECD Education Working Papers, No. 238. OECD Publishing. DOI: 10.1787/19939019

Ralnikova, I. A., Gurova, O. S., & Ippolitova, E. A. (2023). Career prospects of high school students in the context of social change. *Education & Pedagogy Journal*, (4 (8)), 43–57.

Rytivaara, A., & Vehkakoski, T. (2015). What is individual in individualised instruction? Five storylines of meeting individual needs at school. *International Journal of Educational Research*, 73, 12–22. DOI: 10.1016/j.ijer.2015.09.002

Samaha, A. M. (2007). What good is the social model of disability? *The University of Chicago Law Review. University of Chicago. Law School*, 74(4), 1251–1308. DOI: 10.2307/20141862

Schur, L., Han, K., Kim, A., Ameri, M., Blanck, P., & Kruse, D. (2017). Disability at work: A look back and forward. *Journal of Occupational Rehabilitation*, 27(4), 482–497. DOI: 10.1007/s10926-017-9739-5 PMID: 29110160

Stickley, A., Leinsalu, M., Ruchkin, V., Oh, H., Narita, Z., & Koyanagi, A. (2019). Attention-deficit/hyperactivity disorder symptoms and perceived mental health discrimination in adults in the general population. *European Psychiatry*, 56(1), 91–96. DOI: 10.1016/j.eurpsy.2018.12.004 PMID: 30654318

Terzi, L. (2004). The social model of disability: A philosophical critique. *Journal of Applied Philosophy*, 21(2), 141–157. DOI: 10.1111/j.0264-3758.2004.00269.x

Thapar, A., Eyre, O., Patel, V., & Brent, D. (2022). Depression in young people. *Lancet*, 400(10352), 617–631. DOI: 10.1016/S0140-6736(22)01012-1 PMID: 35940184

Weedon, C. (2020). The potential impact and influence of the social model of disability. In Peer, L., & Reid, G. (Eds.), *Special educational needs: A guide for inclusive practice*. Sage Publications.

Williams, D. R., Lawrence, J. A., Davis, B. A., & Vu, C. (2019). Understanding how discrimination can affect health. *Health Services Research*, 54(S2), 1374–1388. DOI: 10.1111/1475-6773.13222 PMID: 31663121

Zendarski, N., Guo, S., Sciberras, E., Efron, D., Quach, J., Winter, L., Bisset, M., Middeldorp, C. M., & Coghill, D. (2022). Examining the educational gap for children with ADHD and subthreshold ADHD. *Journal of Attention Disorders*, 26(2), 282–295. DOI: 10.1177/1087054720972790 PMID: 33317376

KEY TERMS AND DEFINITIONS

Career Prospects: Denotes the potential opportunities and pathways for development, progression, and achievement within a chosen profession or field. These prospects are influenced by various elements, including the job market, educational qualifications, skill levels, work experience, and industry dynamics. They provide individuals with insights into possible job roles, income potential, and long-term career opportunities. A strong correlation between an individual's skills, interests, and market needs can significantly improve their career prospects, thereby enhancing the likelihood of reaching professional aspirations and experiencing job satisfaction. Furthermore, factors such as lifelong learning, networking, and flexibility are essential in bolstering career prospects, as they empower individuals to maintain relevance and competitiveness in a fluid job market. Understanding and investigating career prospects is crucial for effective decision-making, career strategy, and achieving both personal and professional ambitions in a swiftly evolving employment landscape.

Discrimination: Defined as the unfair or biased treatment of individuals or groups based on attributes such as race, gender, disability, age, religion, sexual orientation, or socioeconomic status. This phenomenon encompasses actions or policies that establish obstacles, restrict opportunities, or prevent certain individuals from accessing the resources, rights, and privileges that are available to others. Discrimination can manifest at multiple levels, including individual, institutional, and systemic, and can take forms such as racism, sexism, ableism, or classism. The consequences of discrimination often result in social, economic, and psychological damage, perpetuating inequality and marginalization. It can be overt, as seen in derogatory comments or discriminatory hiring practices, or covert, arising from unconscious biases and stereotypes. Initiatives aimed at combating discrimination emphasize the importance of diversity, equity, and inclusion through legal measures, education, advocacy, and increased awareness. Tackling discrimination is essential for fostering a just society where every individual is afforded dignity, respect, and equal treatment, irrespective of their differences.

Educational Policy: Refers to principles, laws, regulations, and guidelines that regulate the administration and provision of education within a country, state, or educational institution. These policies are intended to ensure that all individuals have access to quality education, promote fairness, and support the overall development of learners. They encompass a wide range of topics, including curriculum standards, teacher qualifications, school funding, assessment strategies, and inclusive practices. The primary purpose of these policies is to define clear objectives for the educational system and to establish processes for achieving these objectives. The creation of educational policies involves various stakeholders, such as government agencies, educators, researchers, and representatives from the community. Effective educational policies are designed to be responsive to the changing needs of society, advancements in technology, and global trends, thereby ensuring that education remains relevant and progressive. Ultimately, the goal is to foster an educational environment that promotes learning, critical thinking, and the well-being of students, preparing them for future academic, professional, and social challenges.

Educational Equity: Defined as the principle of ensuring that all individuals have fair and inclusive access to quality education, regardless of their backgrounds, abilities, or circumstances. This principle aims to confront and eliminate systemic barriers, including discrimination, socioeconomic disparities, and biases, that prevent certain groups from achieving their full educational potential. Educational equity extends beyond the concept of equality, recognizing that some students may require additional resources, support, or accommodations to reach similar outcomes as their peers. It involves the implementation of inclusive policies, differentiated instruction, and targeted interventions to ensure that every student receives the necessary opportunities and support to succeed. The primary goal of educational equity is to create an inclusive learning environment that values diversity and promotes social justice, enabling all students to thrive academically, socially.

Educational Needs: Refer to the particular requirements, skills, knowledge, and support that students need to fulfill their potential in the educational process. These needs can differ significantly among individuals, influenced by factors such as cognitive abilities, language skills, cultural backgrounds, learning preferences, disabilities, and socio-economic conditions. Identifying educational needs requires a comprehensive understanding of both the academic and social-emotional dimensions of a student's development. Addressing these needs involves the implementation of personalized or differentiated instruction, targeted interventions, and accommodations that cater to a range of learning styles and challenges. For instance, students with disabilities may require.

Employment: Defined as the condition of being engaged in work, which may occur through a paid position or self-employment, where individuals carry out tasks or deliver services in exchange for payment. This arrangement typically involves a contractual agreement between an employer and an employee, regulated by labor laws and workplace standards. Employment is instrumental in providing economic security and personal satisfaction, allowing individuals to earn a living, acquire new skills, and contribute to the community. It includes a broad spectrum of job types, from manual labor to professional careers, across various industries such as agriculture, manufacturing, services, and technology. The importance of employment is underscored by its role in driving economic growth and enhancing societal well-being, as it enables individuals to achieve financial autonomy and access essential services like healthcare and education. Furthermore, meaningful employment can elevate self-esteem, foster social inclusion, and create a sense of purpose. Promoting fair and inclusive employment opportunities for everyone is crucial for reducing inequality and strengthening social cohesion.

Inclusive Workforce: Defined by a work environment that wholeheartedly embraces diversity, ensuring that all employees, regardless of their backgrounds, abilities, or characteristics, are valued, respected, and granted equal opportunities for success. This approach surpasses basic legal compliance, actively encouraging diversity in hiring practices, career progression, and workplace culture. An inclusive workforce encompasses individuals from various gender identities, ethnicities, ages, abilities, and other demographic groups, thereby nurturing a sense of belonging and mutual respect. Employers are committed to accessibility, fairness, and providing accommodations that enable every individual to perform at their best. In this inclusive setting, leaders concentrate on establishing policies and practices that address biases and eliminate prejudices.

Inclusive Education: An educational philosophy that aims to provide equal learning opportunities for all students, irrespective of their abilities, backgrounds, or differences. This approach seeks to create a learning environment where every individual feels valued, respected, and supported, thereby fostering a sense of belonging. It involves the modification of teaching practices, curricula, and assessment methods to accommodate the diverse needs of learners, ensuring that those with disabilities, language barriers, or other challenges can fully participate in the classroom experience. The focus is on collaboration among educators, families, and specialists to develop customized support strategies. The focus is not just on integration but on achieving true inclusion, where all students are afforded the same high-quality educational experiences and opportunities for advancement. Inclusive education nurtures empathy, acceptance, and mutual respect among students, preparing them to thrive in a multicultural society. By addressing barriers and promoting equity, inclusive education aims to enable the full engagement and potential of every learner.

Individualized Educational Programs (IEPs): Specifically tailored plans designed to address the distinct educational needs of students with disabilities or special learning requirements. The development of IEPs is a collaborative endeavor that includes educators, parents or guardians, specialists, and, in some cases, the student. These programs provide a comprehensive overview of the student's current academic performance, set learning objectives, and identify the specific services or accommodations necessary to support their educational journey. An IEP features customized teaching methods, specialized interventions, and adjustments to the learning environment or assessments, ensuring that students receive the appropriate support to achieve their full potential. Furthermore, the plan establishes measurable goals and includes periodic assessments to evaluate the student's progress and adapt strategies as required. IEPs are designed to promote equitable access to education and support the overall development of students, recognizing their unique strengths and needs. By prioritizing individualized support, IEPs help foster a more inclusive learning environment where all students can flourish.

Law: Represents a systematic collection of rules and principles set forth by a governing authority to regulate the behaviors and actions of individuals, organizations, and institutions within a given society. It provides a structure for maintaining order, resolving conflicts, protecting individual rights, and promoting social justice. Laws are established through legislative processes and are enforced by judicial bodies, including courts and law enforcement agencies. They encompass a wide array of fields, such as criminal law, civil law, constitutional law, and administrative law. Laws specify acceptable behaviors, detail the consequences of violations, and ensure that all individuals are subject to the same legal standards. The legal system seeks to uphold the rule of law, ensuring that laws are applied fairly and consistently to all members of society. By creating clear

Legislation: The process through which a governing authority, such as a parliament or congress, formulates, enacts, and enforces laws. This process includes the creation of rules and statutes designed to regulate conduct, safeguard rights, and enhance societal welfare. Elected officials, known as legislators, are responsible for proposing, discussing, and approving bills, which become law upon successful completion of the prescribed legal procedures. The significance of legislation lies in its role in maintaining societal order, ensuring justice, and addressing a range of issues, including public health, education, and environmental conservation. It establishes a framework for governmental actions and delineates the duties of citizens, organizations, and institutions. Additionally, legislation prescribes penalties for infractions and sets forth enforcement mechanisms. The effectiveness of legislation hinges on a comprehensive understanding of societal needs, active engagement with stakeholders, and decisions grounded in evidence. It adapts over time to accommodate evolving values, norms, and challenges, serving as a fundamental element of governance and the rule of law.

Local Community: Defined as a collective of individuals residing within a particular geographic area, such as a neighborhood, town, or village, who share mutual interests, social connections, and interactions. This concept extends beyond mere physical proximity, encompassing the social and cultural bonds that unite its members. Individuals within a local community frequently work together to tackle shared challenges, honor traditions, and foster a sense of belonging. These communities are instrumental in shaping the social experiences and identities of their members, affecting their access to resources, services, and opportunities. They are marked by common values, norms, and informal networks that enhance communication, support, and collaboration. Local communities are crucial for promoting social cohesion, civic participation, and resilience in the face of social or economic difficulties. They provide essential environments for individuals to cultivate relationships, contribute to collective welfare, and engage in decision-making processes that influence their everyday lives.

Public Policy: Refers to the comprehensive framework of actions, laws, regulations, and decisions executed by governmental authorities to address societal challenges and enhance the quality of life for citizens. It encompasses a diverse array of fields, such as education, healthcare, economic development, environmental protection, and social welfare. The shaping of public policy is influenced by political ideologies, social values, public opinion, and empirical evidence, with the aim of balancing the needs of individuals, communities, and society as a whole. The policymaking process includes stages such as problem identification, agenda setting, formulation and implementation.

Social Model of Disability: Presents a viewpoint that interprets disability as a consequence of societal obstacles rather than as a result of an individual's impairments or limitations. This perspective contests the conventional medical approach, which prioritizes the diagnosis and treatment of impairments, by highlighting the necessity of fostering inclusive environments that eliminate physical, social, and attitudinal barriers. According to this model, disability arises not merely from an individual's condition but from the absence of accessibility, discriminatory practices, and social exclusion that hinder their engagement in society. It advocates for reforms in policies, infrastructure, education, and societal attitudes to meet diverse needs and advance equality. The model aims to empower individuals by affirming their rights and promoting their full participation in social, economic, and cultural spheres. The Social Model of Disability is essential to disability rights movements and inclusive practices, as it encourages a transition towards perceiving disability as a collective societal responsibility rather than a personal shortcoming.

Student Performance: Defined as the level of success and development demonstrated by students in their academic and extracurricular activities. This concept includes various components such as academic grades, test scores, participation rates, and skill acquisition. Assessment of student performance is commonly conducted through standardized tests, coursework, classroom involvement, and practical projects. Such assessments provide insight into a student's understanding of the curriculum, their learning progress, and their overall engagement in the educational process. This performance serves as a measure of a student's comprehension of the curriculum, their learning trajectory, and their overall involvement in the educational experience. Various factors, such as individual capabilities, the quality of teaching, the learning environment, socio-economic status, and personal drive, significantly influence student performance. In addition to academic achievements, student performance also reflects social and emotional growth, as well as critical thinking and problem-solving skills. Educational institutions and instructors strive to cultivate supportive and inclusive settings that enhance student performance through effective teaching methods, tailored assistance, and engagement strategies. Acknowledging and addressing the diverse needs of students is essential for promoting their development, ensuring equitable learning opportunities, and fostering long-term academic and personal achievements.

Students with Disabilities: Those who encounter physical, cognitive, sensory, or developmental challenges that can affect their ability to fully engage in a standard educational environment. Disabilities can manifest in various forms, including autism spectrum disorder, ADHD, visual or hearing impairments, intellectual disabilities, and mobility limitations. To facilitate meaningful participation in education, these students often need specialized support, accommodations, or adjustments to their learning environments. This assistance may take the form of individualized educational programs, the use of assistive technologies, personalized teaching methods, and additional services such as speech therapy or counseling. The primary objective is to establish an inclusive and equitable learning environment that recognizes and values the unique strengths and requirements of each student. By promoting a supportive educational setting, schools can enable students with disabilities to achieve their academic aspirations, develop social competencies, and enhance their self-confidence, thus preparing them for successful transitions into higher education, careers, and community life.

APPENDIX I: STUDY QUESTIONNAIRE

Table 8. Teachers' Perspectives on the Effectiveness of Educational and Public Policies and Legislation in Promoting Career Transition of Students with ADHD Questionnaire (TPEEPPCLQ)

No	Statements	NAA	SE	ME	GE	VGE
1	To what extent do you feel informed about current educational policies for students with ADHD?					
2	To what extent do you think current public policies are supporting career transitions of students with ADHD?					
3	How well do you understand the legislation related to ADHD in the educational context?					
4	To what extent do you feel supported by school administration in implementing existing policies for students with ADHD?					
5	To what extent do you think current policies align with the career transition needs of students with ADHD?					
6	To what extent do you think the policy resources provided are effective in supporting students with ADHD in their career transitions?					
7	How well do you think teachers are trained to handle ADHD-related policy challenges in career transitions?					
8	To what extent do you think collaboration among teachers, parents, and policymakers is encouraged?					
9	To what extent do you feel that there is adequate support for professional development regarding ADHD following policy initiatives?					
10	To what extent do you find the communication between policymakers and teachers regarding ADHD-related policies sufficient and efficient?					
11	To what extent do you think policies address the individual needs of students with ADHD?					
12	To what extent do you feel empowered to influence policy changes related to ADHD?					
13	To what extent do you feel that the current legislation is in reducing the stigma associated with ADHD?					
14	To what extent do you find the policies related to career transitions for students with ADHD to be inclusive?					
15	To what extent do you feel that policies are regularly updated to reflect new research on ADHD?					
16	To what extent do you think that policies promote equal opportunities for students with ADHD?					

NAA=Not at All, SE=Small Extent, ME=Moderate Extent, GE=Great Extent, VGE=Very Great Extent

APPENDIX II: ADDITIONAL STATISTICS

Table 9. Item-total statistics

No	Statements	Cronbach's Alpha if Item Deleted
1	To what extent do you feel informed about current educational policies for students with ADHD?	.746
2	To what extent do you think current public policies are supporting career transitions of students with ADHD?	.755
3	How well do you understand the legislation related to ADHD in the educational context?	.773
4	To what extent do you feel supported by school administration in implementing existing policies for students with ADHD?	.734
5	To what extent do you think current policies align with the career transition needs of students with ADHD?	.759
6	To what extent do you think the policy resources provided are effective in supporting students with ADHD in their career transitions?	.773
7	How well do you think teachers are trained to handle ADHD-related policy challenges in career transitions?	.720
8	To what extent do you think collaboration among teachers, parents, and policymakers is encouraged?	.685
9	To what extent do you feel that there is adequate support for professional development regarding ADHD following policy initiatives?	.697
10	To what extent do you find the communication between policymakers and teachers regarding ADHD-related policies sufficient and efficient?	.674
11	To what extent do you think policies address the individual needs of students with ADHD?	.701
12	To what extent do you feel empowered to influence policy changes related to ADHD?	.697
13	To what extent do you feel that the current legislation is in reducing the stigma associated with ADHD?	.755
14	To what extent do you find the policies related to career transitions for students with ADHD to be inclusive?	.687
15	To what extent do you feel that policies are regularly updated to reflect new research on ADHD?	.687
16	To what extent do you think that policies promote equal opportunities for students with ADHD?	.787

Table 10. Communalities (extraction method: principal component analysis)

No	Statements	Extraction
1	To what extent do you feel informed about current educational policies for students with ADHD?	.901
2	To what extent do you think current public policies are supporting career transitions of students with ADHD?	.837
3	How well do you understand the legislation related to ADHD in the educational context?	.878
4	To what extent do you feel supported by school administration in implementing existing policies for students with ADHD?	.708
5	To what extent do you think current policies align with the career transition needs of students with ADHD?	.746
6	To what extent do you think the policy resources provided are effective in supporting students with ADHD in their career transitions?	.917
7	How well do you think teachers are trained to handle ADHD-related policy challenges in career transitions?	.589
8	To what extent do you think collaboration among teachers, parents, and policymakers is encouraged?	.836
9	To what extent do you feel that there is adequate support for professional development regarding ADHD following policy initiatives?	.661
10	To what extent do you find the communication between policymakers and teachers regarding ADHD-related policies sufficient and efficient?	.815
11	To what extent do you think policies address the individual needs of students with ADHD?	.863
12	To what extent do you feel empowered to influence policy changes related to ADHD?	.812
13	To what extent do you feel that the current legislation is in reducing the stigma associated with ADHD?	.673
14	To what extent do you find the policies related to career transitions for students with ADHD to be inclusive?	.937
15	To what extent do you feel that policies are regularly updated to reflect new research on ADHD?	.942
16	To what extent do you think that policies promote equal opportunities for students with ADHD?	.699

Chapter 4
Counselors' and Teachers' Perspectives on Psychological Interventions for Students With ADHD During Career Transitioning

ABSTRACT

The study examined the perspectives of secondary school counselors and teachers on the effectiveness of psychological interventions for students with ADHD during career transitioning. The research employed a quantitative research approach. The sample included 18 counselors and 38 teachers. Findings show that both counselors and teachers generally view these interventions positively, but experienced professionals rate them more favorably than their less experienced counterparts. No significant differences were found based on professional orientation or school location, indicating a broad consensus on the value of these interventions across different contexts. Therefore, this study highlights the importance of experience in shaping perspectives towards psychological interventions for students with ADHD during career transitioning, suggesting that enhancing professional development could improve perceptions of the early career professionals working with these students.

DOI: 10.4018/979-8-3693-2635-0.ch004

BACKGROUND

Attention-deficit/hyperactivity disorder (ADHD) is marked by signs such as impulsivity, hyperactivity, and inattention, which can have a substantial influence on a student's academic and social lives (Wilens et al., 2009; Wolraich et al., 2005). Students with ADHD benefit from a variety of psychological interventions that aim to address the problems associated with the disorder (Schultz & Evans, 2015). Turgay et al. (2012) noted that the recognition of ADHD as a condition that frequently continues into adulthood has increased the interest of patients, families, advocates, and professionals in a longitudinal strategy for its management. The authors indicated that this strategy must take into account and tackle the established challenges related to both patients and healthcare systems in the context of long-term mental health treatment, the evolving clinical manifestations of ADHD, and the prevalence of psychiatric comorbidities associated with ADHD. Although pharmacological treatments are frequently employed, psychological approaches have garnered acknowledgement for their efficacy in addressing ADHD symptoms and enhancing overall performance (Fullen et al., 2020). Moore et al. (2016) revealed that the perceived efficacy of school-based interventions for ADHD differs significantly, advocating for adaptable and customized strategies that take into account the broader school environment as well as the fundamental symptoms of ADHD. They also warned that highly personalized interventions may not consistently yield positive outcomes for students with ADHD. DuPaul and Weyandt (2006) identified two primary categories of school-based interventions designed for students with ADHD. The first category consists of proactive or antecedent-based interventions, which emphasize the development of academic and organizational skills. The second category includes reactive or consequent-based interventions, which focus on managing social behavior and classroom conduct. These interventions often employ teachers, peers, parents, computers, and the students themselves as mediators in the treatment process. Interventions addressing core ADHD symptoms across various age groups encompass physical exercise and mind-body approaches, caregiver support, school-based strategies, and executive function interventions (Tourjman et al., 2022). In addition, cognitive behavioral therapy, social skills training, and parent training/education are all types of psychological interventions for managing students with ADHD (Serrano-Troncoso et al., 2013; Stargell et al., 2017). Robb and Findling (2013) indicated that while psychosocial intervention is significant in addressing functional challenges and promoting individual compliance with pharmacotherapy, the predominant emphasis in the literature is on pharmacotherapy as the primary treatment for ADHD. Chronis et al. (2006) noted that there exists substantial evidence supporting behavioral interventions, such as parent training and school-based programs, which have earned the designation of "empirically validated treatments."

Furthermore, they highlighted that social skills training incorporating components of generalization, intensive summer treatment programs, and educational interventions show potential in addressing ADHD. According to the findings of Miranda et al. (2006), the multimodal treatment study of students with ADHD indicates that the most effective approach to treating ADHD involves a multimodal intervention. This often encompasses the use of medication alongside parent training, school-based interventions, and direct child interventions. Raggi and Chronis (2006) also observed that evidence-based methods for treating ADHD, including stimulant medication, behavior therapy, and classroom behavioral interventions, have shown significant effects on behavioral factors such as attention and disruptive behavior in classroom-like environments. Mindfulness-based cognitive-behavioral therapy also have been found to have a positive impact on the treatment of ADHD (Aadil et al., 2017). Mindfulness-based treatments refer to a form of cognitive training that employs several tactics to enhance attention, emotional self-regulation, calmness, and overall well-being (Chiesa et al., 2011).

Mindfulness-based cognitive therapy is an effective treatment for students with ADHD (Gu et al., 2018). Mindfulness-based therapies effectively enhanced attention, decreased inappropriate behaviors, and enhanced self-regulatory capacities in children within general education environments (Ramos et al., 2022). Behavioral parent training (BPT) is also an evidence-based psychological intervention used to support students with ADHD (Hornstra et al., 2021). BPT focuses on instructing parents in more efficient techniques for managing behavior, with the goal of preventing improper conduct, encouraging positive social behavior, and fostering a good parent-child connection (Axelrod & Santagata, 2021). Studies have also demonstrated that BPT has beneficial impacts on the particular student it targets and also has direct implications on the well-being of parents, while also enhancing parent-child connections (Huang et al., 2009; Tømmerås et al., 2018). This intervention can be beneficial in addressing communication challenges experienced by families or schools with a child or student who has ADHD. However, research indicates that the most efficient approach to treating ADHD is a multimodal solution, which often involves the use of medication together with psychological therapy (Pelham & Altszuler, 2020). The multimodal treatment strategy is a methodical and flexible technique that integrates various therapy modules based on the specific requirements and circumstances of the student with ADHD and their family (Drechsler et al., 2020). In instances with more severe ADHD, it is advisable to employ a mix of non-pharmacological and physiotherapy interventions (Serrano-Troncoso et al., 2013). Nonetheless, psychological interventions are also recognized as crucial for addressing the academic, emotional, and behavioral needs of students with ADHD, especially in alleviating burnout and improving self-regulation (Tayebi, 2020). Scholz et al. (2023) indicated that behavioral therapy is a successful intervention for reducing symptoms of inattention in adults suffering from ADHD. They highlighted that brief interventions are particularly advantageous in primary care contexts, owing to their feasibility. DuPaul et al. (1997) argued that due to the variability of ADHD-related behaviors among individuals and across different environments, it is crucial to adopt a personalized approach to assessment and intervention in order to facilitate the academic success of students affected by the disorder. Karlsdóttir et al. (2023) indicated that implementing effective interventions and providing support for students with ADHD can lead to improved well-being among teachers. However, it is essential to offer further training and professional assistance in best practices for ADHD to foster success for both teachers and their students. Vitanza (2014) proposed that school counseling psychologists and other service providers recommending interventions for teachers to implement with students diagnosed with ADHD should consider the various factors that shape teachers' perceptions and their acceptance of these interventions.

School counselors are in a distinctive position to employ strategies that can enhance the learning potential of students with ADHD, according to Shillingford-Butler and Theodore (2012). In a previous study, school counseling psychologists demonstrated a greater understanding, held fewer stigmatizing beliefs, and exhibited more inclusive attitudes towards students with ADHD compared to other school professionals, including teachers (Toye et al., 2019). Ibukun et al. (2015) conducted a cross-sectional study involving 144 Nigerian school teachers in South-West Nigeria and reported that only 16.7% recognized the value of psychological interventions for students with ADHD. Poznanski et al. (2018) emphasized that many teachers frequently perceive themselves as ill-equipped to address the classroom challenges posed by students with ADHD, especially in relation to supporting those with mental health issues. This sense of unpreparedness significantly contributes to teachers' decisions to exit the profession, and there is a notable deficiency in understanding regarding their knowledge of effective management techniques and students' mental health as they enter the classroom environment. Russell et al. (2023) contended that the evidence surrounding current school-based interventions for ADHD is inconsistent. These interventions are often complex and require significant resources, which stands in contrast to teachers' preferences for brief and adaptable strategies that can address various ADHD-related challenges in the classroom. A recent study conducted in rural Ogun State, Nigeria, by Yewande et al. (2024) revealed that primary teachers were largely uninformed about ADHD; although they had observed students exhibiting symptoms associated with the condition, their lack of understanding regarding professional treatment options hindered their ability to effectively manage these students, leading them to treat them similarly to their peers in a traditional educational setting. According to Ojionuka (2016), teachers in Nigeria are entrusted with the pedagogical duty of creating and overseeing a learning atmosphere that supports both learning and inclusivity; and they are essential in recognizing and providing assistance to students who encounter learning difficulties, such as ADHD. Nevertheless, there exists a considerable gap in comparative understanding of the perspectives of Nigerian school counselors and teachers concerning the efficacy, flexibility, and application of psychological interventions for students with ADHD as they navigate career transition. While psychological interventions hold considerable promise, most schoolteachers and counselors may hold some bias against some of them (Eseadi & Diale, 2024). There are also worries about the variability in results, as not all interventions yield the same level of effectiveness for every student with ADHD (Fabiano et al., 2015; Hinshaw et al., 2011). The dearth of ongoing assessment of psychological interventions may further thwart the situation, diminishing their potential influence on career transition outcomes for students with ADHD. Without an understanding of these Nigerian school professionals' perspectives, students with ADHD may continue to experience substantial drawbacks in making successful career transitions, as schools may not deliver the psychological support they require during these crucial phases. It remains unclear how the professional orientations of Nigerian school counselors and teachers, their years of experience, and the urban or rural location of their schools affect their perceptions of the success of psychological interventions within the context of students' career transition. This knowledge gap restricts the capacity of educational policymakers and practitioners to develop or support psychological interventions that effectively cater to the needs of students with ADHD during career transition. In this respect, this study aims to bridge this gap by investigating the perspectives of secondary school counselors and teachers in Nigeria concerning the effectiveness of psychological interventions for students with ADHD, especially in relation to career transitions.

Research Objectives

1. To determine the collective viewpoint of secondary school counselors and teachers on the effectiveness of psychological interventions for students with ADHD during career transitioning.
2. To explore the disparity in the perceived effectiveness of psychological interventions for students with ADHD between counselors and teachers based on their professional orientations (teaching practice orientation & counseling practice orientation).
3. To investigate the disparity between counselors' and teachers' perspectives on the effectiveness of psychological interventions for students with ADHD based on their years of professional experience.

4. To determine if there is a difference in the perspectives of counselors and teachers regarding the effectiveness of psychological interventions for students with ADHD based on their location of practice (urban or rural school).

Research Questions

1. What is the collective viewpoint of secondary school counselors and teachers on the effectiveness of psychological interventions for students with ADHD during career transitioning?
2. Is there a significant disparity in the perceived effectiveness of psychological interventions for students with ADHD between counselors and teachers based on their professional orientations (teaching practice orientation and counseling practice orientation)?
3. Does a significant disparity exist between counselors' and teachers' perspectives on the effectiveness of psychological interventions for students with ADHD based on their years of professional experience?
4. Is there a significant difference in the perspectives of counselors and teachers regarding the effectiveness of psychological interventions for students with ADHD based on their location of practice (urban or rural school)?

Theoretical Framework

The cognitive-behavioral theory offers a significant framework for analyzing the perspectives of school counselors and teachers on the usefulness of psychological interventions for students with ADHD during career transition. This theoretical framework is rooted in a deficit-centered perspective of ADHD, focusing on alleviating symptoms and improving cognitive control over self-regulation as key outcomes of treatment (Champ et al., 2021). Cognitive behavioral therapy (CBT), recognized as an effective intervention within this framework, is used to address the difficulties faced by students with ADHD (Anastopoulos & King, 2015). Evidence from Bramham et al. (2009) indicates that CBT aids individuals in transforming negative thought patterns and addressing behaviors that are frequently associated with ADHD. In CBT sessions, therapists guide clients in acquiring vital skills such as effective time management, improved organizational capabilities, and increased self-awareness (Deupree, 2024). As a holistic approach to psychotherapy, CBT incorporates a diverse array of principles and techniques, leading to the development of various therapies, including Cognitive Therapy, Dialectical Behavioral Therapy, Multimodal Therapy, and Rational Emotive Behavioral Therapy (Grande, 2023). A fundamental technique within CBT is cognitive restructuring, which seeks to transform negative thought processes and foster a more positive outlook on life (Skedel,

2022). The use of this theoretical framework is crucial for critically analyzing the perspectives of teachers and school counselors regarding the efficacy of psychological interventions for students with ADHD during career transition (see Figure 1). By concentrating on therapeutic aims such as alleviating symptoms and fostering self-regulation, this framework serves to evaluate the effectiveness of psychological interventions in preparing students with ADHD for career transitions. Counselors may view psychological interventions as a beneficial approach for tackling ADHD-related behavioral and cognitive difficulties during these transitions, while teachers may assess the interventions based on their effects on academic achievement and classroom behavior. This theoretical approach creates a common platform for understanding how professionals with differing practice orientations evaluate the same interventions from distinct perspectives. Consequently, the study can investigate whether the training background of counselors versus teachers influences their perceptions of psychological interventions' effectiveness in supporting students with ADHD. More experienced counselors and teachers may have observed the long-term effects of cognitive restructuring and self-regulation techniques on students' career transitions and behaviors over time. These veteran professionals might have a more nuanced understanding of the cumulative benefits of psychological interventions on student growth, while those with less experience may prioritize immediate outcomes. By framing the study within CBT, it can explore whether the length of professional experience affects the ability to assess both short-term and long-term effectiveness of psychological interventions. Furthermore, employing CBT as the theoretical framework allows the research to assess whether the flexibility of psychological interventions across various contexts affects how counselors and teachers perceive their effectiveness, as well as how environmental factors related to location influence the perceived success of these interventions.

Figure 1. Study framework

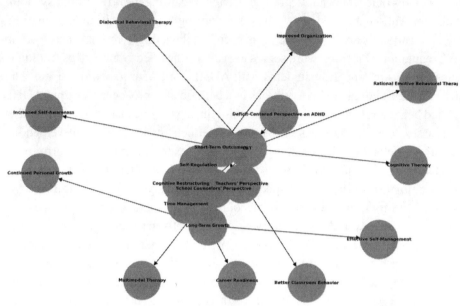

METHODOLOGY

Ethics Statement

Ethical approval for this study was obtained from the relevant institutional review boards. First, it received approval from the Research Ethics Committee of the Faculty of Education, University of Nigeria, Nigeria. It also received additional ethical approval from the Faculty of Education Research Ethics Committee at the University of Johannesburg, South Africa (Sem 2-2020-057). Informed consent was secured from participants. We assured confidentiality and clarified participants' right to withdraw from the study at any given time.

Research Design and Approach

This study used a survey research design. A survey is defined as the process of gathering information from a substantial group of individuals or a specific population, aimed at enhancing scientific understanding or developing theoretical frameworks. Examples of such surveys include opinion polls and questionnaires (Malhotra &

Grover, 1998). According to Kelley et al. (2003), the term 'survey' encompasses various interpretations, but it typically denotes the selection of a sizable sample from a predetermined population, referred to as the 'population of interest.' This population represents the broader group that the researcher aims to study. Subsequently, a limited amount of data is collected from these selected individuals, allowing the researcher to draw inferences about the larger population (Kelley et al., 2003). The research employed a quantitative methodology, which primarily adheres to the confirmatory scientific method, emphasizing hypothesis and theory testing. Quantitative researchers prioritize the articulation of hypotheses, which are then empirically tested to determine their validity. There is a prevailing association of quantitative methods with a natural science or positivist perspective, as noted by Gichuru (2017), which was also embraced in this study.

Research Paradigm

The concept of 'paradigm' refers to a philosophical framework or research philosophy that serves as the foundational theoretical basis for conducting research (Khatri, 2020). These underlying beliefs significantly influence the direction of research on a specific topic. Typically, research is conducted within a singular paradigm, which profoundly impacts the methodologies employed and the outcomes derived (Van Merriënboer & De Bruin, 2014). This particular study is grounded in the positive research paradigm. Positivism is characterized by its proponents' reliance on scientific methods to generate knowledge, asserting that genuine understanding can be achieved through observation and experimentation (Rahi, 2017). Positivist research posits the existence of an objective physical and social world that is independent of human perception, and it is believed that this world can be comprehensively understood, described, and quantified (Gichuru, 2017).

Study Area

This research was conducted in Anambra State. Anambra is a state located in the southeastern region of Nigeria, comprising 21 local government areas, 181 towns, and 330 political wards (Ugwu et al., 2021). The capital city of Anambra State is Awka (Igbokwe et al., 2019).

Population and Sampling

The study involves inclusive school counselors and schoolteachers from selected public secondary schools. A total of 18 school counsellors and 38 inclusive schoolteachers were selected using purposive and convenience sampling techniques.

Purposive and convenience sampling are classified as non-probability sampling techniques. Non-probability sampling is often regarded as advantageous because it ensures representation from all subjects within the population, with sample selection based on individual discretion (Adeoye, 2023). The primary purpose of purposive sampling is to align the sample more closely with the research's aims and objectives, thereby enhancing the study's rigor and the reliability of the data and findings (Campbell et al., 2020). According to Klar & Leeper (2019) purposive sampling can be viewed as a specific form of convenience sampling, as it involves subjective selection of respondents. They further note that convenience sampling is based on untestable assumptions, making it less suitable than probability-based methods, particularly in the context of observational research as opposed to survey-experimental research (Klar & Leeper, 2019). The participants' mean age is 38.69 ± 6.67 years.

Data Collection

The data was collected using a questionnaire. The researchers received help from two postgraduate students to complete the data collection process. The questionnaire used for data collection is called the Counselors' and Teachers' Perspectives on Psychological Interventions and ADHD Questionnaire (CTPPIQ). It is a 17-item scale which measures counselors' and teachers' perceived effectiveness of psychological interventions for students with ADHD during career transitioning. The scale is designed to capture the extent of agreement or perception, with 1 indicating "Strongly disagree" and 5 indicating "Strongly agree." Some examples of item statements in the questionnaire include: "Psychological interventions help to develop coping strategies for students with ADHD during career transition." and "I have observed improvements in students with ADHD due to psychological interventions during career transition." The CTPPIQ has a good internal consistency reliability, with a Cronbach's alpha of 0.73 in the present research.

Data Analysis

Statistical analysis was conducted using Jeffreys' Amazing Statistics Program software (JASP), version 0.18.3. JASP is a free graphical software application compatible with various operating systems, designed to simplify the intricate Bayesian methods (Kelter, 2020). This open-source statistical software is highly effective for conducting exploratory data analysis, as well as frequentist and Bayesian inferential analyses (Perezgonzalez, 2022). The JASP presents multiple visual interpretations of hypothesis tests. (Souza & Borges, 2023). This research employed both descriptive and inferential statistics. Descriptive statistics provide a statistical overview of the data set Sutanapong and Louangrath (2022) which typically includes measures such as mean, median, mode, variance, and standard deviation. Inferential statistics involve making inferences or conclusions based on a collection of observations (Sutanapong & Louangrath, 2022). This type of statistics is utilized to draw generalizations from the sample group that can be applicable to a broader population (Marshall & Jonker, 2011). In this study, descriptive statistics was used to summarize the sociodemographic data, while inferential statistics (t-tests) were used to analyse the research questions at a .05 significance level.

FINDINGS

Table 1. Collective viewpoint of secondary school counselors and teachers on the effectiveness of psychological interventions for students with ADHD during career transitioning

Questionnaire	Group	N	Mean	SD	SE	Coefficient of variation
CTPPIQ	School counsellors	18	3.75	.27	.064	.073
	School teachers	38	3.85	.35	.057	.091

Table 1 shows that school counsellors had a mean score of 3.75 (SD=.27), and the schoolteachers had a mean score of 3.85 (SD=.35) in terms of their collective viewpoint on the effectiveness of psychological interventions for students with ADHD during career transitioning. Figure 2 also demonstrates their collective viewpoint on this issue. The mean scores indicate that both counselors and teachers have a positive perspective on the effectiveness of psychological interventions for students with ADHD during career transitioning.

Figure 2. Collective viewpoint of secondary school counselors and teachers on the effectiveness of psychological interventions for students with ADHD during career transitioning.

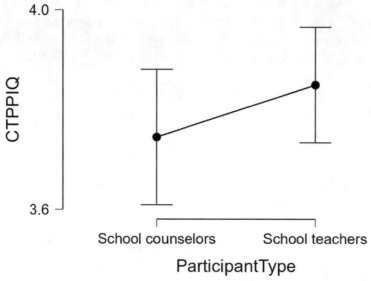

Table 2. Independent samples T-Test on the perceived effectiveness of psychological interventions for students with ADHD between counselors and teachers based on their professional orientations

Variable	T	df	p	Mean Difference	SE Difference	95%CI Lower Upper
Professional Orientations	-1.112	54	.27	-.105	.094	-.294, .084

The t-test analysis in Table 2 revealed that there is no significant disparity in the perceived effectiveness of psychological interventions for students with ADHD during career transitioning between school counselors and teachers based on their professional orientations, $t(54)= -1.112$, $p=.27$, mean difference$=-.105$. Figure 3 elucidates this result of no significant difference between school counselors ($3.75\pm.27$) and teachers ($3.85\pm.35$) based on their professional orientation.

Figure 3. Perceived effectiveness of psychological interventions for students with ADHD between counselors and teachers based on their professional orientations

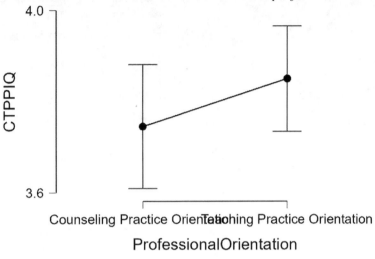

Table 3. Independent samples T-Test on counselors' and teachers' perspectives on the effectiveness of psychological interventions for students with ADHD based on their years of professional experience

Variable	t	df	p	Mean Difference	SE Difference	95%CI Lower Upper
Professional Experience	-2.699	54	.009	-.226	.084	-.393, -.058

The t-test analysis in Table 3 revealed that there is a significant disparity in the perceived effectiveness of psychological interventions for students with ADHD during career transitioning between school counselors and teachers based on their professional experience, $t(54)= -2.699$, $p=.009$, mean difference$=-.226$. Figure 4 further demonstrates this significant disparity, with early career school counselors and teachers (3.69±.30) scoring less than the experienced school counselors and teachers (3.93±.32) on how they perceived the effectiveness of psychological interventions for students with ADHD during career transitioning.

Figure 4. Perceived effectiveness of psychological interventions for students with ADHD between school counselors and teachers based on their professional experience

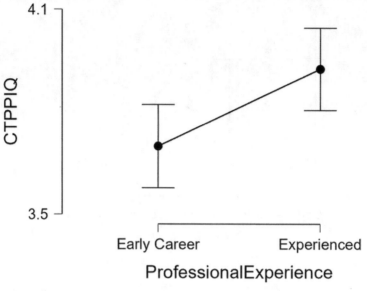

Table 4. Independent samples T-Test on the perceived effectiveness of psychological interventions for students with ADHD between counselors and teachers based on their school location

Variable	T	Df	p	Mean Difference	SE Difference	95%CI Lower Upper
School Location	.077	54	.94	.007	.089	-.172, .185

The t-test analysis in Table 4 revealed that there is no significant difference in the perceived effectiveness of psychological interventions for students with ADHD during career transitioning between school counselors and teachers based on their school location, t(54)=.077, p=.94, mean difference=.007. Figure 5 elucidates this result of no significant difference between school counselors and teachers in rural schools (3.82±.28) and their counterparts in urban schools (3.81±.38).

Figure 5. Perceived effectiveness of psychological interventions for students with ADHD between school counselors and teachers based on their school location

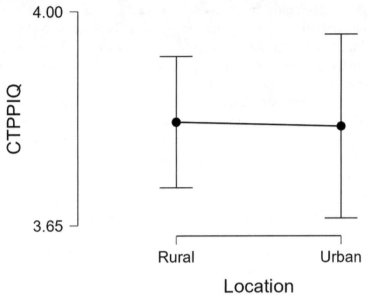

DISCUSSION

This research examined the perspectives of counselors and teachers regarding the effectiveness of psychological interventions for students with ADHD during career transition. The study found that both secondary school counselors and teachers generally view psychological interventions for students with ADHD as effective during career transition, with no significant disparities in perceptions based on professional orientation and school location. Fullen et al. (2020) indicated that psychological interventions for students with ADHD are highly effective. The study revealed that 92% of the studies that implemented various non-pharmacological interventions reported a significant positive effect on either primary or secondary outcomes associated with ADHD. Sonuga-Barke et al. (2013) demonstrated that psychological treatments yield statistically significant outcomes for ADHD. Azeem et al. (2021) revealed that a significant number of school psychologists expressed confidence in the effectiveness of behavior therapy, a psychological intervention which was adopted for students with ADHD, highlighting its potential to improve social and cognitive skills. Earlier on, Call (2011) found that school psychologists assessed the daily report card as being less acceptable and effective compared to the evaluations made by teachers, and they demonstrated a stronger preference for response cost techniques as interventions for ADHD. Zirkelback and Reese (2010) revealed that psychological interventions are beneficial for children and adolescents because they can enhance both their social and intellectual skills. Antshel et al. (2014) indicated that teachers perceived students with ADHD and oppositional defiant disorder as gaining less from CBT intervention. In contrast, those with ADHD who also had comorbid anxiety or depression were viewed as benefiting more from the CBT intervention, according to assessments from teachers. According to DuPaul (2007), intervention strategies implemented within school settings, such as behavioral approaches, adjustments to academic instruction, and programs facilitating communication between home and school, can effectively support students of various age groups diagnosed with ADHD in general education environments. Bussing et al. (2011) noted that students with ADHD also have perceptions about the stigma associated with their condition that significantly affects their willingness to receive treatment interventions. Therefore, it is essential that improvement strategies for these students incorporate psychoeducational interventions aimed at both the students and their parents, focusing on enhancing receptivity to treatment and addressing the stigma surrounding ADHD. According to Moore et al. (2018), self-regulation and individualization are significant components contributing to the effectiveness of academic interventions for students with ADHD. Nevertheless, these components were insufficient on their own; their efficacy was enhanced when they either included personalization for each recipient and were delivered within the classroom context, or when the interventions specifically targeted the enhancement of child relationships.

Our study further revealed that the perceptions of teachers and school counselors regarding the effectiveness of psychological interventions for students with ADHD during career transitioning are more influenced by their professional experience rather than their orientation or school location. Power et al. (2009) found that a teacher's knowledge of ADHD and their years of teaching experience did not significantly influence their ratings of acceptability. Curtis et al. (2006) identified cross-cultural variations in the perception of both behavioral interventions, which were influenced by the nationality of the teachers. Their findings suggest that teachers in the United States regarded psychological interventions as more acceptable, effective, and timely compared to their counterparts in New Zealand. The same study also revealed an interaction effect involving student gender, nationality, and preferences for interventions. These perceptions may have resulted from their professional experience, as our study has pointed out, or the extent of knowledge they possess about the various psychological interventions and the disorder. Ohan et al. (2008) revealed shortcomings in teachers' knowledge concerning ADHD treatment without reference to the school counselors. According to the findings by Vitanza (2014), teachers generally report feeling confident and well-equipped to manage students diagnosed with ADHD; however, they express a desire for further in-service training on the matter. They find students with hyperactive-impulsive characteristics more challenging to handle than those with inattentive traits. While both medication and positive behavioral strategies are seen as effective for inattentive symptoms, teachers tend to favor medication for managing combined symptoms. Moreover, they identify large class sizes and a lack of staff support, particularly the issue of class size, as significant challenges to the effective execution of interventions (Vitanza, 2014). Bussing et al. (2012) found that the willingness to engage with ADHD treatments was significantly influenced by the type of respondent, with lower willingness observed among adolescents compared to adults. This willingness was also linked to feelings of knowledge and the perceived acceptability of treatments, while factors such as stigma, race, gender, and socioeconomic status did not show significant associations. According to Strelow et al. (2020), the most significant factor affecting pre-service teachers' approach to the use of classroom management strategies for students with ADHD is their attitude; knowledge plays a crucial role in shaping these attitudes. To increase the chances of pre-service teachers utilizing effective classroom management strategies in supporting these students, it is necessary to alter their attitudes towards such strategies. For Ikechukwu-Ilomuanya et al. (2015), counselors can assist students to adjust academically through time management counseling intervention.

In the context of feasibility, research indicates that longer interventions do not yield better outcomes than shorter ones, and individual therapy sessions do not prove to be more effective than group sessions (Scholz et al., 2023). Noyes (2017) revealed that teachers regarded the daily report card as the most acceptable, effective, and timely intervention, showing a strong preference for behavioral interventions over medication. According to Labrador-Roca et al. (2020), teachers working with students with ADHD utilized behavior modification techniques, including praise and attention, to promote positive behavior. Conversely, methods such as direct verbal instructions, expulsion, and punishment were applied to mitigate undesirable behavior. The study further indicated that behavior was successfully modified in 68% of instances, while it remained unchanged in 32%. As observed by Antshel (2015), the primary aim of psychosocial interventions for individuals with ADHD is to address functional impairments, with a strong emphasis on the application of behavioral therapy techniques and operant conditioning principles. Smith et al. (2000) provided preliminary evidence supporting the effectiveness, safety, and practicality of various psychotherapeutic interventions for ADHD, including family therapy, behavioral strategies in classrooms, and note-taking skills training. Psychological treatment may be crucial for individuals with ADHD who are willing and developmentally equipped to develop new skills as their symptoms lessen (Weiss et al., 2008). Ojionuka (2016) found that Nigerian school teachers' understanding of ADHD influenced their selection of behavior modification strategies for addressing the characteristic behaviors associated with the disorder. These teachers employed negative disciplinary measures and various interventions aimed at modifying specific negative behaviors linked to ADHD, which suggests a deficiency in their classroom management skills. Staff et al. (2022) demonstrated that both antecedent- and consequent-based strategies were successful in alleviating symptoms and impairments associated with ADHD in the classroom, with encouraging long-term improvements noted in teacher assessments of ADHD. Szép et al. (2021) revealed that various factors, including teachers' perceptions of effectiveness, specialized training for ADHD, perceived disruptions, and their association with either primary or special needs institutions, significantly impacted their implementation of classroom management strategies. Experience was found to have an indirect influence through training. Additionally, challenges such as large class sizes, time constraints, and a high prevalence of students with disabilities were prevalent barriers. This indicates that enhancing perceptions of effectiveness and offering focused ADHD training for educators could substantially improve classroom management (Szép et al., 2021).

According to the findings of Miranda et al. (2006), interventions implemented within the school setting for students with ADHD demonstrate short-term effectiveness in diminishing disruptive behaviors while enhancing both on-task behavior and academic achievement. Misrok and Cooper (2024) reported that there were no statistically significant variations in the perceptions of teachers concerning the need for specialist referrals, regardless of the gender of the students or the nature of their symptoms. Moldavsky et al. (2014) asserted in their research that teachers' feedback indicates a significant inclination towards employing within-school strategies for managing children with ADHD. In a way, these within-school strategies are equivalent to psychological interventions. Kourkoutas et al. (2018) emphasized the necessity for teachers who engage with students displaying challenging behaviors to seek assistance from professionals. This collaboration is essential for enhancing their understanding of the psychological dynamics at play in these students. Weyandt et al. (2009) indicated that the expertise of school counseling psychologists regarding ADHD is notably superior to that of both special and general education teachers; a greater number of years of professional experience correlated negatively with the level of knowledge regarding ADHD. School psychologists engage with a diverse range of students, their parents, and teachers; as such, their training encompasses essential skills such as assessment, intervention, consultation, and counseling. This training is delivered within the framework of a dynamic school environment that is continually adapting to meet evolving needs (Flanagan, 2024). Wiener (2020) contends that school psychologists are pivotal in addressing concerns related to psychological interventions, as they perform assessments that involve the student as an active participant and deliver evidence-based mental health strategies within educational environments. DuPaul et al. (2020) highlighted a considerable disparity between research findings and practical application, indicating that evidence-based treatments frequently fail to be adopted in community and educational environments. In their study, Schatz et al. (2021) found that teachers from various survey samples largely concurred on the efficacy of behavioral classroom management, medication, and their combined use in addressing the needs of students with ADHD. However, it was noted that teachers in 2019 had a somewhat less favorable view of behavioral classroom management compared to their counterparts in 1999. Nevertheless, the perceptions of teachers in both years were consistent with established professional practice guidelines, highlighting a significant necessity for training and support in evidence-based approaches for managing ADHD students in educational settings.

According to the findings of Graczyk et al. (2005), student personnel services professionals, such as school counselors, along with classroom teachers in urban areas, displayed a lack of confidence in the effectiveness of ADHD treatments. The study identified a moderately positive association between the self-confidence of these professionals and their effectiveness ratings for both classroom and mental health interventions. It was also observed that teachers' self-confidence was positively linked to the effectiveness of classroom interventions. However, a negative association was found between teachers' knowledge of ADHD and their perceptions of the effectiveness of classroom and mental health interventions. Furthermore, the study reported that neither the gender of the child nor the subtype of ADHD influenced the effectiveness ratings. In the research by Topping (2011), teachers raised concerns about the decline in the academic achievement of students during transition and school strategies for mitigating the challenge. Grove (2021) documents that participants who availed themselves of psychosocial support conveyed diverse views on its effectiveness. The study did not address the perspectives of teachers or school counselors; however, it highlights the critical need for surveys targeting the views of those benefiting from psychological interventions. Staff et al. (2021) argued that a child's age and class size serve as moderators influencing the effectiveness of various techniques, with both antecedent- and consequent-based methods demonstrating significant efficacy in mitigating problem behaviors in children with ADHD. Overall, it is imperative for professionals to employ psychological interventions that are likely to foster therapeutic benefits, grounded in empirical research findings pertaining to their clients (Fedewa et al., 2015). However, our study is constrained by an uneven sample size, which may hinder the ability to draw unbiased comparisons between the two groups. Also, the geographical limitation of participants to Anambra State, Nigeria, further restricts the generalizability of our findings. Future research should consider a larger, more evenly distributed sample across multiple locations in Nigeria to ensure a more representative analysis. Furthermore, providing training for teachers on the different psychological interventions could prove advantageous for both teachers and students with ADHD. Barkley (2007) emphasized the necessity of further investigation into how parental ADHD influences school interventions, as well as the impact of teacher ADHD and the broader context of the temperamental compatibility between teachers and students. In light of the influence that student-teacher conflict has on the negative correlation between ADHD symptoms and emotional engagement of students in school, it has been proposed that strategies aimed at reducing conflict in the student-teacher relationship be used to foster greater school engagement among students with ADHD, which could result in better long-term outcomes (*see*Rushton et al., 2020). Considering that factors such as academic regulation, self-efficacy in academic settings, emotional regulation, symptoms of ADHD, and both academic and social integration are predictors of school success, it may be beneficial to integrate these components into interventions aimed at students with ADHD to improve their chances of success at school (Stevens et al., 2022). A peer-led program under the guidance of teachers also has the potential to support students with ADHD in averting a decrease in their engagement with school activities (Sibley et al., 2020).

CONCLUSIONS

The study fills a gap in the literature by comparing school counselors' and teachers' perspectives on the effectiveness of psychological interventions for students with ADHD during career transitioning across different professional orientations, professional experiences and school locations. It was shown that psychological interventions are perceived by school counselors and teachers as beneficial in supporting students with ADHD during career transitioning. However, their perceptions are more influenced by their professional experience rather than their orientation or school location. Therefore, there is a need for further training and support for. early-career professional counselors to enhance their confidence in implementing these interventions to support students with ADHD during career transitioning. Future research should explore the specific components of psychological interventions that contribute most to their perceived effectiveness among school counselors and teachers. Future studies should investigate the long-term impacts of these interventions on the career transition success of students with ADHD. Future research should also survey diverse educational contexts to provide a more nuanced perspective on the effectiveness of psychological interventions for students with ADHD during career transitioning.

REFERENCES

Aadil, M., Cosme, R. M., & Chernaik, J. (2017). Mindfulness-Based Cognitive Behavioral Therapy as an Adjunct Treatment of Attention Deficit Hyperactivity Disorder in Young Adults: A Literature Review. *Cureus*, 9(5). Advance online publication. DOI: 10.7759/cureus.1269 PMID: 28775916

Adeoye, M. (2023). Review of Sampling Techniques for Education. *ASEAN Journal for Science Education*, 2(2), 87–94.

Anastopoulos, A. D., & King, K. A. (2015). A cognitive-behavior therapy and mentoring program for college students with ADHD. *Cognitive and Behavioral Practice*, 22(2), 141–151. DOI: 10.1016/j.cbpra.2014.01.002

Antshel, K. M. (2015). Psychosocial interventions in attention-deficit/hyperactivity disorder: Update. *Child and Adolescent Psychiatric Clinics of North America*, 24(1), 79–97. DOI: 10.1016/j.chc.2014.08.002 PMID: 25455577

Antshel, K. M., Faraone, S. V., & Gordon, M. (2014). Cognitive behavioral treatment outcomes in adolescent ADHD. *Journal of Attention Disorders*, 18(6), 483–495. DOI: 10.1177/1087054712443155 PMID: 22628140

Axelrod, M. I., & Santagata, M. L. (2021). Behavioral Parent Training. In Maragakis, A., Drossel, C., & Waltz, T. J. (Eds.), *Applications of Behavior Analysis in Healthcare and Beyond* (pp. 135–154). Springer International Publishing., DOI: 10.1007/978-3-030-57969-2_6

Azeem, A., Faiz, Z., Siddique, M., Ali, M. S., & Warraich, W. (2021). School Psychologists' Perspectives About Effectiveness of Behavior Therapy for Children with Attention Deficit Hyperactivity Disorder in Pakistan. *Humanities & Social Sciences Reviews*, 9(3), 1142–1155. DOI: 10.18510/hssr.2021.93113

Barkley, R. A. (2007). School interventions for attention deficit hyperactivity disorder: Where to from here? *School Psychology Review*, 36(2), 279–286. DOI: 10.1080/02796015.2007.12087945

Bramham, J., Young, S., Bickerdike, A., Spain, D., McCartan, D., & Xenitidis, K. (2009). Evaluation of Group Cognitive Behavioral Therapy for Adults With ADHD. *Journal of Attention Disorders*, 12(5), 434–441. DOI: 10.1177/1087054708314596 PMID: 18310557

Bussing, R., Koro-Ljungberg, M., Noguchi, K., Mason, D., Mayerson, G., & Garvan, C. W. (2012). Willingness to use ADHD treatments: A mixed methods study of perceptions by adolescents, parents, health professionals and teachers. *Social Science & Medicine*, 74(1), 92–100. DOI: 10.1016/j.socscimed.2011.10.009 PMID: 22133584

Bussing, R., Zima, B. T., Mason, D. M., Porter, P. C., & Garvan, C. W. (2011). Receiving treatment for attention-deficit hyperactivity disorder: Do the perspectives of adolescents matter? *The Journal of adolescent health: official publication of the Society for Adolescent Medicine*, 49(1), 7–14. DOI: 10.1016/j.jadohealth.2010.08.014

Call, B. (2011). *Perceptions of acceptability and effectiveness of interventions for ADHD: A comparison of teachers and school psychologists* [James Madison University].

Campbell, S., Greenwood, M., Prior, S., Shearer, T., Walkem, K., Young, S., Bywaters, D., & Walker, K. (2020). Purposive sampling: Complex or simple? Research case examples. *Journal of Research in Nursing*, 25(8), 652–661. DOI: 10.1177/1744987120927206 PMID: 34394687

Champ, R. E., Adamou, M., & Tolchard, B. (2021). The impact of psychological theory on the treatment of Attention Deficit Hyperactivity Disorder (ADHD) in adults: A scoping review. *PLoS One*, 16(12), e0261247. DOI: 10.1371/journal.pone.0261247 PMID: 34932573

Chiesa, A., Calati, R., & Serretti, A. (2011). Does mindfulness training improve cognitive abilities? A systematic review of neuropsychological findings. *Clinical Psychology Review*, 31(3), 449–464. DOI: 10.1016/j.cpr.2010.11.003 PMID: 21183265

Chronis, A. M., Jones, H. A., & Raggi, V. L. (2006). Evidence-based psychosocial treatments for children and adolescents with attention-deficit/hyperactivity disorder. *Clinical Psychology Review*, 26(4), 486–502. DOI: 10.1016/j.cpr.2006.01.002 PMID: 16483703

Curtis, D. F., Pisecco, S., Hamilton, R. J., & Moore, D. W. (2006). Teacher perceptions of classroom interventions for children with ADHD: A cross-cultural comparison of teachers in the United States and New Zealand. *School Psychology Quarterly*, 21(2), 171–196. DOI: 10.1521/scpq.2006.21.2.171

Deupree, S. (2024, May 28). *CBT for ADHD: How It Works, Examples & Effectiveness*. https://www.choosingtherapy.com/cbt-for-adhd/

Drechsler, R., Brem, S., Brandeis, D., Grünblatt, E., Berger, G., & Walitza, S. (2020). ADHD: Current Concepts and Treatments in Children and Adolescents. *Neuropediatrics*, 51(5), 315–335. DOI: 10.1055/s-0040-1701658 PMID: 32559806

DuPaul, G. J. (2007). School-Based Interventions for Students with Attention Deficit Hyperactivity Disorder: Current Status and Future Directions. *School Psychology Review*, 36(2), 183–194. DOI: 10.1080/02796015.2007.12087939

DuPaul, G. J., Eckert, T. L., & McGoey, K. E. (1997). Interventions for students with attention-deficit/hyperactivity disorder: One size does not fit all. *School Psychology Review*, 26(3), 369–381. DOI: 10.1080/02796015.1997.12085872

DuPaul, G. J., Evans, S. W., Mautone, J. A., Owens, J. S., & Power, T. J. (2020). Future directions for psychosocial interventions for children and adolescents with ADHD. *Journal of Clinical Child and Adolescent Psychology*, 49(1), 134–145. DOI: 10.1080/15374416.2019.1689825 PMID: 31799864

DuPaul, G. J., & Weyandt, L. L. (2006). School-Based Interventions for Children and Adolescents with Attention-Deficit/Hyperactivity Disorder: Enhancing Academic and Behavioral Outcomes. *Education & Treatment of Children*, 29(2), 341–358.

Eseadi, C., & Diale, B. M. (2024). *Perspectives on Career Transitioning of Students with Hearing Impairments*. IGI Global., DOI: 10.4018/979-8-3693-2631-2

Fabiano, G. A., Schatz, N. K., Aloe, A. M., Chacko, A., & Chronis-Tuscano, A. (2015). A systematic review of meta-analyses of psychosocial treatment for attention-deficit/hyperactivity disorder. *Clinical Child and Family Psychology Review*, 18(1), 77–97. DOI: 10.1007/s10567-015-0178-6 PMID: 25691358

Fedewa, A. L., Prout, S. M., & Thompson Prout, H. (2015). Ethical and legal issues in psychological interventions with children and adolescents. In Prout, H. T., & Fedewa, A. L. (Eds.), *Counseling and psychotherapy with children and adolescents: Theory and practice for school and clinical settings* (5th ed., pp. 25–59). John Wiley & Sons Inc. DOI: 10.1002/9781394259496.ch2

Flanagan, R. (2024). School psychology: Training individuals for one of the best kept secrets in professional psychology. In *Psychologists in Making* (pp. 36–52). Routledge.

Fullen, T., Jones, S. L., Emerson, L. M., & Adamou, M. (2020). Psychological Treatments in Adult ADHD: A Systematic Review. *Journal of Psychopathology and Behavioral Assessment*, 42(3), 500–518. DOI: 10.1007/s10862-020-09794-8

Gichuru, M. J. (2017). *The Interpretive Research Paradigm: A Critical Review Of Is Research Methodologies*. https://www.semanticscholar.org/paper/The-Interpretive-Research-Paradigm%3A-A-Critical-Of-Gichuru/0cb387722749cf86228d58c510e35b8f38726e1c

Graczyk, P. A., Atkins, M. S., Jackson, M. M., Letendre, J. A., Kim-Cohen, J., Baumann, B. L., & Mccoy, J. (2005). Urban Educators' Perceptions of Interventions for Students with Attention Deficit Hyperactivity Disorder: A Preliminary Investigation. *Behavioral Disorders*, 30(2), 95–104. DOI: 10.1177/019874290503000203

Grande, D. (2023, July 20). *Cognitive Behavioral Therapy: How It Works & What To Expect*. https://www.choosingtherapy.com/cognitive-behavioral-therapy/

Grove, Z. B. (2021). *Perceptions of support among university students diagnosed with Attention-Deficit/Hyperactivity Disorder (ADHD)*. University of the Witwatersrand., http://hdl.handle.net/10539/35614

Gu, Y., Xu, G., & Zhu, Y. (2018). A Randomized Controlled Trial of Mindfulness-Based Cognitive Therapy for College Students with ADHD. *Journal of Attention Disorders*, 22(4), 388–399. DOI: 10.1177/1087054716686183 PMID: 28038496

Hinshaw, S. P., Scheffler, R. M., Fulton, B. D., Aase, H., Banaschewski, T., Cheng, W., Mattos, P., Holte, A., Levy, F., Sadeh, A., Sergeant, J. A., Taylor, E., & Weiss, M. D. (2011). International variation in treatment procedures for ADHD: Social context and recent trends. *Psychiatric Services (Washington, D.C.)*, 62(5), 459–464. DOI: 10.1176/ps.62.5.pss6205_0459 PMID: 21532069

Hornstra, R., Van Der Oord, S., Staff, A. I., Hoekstra, P. J., Oosterlaan, J., Van Der Veen-Mulders, L., Luman, M., & Van Den Hoofdakker, B. J. (2021). Which Techniques Work in Behavioral Parent Training for Children with ADHD? A Randomized Controlled Microtrial. *Journal of Clinical Child and Adolescent Psychology*, 50(6), 888–903. DOI: 10.1080/15374416.2021.1955368 PMID: 34424102

Huang, H.-L., Lu, C.-H., Tsai, H.-W., Chao, C.-C., Ho, T.-Y., Chuang, S.-F., Tsai, C.-H., & Yang, P.-C. (2009). Effectiveness of Behavioral Parent Therapy in Preschool Children With Attention-Deficit Hyperactivity Disorder. *The Kaohsiung Journal of Medical Sciences*, 25(7), 357–365. DOI: 10.1016/S1607-551X(09)70528-5 PMID: 19605327

Ibukun, A., Oluyemi, O., Abidemi, B., Suraj, A., & Ola, F. (2015). Literacy about Attention-deficit/Hyperactivity Disorder among primary school teachers in Lagos, Nigeria. *British Journal of Medicine and Medical Research*, 8(8), 684–691. DOI: 10.9734/BJMMR/2015/18089

Igbokwe, E. C., Emengini, E. J., & Ojiako, J. C. (2019). Evaluation of Development Dynamics of Awka Capital Territory, Anambra State, using Remote Sensing. *International Journal of Engineering Science and Computing*, 9(4), 21719–21728.

Ikechukwu-Ilomuanya, A. B., Eze, J., & Eseadi, C. (2015). Effect of time management counseling on academic adjustment of deviant in-school adolescent in Nsukka urban in Enugu State. *Educational Psychologist*, 9(1), 70–76.

Karlsdóttir, E., Gudmundsdottir, B. G., & Sveinbjörnsdóttir, B. (2023). Use of School-Based Interventions for ADHD, Professional Support, and Burnout Symptoms among Teachers in Iceland. *Journal of Attention Disorders*, 27(14), 1583–1595. DOI: 10.1177/10870547231187149 PMID: 37449377

Kelley, K., Clark, B., Brown, V., & Sitzia, J. (2003). Good practice in the conduct and reporting of survey research. *International Journal for Quality in Health Care : Journal of the International Society for Quality in Health Care*, 15(3), 261–266. DOI: 10.1093/intqhc/mzg031 PMID: 12803354

Kelter, R. (2020). Bayesian alternatives to null hypothesis significance testing in biomedical research: A non-technical introduction to Bayesian inference with JASP. *BMC Medical Research Methodology*, 20(1), 142. DOI: 10.1186/s12874-020-00980-6 PMID: 32503439

Khatri, K. K. (2020). Research Paradigm: A Philosophy of Educational Research. *International Journal of English Literature and Social Sciences*, 5(5), 1435–1440. DOI: 10.22161/ijels.55.15

Klar, S., & Leeper, T. (2019). *Identities and Intersectionality: A Case for Purposive Sampling in Survey-Experimental Research.*, DOI: 10.1002/9781119083771.ch21

Kourkoutas, E., Stavrou, P.-D., & Plexousakis, S. (2018). Teachers' emotional and educational reactions toward children with behavioral problems: Implication for school-based counseling work with teachers. *Journal of Psychology and Behavioural Science*, 6(2), 17–34. DOI: 10.15640/jpbs.v6n2a3

Labrador-Roca, V., Vázquez, J. H., & Yuba, E. I. (2020). The effects of educational intervention on the behaviour of students with ADHD. *Journal of Physical Education and Sport*, 20(5), 2595–2606. DOI: 10.7752/jpes.2020.05354

Malhotra, M. K., & Grover, V. (1998). An assessment of survey research in POM: From constructs to theory. *Journal of Operations Management*, 16(4), 407–425. DOI: 10.1016/S0272-6963(98)00021-7

Marshall, G., & Jonker, L. (2011). An introduction to inferential statistics: A review and practical guide. *Radiography*, 17(1), e1–e6. DOI: 10.1016/j.radi.2009.12.006

Miranda, A., Jarque, S., & Tarraga, R. (2006). Interventions in School Settings for Students With ADHD. *Exceptionality*, 14(1), 35–52. DOI: 10.1207/s15327035ex1401_4

Misrok, A., & Cooper, J. M. (2024). ADHD in Schools: Examining the Role of Gender and Symptom Presentation in Teacher-Initiated Referrals. *Contemporary School Psychology*, •••, 1–16. DOI: 10.1007/s40688-024-00518-3

Moore, D. A., Gwernan-Jones, R., Richardson, M., Racey, D., Rogers, M., Stein, K., Thompson-Coon, J., Ford, T. J., & Garside, R. (2016). The experiences of and attitudes toward non-pharmacological interventions for attention-deficit/hyperactivity disorder used in school settings: A systematic review and synthesis of qualitative research. *Emotional & Behavioural Difficulties*, 21(1), 61–82. DOI: 10.1080/13632752.2016.1139296

Moore, D. A., Russell, A. E., Matthews, J., Ford, T. J., Rogers, M., Ukoumunne, O. C., Kneale, D., Thompson-Coon, J., Sutcliffe, K., Nunns, M., Shaw, L., & Gwernan-Jones, R. (2018). School-based interventions for attention-deficit/hyperactivity disorder: A systematic review with multiple synthesis methods. *Review of Education*, 6(3), 209–263. DOI: 10.1002/rev3.3149

Noyes, A. (2017). *Pre-Service teachers' perceptions of the acceptability of interventions for ADHD and knowledge of evidence-based practice.*(Master's thesis, Mount Saint Vincent University, Nova Scotia)

Ohan, J. L., Cormier, N., Hepp, S. L., Visser, T. A., & Strain, M. C. (2008). Does knowledge about attention-deficit/hyperactivity disorder impact teachers' reported behaviors and perceptions? *School Psychology Quarterly*, 23(3), 436–449. DOI: 10.1037/1045-3830.23.3.436

Ojionuka, A. N. (2016). *Nigerian Educators' Attention-Deficit Hyperactivity Disorder Knowledge and Classroom Behavior Management Practices*. Walden Dissertations and Doctoral Studies. 2224. https://scholarworks.waldenu.edu/dissertations/2224

Pelham, W. E. J., & Altszuler, A. R. (2020). Combined Treatment for Children with Attention-Deficit/Hyperactivity Disorder: Brief History, the Multimodal Treatment for Attention-Deficit/Hyperactivity Disorder Study, and the Past 20 Years of Research. *Journal of Developmental and Behavioral Pediatrics*, 41(2S), S88–S98. DOI: 10.1097/DBP.0000000000000777 PMID: 31996571

Perezgonzalez, J. (2022). *Frequentist-Bayesian analyses in parallel using JASP - A tutorial*. OSF. https://doi.org/DOI: 10.31234/osf.io/vkb2c

Power, T. J., Tresco, K. E., & Cassano, M. C. (2009). School-based interventions for students with attention-deficit/hyperactivity disorder. *Current Psychiatry Reports*, 11(5), 407–414. DOI: 10.1007/s11920-009-0061-6 PMID: 19785983

Poznanski, B., Hart, K. C., & Cramer, E. (2018). Are Teachers Ready? Preservice Teacher Knowledge of Classroom Management and ADHD. *School Mental Health*, 10(3), 301–313. DOI: 10.1007/s12310-018-9259-2

Raggi, V. L., & Chronis, A. M. (2006). Interventions to address the academic impairment of children and adolescents with ADHD. *Clinical Child and Family Psychology Review*, 9(2), 85–111. DOI: 10.1007/s10567-006-0006-0 PMID: 16972189

Rahi, S. (2017). Research Design and Methods: A Systematic Review of Research Paradigms, Sampling Issues and Instruments Development. *International Journal of Economics & Management Sciences*, 6(2), 1000403. DOI: 10.4172/2162-6359.1000403

Ramos, M. C., Macphee, F. L., Merrill, B. M., Altszuler, A. R., Raiker, J. S., Gnagy, E. M., Greiner, A. R., Parent, J., Coles, E. K., Burger, L., & Pelham, W. E.Jr. (2022). Mindfulness as an Adjunct to Behavior Modification for Elementary-aged Children with ADHD. *Research on Child and Adolescent Psychopathology*, 50(12), 1573–1588. DOI: 10.1007/s10802-022-00947-9 PMID: 35802209

Robb, A., & Findling, R. L. (2013). Challenges in the Transition of Care for Adolescents with Attention-Deficit/Hyperactivity Disorder. *Postgraduate Medicine*, 125(4), 131–140. DOI: 10.3810/pgm.2013.07.2685 PMID: 23933901

Rushton, S., Giallo, R., & Efron, D. (2020). ADHD and emotional engagement with school in the primary years: Investigating the role of student–teacher relationships. *The British Journal of Educational Psychology*, 90(S1), 193–209. DOI: 10.1111/bjep.12316 PMID: 31654412

Russell, A. E., Dunn, B., Hayes, R., Moore, D., Kidger, J., Sonuga-Barke, E., Pfiffner, L., & Ford, T. (2023). Investigation of the feasibility and acceptability of a school-based intervention for children with traits of ADHD: Protocol for an iterative case-series study. *BMJ Open*, 13(2), e065176. DOI: 10.1136/bmjopen-2022-065176 PMID: 36787977

Schatz, N. K., Fabiano, G. A., Raiker, J. S., Hayes, T. B., & Pelham, W. E.Jr. (2021). Twenty-year trends in elementary teachers' beliefs about best practices for students with ADHD. *School Psychology*, 36(4), 203–213. DOI: 10.1037/spq0000442 PMID: 34292041

Scholz, L., Werle, J., Philipsen, A., Schulze, M., Collonges, J., & Gensichen, J. (2023). Effects and feasibility of psychological interventions to reduce inattention symptoms in adults with ADHD: A systematic review. *Journal of Mental Health (Abingdon, England)*, 32(1), 307–320. DOI: 10.1080/09638237.2020.1818189 PMID: 32954909

Schultz, B. K., & Evans, S. W. (2015). *A Practical Guide to Implementing School-Based Interventions for Adolescents with ADHD*. Springer., DOI: 10.1007/978-1-4939-2677-0

Serrano-Troncoso, E., Guidi, M., & Alda-Díez, J. Á. (2013). Is psychological treatment efficacious for attention deficit hyperactivity disorder (ADHD)? Review of nonpharmacological treatments in children and adolescents with ADHD. *Actas Españolas de Psiquiatría*, 41(1), 1. PMID: 23440535

Shillingford-Butler, M. A., & Theodore, L. (2012). Students Diagnosed with Attention Deficit Hyperactivity Disorder: Collaborative Strategies for School Counselors. *Professional School Counseling*, 16(2, suppl), 2156759X12016002S05. Advance online publication. DOI: 10.1177/2156759X12016002S05

Sibley, M. H., Morley, C., Rodriguez, L., Coxe, S. J., Evans, S. W., Morsink, S., & Torres, F. (2020). A peer-delivered intervention for high school students with impairing ADHD symptoms. *School Psychology Review*, 49(3), 275–290. DOI: 10.1080/2372966X.2020.1720803

Skedel, R. (2022, March 31). *Cognitive Restructuring: How It Works, Tips, & Effectiveness*. ChoosingTherapy.Com. https://www.choosingtherapy.com/cognitive-restructuring/

Smith, B. H., Waschbusch, D. A., Willoughby, M. T., & Evans, S. (2000). The efficacy, safety, and practicality of treatments for adolescents with attention-deficit/hyperactivity disorder (ADHD). *Clinical Child and Family Psychology Review*, 3(4), 243–267. DOI: 10.1023/A:1026477121224 PMID: 11225739

Sonuga-Barke, E. J., Brandeis, D., Cortese, S., Daley, D., Ferrin, M., Holtmann, M., Stevenson, J., Danckaerts, M., Van der Oord, S., Döpfner, M., Dittmann, R. W., Simonoff, E., Zuddas, A., Banaschewski, T., Buitelaar, J., Coghill, D., Hollis, C., Konofal, E., Lecendreux, M., & Sergeant, J. (2013). Nonpharmacological interventions for ADHD: Systematic review and meta-analyses of randomized controlled trials of dietary and psychological treatments. *The American Journal of Psychiatry*, 170(3), 275–289. DOI: 10.1176/appi.ajp.2012.12070991 PMID: 23360949

Souza, R., & Borges, E. M. (2023). Teaching Descriptive Statistics and Hypothesis Tests Measuring Water Density. *Journal of Chemical Education*, 100(11), 4438–4448. Advance online publication. DOI: 10.1021/acs.jchemed.3c00402

Staff, A. I., van den Hoofdakker, B. J., van der Oord, S., Hornstra, R., Hoekstra, P. J., Twisk, J. W., Oosterlaan, J., & Luman, M. (2021). Effectiveness of specific techniques in behavioral teacher training for childhood ADHD: A randomized controlled microtrial. *Journal of Clinical Child and Adolescent Psychology*, 50(6), 763–779. DOI: 10.1080/15374416.2020.1846542 PMID: 33471581

Staff, A. I., van der Oord, S., Oosterlaan, J., Hornstra, R., Hoekstra, P. J., van den Hoofdakker, B. J., & Luman, M. (2022). Effectiveness of Specific Techniques in Behavioral Teacher Training for Childhood ADHD Behaviors: Secondary Analyses of a Randomized Controlled Microtrial. *Research on Child and Adolescent Psychopathology*, 50(7), 867–880. DOI: 10.1007/s10802-021-00892-z PMID: 35015187

Stargell, N. A., Barker, L. A., Kress, V. E., & Bullock, M. L. (2017). Counseling Youth With Attention-Deficit/Hyperactivity Disorder (ADHD). *American Counseling Association Practice Briefs,* 1-5. The Center for Counseling Practice, Policy, and Research. https://www.counseling.org/docs/default-source/practice-briefs/counseling-youth-with-adhd.pdf

Stevens, A. E., Abu-Ramadan, T. M., & Hartung, C. M. (2022). Promoting academic success in college students with ADHD and LD: A systematic literature review to identify intervention targets. *Journal of American College Health*, 70(8), 2342–2355. DOI: 10.1080/07448481.2020.1862127 PMID: 33577411

Strelow, A. E., Dort, M., Schwinger, M., & Christiansen, H. (2020). Influences on pre-service teachers' intention to use classroom management strategies for students with ADHD: A model analysis. *International Journal of Educational Research*, 103, 101627. DOI: 10.1016/j.ijer.2020.101627

Sutanapong, C., & Louangrath, P. I. (2022). Descriptive and Inferential Statistics. *International Journal of Research & Methodology in Social Science*, 1(1), 22–35.

Szép, A., Dantchev, S., Zemp, M., Schwinger, M., Chavanon, M.-L., & Christiansen, H. (2021). Facilitators and Barriers of Teachers' Use of Effective Classroom Management Strategies for Students with ADHD: A Model Analysis Based on Teachers' Perspectives. *Sustainability (Basel)*, 13(22), 22. Advance online publication. DOI: 10.3390/su132212843

Tayebi, S. (2020). The effectiveness of social component intervention program on school burnout and academic self-regulation in students with ADHD. *International Journal of Schooling*, 2(3), 59–74.

Tømmerås, T., Kjøbli, J., & Forgatch, M. (2018). Benefits of Child Behavior Interventions for Parent Well-Being. *Family Relations*, 67(5), 644–659. DOI: 10.1111/fare.12344

Topping, K. (2011). Primary–secondary transition: Differences between teachers' and children's perceptions. *Improving Schools*, 14(3), 268–285. DOI: 10.1177/1365480211419587

Tourjman, V., Louis-Nascan, G., Ahmed, G., DuBow, A., Côté, H., Daly, N., Daoud, G., Espinet, S., Flood, J., Gagnier-Marandola, E., Gignac, M., Graziosi, G., Mansuri, Z., & Sadek, J. (2022). Psychosocial Interventions for Attention Deficit/Hyperactivity Disorder: A Systematic Review and Meta-Analysis by the CADDRA Guidelines Work GROUP. *Brain Sciences*, 12(8), 1023. DOI: 10.3390/brainsci12081023 PMID: 36009086

Toye, M. K., Wilson, C., & Wardle, G. A. (2019). Education professionals' attitudes towards the inclusion of children with ADHD: The role of knowledge and stigma. *Journal of Research in Special Educational Needs*, 19(3), 184–196. DOI: 10.1111/1471-3802.12441

Turgay, A., Goodman, D. W., Asherson, P., Lasser, R. A., Babcock, T. F., Pucci, M. L., & Barkley, R.ADHD Transition Phase Model Working Group. (2012). Lifespan persistence of ADHD: The life transition model and its application. *The Journal of Clinical Psychiatry*, 73(2), 10337. DOI: 10.4088/JCP.10m06628 PMID: 22313720

Ugwu, C. I., Chukwulobelu, U., Igboekwu, C., Emodi, N., Anumba, J. U., Ugwu, S. C., Ezeobi, C. L., Ibeziako, V., & Nwakaogor, G. U. (2021). Geo-Spatial Mapping of Tuberculosis Burden in Anambra State, South-East Nigeria. *Journal of Tuberculosis Research*, 9(1), 1. Advance online publication. DOI: 10.4236/jtr.2021.91004

Van Merriënboer, J., & De Bruin, A. (2014). Research paradigms and perspectives on learning. In *Handbook of Research for Educational Communications and Technology*. DOI: 10.1007/978-1-4614-3185-5_2

Vitanza, B. S. (2014). *Attention-deficit hyperactivity disorder: Teachers' perceptions and acceptability of interventions.* (Doctoral Dissertation, Philadelphia College of Osteopathic Medicine). https://digitalcommons.pcom.edu/psychology_dissertations/315

Weiss, M., Safren, S. A., Solanto, M. V., Hechtman, L., Rostain, A. L., Ramsay, J. R., & Murray, C. (2008). Research forum on psychological treatment of adults with ADHD. *Journal of Attention Disorders*, 11(6), 642–651. DOI: 10.1177/1087054708315063 PMID: 18417729

Weyandt, L. L., Fulton, K. M., Schepman, S. B., Verdi, G. R., & Wilson, K. G. (2009). Assessment of teacher and school psychologist knowledge of Attention-Deficit/Hyperactivity Disorder. *Psychology in the Schools*, 46(10), 951–961. DOI: 10.1002/pits.20436

Wiener, J. (2020). The role of school psychologists in supporting adolescents with ADHD. *Canadian Journal of School Psychology*, 35(4), 299–310. DOI: 10.1177/0829573520923536

Wilens, T. E., Biederman, J., Faraone, S. V., Martelon, M., Westerberg, D., & Spencer, T. J. (2009). Presenting ADHD Symptoms, Subtypes, and Comorbid Disorders in Clinically Referred Adults With ADHD. *The Journal of Clinical Psychiatry*, 70(11), 15333. DOI: 10.4088/JCP.08m04785pur PMID: 20031097

Wolraich, M. L., Wibbelsman, C. J., Brown, T. E., Evans, S. W., Gotlieb, E. M., Knight, J. R., Ross, E. C., Shubiner, H. H., Wender, E. H., & Wilens, T. (2005). Attention-deficit/hyperactivity disorder among adolescents: A review of the diagnosis, treatment, and clinical implications. *Pediatrics*, 115(6), 1734–1746. DOI: 10.1542/peds.2004-1959 PMID: 15930238

Yewande, O. S., Oluwaseun, A. A., & Cynthia, O. A. (2024). Perception of Teachers on Students with Attention Deficit Hyperactivity Disorder (ADHD): A Sociological Investigation. *International Journal of Social Sciences & Educational Studies*, 10(4), 10–24. DOI: 10.23918/ijsses.v10i4p10

ADDITIONAL READINGS

Ahmed, R., Borst, J., Wei, Y. C., & Aslani, P. (2017). Parents' Perspectives About Factors Influencing Adherence to Pharmacotherapy for ADHD. *Journal of Attention Disorders*, 21(2), 91–99. DOI: 10.1177/1087054713499231 PMID: 23995052

Algadheeb, N. A. (2015). Professional/Career Orientation, Awareness, and Their Relationship to Locus of Control. *Journal of College Teaching and Learning*, 12(1), 13–38. DOI: 10.19030/tlc.v12i1.9067

Andrade, E. M., Geha, L. M., Duran, P., Suwwan, R., Machado, F., & do Rosário, M. C. (2016). Quality of life in caregivers of ADHD children and diabetes patients. *Frontiers in Psychiatry*, 7, 127. DOI: 10.3389/fpsyt.2016.00127 PMID: 27504099

Antshel, K. M. (2015). Psychosocial interventions in attention-deficit/hyperactivity disorder: Update. *Child and Adolescent Psychiatric Clinics of North America*, 24(1), 79–97. DOI: 10.1016/j.chc.2014.08.002 PMID: 25455577

Babinski, D. E., & Sibley, M. H. (2022). Family-based treatments for attention-deficit/hyperactivity disorder: A review of family functioning outcomes in randomized controlled trials from 2010 to 2019. *Journal of Marital and Family Therapy*, 48(1), 83–106. DOI: 10.1111/jmft.12572 PMID: 34779516

Bikic, A., Reichow, B., McCauley, S. A., Ibrahim, K., & Sukhodolsky, D. G. (2017). Meta-analysis of organizational skills interventions for children and adolescents with attention-deficit/hyperactivity disorder. *Clinical Psychology Review*, 52, 108–123. DOI: 10.1016/j.cpr.2016.12.004 PMID: 28088557

Boerner, K. E., Pearl-Dowler, L., Holsti, L., Wharton, M. N., Siden, H., & Oberlander, T. F. (2023). Family perspectives on in-home multimodal longitudinal data collection for children who function across the developmental spectrum. *Journal of Developmental and Behavioral Pediatrics*, 44(4), e284–e291. DOI: 10.1097/DBP.0000000000001183 PMID: 37074803

Bondopadhyay, U., Diaz-Orueta, U., & Coogan, A. N. (2022). A systematic review of sleep and circadian rhythms in children with attention deficit hyperactivity disorder. *Journal of Attention Disorders*, 26(2), 149–224. DOI: 10.1177/1087054720978556 PMID: 33402013

Cairncross, M., & Miller, C. J. (2020). The Effectiveness of Mindfulness-Based Therapies for ADHD: A Meta-Analytic Review. *Journal of Attention Disorders*, 24(5), 627–643. DOI: 10.1177/1087054715625301 PMID: 26838555

Canits, I., Bernoster, I., Mukerjee, J., Bonnet, J., Rizzo, U., & Rosique-Blasco, M. (2019). Attention-deficit/hyperactivity disorder (ADHD) symptoms and academic entrepreneurial preference: Is there an association? *Small Business Economics*, 53(2), 369–380. DOI: 10.1007/s11187-018-0057-x

Carr, A. W., Bean, R. A., & Nelson, K. F. (2020). Childhood attention-deficit hyperactivity disorder: Family therapy from an attachment-based perspective. *Children and Youth Services Review*, 119, 105666. DOI: 10.1016/j.childyouth.2020.105666

Chokka, P., Bender, A., Brennan, S., Ahmed, G., Corbière, M., Dozois, D. J. A., Habert, J., Harrison, J., Katzman, M. A., McIntyre, R. S., Liu, Y. S., Nieuwenhuijsen, K., & Dewa, C. S. (2023). Practical pathway for the management of depression in the workplace: A Canadian perspective. *Frontiers in Psychiatry*, 14, 1207653. DOI: 10.3389/fpsyt.2023.1207653 PMID: 37732077

Ciesielski, H. A., Tamm, L., Vaughn, A. J., Cyran, J. E., & Epstein, J. N. (2019). Academic skills groups for middle school children with ADHD in the outpatient mental health setting: An open trial. *Journal of Attention Disorders*, 23(4), 409–417. DOI: 10.1177/1087054715584055 PMID: 25926629

Cole, A. M., Chan, E. S., Gaye, F., Harmon, S. L., & Kofler, M. J. (2024). The role of working memory and organizational skills in academic functioning for children with attention-deficit/hyperactivity disorder. *Neuropsychology*, 38(6), 487–500. DOI: 10.1037/neu0000960 PMID: 38990684

Connolly, J. J., Glessner, J. T., Elia, J., & Hakonarson, H. (2015). ADHD & Pharmacotherapy: past, present and future: A review of the changing landscape of drug therapy for attention deficit hyperactivity disorder. *Therapeutic Innovation & Regulatory Science*, 49(5), 632–642. DOI: 10.1177/2168479015599811 PMID: 26366330

Corbisiero, S., Bitto, H., Newark, P., Abt-Mörstedt, B., Elsässer, M., Buchli-Kammermann, J., Künne, S., Nyberg, E., Hofecker-Fallahpour, M., & Stieglitz, R. D. (2018). A comparison of cognitive-behavioral therapy and pharmacotherapy vs. pharmacotherapy alone in adults with attention-deficit/hyperactivity disorder (ADHD): A randomized controlled trial. *Frontiers in Psychiatry*, 9, 571. DOI: 10.3389/fpsyt.2018.00571 PMID: 30505283

Daley, D., Van Der Oord, S., Ferrin, M., Cortese, S., Danckaerts, M., Doepfner, M., Van den Hoofdakker, B. J., Coghill, D., Thompson, M., Asherson, P., Banaschewski, T., Brandeis, D., Buitelaar, J., Dittmann, R. W., Hollis, C., Holtmann, M., Konofal, E., Lecendreux, M., Rothenberger, A., & Sonuga-Barke, E. J. (2018). Practitioner review: Current best practice in the use of parent training and other behavioral interventions in the treatment of children and adolescents with attention deficit hyperactivity disorder. *Journal of Child Psychology and Psychiatry, and Allied Disciplines*, 59(9), 932–947. DOI: 10.1111/jcpp.12825 PMID: 29083042

Dekkers, T. J., Groenman, A. P., Wessels, L., Kovshoff, H., Hoekstra, P. J., & van den Hoofdakker, B. J. (2022). Which factors determine clinicians' policy and attitudes towards medication and parent training for children with Attention-Deficit/Hyperactivity Disorder? *European Child & Adolescent Psychiatry*, 31(3), 1–11. DOI: 10.1007/s00787-021-01735-4 PMID: 33585968

Dort, M., Strelow, A. E., Schwinger, M., & Christiansen, H. (2020). Working with children with ADHD—A latent profile analysis of teachers' and psychotherapists' attitudes. *Sustainability (Basel)*, 12(22), 9691. DOI: 10.3390/su12229691

DosReis, S., Park, A., Ng, X., Frosch, E., Reeves, G., Cunningham, C., Janssen, E. M., & Bridges, J. F. (2017). Caregiver treatment preferences for children with a new versus existing attention-deficit/hyperactivity disorder diagnosis. *Journal of Child and Adolescent Psychopharmacology*, 27(3), 234–242. DOI: 10.1089/cap.2016.0157 PMID: 27991834

DuPaul, G. J., Evans, S. W., Mautone, J. A., Owens, J. S., & Power, T. J. (2019). Future directions for psychosocial interventions for children and adolescents with ADHD. *Journal of Clinical Child and Adolescent Psychology*, 49(1), 134–145. DOI: 10.1080/15374416.2019.1689825 PMID: 31799864

Durand, G., & Arbone, I. S. (2022). Exploring the relationship between ADHD, its common comorbidities, and their relationship to organizational skills. *PeerJ*, 10, e12836. DOI: 10.7717/peerj.12836 PMID: 35116205

Eisenberg, D., & Schneider, H. (2007). Perceptions of academic skills of children diagnosed with ADHD. *Journal of Attention Disorders*, 10(4), 390–397. DOI: 10.1177/1087054706292105 PMID: 17449838

Español-Martín, G., Pagerols, M., Prat, R., Rivas, C., Ramos-Quiroga, J. A., Casas, M., & Bosch, R. (2023). The impact of attention-deficit/hyperactivity disorder and specific learning disorders on academic performance in Spanish children from a low-middle-and a high-income population. *Frontiers in Psychiatry*, 14, 1136994. DOI: 10.3389/fpsyt.2023.1136994 PMID: 37124266

Evans, S. W., Owens, J. S., Wymbs, B. T., & Ray, A. R. (2017). Evidence-based psychosocial treatments for children and adolescents with attention deficit/hyperactivity disorder. *Journal of Clinical Child and Adolescent Psychology*, 47(2), 157–198. DOI: 10.1080/15374416.2017.1390757 PMID: 29257898

Fiksdal, B. L. (2014). A comparison of the effectiveness of a token economy system, a response cost condition, and a combination condition in reducing problem behaviors and increasing student academic engagement and performance in two first grade classrooms.(Master's thesis, Minnesota State University, Mankato). Cornerstone: A Collection of Scholarly and Creative Works for Minnesota State University, Mankato. https://cornerstone.lib.mnsu.edu/etds/343/

Gaitantzi, Z. (2021). School Based Interventions made in Elementary School for Children with ADHD (Dissertation). Retrieved from https://urn.kb.se/resolve?urn=urn:nbn:se:hj:diva-54689

Gatti, U., Grattagliano, I., & Rocca, G. (2018). Evidence-based psychosocial treatments of conduct problems in children and adolescents: An overview. *Psychiatry, Psychology, and Law : an Interdisciplinary Journal of the Australian and New Zealand Association of Psychiatry, Psychology and Law*, 26(2), 171–193. DOI: 10.1080/13218719.2018.1485523 PMID: 31984071

Gerber, W. D., Gerber-von Müller, G., Andrasik, F., Niederberger, U., Siniatchkin, M., Kowalski, J. T., Petermann, U., & Petermann, F. (2012). The impact of a multimodal summer camp training on neuropsychological functioning in children and adolescents with ADHD: An exploratory study. *Child Neuropsychology*, 18(3), 242–255. DOI: 10.1080/09297049.2011.599115 PMID: 21824010

Geurts, D. E., Schellekens, M. P., Janssen, L., & Speckens, A. E. (2021). Mechanisms of change in mindfulness-based cognitive therapy in adults with ADHD. *Journal of Attention Disorders*, 25(9), 1331–1342. DOI: 10.1177/1087054719896865 PMID: 31904295

Gu, Y., Xu, G., & Zhu, Y. (2018). A randomized controlled trial of mindfulness-based cognitive therapy for college students with ADHD. *Journal of Attention Disorders*, 22(4), 388–399. DOI: 10.1177/1087054716686183 PMID: 28038496

Hahn-Markowitz, J., Berger, I., Manor, I., & Maeir, A. (2018). Cognitive-functional (Cog-Fun) dyadic intervention for children with ADHD and their parents: Impact on parenting self-efficacy. *Physical & Occupational Therapy in Pediatrics*, 38(4), 444–456. DOI: 10.1080/01942638.2018.1441939 PMID: 29494784

Hepark, S., Janssen, L., de Vries, A., Schoenberg, P. L., Donders, R., Kan, C., & Speckens, A. E. (2019). The efficacy of adapted MBCT on core symptoms and executive functioning in adults with ADHD: A preliminary randomized controlled trial. *Journal of Attention Disorders*, 23(4), 351–362. DOI: 10.1177/1087054715613587 PMID: 26588940

Iznardo, M., Rogers, M. A., Volpe, R. J., Labelle, P. R., & Robaey, P. (2020). The effectiveness of daily behavior report cards for children with ADHD: A Meta-Analysis. *Journal of Attention Disorders*, 24(12), 1623–1636. DOI: 10.1177/1087054717734646 PMID: 29135352

Janssen, L., de Vries, A. M., Hepark, S., & Speckens, A. E. (2020). The feasibility, effectiveness, and process of change of mindfulness-based cognitive therapy for adults with ADHD: A mixed-method pilot study. *Journal of Attention Disorders*, 24(6), 928–942. DOI: 10.1177/1087054717727350 PMID: 28853328

Johnston, C., & Park, J. L. (2015). Interventions for attention-deficit hyperactivity disorder: A year in review. *Current Developmental Disorders Reports*, 2(1), 38–45. DOI: 10.1007/s40474-014-0034-2

Kim, M., King, M. D., & Jennings, J. (2019). ADHD remission, inclusive special education, and socioeconomic disparities. *SSM - Population Health*, 8, 100420. DOI: 10.1016/j.ssmph.2019.100420 PMID: 31431914

Kok, F. M., Groen, Y., Fuermaier, A. B., & Tucha, O. (2020). The female side of pharmacotherapy for ADHD—A systematic literature review. *PLoS One*, 15(9), e0239257. DOI: 10.1371/journal.pone.0239257 PMID: 32946507

Lee, C. S., Ma, M. T., Ho, H. Y., Tsang, K. K., Zheng, Y. Y., & Wu, Z. Y. (2017). The effectiveness of mindfulness-based intervention in attention on individuals with ADHD: A systematic review. *Hong Kong Journal of Occupational Therapy*, 30(1), 33–41. DOI: 10.1016/j.hkjot.2017.05.001 PMID: 30186078

Li, L., Zhu, N., Zhang, L., Kuja-Halkola, R., D'Onofrio, B. M., Brikell, I., Lichtenstein, P., Cortese, S., Larsson, H., & Chang, Z. (2024). ADHD pharmacotherapy and mortality in individuals with ADHD. *Journal of the American Medical Association*, 331(10), 850–860. DOI: 10.1001/jama.2024.0851 PMID: 38470385

Liu, T. L., Hsiao, R. C., Chou, W. J., & Yen, C.-F. (2024). Parenting stress, anxiety, and sources of acquiring knowledge in Taiwanese caregivers of children with attention-deficit/hyperactivity disorder. *BMC Public Health*, 24(1), 1675. DOI: 10.1186/s12889-024-18761-x PMID: 38914984

Lovell, B., Moss, M., & Wetherell, M. A. (2012). With a little help from my friends: Psychological, endocrine and health corollaries of social support in parental caregivers of children with autism or ADHD. *Research in Developmental Disabilities*, 33(2), 682–687. DOI: 10.1016/j.ridd.2011.11.014 PMID: 22186636

Machlin, L., McLaughlin, K. A., & Sheridan, M. A. (2020). Brain structure mediates the association between socioeconomic status and attention-deficit/hyperactivity disorder. *Developmental Science*, 23(1), e12844. DOI: 10.1111/desc.12844 PMID: 31056844

Meijer, W. M., Faber, A., van den Ban, E., & Tobi, H. (2009). Current issues around the pharmacotherapy of ADHD in children and adults. *Pharmacy World & Science*, 31(5), 509–516. DOI: 10.1007/s11096-009-9302-3 PMID: 19562500

Mészáros, A., Czobor, P., Bálint, S., Komlósi, S., Simon, V., & Bitter, I. (2009). Pharmacotherapy of adult attention deficit hyperactivity disorder (ADHD): A meta-analysis. *The International Journal of Neuropsychopharmacology*, 12(8), 1137–1147. DOI: 10.1017/S1461145709990198 PMID: 19580697

Miller, A. C., Keenan, J. M., Betjemann, R. S., Willcutt, E. G., Pennington, B. F., & Olson, R. K. (2013). Reading comprehension in children with ADHD: Cognitive underpinnings of the centrality deficit. *Journal of Abnormal Child Psychology*, 41(3), 473–483. DOI: 10.1007/s10802-012-9686-8 PMID: 23054132

Moore, D. A., Whittaker, S., & Ford, T. J. (2016). Daily report cards as a school-based intervention for children with attention-deficit/hyperactivity disorder. *Support for Learning*, 31(1), 71–83. DOI: 10.1111/1467-9604.12115

Nolan, J. D., & Filter, K. J. (2012). A function-based classroom behavior intervention using non-contingent reinforcement plus response cost. *Education & Treatment of Children*, 35(3), 419–430. DOI: 10.1353/etc.2012.0017

Perry, R., Ford, T., O'Mahen, H., & Russell, A. E. (2020). Prioritizing targets for school-based ADHD interventions: a Delphi survey. Survey data.

Perugi, G., Pallucchini, A., Rizzato, S., Pinzone, V., & De Rossi, P. (2019). Current and emerging pharmacotherapy for the treatment of adult attention deficit hyperactivity disorder (ADHD). *Expert Opinion on Pharmacotherapy*, 20(12), 1457–1470. DOI: 10.1080/14656566.2019.1618270 PMID: 31112441

Pfiffner, L. J., & Haack, L. M. (2014). Behavior management for school-aged children with ADHD. *Child and Adolescent Psychiatric Clinics of North America*, 23(4), 731–746. DOI: 10.1016/j.chc.2014.05.014 PMID: 25220083

Pond, E., Fowler, K., & Hesson, J. (2019). The influence of socioeconomic status on psychological distress in Canadian adults with ADD/ADHD. *Journal of Attention Disorders*, 23(9), 940–948. DOI: 10.1177/1087054716653214 PMID: 27288904

Preston, A. S., Heaton, S. C., McCann, S. J., Watson, W. D., & Selke, G. (2009). The role of multidimensional attentional abilities in academic skills of children with ADHD. *Journal of Learning Disabilities*, 42(3), 240–249. DOI: 10.1177/0022219408331042 PMID: 19264927

Romadona, N. F., Listiana, A., & Kurniati, E. (2016, November). Behavior management to improve social skills and academic achievement of children with attention deficit/hyperactivity disorder (ADHD). In *3rd International Conference on Early Childhood Education (ICECE 2016)* (pp. 359-363). Atlantis Press.

Rowland, A. S., Skipper, B. J., Rabiner, D. L., Qeadan, F., Campbell, R. A., Naftel, A. J., & Umbach, D. M. (2018). Attention-deficit/hyperactivity disorder (ADHD): Interaction between socioeconomic status and parental history of ADHD determines prevalence. *Journal of Child Psychology and Psychiatry, and Allied Disciplines*, 59(3), 213–222. DOI: 10.1111/jcpp.12775 PMID: 28801917

Russell, A. E., Ford, T., Williams, R., & Russell, G. (2016). The association between socioeconomic disadvantage and attention deficit/hyperactivity disorder (ADHD): A systematic review. *Child Psychiatry and Human Development*, 47(3), 440–458. DOI: 10.1007/s10578-015-0578-3 PMID: 26266467

Shrestha, M., Lautenschleger, J., & Soares, N. (2020). Non-pharmacologic management of attention-deficit/hyperactivity disorder in children and adolescents: A review. *Translational Pediatrics*, 9(S1, Suppl 1), S114–S124. DOI: 10.21037/tp.2019.10.01 PMID: 32206589

Smalley, S. L., Loo, S. K., Hale, T. S., Shrestha, A., McGough, J., Flook, L., & Reise, S. (2009). Mindfulness and attention deficit hyperactivity disorder. *Journal of Clinical Psychology*, 65(10), 1087–1098. DOI: 10.1002/jclp.20618 PMID: 19681107

Susmarini, D., Ninh, D. T., & Shin, H. (2024). Family resilience and caregiver's well-being across different age groups of children with ADHD in the United States: A cross-sectional study. *Child Health Nursing Research*, 30(2), 97–107. DOI: 10.4094/chnr.2024.003 PMID: 38712459

Thorell, L. B. (2007). Do delay aversion and executive function deficits make distinct contributions to the functional impact of ADHD symptoms? A study of early academic skill deficits. *Journal of Child Psychology and Psychiatry, and Allied Disciplines*, 48(11), 1061–1070. DOI: 10.1111/j.1469-7610.2007.01777.x PMID: 17995481

Tresco, K. E., Lefler, E. K., & Power, T. J. (2010). Psychosocial interventions to improve the school performance of students with attention-deficit/hyperactivity disorder. *Mind & Brain : the Journal of Psychiatry*, 1(2), 69–74. PMID: 21152355

Truchlicka, M., McLaughlin, T. F., & Swain, J. C. (1998). Effects of token reinforcement and response cost on the accuracy of spelling performance with middle-school special education students with behavior disorders. *Behavioral Interventions*, 13(1), 1–10. DOI: 10.1002/(SICI)1099-078X(199802)13:1<1::AID-BIN1>3.0.CO;2-Z

Tsibizova, T. (2019). Aiding the Transition of students from School into Technical University. In *Handbook of Research on Engineering Education in a Global Context* (pp. 154–164). IGI Global. DOI: 10.4018/978-1-5225-3395-5.ch014

Vacher, C., Goujon, A., Romo, L., & Purper-Ouakil, D. (2020). Efficacy of psychosocial interventions for children with ADHD and emotion dysregulation: A systematic review. *Psychiatry Research*, 291, 113151. DOI: 10.1016/j.psychres.2020.113151 PMID: 32619822

Vasko, J. M., Oddo, L. E., Meinzer, M. C., Garner, A., & Chronis-Tuscano, A. (2020). Psychosocial interventions for college students with ADHD: Current status and future directions. *The ADHD Report*, 28(4), 5–12. DOI: 10.1521/adhd.2020.28.4.5

Wodka, E. L., Mark Mahone, E., Blankner, J. G., Gidley Larson, J. C., Fotedar, S., Denckla, M. B., & Mostofsky, S. H. (2007). Evidence that response inhibition is a primary deficit in ADHD. *Journal of Clinical and Experimental Neuropsychology*, 29(4), 345–356. DOI: 10.1080/13803390600678046 PMID: 17497558

Zylowska, L., Ackerman, D. L., Yang, M. H., Futrell, J. L., Horton, N. L., Hale, T. S., Pataki, C., & Smalley, S. L. (2008). Mindfulness meditation training in adults and adolescents with ADHD: A feasibility study. *Journal of Attention Disorders*, 11(6), 737–746. DOI: 10.1177/1087054707308502 PMID: 18025249

KEY TERMS AND DEFINITIONS

Academic Skills: The crucial competencies and knowledge necessary for effective learning and success in educational contexts. These skills include reading comprehension, writing expertise, mathematical reasoning, critical thinking, and problem-solving abilities. They establish the foundation of a student's educational experience, facilitating the understanding, analysis, and application of information across various subjects. The development of strong academic skills is essential for achieving high levels of performance in school, enhancing self-confidence, and preparing for future academic and professional endeavors. Schools are instrumental in promoting these skills through effective teaching practices, individualized support, and engaging educational activities. Additionally, strong academic skills foster lifelong learning, enabling individuals to adapt to new challenges and opportunities throughout their lives.

Behavior Modification: A therapeutic method aimed at altering maladaptive behaviors by employing principles derived from behavioral psychology, with a particular emphasis on operant conditioning. This approach utilizes both positive and negative reinforcement, as well as punishment and various other techniques, to promote desirable behaviors while reducing those that are undesirable. Such techniques are frequently applied in educational, clinical, and domestic environments to tackle a diverse array of issues, including behavioral disorders, anxiety, and attention-related difficulties. The methodology prioritizes the establishment of clear objectives, consistency in application, and the systematic monitoring of progress. By reinforcing appropriate behaviors and discouraging inappropriate ones, Behavior Modification seeks to enhance individuals' self-regulation and improve their adaptability to their surroundings.

Caregiver Support: Refers to the various forms of assistance, resources, and guidance offered to individuals tasked with the care and well-being of others, particularly children, the elderly, or those with disabilities. This support may encompass emotional encouragement, access to essential information, respite care, and training in caregiving practices. Effective caregiver support enables caregivers to manage their duties more efficiently, reduce stress levels, and enhance their ability to provide high-quality care. In the realm of education, caregiver support also includes facilitating parents or guardians in their engagement with their child's educational journey, promoting collaboration with educators, and fostering a nurturing home environment. By delivering both practical and emotional support, caregivers are empowered to prioritize their own well-being while successfully fulfilling their caregiving responsibilities.

Classroom Behavioral Interventions: Refer to a set of strategies and techniques that educators utilize to manage and enhance student behavior effectively. The goal of these interventions is to establish a positive educational environment, decrease instances of disruptive behavior, and foster student engagement. Examples of such interventions include defining clear behavioral expectations, applying positive reinforcement, utilizing behavior charts, and teaching social-emotional skills. These interventions can be proactive, aimed at preventing behavioral problems, or reactive, addressing issues as they occur. Educators often adapt these strategies to suit the diverse needs of their students, thereby cultivating a supportive and inclusive classroom atmosphere. Effective behavioral interventions assist students in developing self-regulation, improving their focus, and enriching their overall educational experience.

Daily Report Card (DRC): An effective behavior management tool utilized to track and encourage specific behaviors among students during the school day. It involves the establishment of explicit behavioral targets, such as attentiveness, task completion, or compliance with instructions, and the evaluation of the student's performance against these targets. Teachers provide feedback on a report card or sheet, which is then shared with the student and their parents on a daily basis. The DRC promotes accountability among students, ensures regular communication between teachers and parents, and reinforces positive behaviors through rewards or recognition. This strategy is especially advantageous for students with behavioral or attention-related challenges, as it fosters consistency in behavior management and supports both academic and social advancement.

Family Therapy: A form of psychological counseling that focuses on families as a unified group to address and resolve conflicts, improve communication, and enhance relationships. This approach centers on understanding the dynamics, patterns, and roles within the family that may contribute to conflicts or dysfunction. Therapists apply various techniques to facilitate open communication, foster empathy, and help family members articulate their feelings in a constructive manner. The aim of family therapy is to tackle issues such as conflicts between parents and children, marital challenges, substance abuse, or mental health issues that impact the entire family. The overarching goal is to create healthier relationships, promote understanding, and support the well-being of all family members.

Structured Mental Health Interventions: Designed to tackle and alleviate psychological and emotional issues. Their purpose is to enhance mental well-being, manage symptoms, and improve the overall quality of life for individuals. These interventions may include various therapeutic approaches, such as cognitive-behavioral therapy, as well as medication, counseling, support groups, and psychoeducation. They are tailored to address the specific needs of individuals, focusing on conditions like anxiety, depression, trauma, or substance abuse. Such interventions can be provided in clinical settings, educational institutions, or community programs, often facilitated by mental health professionals. The ultimate goal is to furnish individuals with coping mechanisms, emotional support, and effective strategies for managing their mental health.

Mindfulness-Based Cognitive-Behavioral Therapy (MB-CBT): An innovative therapeutic approach that synthesizes cognitive-behavioral methods with mindfulness practices. Its central aim is to aid individuals in managing negative thoughts and emotions by promoting awareness and acceptance of the present moment. In MB-CBT, clients are encouraged to recognize and challenge their automatic negative thought patterns while engaging in mindfulness exercises that foster a non-judgmental attitude. This integrative approach effectively mitigates stress, anxiety, and depression, while enhancing emotional regulation. Mindfulness techniques, including meditation, breathing exercises, and body scans, are incorporated alongside traditional CBT practices such as cognitive restructuring and behavioral activation. MB-CBT ultimately empowers individuals to disrupt negative thinking patterns, build resilience, and enhance their overall mental health.

Organizational Skills: Defined as the capabilities that assist individuals in effectively planning, prioritizing, and managing their various tasks and responsibilities. These skills include essential elements such as time management, goal setting, task prioritization, and the ability to maintain an organized environment. With strong organizational skills, students can effectively manage their academic workloads, meet deadlines, and reduce stress. The development of these skills is crucial for achieving success across educational, professional, and everyday life scenarios. They enable individuals to work more efficiently, maintain focus, and complete tasks punctually. Educators and parents often emphasize the importance of teaching these skills to students, as they contribute to fostering independence and self-discipline. The relevance of organizational skills extends beyond academic contexts, playing a vital role in enhancing productivity and effectiveness in both professional and personal life.

Response Cost Techniques: Behavioral interventions designed to diminish unwanted behaviors by withdrawing a privilege or reward in response to such behaviors. This approach entails the forfeiture of a previously acquired reinforcer, which may include points, tokens, or privileges, as a penalty for inappropriate conduct. For instance, in an educational environment, a student might lose points from a reward system for speaking out of turn. The primary objective of this technique is to deter negative behavior by linking it to an immediate and consistent consequence. Response cost is frequently integrated into a comprehensive behavior management strategy and proves most effective when paired with positive reinforcement for appropriate behaviors. The ultimate aim is to foster self-discipline and encourage constructive behavioral transformation.

School-Based Interventions: Refer to a set of strategies and programs implemented within educational settings to meet the academic, behavioral, and social-emotional needs of students. These initiatives are crafted to foster student growth, enhance educational outcomes, and cultivate a positive atmosphere within the school. Examples of such interventions include tutoring services, counseling programs, behavior management strategies, peer support networks, and activities focused on social-emotional learning. The primary objective of school-based interventions is to facilitate early detection and assistance for students encountering challenges such as learning disabilities, emotional struggles, or behavioral concerns. These efforts typically involve collaboration among educators, counselors, psychologists, and parents to establish a unified support framework. By addressing multiple dimensions of student well-being, school-based interventions advocate for a comprehensive educational approach that improves academic performance, social competencies, and overall mental health.

Socioeconomic Status (SES): Defined as the social and economic rank of an individual or family within society, influenced by elements such as income, educational attainment, job type, and resource accessibility. SES affects numerous dimensions of life, including health outcomes, educational opportunities, living environments, and chances for personal advancement. Those with a high socioeconomic status generally have superior access to quality education, healthcare services, housing, and social networks, while individuals with a low socioeconomic status often encounter financial difficulties, limited opportunities, and heightened exposure to stress and health risks. SES is a significant contributor to social inequality and can greatly affect an individual's experiences, lifestyle, and overall health. Addressing the disparities associated with SES is vital for advancing social equity and minimizing inequalities in access to essential services.

Student Personnel Services: Represent a broad spectrum of support services aimed at enhancing the academic, social, and emotional well-being of students within educational institutions. These services include counseling, career guidance, health services, extracurricular involvement, and support for special education. The primary aim of these services is to foster a supportive environment that addresses the holistic needs of students, thereby aiding them in realizing their academic potential and personal growth. Professionals such as counselors, social workers, and health staff work in concert to offer personalized support and interventions. By focusing on different aspects of students' lives, these services promote a constructive school experience and lay the groundwork for future success.

Pharmacotherapy: The practice of treating both medical and psychological disorders through the administration of medications. This approach utilizes prescribed drugs to manage or reduce the symptoms associated with a variety of health concerns, encompassing physical ailments, mental health issues, and chronic diseases. In the realm of mental health, pharmacotherapy is frequently employed to address conditions such as depression, anxiety, bipolar disorder, and ADHD, with medications aimed at restoring balance in brain chemistry to enhance mood, concentration, or behavior. The primary objective of pharmacotherapy is to improve the quality of life for patients, often integrated into a broader treatment strategy that may also involve therapy or modifications in lifestyle. Effective pharmacotherapy necessitates diligent oversight and adjustments by healthcare professionals to ensure optimal results and to mitigate possible adverse effects.

Psychosocial Interventions: Refers to a range of structured activities and therapeutic techniques aimed at addressing the psychological and social challenges that individuals face. These interventions are designed to enhance mental health, emotional well-being, and social functioning by targeting issues such as stress, anxiety, depression, and relationship problems. Common examples include cognitive-behavioral therapy (CBT), counseling, group therapy, and social skills training. The focus of psychosocial interventions is to help individuals develop effective coping strategies, increase self-awareness, and improve their relationships with others. These interventions are often applied in educational, healthcare, and community settings to assist children, adolescents, and adults in navigating various life challenges. The primary objective is to empower individuals to cultivate resilience, promote positive behaviors, and lead healthier, more satisfying lives.

Professional Orientation: Intricately linked to a person's perspective on specific career interests or roles. It embodies the patterns and actions that signify an individual's inclination to engage in or commit to a particular profession. This orientation is shaped by a multitude of factors, including educational and social experiences, which inform an individual's preferences for various activities and career paths.

APPENDIX I: STUDY QUESTIONNAIRE

Table 5. Counselors' and teachers' perspectives on psychological interventions and ADHD questionnaire (TCPPIQ)

No	Statements	SD	D	UD	D	SD
1	I feel that psychological interventions are effective for students with ADHD who have career transition-related burnout.					
2	The use of psychological interventions increases students' focus and attention during career transition.					
3	Psychological interventions support the emotional well-being of students with ADHD.					
4	I have observed improvements in students with ADHD due to psychological interventions during career transition.					
5	Psychological interventions help to develop coping strategies for students with ADHD during career transition.					
6	I feel counselors have the capacity to implement psychological interventions for students with ADHD during their career transition.					
7	Psychological interventions enhance the career transition outcomes for students with ADHD.					
8	I think that training in psychological interventions is essential for teachers of students with ADHD.					
9	Psychological interventions can be adapted for individual student needs.					
10	I see psychological interventions as a vital part of the educational process for students with ADHD.					
11	The effectiveness of psychological interventions can vary among students with ADHD.					
12	Psychological interventions address not only academic issues but also behavioral issues of students with ADHD.					
13	I feel that parents should be involved in the psychological interventions of their children with ADHD.					
14	Psychological interventions help in reducing classroom disruptions caused by ADHD.					
15	I receive adequate support and resources for implementing psychological interventions for students with ADHD.					
16	Continuous assessment of the effectiveness of psychological interventions for students with ADHD is necessary.					
17	I would recommend psychological interventions to other educators of students with ADHD.					

SD=Strongly Disagree, D=Disagree, UD=Undecided, A=Agree, SA=Strongly Agree

APPENDIX II: ADDITIONAL STATISTICS

Table 6. Item-total statistics

No	Statements	Cronbach's Alpha if Item Deleted
1	I feel that psychological interventions are effective for students with ADHD who have career transition-related burnout.	.716
2	The use of psychological interventions increases students' focus and attention during career transition.	.727
3	Psychological interventions support the emotional well-being of students with ADHD.	.747
4	I have observed improvements in students with ADHD due to psychological interventions during career transition.	.711
5	Psychological interventions help to develop coping strategies for students with ADHD during career transition.	.727
6	I feel counselors have the capacity to implement psychological interventions for students with ADHD during their career transition.	.725
7	Psychological interventions enhance the career transition outcomes for students with ADHD.	.707
8	I think that training in psychological interventions is essential for teachers of students with ADHD.	.704
9	Psychological interventions can be adapted for individual student needs.	.749
10	I see psychological interventions as a vital part of the educational process for students with ADHD.	.749
11	The effectiveness of psychological interventions can vary among students with ADHD.	.718
12	Psychological interventions address not only academic issues but also behavioral issues of students with ADHD.	.697
13	I feel that parents should be involved in the psychological interventions of their children with ADHD.	.705
14	Psychological interventions help in reducing classroom disruptions caused by ADHD.	.699
15	I receive adequate support and resources for implementing psychological interventions for students with ADHD.	.711
16	Continuous assessment of the effectiveness of psychological interventions for students with ADHD is necessary.	.709
17	I would recommend psychological interventions to other educators of students with ADHD.	.717

Table 7. Communalities (extraction method: principal component analysis)

No	Statements	Extraction
1	I feel that psychological interventions are effective for students with ADHD who have career transition-related burnout.	.524
2	The use of psychological interventions increases students' focus and attention during career transition.	.771
3	Psychological interventions support the emotional well-being of students with ADHD.	.794
4	I have observed improvements in students with ADHD due to psychological interventions during career transition.	.711
5	Psychological interventions help to develop coping strategies for students with ADHD during career transition.	.755
6	I feel counselors have the capacity to implement psychological interventions for students with ADHD during their career transition.	.663
7	Psychological interventions enhance the career transition outcomes for students with ADHD.	.737
8	I think that training in psychological interventions is essential for teachers of students with ADHD.	.598
9	Psychological interventions can be adapted for individual student needs.	.907
10	I see psychological interventions as a vital part of the educational process for students with ADHD.	.919
11	The effectiveness of psychological interventions can vary among students with ADHD.	.731
12	Psychological interventions address not only academic issues but also behavioral issues of students with ADHD.	.735
13	I feel that parents should be involved in the psychological interventions of their children with ADHD.	.735
14	Psychological interventions help in reducing classroom disruptions caused by ADHD.	.656
15	I receive adequate support and resources for implementing psychological interventions for students with ADHD.	.749
16	Continuous assessment of the effectiveness of psychological interventions for students with ADHD is necessary.	.693
17	I would recommend psychological interventions to other educators of students with ADHD.	.584

Chapter 5
Educational Psychologists' Perspectives on Practice Guidelines for Students With ADHD During Career Transitioning

ABSTRACT

This study examined educational psychologists' perspectives on practice guidelines for supporting students with ADHD during career transitioning. The study used a survey design with a sample of 32 educational psychologists from public secondary schools in Delta State, Nigeria. The data collection instrument was a questionnaire, which demonstrated good reliability. The findings indicate a positive perspective among educational psychologists on practice guidelines for supporting students with ADHD during career transitioning. Statistical analysis further revealed that factors such as gender, years of experience, or school location did not significantly affect the psychologists' perspectives on the guidelines. The findings suggest that current practice guidelines are considered relevant by educational psychologists, regardless of their background or work environment.

DOI: 10.4018/979-8-3693-2635-0.ch005

BACKGROUND

Globally, around 16 per cent of college students have been diagnosed with attention-deficit/hyperactivity disorder (ADHD), which adversely impacts their social interactions and learning outcomes (Pesantez, 2021). School-based professionals, such as educational psychologists, play a crucial role in bridging the gap between the many systems that support students (Keller-Margulis et al., 2020) including those with ADHD. It is essential for school professionals like educational psychologists to understand both the characteristics and implications of this disorder, as well as to possess the necessary skills and competencies to conduct psychoeducational screenings, assessments, and interventions in a prompt and evidence-based manner (Brock et al., 2009, Eseadi & Diale, 2024). DuPaul and Jimerson (2014) emphasized that students diagnosed with ADHD often experience persistent behavioral challenges that adversely affect their academic and social performance within educational environments. These challenges not only hinder the students' academic success but also pose considerable obstacles for educational psychologists and other professionals who support this group. These professionals cannot afford to ignore the various issues and are therefore responsible for implementing practice guidelines to support students with ADHD. The goal is to ensure a conducive environment that fosters inclusive education. Salhiya (2021) highlighted the necessity of taking into account underlying factors, comorbidities, and functional impairments in the treatment of students with ADHD. The author advocated the use of culturally tailored psychological assessments, the mitigation of side effects, and the careful adjustment of medication when required. Furthermore, the author emphasized the importance of prioritizing evidence-based behavioral therapies and integrated approaches, while also proposing that a combination of nutritious diets, traditional healing practices, and effective therapeutic interventions could provide the most holistic treatment for students with ADHD (Salhiya, 2021). In their study, Weis et al. (2019) revealed that psychologists exhibited a tendency to overlook the assessment of students' impairment areas and failed to consider alternative explanations for self-reported symptoms of ADHD. The authors expressed concerns that an excessive dependence on self-reports, coupled with insufficient adherence to DSM-5 criteria, may undermine the reliability of ADHD diagnoses and the suitability of subsequent medication and accommodations during career transition. According to Lonergan (2010), various factors can affect the assessment, diagnosis, and treatment of students diagnosed with ADHD. These factors encompass the subjective nature of diagnosis, limited availability of resources, the influence of medical interventions, the repercussions of the ADHD label, and a lack of compliance with practice guidelines.

There are established guidelines aimed at providing a framework for the effective and thorough assessment, diagnosis, and management of ADHD (May et al., 2023a, 2023b; Shah et al., 2019; Wolraich et al., 2019). In 2011 and 2019, respectively, the American Academy of Pediatrics released revised clinical practice guidelines on ADHD, initially created in 2000 (Eom & Kim, 2024). New ADHD studies and the Diagnostic and Statistical Manual of Mental Disorders, fifth edition (DSM-5) have also added to our knowledge of practice guidelines for managing ADHD (American Psychiatric Association, 2013; Eom & Kim, 2024; May et al., 2023a; Shah et al., 2019). Furthermore, the Society of Developmental and Behavioral Pediatrics (SDBP) has published an additional clinical practice guideline for effectively addressing ADHD (Barbaresi et al., 2020; Eom & Kim, 2024). The practice guidelines emphasized the significance of individualized education plans, behavioral treatments, and accommodating the distinct characteristics of students with ADHD. By following these guidelines, educational psychologists can significantly enhance their effectiveness in supporting students with ADHD during career transitioning. The acceptance and success of practice guidelines within the school context rely on the perspectives of school-based professionals such as educational psychologists, as they are the ones who first apply these guidelines in delivering school-based interventions (Paulus et al., 2016). School-based interventions have a significant influence on assisting students with ADHD (Power et al., 2009). The school-based interventions entail the cooperative efforts of teachers, parents, and mental health experts (Schultz & Evans, 2015), while also addressing the specific academic and career needs of students with ADHD. These services are referred to as any intervention, program, or strategy implemented in a school environment that has been developed specifically to impact students' emotional, behavioral, or social functioning (Rones & Hoagwood, 2000). According to prior research, school-based interventions for ADHD are successful in the short term for decreasing problematic conduct and enhancing focused behavior and academic achievement in students with ADHD (Miranda et al., 2006). According to the Educational Psychology Association of South Africa (2024), it is crucial for educational psychologists to confine their practice to domains that align with their competencies, which are determined by their formal education, training, supervised experience, and relevant professional experience.

Educational psychologists must prioritize the involvement of students and their families in their work. By employing a range of approaches, tools, and support systems, they can effectively capture the views and preferences of these individuals, ensuring that their aspirations are fairly represented in assessments, consultations, and discussions, while also addressing specific individual and contextual needs (Joint Professional Liaison Group, 2020). The Health Professions Council of South

Africa (2019; 2024) states that Educational Psychologists are equipped with a robust understanding of learning theory, developmental psychology, and psychopathology. Their expertise extends to neurodevelopment, cognitive functioning, and family dynamics, which empowers them to facilitate individual, group, and family therapy, offer psychological consultations, and implement various interventions aimed at addressing developmental and learning challenges throughout an individual's life. Implementing various guidelines, such as altering a student's seating arrangement or rewarding a student for good performance, has, more often than not, improved the academic success of students with ADHD (Gaastra et al., 2016). In the United Kingdom, the responsibilities of educational psychologists are typically divided into five distinct categories: assessment, consultation, intervention, research, and training (Fallon et al., 2010). Their job can be carried out at one of three levels: individual, group, or systemic (Lyons et al., 2024). Talapatra et al. (2020) emphasized the significance of various instructional methods—namely direct, informal, and experiential—in the provision of transition services by educational psychologists. The growing incidence of ADHD among Nigerian students presents significant challenges for educational psychologists who are charged with the responsibility of providing various psychological and educational support services to all students, their disabilities notwithstanding. While Nigerian educational psychologists are crucial in facilitating the career transition of students with ADHD, it is unclear whether their assessments of the effectiveness of current practice guidelines would vary by factors such as their years of experience, gender, and practice in urban or rural areas. In Delta State, Nigeria, the absence of a well-coordinated approach to supporting students with ADHD during career transition raises concerns about the adequacy and consistency of the guidance provided by educational psychologists and other school-based professionals. The lack of cohesive practice guidelines may lead to disparities in the support available to these students, further complicating their navigation of career transition. The existing yet unexplored perspectives of educational psychologists might serve as a potential barrier to the successful implementation of practice guidelines in schools. Thus, there is a need to explore the perspectives of educational psychologists on practice guidelines for assisting Nigerian students with ADHD during career transition. The present research aims to examine educational psychologists' perspectives on practice guidelines for students with ADHD in Delta State, Nigeria.

Research Objectives

1. To investigate the mean perspective of educational psychologists on practice guidelines for supporting students with ADHD during career transitioning.

2. To examine the differences in the mean perspectives of educational psychologists on practice guidelines for supporting students with ADHD during career transitioning based on years of experience.
3. To examine the disparity between the mean perspectives of male and female educational psychologists on practice guidelines for supporting students with ADHD during career transitioning.
4. To examine the differences between the mean perspectives of rural and urban educational psychologists on practice guidelines for supporting students with ADHD during career transitioning.

Research Questions

1. What is the mean perspective of educational psychologists on practice guidelines for supporting students with ADHD during career transitioning?
2. Do significant differences exist in the mean perspectives of educational psychologists on practice guidelines for supporting students with ADHD during career transitioning based on years of experience?
3. Do mean perspectives of male and female educational psychologists significantly differ on practice guidelines for supporting students with ADHD during career transitioning?
4. Do significant differences exist in the mean perspectives of rural and urban educational psychologists on practice guidelines for supporting students with ADHD during career transitioning?

Theoretical Framework

This research seeks to examine educational psychologists' perspectives on practice guidelines for supporting students with ADHD during career transitions in Delta State, Nigeria, through the lens of Social Learning Theory (SLT). SLT, as proposed by Albert Bandura, emphasizes the role of observation, imitation, and modeling in learning, highlighting the interaction between individuals, their environment, and behavior (Rumjaun & Narod, 2020; Gibson, 2004). Educational psychologists develop their understanding of practice guidelines for ADHD support through these social and professional interactions. By observing and engaging with colleagues, students, and educational systems, these professionals continuously refine their approaches to addressing the unique needs of students with ADHD. SLT serves as a critical framework for understanding the formation of these perspectives, as it posits that knowledge is acquired within a social context, influenced by interactions with others (Nabavi & Bijandi, 2015). In this context, SLT helps explain variations in psychologists' perspectives based on factors such as years of experience, gender, and work environment. For instance, psychologists with more experience may have observed a broader range of strategies and insights from their colleagues, resulting in a more nuanced understanding of effective practice guidelines. Similarly, SLT provides a basis for investigating potential gender-based differences in perspectives, considering how male and female psychologists might model their practices differently based on social expectations and professional experiences. Furthermore, the theory offers insight into how the distinct social environments of rural and urban psychologists may lead to differences in their approaches to supporting students with ADHD. Urban psychologists, with greater access to resources and professional networks, may model practices differently from their rural counterparts, who may operate in more isolated and resource-constrained environments. Overall, SLT provides a robust theoretical framework for exploring how educational psychologists in Delta State form their perspectives on practice guidelines for ADHD students, shaped by their professional interactions and social learning experiences (see Figure 1).

Figure 1. Study framework

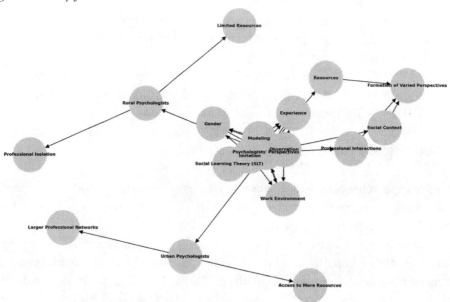

METHODOLOGY

Ethics Statement

Ethical approval for this study was obtained from the relevant institutional review boards. First, it received approval from the Research Ethics Committee of the Faculty of Education, University of Nigeria, Nigeria. It also received additional ethical approval from the Faculty of Education Research Ethics Committee at the University of Johannesburg, South Africa (Sem 2-2020-057). Informed consent was secured from participants. We assured confidentiality and clarified participants' right to withdraw from the study at any given time.

Research Design and Approach

The study employed a survey research design. This type of research is characterized as a specific form of field study that focuses on gathering data from a sample of elements selected from a well-defined population using a questionnaire (Visser et al., 2000). Survey research is classified as a non-experimental approach that seeks to collect information about the occurrence, distribution, and relationships among variables within a predetermined population (Coughlan et al., 2013). Descriptive survey research utilizes a methodical inquiry into current conditions through the collection and analysis of empirical data, which aids in the advancement of knowledge and interpretation of data (Kumar & Mehta, 2013). This research design can also integrate qualitative methodologies, akin to the approach utilized in this study. Quantitative methods yield reliable data and enable extensive generalizations across a population, thus providing a clearer understanding of the social phenomena being examined (Gallagher, 2013).

Research Paradigm

Research paradigms and designs in the academic field are essential for conducting effective research endeavors (Kumatongo & Muzata, 2021). This study is grounded in the positivist research paradigm. The term positivism holds significant importance in the human sciences, largely due to its valued assertion of objective knowledge (Jaja et al., 2022). Positivist approaches, particularly single studies, provide a reliable and systematic methodology for research, playing a vital role in pluralist research frameworks within information systems (Shanks & Parr, 2003). This philosophical stance, rooted in David Hume's understanding of reality, maintains that real events can be observed through empirical means and explained via logical analysis, including theory-based predictions (Kaboub, 2007). The aim of the positivist perspective is to accurately represent the phenomena experienced by individuals (Tavakol et al., 2006).

Study Area

This research was conducted in Delta State in the South-south zone of Nigeria. Delta State is one of the thirty-six states that make up the Federal Republic of Nigeria, consisting of twenty-five Local Government Areas. The capital city of Delta State is Asaba (Ikpo, 2011). Geographically, Delta State is situated to the north of Edo State, to the east of Anambra and Rivers States, to the south of Bayelsa State and the Atlantic Ocean, and the west of Ondo State (Balogun & Onokerhoraye, 2022).

Population and Sampling

The choice of sampling methods is influenced by the study's objectives and the specific research question, especially when a reliable answer regarding the population of interest is required (Shorten & Moorley, 2014). Sampling techniques are generally divided into two categories: probability and non-probability (Amir et al., 2020). This research adopted the non-probability sampling method. This method involves selecting the sample population through a non-systematic process, which does not ensure equal opportunities for every individual within the target population (Elfil & Negida, 2017). Non-probability sampling encompasses techniques such as accidental sampling, purposive sampling, and quota sampling, among others (Burger & Silima, 2006). The study involves educational psychologists from selected public secondary schools. A total of 32 educational psychologists were selected using purposive and convenience sampling techniques. A convenience sample consists of individuals who are readily accessible to the researcher and are likely to provide the necessary information (Mweshi & Sakyi, 2020). Purposive sampling operates on the principle that identifying the most relevant cases for the study yields the most valuable data, with research outcomes being directly influenced by the selected cases (Mweshi & Sakyi, 2020).

Data Collection

The data was collected using a questionnaire. The researchers received help from two postgraduate students to complete the data collection process. The questionnaire used for data collection is called the Educational Psychologists' Perspectives on Practice Guidelines for Students with ADHD Questionnaire (EPPPGSAQ). It is a 22-item scale, with response options ranging from Not at all (1) to Very great extent (5). This scale measures educational psychologists' perspectives on practice guidelines for supporting students with ADHD during career transitioning. The scale is designed to capture the extent of agreement or perception, with 1 indicating "Not at All" and 5 indicating "Great Extent." Some examples of item statements in the questionnaire include: "To what extent do you follow practice guidelines for ADHD in your work?", "To what extent do you feel confident are you in your ability to support students with ADHD in their career transition using existing guidelines?" and " To what extent do you consider ADHD guidelines to be important in your role as an educational psychologist?" The EPPPGSAQ has a good internal consistency reliability, with a Cronbach's alpha of 0.93 in the present research.

Data Analysis

Statistical analysis was conducted using Statistical Package for the Social Sciences (SPSS), version 27. SPSS is a prominent Windows-based software utilized for data entry, analysis, and the generation of tables and graphs, particularly suited for handling extensive datasets and conducting statistical analyses in the field of social sciences (Kumar & Mehta, 2013). As a statistical package designed for social sciences, SPSS serves as a robust instrument capable of executing a wide array of data analyses applicable not only to social sciences but also to natural sciences and business contexts (Singh, 2015). The software is regularly updated, allowing users to derive statistics that range from basic descriptive measures to intricate analyses of multivariate matrices (Alili & Krstev, 2019). SPSS provides a rapid visual modeling environment that accommodates both simple and highly complex models (Williams, 2024). It is frequently employed for data management, descriptive statistics, inferential statistics, and data visualization (Eval Community, 2016). Descriptive statistics yield critical insights, such as mean, median, and mode, regarding the variables under examination (Park, 2015). In this context, descriptive statistics were utilized to examine sociodemographic data, while univariate analysis was employed to respond to the research questions at a significance level of .05, focusing on the investigation of each variable (Cleff, 2014).

FINDINGS

Table 1. Mean perspective of educational psychologists on practice guidelines for supporting students with ADHD during career transitioning

Gender	Experience	School Location	Mean	Std. Deviation	N
Male Educational Psychologists	Early Career Psychologists	Rural Schools	3.23	.13	5
		Urban Schools	3.32	.28	5
		Total	3.27	.21	10
	Experienced Psychologists	Rural Schools	3.32	.00	2
		Total	3.32	.00	2
	Total	Rural Schools	3.25	.11	7
		Urban Schools	3.32	.28	5
		Total	3.28	.19	12
Female Educational Psychologists	Early Career Psychologists	Rural Schools	3.48	.19	7
		Urban Schools	3.31	.15	6
		Total	3.40	.19	13
	Experienced Psychologists	Rural Schools	3.24	.12	4
		Urban Schools	3.06	.25	3
		Total	3.16	.19	7
	Total	Rural Schools	3.39	.21	11
		Urban Schools	3.23	.21	9
		Total	3.32	.22	20
Total	Early Career Psychologists	Rural Schools	3.38	.21	12
		Urban Schools	3.31	.20	11
		Total	3.35	.21	23
	Experienced Psychologists	Rural Schools	3.27	.10	6
		Urban Schools	3.06	.25	3
		Total	3.19	.18	9
	Total	Rural Schools	3.34	.19	18
		Urban Schools	3.26	.23	14
		Total	3.30	.21	32

The overall mean perspective of educational psychologists, considering all variables, is 3.30 with a standard deviation of 0.21, as shown in the last row of Table 1. This result indicates a generally positive perspective by educational psychologists on practice guidelines for supporting students with ADHD during career transitioning. To further illustrate this result, Figures 2 and 3 are used as representations of the mean perspectives for rural and urban educational psychologists across gender and years of experience, respectively. These figures illustrate the estimated marginal means.

Figure 2. Mean perspective of rural educational psychologists on practice guidelines for supporting students with ADHD during career transitioning

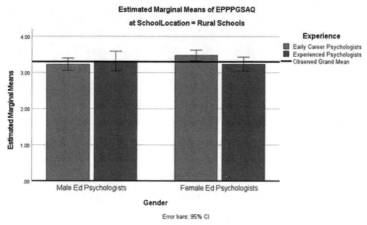

Figure 3. Mean perspective of urban educational psychologists on practice guidelines for supporting students with ADHD during career transitioning

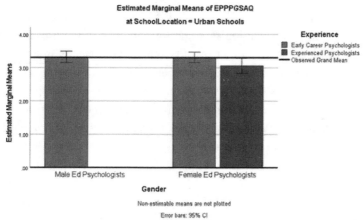

Table 2. Univariate results on the perspective of educational psychologists on practice guidelines for supporting students with ADHD during career transitioning by gender, years of experience and school location

Source	Type III Sum of Squares	Df	Mean Square	F	Sig.
Corrected Model	.444ª	6	.074	2.083	.092
Intercept	233.220	1	233.220	6563.239	.000
Gender	.001	1	.001	.037	.850
Experience	.060	1	.060	1.700	.204
School Location	.028	1	.028	.786	.384
Error	.888	25	.036		
Total	350.653	32			
Corrected Total	1.332	31			

According to Table 2, the effect of years of experience on the mean perspectives of educational psychologists on practice guidelines for supporting students with ADHD during career transitioning is not statistically significant, with a p-value of .204 (F = 1.700). This suggests that there is no significant difference in the perspectives of educational psychologists on practice guidelines for supporting students with ADHD during career transitioning based on the years of experience of the psychologists. Table 2 also indicates that gender does not have a statistically significant effect on the mean perspectives of educational psychologists on practice guidelines for supporting students with ADHD during career transitioning, with a p-value of 0.850 (F = 0.037). Therefore, there is no significant difference in the perspectives of male and female educational psychologists regarding practice guidelines for supporting students with ADHD during career transitioning. The analysis in Table 2 further shows that school location (rural vs. urban) does not significantly affect the mean perspectives of educational psychologists on practice guidelines for supporting students with ADHD during career transitioning, with a p-value of 0.384 (F = 0.786). Thus, there is no significant difference in the perspectives of educational psychologists on practice guidelines for supporting students with ADHD during career transitioning based on whether the psychologists are from rural or urban schools.

DISCUSSION

This research sought to examine the views of educational psychologists on the practice guidelines for students with ADHD in the context of career transitioning. It also analyzed how various factors, including the gender of the educational psychologists, their location, and their years of experience, could affect their perceptions of practice guidelines in view of supporting the career transitioning of these students. This study found a generally positive perspective by educational psychologists on practice guidelines for supporting students with ADHD during career transitioning. Talapatra et al. (2020) observed that educational psychologists possess significant potential to enhance the transition process for students with disabilities; however, their participation in this area is frequently minimal. Furthermore, the study by Hill and Turner (2016) focused solely on the perspectives of educational psychologists, revealing that they are infrequently involved in the assessment of ADHD, while regular students are more often able to access psychological interventions. DeBonis et al. (2000) revealed that educational psychologists reported a low frequency of utilizing general practices intended to systematically improve executive functions in contextually appropriate manners. Nevertheless, considering the significant population of students receiving prescriptions for psychotropic medications, a primary challenge for educational psychologists is to maintain the quality and continuity of care for these students, all while complying with applicable legal and ethical standards (Shahidullah, 2014). Rutter and Atkinson (2022) highlighted the competencies of educational psychologists in cognitive behavioral therapy when working with children, young people, and adults. In an earlier study, Borick (2011) noted that a significant number of educational psychologists were actively conducting assessments and providing interventions for ADHD, suggesting a favorable attitude towards guidelines aimed at supporting these students. The majority of respondents, in a study by Maksić (2018), specifically educational psychologists, maintained an optimistic perspective regarding their anticipated engagement in clinical practices. Despite this, Dryer et al. (2013) had shown minimal evidence of widespread interdisciplinary collaboration and adherence to ADHD practice guidelines among various professionals. Tree (2008) reported that psychologists were less frequently involved in current practices for determining placements for students with ADHD. The author further clarified that schools typically adhered to federal guidelines and recommendations from researchers regarding placement decisions, particularly when educational psychologists were involved. Similarly, Ogg et al. (2013) found that psychologists most frequently adhered to recommended guidelines for diagnosis, impairment, and intervention development, while they were less likely to follow guidelines related to progress monitoring, outcome evaluation, and integrity assessment. Current guidelines in this regard reflect the available evidence that is pertinent to inform clinical practice (Shah et al., 2019).

Factors such as the number of years of experience, gender, and geographical setting (whether rural or urban) did not influence psychologists' views of practice guidelines concerning the career transitioning of students with ADHD. Prior research indicated that school professionals who possess greater years of experience and advanced training have provided consultation services to a larger number of students and have facilitated more in-programs compared to their less experienced or less trained counterparts (Curtis et al., 2006). The findings of Talapatra et al. (2020) showed that the prior experience of educational psychologists in working with individuals with disabilities served as a significant predictor of their performance in transition-related professional activities. Borick (2011) identified a correlation between the years of experience of psychologists and their confidence in their training to evaluate and implement interventions for students with ADHD. Koonce (2007) demonstrated significant regional disparities in the selection of instruments and procedures by psychologists. Reschly and Connolly (1990) indicated that there was minimal evidence supporting a more generalized role for rural educational psychologists, along with distinct continuing education requirements between rural and urban populations. According to Graves et al. (2014), notable disparities exist in demographics, practices, and challenges encountered by educational psychologists in urban environments. Findings from Wnek et al. (2008) emphasized a consistent perception among psychologists across the United States, irrespective of the demographic backgrounds of the respondents. It was observed that rural school professionals typically had less experience and were engaged in a higher number of special education reevaluations while conducting fewer consultations compared to their urban and suburban counterparts (Curtis et al., 2006). Goforth et al. (2017) found that rural educational psychologists managed a greater number of schools, possessed fewer years of experience, and dedicated significantly more time to travel, yet they had comparable access to various interventions and professional development resources. Although our research indicates no significant differences in the views of educational psychologists regarding practice guidelines for assisting students with ADHD during career transitions based on their rural or urban affiliations, the implementation of these clinical practice guidelines may present some challenges for psychologists in rural settings. Clopton and Knesting (2006) argued that educational psychologists in rural regions encounter issues such as limited community support services, feelings of professional isolation, inadequate workspace, and extensive travel time. Educational psychologists recognize their capabilities in facilitating the transition process; however, they encounter obstacles such as inadequate resource distribution, insufficient training, and limited understanding of the empirical evidence supporting transition services, which hinder their ability to engage effectively, according to Ducharme et al. (2020). May et al. (2023b) indicated that practice guidelines could be utilized to enhance the training of psychologists, thereby ensuring that individuals with ADHD receive consistent and evidence-based support in clinical environments. Educational psychologists are recognized as specialists in assessment, data collection, interventions, research, and professional development, which positions them effectively to lead and facilitate the individualized transition planning process (Rutner, 2022). As scientist-practitioners, educational psychologists strive to implement empirically-based methodologies within educational environments (Froese & Montgomery, 2014). They can serve as valuable partners in the assessment and treatment of both prevalent and less common disorders, free from the limitations typically associated with managed care (Wodrich & Landau, 1999). Furthermore, educational psychologists are uniquely positioned to facilitate the implementation of school-based adjunctive treatments for students with ADHD (Shahidullah et al., 2014). Smith (1999) demonstrated that educational psychologists are assured in their skills to provide various services, including consultation, intervention, and assessment, for students with ADHD. Evidence indicates that educational psychologists provide a more comprehensive perspective, placing a strong emphasis on the social and emotional well-being of the child (Atkinson et al., 2022). The transition experience for individuals with ADHD is often suboptimal, and adherence to clear recommendations is essential for ensuring an effective transition (Young et al., 2016).

CONCLUSIONS

The study has revealed that educational psychologists hold a predominantly favorable perspective regarding practice guidelines aimed at assisting students with ADHD during their career transitions. The study found that there is no significant difference in the perspectives of educational psychologists on practice guidelines for supporting students with ADHD during career transitioning based on the gender, years of experience and school location of the psychologists. This suggests that educational psychologists recognize the importance and effectiveness of these guidelines in supporting students with ADHD during career transitioning. The positive perspectives of educational psychologists can encourage ongoing development and refinement of practice guidelines for supporting students with ADHD, knowing they are well-received by practitioners.

REFERENCES

Alili, A., & Krstev, D. (2019). Using SPSS for research and data analysis. *Knowledge–International Journal, 32*(3). https://eprints.ugd.edu.mk/29545/1/KIJ%2C%20Vol.%2032.3%20%282%29.pdf

American Psychiatric Association. (2013). *Diagnostic and statistical manual of mental disorders: DSM-5* (5th ed.). American Psychiatric Association.

Amir, N., Jabeen, F., & Niaz, S. (2020, November). *A Brief Review of Conditions, Circumstances and Applicability of Sampling Techniques in Computer Science Domain*. 2020 IEEE 23rd International Multitopic Conference (INMIC), Bahawalpur, Pakistan. DOI: 10.1109/INMIC50486.2020.9318209

Atkinson, C., Barrow, J., & Norris, S. (2022). Assessment practices of educational psychologists and other educational professionals. *Educational Psychology in Practice*, 38(4), 347–363. DOI: 10.1080/02667363.2022.2109005

Balogun, V. S., & Onokerhoraye, A. G. (2022). Climate change vulnerability mapping across ecological zones in Delta State, Niger Delta Region of Nigeria. *Climate Services*, 27, 100304. DOI: 10.1016/j.cliser.2022.100304

Barbaresi, W. J., Campbell, L., Diekroger, E. A., Froehlich, T. E., Liu, Y. H., O'Malley, E., Pelham, W. E., Power, T. J., Zinner, S. H., & Chan, E. (2020). Society for Developmental and Behavioral Pediatrics Clinical Practice Guideline for the Assessment and Treatment of Children and Adolescents with Complex Attention-Deficit/Hyperactivity Disorder. *Journal of Developmental and Behavioral Pediatrics*, 41(2S), S35–S57. DOI: 10.1097/DBP.0000000000000770 PMID: 31996577

Borick, T. J. (2011). *Assessment and intervention practices for attention deficit hyperactivity disorder (ADHD): A national survey of school psychologists*. Indiana University of Pennsylvania.

Brock, S. E., Jimerson, S. R., & Hansen, R. L. (2009). *Identifying, Assessing, and Treating ADHD at School* (1st ed.). Springer., DOI: 10.1007/978-1-4419-0501-7

Burger, A., & Silima, T. (2006). Sampling and sampling design. *Journal of Public Administration*, 41(3), 656–668. DOI: 10.10520/EJC51475

Cleff, T. (2014). Univariate Data Analysis. In *Exploratory Data Analysis in Business and Economics* (pp. 23–60). Springer Cham., DOI: 10.1007/978-3-319-01517-0_3

Clopton, K. L., & Knesting, K. (2006). Rural school psychology: Re-opening the discussion. *Journal of Research in Rural Education*, 21(5), 1–11.

Coughlan, M., Cronin, P., & Ryan, F. (2013). Survey research: Process and limitations. *International Journal of Therapy and Rehabilitation*, 16(1), 9–15. Advance online publication. DOI: 10.12968/ijtr.2009.16.1.37935

Curtis, D. F., Pisecco, S., Hamilton, R. J., & Moore, D. W. (2006). Teacher perceptions of classroom interventions for children with ADHD: A cross-cultural comparison of teachers in the United States and New Zealand. *School Psychology Quarterly*, 21(2), 171–196. DOI: 10.1521/scpq.2006.21.2.171

DeBonis, D., Ylvisaker, M., & Kundert, D. (2000). The relationship between ADHD theory and practice: A preliminary investigation. *Journal of Attention Disorders*, 4(3), 161–173. DOI: 10.1177/108705470000400303

Dryer, M., Kiernan, M., & Tyson, G. (2013). Do professions differ in their beliefs about the causes and treatment of attention-deficit hyperactivity disorder? *ADHD: Cognitive Symptoms, Genetics and Treatment Outcomes*, 61–79.

Ducharme, D., Roach, A. T., & Wellons, Q. D. (2020). The role of school psychologists in employment-focused transition services. *Journal of Applied School Psychology*, 36(4), 376–400. DOI: 10.1080/15377903.2020.1749205

DuPaul, G. J., & Jimerson, S. R. (2014). Assessing, understanding, and supporting students with ADHD at school: contemporary science, practice, and policy. *School psychology quarterly: the official journal of the Division of School Psychology, American Psychological Association*, 29(4), 379–384. DOI: 10.1037/spq0000104

Educational Psychology Association of South Africa. (2024, September 30). The Scope of Practice of Educational Psychologists. https://www.epassa.net/2024/09/30/the-scope-of-practice-of-educational-psychologists/

Elfil, M., & Negida, A. (2017). Sampling methods in Clinical Research; an Educational Review. *Emergency (Tehran, Iran)*, 5(1), e52. https://www.ncbi.nlm.nih.gov/pmc/articles/PMC5325924/ PMID: 28286859

Eom, T. H., & Kim, Y.-H. (2024). Clinical practice guidelines for attention-deficit/hyperactivity disorder: Recent updates. *Clinical and Experimental Pediatrics*, 67(1), 26–34. DOI: 10.3345/cep.2021.01466 PMID: 37321571

Eseadi, C., & Diale, B. M. (2024). *Perspectives on Career Transitioning of Students with Hearing Impairments*. IGI Global., DOI: 10.4018/979-8-3693-2631-2

Eval Community. (2016). *Utilizing SPSS (Statistical Package for the Social Sciences) for Effective Data Analysis in Monitoring and Evaluation*. https://www.evalcommunity.com/career-center/using-spss-in-monitoring-and-evaluation/

Fallon, K., Woods, K., & Rooney, S. (2010). A discussion of the developing role of educational psychologists within Children's services. *Educational Psychology in Practice*, 26(1), 1–23. DOI: 10.1080/02667360903522744

Froese, K. A., & Montgomery, J. (2014). From research to practice: The process of training school psychologists as knowledge transfer professionals. *Procedia: Social and Behavioral Sciences*, 141, 375–381. DOI: 10.1016/j.sbspro.2014.05.066

Gaastra, G. F., Groen, Y., Tucha, L., & Tucha, O. (2016). The Effects of Classroom Interventions on Off-Task and Disruptive Classroom Behavior in Children with Symptoms of Attention-Deficit/Hyperactivity Disorder: A Meta-Analytic Review. *PLoS One*, 11(2), e0148841. DOI: 10.1371/journal.pone.0148841 PMID: 26886218

Gallagher, M. (2013). 9. Capturing Meaning and Confronting Measurement. In Mosley, L. (Ed.), *Interview Research in Political Science* (pp. 181–195). Cornell University Press., DOI: 10.7591/9780801467974-012

Gibson, S. K. (2004). Social Learning (Cognitive) Theory and Implications for Human Resource Development. *Advances in Developing Human Resources*, 6(2), 193–210. DOI: 10.1177/1523422304263429

Goforth, A. N., Yosai, E. R., Brown, J. A., & Shindorf, Z. R. (2017). A multi-method inquiry of the practice and context of rural school psychology. *Contemporary School Psychology*, 21(1), 58–70. DOI: 10.1007/s40688-016-0110-1

Graves, S.Jr, Proctor, S., & Aston, C. (2014). Professional Roles and Practices of School Psychologists In Urban Schools. *Psychology in the Schools*, 51(4), 384–394. DOI: 10.1002/pits.21754

Health Professions Council of South Africa. (2019, February). Minimum standards for the training of Educational Psychology. https://www.hpcsa.co.za/Content/upload/psb/guidelines/Minimum_standards_for_the_training_of_Educational_Psychology.pdf

Health Professions Council of South Africa. (2024, January). Guidelines to Prepare for The National Board Examination for Educational Psychology. https://www.hpcsa.co.za/Content/upload/professional_boards/psb/examinations/Board_Examination_Guidelines_Educational_Psychology_January_2024_revised.pdf

Hill, V., & Turner, H. (2016). Educational psychologists' perspectives on the medicalisation of childhood behaviour: A focus on Attention Deficit Hyperactive Disorder (ADHD). *Educational and Child Psychology*, 33(2), 12–29. DOI: 10.53841/bpsecp.2016.33.2.12

Ikpo, N. (2011, February 12). IBB & Delta State creation: How Asaba became the capital. *Vanguard News*. https://www.vanguardngr.com/2011/02/ibb-delta-state-creation-how-asaba-became-the-capital-by-nosike-ikpo/

Jaja, I., Cornelius, A., & Idoniboye, O. (2022). A Critique of the Positivist Paradigm in Human Sciences. *International Journal of Research and Innovation in Social Science*, 6(3), 224–229.

Joint Professional Liaison Group. (2020, June). Guidance for Educational Psychologists providing advice and information for Education, Health and Care Needs Assessments. /https://www.aep.org.uk/system/files?alId=11433&file=2022-03%2FGuidance+for+EPs+providing+advice+for+EHCNA+June+2020.pdf

Kaboub, F. (2007). Positivist paradigm. *Encyclopaedia of Counselling*, 2(2), 343. https://personal.denison.edu/~kaboubf/Pub/2008-Positivist-Paradigm.pdf

Keller-Margulis, M. A., Ochs, S., Nowell, K. P., & Mire, S. S. (2020). Role of the school-based professional in linking systems of care. In *Pediatric health conditions in schools: A clinician's guide for working with children, families, and educators* (pp. 61–77). Oxford University Press., DOI: 10.1093/med-psych/9780190687281.003.0004

Koonce, D. A. (2007). Attention deficit hyperactivity disorder assessment practices by practicing school psychologists: A national survey. *Journal of Psychoeducational Assessment*, 25(4), 319–333. https://doi.org/10.1um177/0734282906298264. DOI: 10.1177/0734282906298264

Kumar, A., & Mehta, P. (2013). Meaning of the term- descriptive survey research method. *International Journal of Research in Social Sciences and Humanities*, 3(1), 16–22.

Kumatongo, B., & Muzata, K. K. (2021). Research Paradigms and Designs with their Application in Education. *Journal of Lexicography and Terminology*, 5(1), 16–32.

Lonergan, C. (2010). *The perspectives of educational psychologists, teachers, parents, and healthcare professionals on the assessment diagnosis and treatment of children with a diagnosis of ADHD in one English local authority*. Institute of Education, University of London.

Lyons, A., Thomas, G., Octigan, S., & Orme, J. (2024). Developing best practice guidance for educational psychologists gaining consent across the 0-25 age range. *Educational Psychology in Practice*, •••, 1–19. DOI: 10.1080/02667363.2024.2403072

Maksić, S. (2018). *Professional role, status and identity of the school psychologist in Serbia*. IPIR - Repository of the Institute for Educational Research., DOI: 10.20544/teacher.15.01

May, T., Birch, E., Chaves, K., Cranswick, N., Culnane, E., Delaney, J., Derrick, M., Eapen, V., Edlington, C., Efron, D., Ewais, T., Garner, I., Gathercole, M., Jagadheesan, K., Jobson, L., Kramer, J., Mack, M., Misso, M., Murrup-Stewart, C., & Bellgrove, M. (2023a). The Australian evidence-based clinical practice guideline for attention deficit hyperactivity disorder. *The Australian and New Zealand Journal of Psychiatry*, 57(8), 1101–1116. DOI: 10.1177/00048674231166329 PMID: 37254562

May, T., Murrup-Stewart, C., & Bellgrove, M. (2023b). Australian Evidence-Based Clinical Practice Guideline for Attention Deficit Hyperactivity Disorder: The Role of Psychologists. *The Australian and New Zealand Journal of Psychiatry*, 33(1), 18–34. DOI: 10.1177/00048674231166329

Miranda, A., Jarque, S., & Tarraga, R. (2006). Interventions in School Settings for Students With ADHD. *Exceptionality*, 14(1), 35–52. DOI: 10.1207/s15327035ex1401_4

Mweshi, G. K., & Sakyi, K. (2020). Application of sampling methods for the research design. *Archives of Business Research*, 8(11), 180–193. DOI: 10.14738/abr.811.9042

Nabavi, R. T., & Bijandi, M. (2012). *Bandura's Social Learning Theory & Social Cognitive Learning Theory*. ResearchGate, https://www.researchgate.net/publication/267750204_Bandura's_Social_Learning_Theory_Social_Cognitive_Learning_Theory#fullTextFileContent

Ogg, J., Fefer, S., Sundman-Wheat, A., McMahan, M., Stewart, T., Chappel, A., & Bateman, L. (2013). School-Based Assessment of ADHD: Purpose, Alignment With Best Practice Guidelines, and Training. *Journal of Applied School Psychology*, 29(4), 305–327. DOI: 10.1080/15377903.2013.836775

Park, H. M. (2015). *Univariate Analysis and Normality Test Using SAS, Stata, and SPSS*. The Trustees of Indiana University. https://hdl.handle.net/2022/19742

Paulus, F. W., Ohmann, S., & Popow, C. (2016). Practitioner Review: School-based interventions in child mental health. *Journal of Child Psychology and Psychiatry, and Allied Disciplines*, 57(12), 1337–1359. DOI: 10.1111/jcpp.12584 PMID: 27445203

Pesantez, N. (2021, November 22). Study: One in Six College Freshmen Has ADHD — Most with Comorbidities. *ADDitude*. https://www.additudemag.com/statistics-about-college-students-adhd-rates-news/

Power, T. J., Tresco, K. E., & Cassano, M. C. (2009). School-based interventions for students with attention-deficit/hyperactivity disorder. *Current Psychiatry Reports*, 11(5), 407–414. DOI: 10.1007/s11920-009-0061-6 PMID: 19785983

Reschly, D. J., & Connolly, L. M. (1990). Comparisons of School Psychologists in the City and Country: Is There a "Rural" School Psychology? *School Psychology Review*, 19(4), 534–549. DOI: 10.1080/02796015.1990.12087356

Rones, M., & Hoagwood, K. (2000). School-based mental health services: A research review. *Clinical Child and Family Psychology Review*, 3(4), 223–241. DOI: 10.1023/A:1026425104386 PMID: 11225738

Rumjaun, A., & Narod, F. (2020). Social Learning Theory—Albert Bandura. In Akpan, B., & Kennedy, T. J. (Eds.), *Science Education in Theory and Practice: An Introductory Guide to Learning Theory* (pp. 85–99). Springer International Publishing., DOI: 10.1007/978-3-030-43620-9_7

Rutner, K. F. (2022). *The Integral Role of the School Psychologist: A Multi-Tiered Approach to Supporting Students with Disabilities for Post-Secondary Transition.* (Doctoral Dissertation, Alliant International University, San Diego).

Rutter, S., & Atkinson, C. (2022). Educational psychologists' use of cognitive behavioural therapy in professional practice. *Educational and Child Psychology*, 39(3), 113–128. DOI: 10.53841/bpsecp.2022.39.3.113

Salhiya, R. D. (2021). Counseling Practice Guideline for the Evaluation, Diagnosis, and Treatment of Attention-Deficit/Hyperactivity Disorder for Children. *Journal of Research in Humanities and Social Science*, 9(1), 33–41.

Schultz, B. K., & Evans, S. W. (2015). *A practical guide to implementing school-based interventions for adolescents with ADHD*. Springer., DOI: 10.1007/978-1-4939-2677-0

Shah, R., Grover, S., & Avasthi, A. (2019). Clinical Practice Guidelines for the Assessment and Management of Attention-Deficit/Hyperactivity Disorder. *Indian Journal of Psychiatry*, 61(8, Suppl 2), 176–193. DOI: 10.4103/psychiatry.IndianJPsychiatry_543_18 PMID: 30745695

Shahidullah, J. D. (2014). Medication-related practice roles: An ethical and legal primer for school psychologists. *Contemporary School Psychology*, 18(2), 127–132. DOI: 10.1007/s40688-014-0013-y

Shahidullah, J. D., Voris, D. S., Hicks, T., & Carlson, J. S. (2014). The importance and need for implementing school-based supports as adjuncts to pharmacotherapy for students diagnosed with ADHD. *Research and Practice in the Schools : The Official Journal of the Texas Association of School Psychologists*, 2(1), 31–40.

Shanks, G., & Parr, A. (2003). Positivist, Single Case Study Research in Information Systems: A Critical Analysis. In C. Ciborra, R. Mercurio, M. De Marco, M. Martinez, & A. Carignani (Eds.), *New Paradigms in Organizations, Markets & Society:Proceedings of the 11th European Conference on Information Systems (ECIS 2003)* (pp. 1 - 12). Department of Information Systems, London School of Economics.

Shorten, A., & Moorley, C. (2014). Selecting the sample. *Evidence-Based Nursing*, 17(2), 32–33. DOI: 10.1136/eb-2014-101747 PMID: 24561511

Singh, A. (2015). SPSS - An Overview. In *Extension Research Methodology*. Agrotech Publishing Academy.

Smith, A. L. (1999). *School psychologists and attention-deficit/hyperactivity disorder: A survey of training, knowledge, practice, and attitude*. Ball State University.

Talapatra, D., Wilcox, G., Roof, H., & Hutchinson, C. (2020). Transition planning for students with disabilities: Perspectives of Canadian and American school psychologists. *International Journal of School & Educational Psychology, 8*(sup1), 49–64. DOI: 10.1080/21683603.2018.1558136

Tavakol, M., Torabi, S., & Akbar Zeinaloo, A. (2006). Grounded Theory in Medical Education Research. *Medical Education Online*, 11(1), 4607. DOI: 10.3402/meo.v11i.4607 PMID: 28253770

Tree, T. (2008). School-Based Services for Children with Attention-Deficit/Hyperactivity Disorder. *All Graduate Theses and Dissertations*. DOI: 10.26076/d815-426b

Visser, P. S., Krosnick, J. A., & Lavrakas, P. J. (2000). Survey research. In Reis, H. T., & Judd, C. M. (Eds.), *Handbook of research methods in social and personality psychology* (pp. 223–252). Cambridge University Press.

Weis, R., Till, C. H., & Erickson, C. P. (2019). ADHD assessment in college students: Psychologists' adherence to DSM-5 criteria and multi-method/multi-informant assessment. *Journal of Psychoeducational Assessment*, 37(2), 209–225. DOI: 10.1177/0734282917735152

Williams, K. (2024, March 20). What is SPSS? Definition, Features, Types, and Use Cases. *SurveySparrow*. https://surveysparrow.com/blog/what-is-spss/

Wnek, A. C., Klein, G., & Bracken, B. A. (2008). Professional Development Issues for School Psychologists: What's Hot, What's Not in the United States. *School Psychology International*, 29(2), 145–160. DOI: 10.1177/0143034308090057

Wodrich, D. L., & Landau, S. (1999). School psychologists: Strategic allies in the contemporary practice of primary care pediatrics. *Clinical Pediatrics*, 38(10), 597–606. DOI: 10.1177/000992289903801005 PMID: 10544866

Wolraich, M. L., Hagan, J. F.Jr, Allan, C., Chan, E., Davison, D., Earls, M., Evans, S. W., Flinn, S. K., Froehlich, T., Frost, J., Holbrook, J. R., Lehmann, C. U., Lessin, H. R., Okechukwu, K., Pierce, K. L., Winner, J. D., & Zurhellen, W. (2019). Clinical practice guideline for the diagnosis, evaluation, and treatment of attention-deficit/ hyperactivity disorder in children and adolescents. *Pediatrics*, 144(4), e20192528. DOI: 10.1542/peds.2019-2528 PMID: 31570648

Young, S., Adamou, M., Asherson, P., Coghill, D., Colley, B., Gudjonsson, G., Hollis, C., McCarthy, J., Müller, U., Paul, M., Pitts, M., & Arif, M. (2016). Recommendations for the transition of patients with ADHD from child to adult healthcare services: A consensus statement from the UK adult ADHD network. *BMC Psychiatry*, 16(1), 301. DOI: 10.1186/s12888-016-1013-4 PMID: 27561259

ADDITIONAL READINGS

Amer, Y. S., Al-Joudi, H. F., Varnham, J. L., Bashiri, F. A., Hamad, M. H., Al Salehi, S. M., Daghash, H. F., & Albatti, T. H. (2019). Appraisal of clinical practice guidelines for the management of attention deficit hyperactivity disorder (ADHD) using the AGREE II Instrument: A systematic review. *PLoS One*, 14(7), e0219239. DOI: 10.1371/journal.pone.0219239 PMID: 31276528

Anbarasan, D., Kitchin, M., & Adler, L. A. (2020). Screening for adult ADHD. *Current Psychiatry Reports*, 22(12), 1–5. DOI: 10.1007/s11920-020-01194-9 PMID: 33095375

Andersen, A. C., Sund, A. M., Thomsen, P. H., Lydersen, S., Young, S., & Nøvik, T. S. (2022). Cognitive behavioral group therapy for adolescents with ADHD: A study of satisfaction and feasibility. *Nordic Journal of Psychiatry*, 76(4), 280–286. DOI: 10.1080/08039488.2021.1965212 PMID: 34410203

Auvin, S., Wirrell, E., Donald, K. A., Berl, M., Hartmann, H., Valente, K. D., Van Bogaert, P., Cross, J. H., Osawa, M., Kanemura, H., Aihara, M., Guerreiro, M. M., Samia, P., Vinayan, K. P., Smith, M. L., Carmant, L., Kerr, M., Hermann, B., Dunn, D., & Wilmshurst, J. M. (2018). Systematic review of the screening, diagnosis, and management of ADHD in children with epilepsy. Consensus paper of the Task Force on Comorbidities of the ILAE Pediatric Commission. *Epilepsia*, 59(10), 1867–1880. DOI: 10.1111/epi.14549 PMID: 30178479

Bied, A., Biederman, J., & Faraone, S. (2017). Parent-based diagnosis of ADHD is as accurate as a teacher-based diagnosis of ADHD. *Postgraduate Medicine*, 129(3), 375–381. DOI: 10.1080/00325481.2017.1288064 PMID: 28271921

Bishry, Z., Ramy, H. A., El-Shahawi, H. H., El-Sheikh, M. M., El-Missiry, A. A., & El-Missiry, M. A. (2018). Screening for ADHD in a sample of Egyptian adolescent school students. *Journal of Attention Disorders*, 22(1), 58–65. DOI: 10.1177/1087054714533190 PMID: 24891559

Bussing, R., Koro-Ljungberg, M., Gagnon, J. C., Mason, D. M., Ellison, A., Noguchi, K., Garvan, C. W., & Albarracin, D. (2016). Feasibility of school-based ADHD interventions: A mixed-methods study of perceptions of adolescents and adults. *Journal of Attention Disorders*, 20(5), 400–413. DOI: 10.1177/1087054713515747 PMID: 24448222

Capuzzi, E., Capellazzi, M., Caldiroli, A., Cova, F., Auxilia, A. M., Rubelli, P., & Clerici, M. (2022, January). Screening for ADHD symptoms among criminal offenders: Exploring the association with clinical features. [). MDPI.]. *Health Care*, 10(2), 180. PMID: 35206795

Chamberlain, S. R., Cortese, S., & Grant, J. E. (2021). Screening for adult ADHD using brief rating tools: What can we conclude from a positive screen? Some caveats. *Comprehensive Psychiatry*, 106, 152224. DOI: 10.1016/j.comppsych.2021.152224 PMID: 33581449

Cherkasova, M. V., French, L. R., Syer, C. A., Cousins, L., Galina, H., Ahmadi-Kashani, Y., & Hechtman, L. (2020). Efficacy of cognitive behavioral therapy with and without medication for adults with ADHD: A randomized clinical trial. *Journal of Attention Disorders*, 24(6), 889–903. DOI: 10.1177/1087054716671197 PMID: 28413900

Cheung, K., & Theule, J. (2016). Parental psychopathology in families of children with ADHD: A meta-analysis. *Journal of Child and Family Studies*, 25(12), 3451–3461. DOI: 10.1007/s10826-016-0499-1

Claesdotter, E., Cervin, M., Åkerlund, S., Råstam, M., & Lindvall, M. (2018). The effects of ADHD on cognitive performance. *Nordic Journal of Psychiatry*, 72(3), 158–163. DOI: 10.1080/08039488.2017.1402951 PMID: 29161919

Climie, E. A., & Mastoras, S. M. (2015). ADHD in schools: Adopting a strengths-based perspective. *Canadian Psychology*, 56(3), 295–300. DOI: 10.1037/cap0000030

Coelho, L. F., Barbosa, D. L. F., Rizzutti, S., Bueno, O. F. A., & Miranda, M. C. (2017). Group cognitive behavioral therapy for children and adolescents with ADHD. *Psicologia: Reflexão e Crítica*, 30(1), 11. DOI: 10.1186/s41155-017-0063-y PMID: 32026094

Cornell, H. R., Lin, T. T., & Anderson, J. A. (2018). A systematic review of play-based interventions for students with ADHD: Implications for school-based occupational therapists. *Journal of Occupational Therapy, Schools & Early Intervention*, 11(2), 192–211. DOI: 10.1080/19411243.2018.1432446

Dark, C., Homman-Ludiye, J., & Bryson-Richardson, R. J. (2018). The role of ADHD associated genes in neurodevelopment. *Developmental Biology*, 438(2), 69–83. DOI: 10.1016/j.ydbio.2018.03.023 PMID: 29608877

Do Austerman, J. O. S. E. P. H. (2015). ADHD and behavioral disorders: Assessment, management, and an update from DSM-5. *Cleveland Clinic Journal of Medicine*, 82(11 suppl 1), 3. DOI: 10.3949/ccjm.82.s1.01 PMID: 26555810

Doernberg, E., & Hollander, E. (2016). Neurodevelopmental disorders (ASD and ADHD): Dsm-5, icd-10, and icd-11. *CNS Spectrums*, 21(4), 295–299. DOI: 10.1017/S1092852916000262 PMID: 27364515

DuPaul, G. J., & Langberg, J. M. (2015). Educational impairments in children with ADHD. In Barkley, R. A. (Ed.), *Attention-deficit hyperactivity disorder: A handbook for diagnosis and treatment* (4th ed., pp. 169–190). The Guilford Press.

Efron, D., Nicholson, J. M., Anderson, V., Silk, T., Ukoumunne, O. C., Gulenc, A., Hazell, P., Jongeling, B., & Sciberras, E. (2020). ADHD at age 7 and functional impairments at age 10. *Pediatrics*, 146(5), e20201061. DOI: 10.1542/peds.2020-1061 PMID: 33023991

Evans, S. W., Langberg, J. M., Schultz, B. K., Vaughn, A., Altaye, M., Marshall, S. A., & Zoromski, A. K. (2016). Evaluation of a school-based treatment program for young adolescents with ADHD. *Journal of Consulting and Clinical Psychology*, 84(1), 15–30. DOI: 10.1037/ccp0000057 PMID: 26501496

Goodman, D. W., & Mattingly, G. (2023). Practice guidelines development: The APSARD United States guidelines for the diagnosis and treatment of ADHD in adults. *Psychiatric Annals*, 53(10), 449–454. DOI: 10.3928/00485713-20230911-05

Gordon, C. T., & Fabiano, G. A. (2019). The transition of youth with ADHD into the workforce: Review and future directions. *Clinical Child and Family Psychology Review*, 22(3), 316–347. DOI: 10.1007/s10567-019-00274-4 PMID: 30725305

Haugan, A. L. J., Sund, A. M., Young, S., Thomsen, P. H., Lydersen, S., & Nøvik, T. S. (2022). Cognitive behavioral group therapy as addition to psychoeducation and pharmacological treatment for adolescents with ADHD symptoms and related impairments: A randomised controlled trial. *BMC Psychiatry*, 22(1), 375. DOI: 10.1186/s12888-022-04019-6 PMID: 35655149

Hill, V. C., & Turner, H. (2016). Educational psychologists' perspectives on the medicalization of childhood behavior: A focus on Attention Deficit Hyperactive Disorder (ADHD). *Educational and Child Psychology*, 33(2), 12–29. DOI: 10.53841/bpsecp.2016.33.2.12

Jensen, C. M., Amdisen, B. L., Jørgensen, K. J., & Arnfred, S. M. (2016). Cognitive behavioral therapy for ADHD in adults: Systematic review and meta-analyses. *Attention Deficit and Hyperactivity Disorders*, 8(1), 3–11. DOI: 10.1007/s12402-016-0188-3 PMID: 26801998

Johnston, C., & Chronis-Tuscano, A. (2015). Families and ADHD. In R. A. Barkley (Ed.), *Attention-deficit hyperactivity disorder: A handbook for diagnosis and treatment* (4th ed., pp. 191–209). The Guilford Press. Koutsoklenis, A., & Honkasilta, J. (2023). ADHD in the DSM-5-TR: what has changed and what has not. *Frontiers in Psychiatry, 13*, 1064141.

Karlsdóttir, E. (2019). *School-based treatment for ADHD, professional support and teacher burnout* (Doctoral dissertation).

Mccullough, L. (2019). *Adults with ADHD: Perceptions of college resources to assist with career decisions* (Order No. 27735070). Available from ProQuest Dissertations & Theses Global. (2339172810). https://www.proquest.com/dissertations-theses/adults-with-adhd-perceptions-college-resources/docview/2339172810/se-2

Moffitt, T. E., Houts, R., Asherson, P., Belsky, D. W., Corcoran, D. L., Hammerle, M., Harrington, H. L., Hogan, S., Meier, M. H., Polanczyk, G. V., Poulton, R., Ramrakha, S., Sugden, K., Williams, B., Rohde, L. A., & Caspi, A. (2015). Is adult ADHD a childhood-onset neurodevelopmental disorder? Evidence from a four-decade longitudinal cohort study. *The American Journal of Psychiatry*, 172(10), 967–977. DOI: 10.1176/appi.ajp.2015.14101266 PMID: 25998281

Mohamed, S. M., Butzbach, M., Fuermaier, A. B. M., Weisbrod, M., Aschenbrenner, S., Tucha, L., & Tucha, O. (2021). Basic and complex cognitive functions in Adult ADHD. *PLoS One*, 16(9), e0256228. DOI: 10.1371/journal.pone.0256228 PMID: 34473722

Montagna, A., Karolis, V., Batalle, D., Counsell, S., Rutherford, M., Arulkumaran, S., Happe, F., Edwards, D., & Nosarti, C. (2020). ADHD symptoms and their neurodevelopment correlates in children born very preterm. *PLoS One*, 15(3), e0224343. DOI: 10.1371/journal.pone.0224343 PMID: 32126073

Nøvik, T. S., Haugan, A. L. J., Lydersen, S., Thomsen, P. H., Young, S., & Sund, A. M. (2020). Cognitive–behavioral group therapy for adolescents with ADHD: Study protocol for a randomised controlled trial. *BMJ Open*, 10(3), e032839. DOI: 10.1136/bmjopen-2019-032839 PMID: 32213517

Peterson, B. S., Trampush, J., Brown, M., Maglione, M., Bolshakova, M., Rozelle, M., Miles, J., Pakdaman, S., Yagyu, S., Motala, A., & Hempel, S. (2024). Tools for the diagnosis of ADHD in children and adolescents: A systematic review. *Pediatrics*, 153(4), e2024065854. DOI: 10.1542/peds.2024-065854 PMID: 38523599

Philipsen, A., Jans, T., Graf, E., Matthies, S., Borel, P., Colla, M., & van Elst, L. T. (2015). Effects of group psychotherapy, individual counseling, methylphenidate, and placebo in the treatment of adult attention-deficit/hyperactivity disorder: A randomized clinical trial. *JAMA Psychiatry*, 72(12), 1199–1210. DOI: 10.1001/jamapsychiatry.2015.2146 PMID: 26536057

Rigler, T., Manor, I., Kalansky, A., Shorer, Z., Noyman, I., & Sadaka, Y. (2016). New DSM-5 criteria for ADHD—Does it matter? *Comprehensive Psychiatry*, 68, 56–59. DOI: 10.1016/j.comppsych.2016.03.008 PMID: 27234183

Rogers, M., & Tannock, R. (2018). Are classrooms meeting the basic psychological needs of children with ADHD symptoms? A self-determination theory perspective. *Journal of Attention Disorders*, 22(14), 1354–1360. DOI: 10.1177/1087054713508926 PMID: 24327276

Roselló, B., Berenguer, C., Baixauli, I., Mira, Á., Martinez-Raga, J., & Miranda, A. (2020). Empirical examination of executive functioning, ADHD associated behaviors, and functional impairments in adults with persistent ADHD, remittent ADHD, and without ADHD. *BMC Psychiatry*, 20(1), 1–12. DOI: 10.1186/s12888-020-02542-y PMID: 32204708

Roy, A., Oldehinkel, A. J., & Hartman, C. A. (2017). Cognitive functioning in adolescents with self-reported ADHD and depression: Results from a population-based study. *Journal of Abnormal Child Psychology*, 45(1), 69–81. DOI: 10.1007/s10802-016-0160-x PMID: 27138748

Royal, C., Wade, W., & Nickel, H. (2015). Career development and vocational behavior of adults with attention-deficit/hyperactivity disorder [ADHD]. *Career Planning and Adult Development Journal*, 31(4), 54–63.

Samosh, D., Lilius, J., & Atwood, K. (2024). ADHD and Career Success: Barriers, Facilitators, and Future Research Directions. In *Neurodiversity and Work: Employment, Identity, and Support Networks for Neurominorities* (pp. 257–281). Springer Nature Switzerland. DOI: 10.1007/978-3-031-55072-0_12

Sasser, T., Schoenfelder, E. N., & Stein, M. A. (2017). Targeting functional impairments in the treatment of children and adolescents with ADHD. *CNS Drugs*, 31(2), 97–107. DOI: 10.1007/s40263-016-0400-1 PMID: 27943133

Shabanpour, A., & Mohammadyfar, M. A., TalePesand, S., & Rezaei, A. M. (2017). Comparison of the effectiveness of three methods of cognitive-behavioral therapy (individual counseling, group counseling and parent education) on reduction of ADHD syndrome. *Eurasian Journal of Biosciences*, 11(1).

Shaikh, A. (2018). Group therapy for improving self-esteem and social functioning of college students with ADHD. *Journal of College Student Psychotherapy*, 32(3), 220–241. DOI: 10.1080/87568225.2017.1388755

Sibley, M. H., Altszuler, A. R., Morrow, A. S., & Merrill, B. M. (2014). Mapping the academic problem behaviors of adolescents with ADHD. *School Psychology Quarterly*, 29(4), 422–437. DOI: 10.1037/spq0000071 PMID: 24933215

Silverstein, M. J., Faraone, S. V., Leon, T. L., Biederman, J., Spencer, T. J., & Adler, L. A. (2020). The relationship between executive function deficits and dsm-5-defined ADHD symptoms. *Journal of Attention Disorders*, 24(1), 41–51. DOI: 10.1177/1087054718804347 PMID: 30296883

Steinberg, E. A., & Drabick, D. A. (2015). A developmental psychopathology perspective on ADHD and comorbid conditions: The role of emotion regulation. *Child Psychiatry and Human Development*, 46(6), 951–966. DOI: 10.1007/s10578-015-0534-2 PMID: 25662998

Suhr, J. A., Cook, C., & Morgan, B. (2017). Assessing functional impairment in ADHD: Concerns for validity of self-report. *Psychological Injury and Law*, 10(2), 151–160. DOI: 10.1007/s12207-017-9292-8

Toye, M. K., Wilson, C., & Wardle, G. A. (2019). Education professionals' attitudes towards the inclusion of children with ADHD: The role of knowledge and stigma. *Journal of Research in Special Educational Needs*, 19(3), 184–196. DOI: 10.1111/1471-3802.12441

Wiener, J. (2020). The role of school psychologists in supporting adolescents with ADHD. *Canadian Journal of School Psychology*, 35(4), 299–310. DOI: 10.1177/0829573520923536

Wolraich, M. L., Hagan, J. F.Jr, Allan, C., Chan, E., Davison, D., Earls, M., Evans, S. W., Flinn, S. K., Froehlich, T., Frost, J., Holbrook, J. R., Lehmann, C. U., Lessin, H. R., Okechukwu, K., Pierce, K. L., Winner, J. D., & Zurhellen, W. (2019). Clinical practice guideline for the diagnosis, evaluation, and treatment of attention-deficit/hyperactivity disorder in children and adolescents. *Pediatrics*, 144(4), e20192528. DOI: 10.1542/peds.2019-2528 PMID: 31570648

KEY TERMS AND DEFINITIONS

Academic Needs: Refer to the specific requirements, resources, and support systems essential for students to thrive in their educational pursuits. These needs can differ significantly based on various factors, including individual learning styles, abilities, interests, and challenges faced. Key components of academic needs encompass effective teaching strategies, personalized instruction, access to educational materials, and nurturing learning environments. Students with disabilities or learning challenges may necessitate additional accommodations, such as tailored curricula, assistive technologies, or specialized support interventions. Addressing academic needs is vital for fostering student engagement, self-esteem, and overall success in the educational setting. The roles of teachers, parents, and support personnel are critical in recognizing and fulfilling these needs, ensuring that all students have the opportunity to achieve their maximum potential.

Career Needs: Refer to the array of skills, resources, information, and support that individuals must possess to fulfill their career aspirations and successfully navigate the job market. These needs can differ significantly based on personal interests, skill sets, educational qualifications, and current industry dynamics. Essential elements of career needs include access to relevant training programs, mentorship, career counseling services, effective job search techniques, and opportunities for professional development and advancement. To adequately address these needs, it is important to provide guidance in career exploration, planning, decision-making, and skill acquisition. By addressing career needs, individuals are better equipped to make informed choices, achieve job satisfaction, and adapt to shifts in the job market, ultimately leading to successful and fulfilling career paths.

Clinical Practice Guidelines: Meticulously formulated recommendations intended to aid healthcare professionals in making well-informed decisions regarding patient care. These guidelines are grounded in evidence derived from clinical research, expert consensus, and established best practices within the medical and psychological domains. They provide standardized procedures for the diagnosis, treatment, and management of specific health conditions. The primary objective of clinical practice guidelines is to enhance the quality and uniformity of care, minimize variability in treatment methods, and ensure patient safety. They encompass various facets of healthcare, including assessment techniques, intervention approaches, and follow-up procedures. By following these guidelines, practitioners can deliver evidence-based, effective, and ethically sound care that is customized to meet the individual needs of each patient.

Cognitive Functioning: Refers to the array of mental processes that facilitate knowledge acquisition, reasoning, memory retention, and problem-solving. This includes capabilities such as attention, memory, comprehension of language, decision-making, and executive functioning. Such cognitive abilities are vital for performing daily tasks, engaging in learning, communicating effectively, and adjusting to new environments. Individual differences in cognitive abilities can be influenced by various factors, including age, educational experiences, health conditions, and the development of the brain. Cognitive impairments may occur due to conditions such as dementia, traumatic brain injuries, or learning disabilities. Strategies to enhance cognitive functioning include cognitive training, therapeutic approaches, and the creation of environments that encourage mental agility and effective problem-solving.

Diagnosis: Refers to the systematic process of determining a specific condition, disorder, or issue through a comprehensive evaluation of symptoms, behaviors, and pertinent information. In both medical and psychological fields, this process entails gathering data via assessments, observations, interviews, and standardized testing to gain insight into an individual's health status. Professionals, including physicians, psychologists, and therapists, rely on established diagnostic criteria such as the DSM-5 or ICD-10 to classify and identify conditions such as depression, ADHD, or learning disabilities. An accurate diagnosis is essential for developing effective treatment or intervention strategies that are customized to meet the unique needs of the individual. It clarifies the underlying problems and informs decisions regarding suitable support, therapies, or medications, thereby assisting individuals in managing or overcoming their difficulties.

Diagnostic and Statistical Manual of Mental Disorders, (DSM-5): An extensive resource published by the American Psychiatric Association (APA). It establishes standardized criteria for the diagnosis of mental health disorders, detailing symptoms, prevalence rates, and related characteristics. The DSM-5 is an essential tool for mental health practitioners, enabling them to accurately identify and categorize a diverse array of psychological conditions, including mood disorders, anxiety disorders, personality disorders, and neurodevelopmental disorders. This manual supports consistent diagnosis, informs treatment strategies, and facilitates research within the domains of psychology and psychiatry. Furthermore, the DSM-5 incorporates the latest insights and findings in mental health, assisting clinicians in implementing evidence-based practices.

Educational Psychologists: Experts who investigate the dynamics of learning and development in educational settings. They aim to understand the psychological factors that influence learning, behavior, and the development of children and adolescents. Their work involves assessing the cognitive, emotional, and social needs of students and providing actionable recommendations to enhance educational achievements. These professionals work in partnership with teachers, parents, and school administrators to design effective interventions, assist students with special needs, and establish conducive learning environments. Utilizing psychological assessments and strategies grounded in research, educational psychologists address issues such as learning disabilities, behavioral challenges, and emotional difficulties. Their ultimate mission is to improve the learning experiences of students, promote mental health, and support their holistic development.

Family Dynamics: Refer to the established patterns of interaction, relationships, and roles within a family system. These dynamics are instrumental in shaping how family members communicate, resolve conflicts, provide support, and navigate challenges. Influencing factors include parenting styles, cultural values, economic status, and the presence of stressors or mental health issues. Healthy family dynamics are characterized by open communication, mutual respect, and emotional support, fostering an environment that encourages personal growth and development. In contrast, unhealthy dynamics, such as persistent conflict, ineffective communication, or rigid roles, can lead to increased stress and psychological challenges. Understanding family dynamics is vital for therapists in addressing family-related issues and promoting healthier, more supportive relationships.

Functional Impairments: Refer to the restrictions or difficulties experienced in performing daily activities and tasks due to various physical, cognitive, emotional, or psychological conditions. These impairments have a significant impact on vital areas of functioning, such as self-care, mobility, communication, social interactions, and work-related duties. They may arise from conditions such as mental disorders, developmental disabilities, physical injuries, or chronic health conditions. Assessing functional impairments is important for professionals to understand the influence of a condition on an individual's daily life and to create targeted interventions that can improve their quality of life. Supportive strategies, therapeutic interventions, and necessary accommodations play a critical role in assisting individuals to overcome or adapt to these challenges, ultimately fostering greater independence and well-being.

Group Therapy: A form of psychological treatment where a therapist leads a small group of individuals who face similar challenges or concerns. This therapeutic approach allows participants to share their thoughts and feelings, gain insights from the experiences of others, and develop social and coping skills in a supportive setting. It is commonly employed to address issues such as depression, anxiety, addiction, grief, and social difficulties. The group context fosters a sense of community and diminishes feelings of isolation, encouraging members to learn from each other and provide mutual support. Through facilitated discussions, role-playing, and feedback, individuals can enhance their self-awareness, empathy, and the quality of their relationships.

Individual Therapy: Often referred to as one-on-one therapy, entails a confidential and direct engagement between a therapist and a client. This therapeutic approach emphasizes the exploration of the client's personal challenges, thoughts, and feelings, aiming to promote healing, personal development, and effective problem-solving. The therapist assists the client in recognizing behavioral patterns, comprehending underlying emotions, and cultivating healthier coping mechanisms. This form of therapy is beneficial for a variety of issues, including depression, anxiety, trauma, and relationship difficulties. The private environment fosters a sense of safety for clients to discuss sensitive matters, receive tailored support, and progress at their own pace toward their objectives and enhanced well-being.

Neurodevelopment: The term used to describe the evolution and maturation of the brain and nervous system, which in turn influences cognitive, emotional, and behavioral functions. This developmental begins in the prenatal stage and continues through early adulthood, shaping how individuals perceive, process, and react to their environment. The process is shaped by a combination of genetic factors, early life experiences, and environmental conditions. Healthy neurodevelopment is critical for effective learning, social interactions, and adaptive behaviors. Disruptions in this process can result in conditions such as autism spectrum disorder (ASD), Attention-Deficit/Hyperactivity Disorder (ADHD), or intellectual disabilities. Gaining insights into neurodevelopment is vital for professionals to formulate interventions and support systems that promote optimal growth and well-being for those facing neurodevelopmental challenges.

Psychopathology: Refers to the scientific examination of mental disorders, encompassing their origins, progression, symptoms, and impacts on behavior and cognitive functions. This field investigates various conditions, including depression, anxiety disorders, schizophrenia, bipolar disorder, and personality disorders. The primary objective of psychopathology is to comprehend the biological, psychological, and social influences that lead to these disorders, as well as to establish effective methods for their diagnosis, treatment, and management. By analyzing patterns of atypical thoughts, emotions, and behaviors, mental health practitioners can achieve more precise diagnoses and formulate appropriate therapeutic strategies. Ultimately, psychopathology plays a crucial role in enhancing the understanding of mental health, diminishing stigma, and advocating for evidence-based interventions for those facing psychological challenges.

School-Based Professionals: A collective of educators and support staff who function within schools to address the diverse academic, social, and emotional needs of students. This group comprises teachers, school counselors, social workers, educational psychologists, special education staff, and administrators. Their collective aim is to foster a safe and supportive educational environment, identify and address various challenges, and provide resources that facilitate student achievement. These professionals collaborate to formulate individualized education plans, carry out assessments, and implement interventions for students encountering academic or behavioral difficulties. By promoting a positive school climate, they support student well-being, engagement, and academic success, ensuring that all students receive the necessary assistance.

Screening: An initial evaluative procedure designed to identify individuals who may have particular issues, conditions, or needs that warrant additional assessment or intervention. In educational and healthcare contexts, screening tools are utilized to identify early signs of learning difficulties, developmental delays, mental health issues, or physical health problems. This process is usually brief and focuses on critical indicators, aiding professionals in deciding whether a more detailed assessment or diagnosis is required. For example, schools commonly employ screening methods to detect students who may struggle with reading or show behavioral difficulties. By conducting early screenings, timely support and interventions can be provided, leading to improved outcomes and the prevention of more significant issues in the future.

APPENDIX I: STUDY QUESTIONNAIRE

Table 3. Educational psychologists' perspectives on practice guidelines for students with ADHD questionnaire (EPPPGSAQ)

No	Statements	NAA	SE	ME	GE	VGE
1	To what extent do you follow practice guidelines for ADHD in your work?					
2	To what extent do you often incorporate ADHD guidelines into student career transition planning?					
3	To what extent do you find the current ADHD guidelines effective in supporting the career transition of students?					
4	To what extent do you feel prepared to implement ADHD guidelines?					
5	To what extent do you understand ADHD guidelines for educational settings?					
6	To what extent do you frequently update your knowledge about ADHD guidelines?					
7	To what extent do you feel confident are you in your ability to support students with ADHD in their career transition using existing guidelines?					
8	To what extent do ADHD guidelines influence your practice?					
9	To what extent do you often collaborate with others using ADHD guidelines?					
10	To what extent do you consider ADHD guidelines to be important in your role as an educational psychologist?					
11	To what extent do you perceive the impact of ADHD guidelines on student outcomes?					
12	To what extent do you find current ADHD guidelines accessible?					
13	To what extent do you often participate in training on ADHD guidelines?					
14	To what extent do you communicate ADHD guidelines to colleagues?					
15	To what extent do you consider ADHD guidelines to be effective in addressing career transitions?					
16	To what extent do you rate your knowledge of ADHD intervention guidelines?					
17	To what extent do you often evaluate the effectiveness of ADHD guidelines?					
18	To what extent are your colleagues supportive of implementing ADHD guidelines?					
19	To what extent do you perceive the role of ADHD guidelines in educational policy?					
20	To what extent do you often reflect on your practice in terms of ADHD guidelines?					
21	To what extent do you perceive challenges in implementing ADHD guidelines?					
22	To what extent do you rate the clarity of ADHD guidelines?					

NAA=Not at All, SE=Small Extent, ME=Moderate Extent, GE=Great Extent, VGE=Very Great Extent

APPENDIX II: ADDITIONAL STATISTICS

Table 4. Item-total statistics

No	Statements	Cronbach's Alpha if Item Deleted
1	To what extent do you follow practice guidelines for ADHD in your work?	.925
2	To what extent do you often incorporate ADHD guidelines into student career transition planning?	.922
3	To what extent do you find the current ADHD guidelines effective in supporting the career transition of students?	.921
4	To what extent do you feel prepared to implement ADHD guidelines?	.923
5	To what extent do you understand ADHD guidelines for educational settings?	.924
6	To what extent do you frequently update your knowledge about ADHD guidelines?	.925
7	To what extent do you feel confident are you in your ability to support students with ADHD in their career transition using existing guidelines?	.922
8	To what extent do ADHD guidelines influence your practice?	.921
9	To what extent do you often collaborate with others using ADHD guidelines?	.924
10	To what extent do you consider ADHD guidelines to be important in your role as an educational psychologist?	.926
11	To what extent do you perceive the impact of ADHD guidelines on student outcomes?	.924
12	To what extent do you find current ADHD guidelines accessible?	.923
13	To what extent do you often participate in training on ADHD guidelines?	.925
14	To what extent do you communicate ADHD guidelines to colleagues?	.924
15	To what extent do you consider ADHD guidelines to be effective in addressing career transitions?	.925
16	To what extent do you rate your knowledge of ADHD intervention guidelines?	.924
17	To what extent do you often evaluate the effectiveness of ADHD guidelines?	.923
18	To what extent are your colleagues supportive of implementing ADHD guidelines?	.934
19	To what extent do you perceive the role of ADHD guidelines in educational policy?	.934
20	To what extent do you often reflect on your practice in terms of ADHD guidelines?	.932
21	To what extent do you perceive challenges in implementing ADHD guidelines?	.931
22	To what extent do you rate the clarity of ADHD guidelines?	.931

Table 5. Communalities (extraction method: principal component analysis)

No	Statements	Extraction
1	To what extent do you follow practice guidelines for ADHD in your work?	.963
2	To what extent do you often incorporate ADHD guidelines into student career transition planning?	.813
3	To what extent do you find the current ADHD guidelines effective in supporting the career transition of students?	.896
4	To what extent do you feel prepared to implement ADHD guidelines?	.781
5	To what extent do you understand ADHD guidelines for educational settings?	.714
6	To what extent do you frequently update your knowledge about ADHD guidelines?	.963
7	To what extent do you feel confident are you in your ability to support students with ADHD in their career transition using existing guidelines?	.813
8	To what extent do ADHD guidelines influence your practice?	.896
9	To what extent do you often collaborate with others using ADHD guidelines?	.899
10	To what extent do you consider ADHD guidelines to be important in your role as an educational psychologist?	.775
11	To what extent do you perceive the impact of ADHD guidelines on student outcomes?	.948
12	To what extent do you find current ADHD guidelines accessible?	.927
13	To what extent do you often participate in training on ADHD guidelines?	.738
14	To what extent do you communicate ADHD guidelines to colleagues?	.848
15	To what extent do you consider ADHD guidelines to be effective in addressing career transitions?	.806
16	To what extent do you rate your knowledge of ADHD intervention guidelines?	.948
17	To what extent do you often evaluate the effectiveness of ADHD guidelines?	.927
18	To what extent are your colleagues supportive of implementing ADHD guidelines?	.949
19	To what extent do you perceive the role of ADHD guidelines in educational policy?	.949
20	To what extent do you often reflect on your practice in terms of ADHD guidelines?	.697
21	To what extent do you perceive challenges in implementing ADHD guidelines?	.958
22	To what extent do you rate the clarity of ADHD guidelines?	.958

Chapter 6
Perspectives on School Support Services for Students With ADHD:
Student Survey

ABSTRACT

This predictive correlational survey investigated the perceived effectiveness of school support services for students with ADHD during career transition, focusing on the predictive influence of gender, school location, and grade level. The study participants were 62 students drawn purposively from junior and senior secondary grades. Data were collected using the School Support Services for Students with ADHD Questionnaire (SSSSAQ). The findings revealed a generally low perception of the effectiveness of school support services among students with ADHD during career transition, with an overall mean score of 2.25. The study concludes that gender, school location, and grade level do not significantly predict the perceived effectiveness of school support services among students with ADHD during career transition. The study elucidates the inadequacies in current support services for students with ADHD, highlighting the need for increased efforts towards providing effective school support services to foster career transition for these students.

BACKGROUND

Every institution requires a support system, which often serves as the backbone for its operations (Eseadi, 2023; Onyishi, 2024). According to Eseadi and Diale (2024), institutional support comprises a wide variety of activities and resources that institutions utilize to promote effective management, operational success, and enduring growth. In the context of students with disabilities, this support includes a diverse set of services and accommodations. In a school setting, recognizing the diverse perspectives and attitudes within the support system significantly influences the overall success and achievements of students. It is important to note that students with attention-deficit/hyperactivity disorder (ADHD) consistently face challenges in the academic environment, as the characteristics of the disorder limit their ability to succeed. They face a heightened risk of experiencing academic underperformance, facing social isolation, and potentially dropping out of school before completion (Oke et al., 2019; Sciberras et al., 2009). To tackle the difficulties encountered by students with ADHD, educational institutions have established support services aimed at assisting them. When determining the most effective ways to support students' success, it is crucial to consider their perspectives. Some examples of school support services include appropriate accommodations (Gregg, 2009), psychosocial interventions (Wolf, et al., 2009), and academic interventions (Weyandt et al., 2008). The academic interventions may include tutoring, individualized education plans, and coaching (DuPaul et al., 2014). Norvilitis and Fang (2005) revealed that 68% of American students and 85% of Chinese students believed that educational institutions lack adequate support services for students with ADHD. In another study, students indicated that ADHD coaching contributed to their improved self-regulation, resulting in enhanced academic experiences and outcomes (Parker et al., 2013). The authors also indicated that students viewed ADHD coaching as a distinctive service that fostered the development of more constructive beliefs, positive emotions, and self-regulated behaviors. According to Fabiano et al. (2024), subpar academic achievements are often attributed to the dearth of evidence-based intervention services in school settings, a diminished appreciation for the relevance of general education environments in offering behavioral support, and an undue emphasis on assessment and classification over intervention. The authors advocated for the integration of ADHD screening, intervention, and maintenance within Multi-Tiered Systems of Support in general education, suggesting that special education eligibility should be limited to students who need more intensive support. Hart et al. (2017) showed that there is a decline in behavioral support for students with ADHD during their transition. Grove (2021) identified ADHD medication as the main therapeutic support for students with ADHD, who found it beneficial for improving concentration, despite facing physical and socio-emotional side effects. Most of the students did not participate in psychosocial support systems, preferring to depend on their own capabilities. Those who did engage with these systems expressed a range of opinions. These students recounted the academic strategies they implemented and conveyed a need for more tutorials, support groups, and greater social awareness about ADHD in the context of higher education.

Golson et al. (2022) highlighted the importance of involving students with ADHD in the decision-making processes regarding support services in their schools. According to the authors, these students' perspectives demonstrate a clear preference for the inclusion of parents and interdisciplinary community professionals in such services. However, these students are often overlooked in the planning stages despite their awareness of the advantages and possible ways of improving these services. In their study, Mytkowicz and Goss (2012) examined how students with ADHD perceived the outcomes of their involvement in support programs. The authors revealed that students noted improvements in self-authorship, self-determination, metacognitive awareness, academic competencies, and their self-perception as learners. The authors attributed these improvements to mentoring relationships and metacognitive conversations with faculty, emphasizing the importance of a metacognitive, dialogic framework, the role of caring and supportive mentorship, and the need to merge emotional and cognitive components in support programs tailored for students with ADHD. DuPaul et al. (2014) revealed a significant disparity between the documented effective services for students with ADHD and the actual services provided in educational settings. Similarly, Moore et al. (2017) indicated that evidence is scarce concerning school-based intervention services aimed at assisting students with ADHD. Various factors can affect how students with ADHD perceive and access school support services. Factors such as socioeconomic status, cultural and linguistic backgrounds, and government policies may play a role in determining the availability of these services for students with ADHD (Zendarski et al., 2020). A comprehensive understanding of these factors will enable schools to customize their approaches to providing support services and making them more effective for students with ADHD. This understanding will also inform future strategies aimed at enhancing support services for these students. There is a significant lack of literature addressing the perception of Nigerian students with ADHD, concerning the school support services available. The scarcity of literature highlights the critical need to conduct studies to understand how these students perceive the various school support services intended to aid them. Loe and Feldman (2007) emphasized the necessity for research to assess whether current or novel intervention services can enhance skills in reading, writing, and mathematics, decrease grade retention, minimize expulsions and detentions, improve graduation rates, and increase the likelihood of students with ADHD completing postsecondary education. In Nigeria, current school support services appear to be failing to adequately cater to the career transition needs of these students rendering them susceptible to poor academic performance and other negative outcomes (*see* Lasisi et al., 2017; Oke et al., 2019). Existing secondary school services frameworks in Nigeria seem not to be placing sufficient emphasis on the necessity of specialized support services for students with ADHD. As a result, many public secondary schools operate without the requisite resources and adequately trained personnel to deliver effective support services to students across board. This situation is further complicated by cultural stigmas, myths, and misconceptions surrounding disabilities such as ADHD (Olatunji et al., 2023), which may discourage these students from seeking help or advocating for means of meeting their support needs in schools. Therefore, it is essential to gather insights directly from students with ADHD about their experiences with school support services during career transition. Conducting a survey that focuses on student perspectives can highlight the strengths and weaknesses of the current support systems available to these students. The present study aims to investigate students' perceptions of school support services available for students with ADHD in Abia State, Nigeria.

Research Objectives

1. To ascertain the mean perspectives on the effectiveness of school support services for students with ADHD during career transitioning.
2. To examine the extent gender predicts the perceived effectiveness of school support services for students with ADHD during career transitioning.
3. To examine the extent school location predicts the perceived effectiveness of school support services for students with ADHD during career transitioning.
4. To examine the extent grade level predicts the perceived effectiveness of school support services for students with ADHD during career transitioning.

Research Questions

1. What is the mean perspective on the effectiveness of school support services for students with ADHD during career transitioning?
2. To what extent does gender (male and female) predict the perceived effectiveness of school support services for students with ADHD during career transitioning?
3. To what extent does school location (rural and urban) predict the perceived effectiveness of school support services for students with ADHD during career transitioning?
4. To what extent does grade level (junior and senior grades) predict the perceived effectiveness of school support services for students with ADHD during career transitioning?

Theoretical Framework

Our research adopts the ecological systems theory propounded by Urie Bronfenbrenner, which posits that an individual's growth is shaped by five interconnected systems: the microsystem, mesosystem, exosystem, macrosystem, and chronosystem (Härkönen, 2007). Rogers et al. (2015) revealed that the ecological systems theory delineates the multiple factors influencing the functioning of students with ADHD within the school environment, addressing aspects at the child, classroom, and family levels. Denis (2012) stated that when an entity is socially constructed or shaped by perceptions, the norms related to that constructed entity are affected by the existing systems within a social context. The theory presents an integrative framework for understanding the ways in which various environmental and individual factors affect students' perceptions of the support services provided by schools. This theoretical framework underscores the importance of the microsystem, which includes immediate contexts like the school setting, where students with ADHD interact closely with educators, counselors, and fellow students. These everyday engagements are crucial in forming the students' experiences and play a vital role in determining their perceptions of the support services available to them. By investigating students' perspectives on the support they receive, the study delves into the microsystem, facilitating an analysis of how these direct interactions within the school context shape their opinions regarding the services aimed at supporting their career transitions. The mesosystem encompasses the relationships among the different systems that an individual engages with, including home, educational institutions, and wider societal norms. Gender plays a crucial role in this context, as it frequently influences students' experiences within the educational setting through established cultural norms and societal expectations. For instance, boys and girls diagnosed with ADHD may encounter distinct challenges and varying degrees of support shaped by these gender-specific societal standards. By concentrating on the mesosystem, the theory offers a framework for examining how gendered interactions within these interconnected systems affect students' views on the support services available to them. The research also explores how the geographical location of schools affects students' views on the effectiveness of support services. This aspect is connected to Bronfenbrenner's exosystem, which encompasses broader community influences that indirectly shape an individual's experiences. For instance, the availability of resources in urban compared to rural schools may influence the quality and accessibility of support services. By analyzing how these location-related differences affect students' perceptions, the study utilizes the exosystem framework to understand how community contexts inform students' opinions on school support services. The research investigates the role of grade level as a determinant of perceived support service effectiveness, aligning with Bronfenbrenner's chronosystem. This framework considers the changes and transitions in an individual's life over time, illustrating how perceptions may shift as students advance through various educational stages. As students with ADHD progress through different grades, their requirements and interactions with support services are likely to evolve, reflecting their developmental milestones and growing autonomy. This temporal aspect of the chronosystem enables the study to assess how perceptions of support services may change as students move through their educational journey, offering valuable insights into how these services can be tailored to meet the changing needs of students (see Figure 1).

Figure 1. Study framework

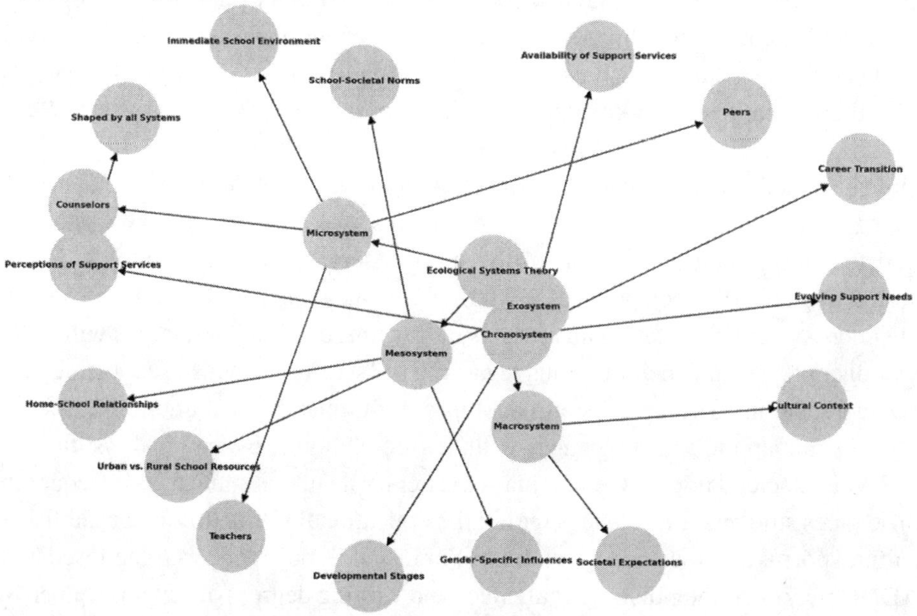

METHODOLOGY

Ethics Statement

Ethical approval for this study was obtained from the relevant institutional review boards. First, it received approval from the Research Ethics Committee of the Faculty of Education, University of Nigeria, Nigeria. It also received additional ethical approval from the Faculty of Education Research Ethics Committee at the University of Johannesburg, South Africa (Sem 2-2020-057). Informed assent was secured from participants, while written informed consent was obtained from their parents/guardians. We assured confidentiality and clarified participants' right to withdraw from the study at any given time.

Research Design and Approach

Research design outlines the methodologies employed in a study, detailing the timing and conditions under which data will be collected (Hassan, 2016). Correlational research represents a form of non-experimental inquiry that aids in predicting and elucidating the relationships between variables (Seeram, 2019). The objective of correlational studies is to investigate whether variations in the characteristics of a population exist based on the exposure of its subjects to a particular event within a naturalistic context (Lau, 2017). The results derived from correlational research can inform the understanding of prevalence and interrelations among variables, as well as enable the forecasting of events based on existing data and insights (Curtis et al., 2016). This research employed a predictive correlational survey research design. Correlational research is classified as a quantitative research method (Asamoah, 2014). The study adopted a quantitative research approach. A quantitative research framework can be categorized into three types: experiments, quasi-experiments, and non-experiments (Jopling, 2019).

Research Paradigm

This study is grounded in the positivist research paradigm. A paradigm can be defined as a conceptual framework that serves as a model from which specific, coherent traditions of scientific inquiry emerges (Somekh & Lewin, 2004). Quantitative methodology is commonly characterized as a method of conducting social research that employs a natural science perspective, particularly a positivist approach, to examine social phenomena (Bryman, 1984). Advocates of quantitative methods maintain assumptions that align with a positivist philosophy (Onwuegbuzie, 2000). The positivist and interpretivist paradigms form the foundation for quantitative and qualitative methods, respectively (Howe, 1988). The positivist approach adheres to a structured quantitative research process, emphasizing the numerical measurement of social phenomena, while the interpretivist and social constructionist approaches aim to understand social reality by exploring and generating knowledge through qualitative research (Akhter & Ferdous, 2019). Positivism encompasses a range of ideological and philosophical stances that are typically linked to quantitative research. It is characterized by a belief in an objective reality and the endeavor to substantiate priori theories through empirical evidence, which is predominantly quantitative in nature (Baltes & Ralph, 2022).

Study Area

This research was conducted in Abia State in the South-east zone of Nigeria. Abia State is located in the southeastern region of Nigeria (Igboekwe & Nwankwo, 2011). The capital city of Abia State is Umuahia (Onyeonoro et al., 2023). It shares its northern border with Enugu State, its southern border with Rivers State, its eastern borders with Cross River and Akwa Ibom States, and its western border with Imo State (Igboekwe & Nwankwo, 2011)

Population and Sampling

The study involves 62 students across junior and senior secondary school grades from selected public secondary schools. Non-probability sampling diverges from the established principles of probability sampling, signifying that the inclusion of units occurs with probabilities that are either unknown or known to be zero for some (Wolf et al., 2016). Convenience and purposive sampling are two prominent forms of non-probability sampling methods. The purposive sampling approach is particularly effective for examining specific cultural domains, especially when engaging with experts who possess relevant knowledge (Tongco, 2007). It is essential to differentiate between convenience sampling and purposive sampling, as convenience sampling is a non-probabilistic method that can be applied in both qualitative and quantitative research, although it is more commonly associated with quantitative studies (Suen et al., 2014). A total of 33 (53.2%) junior-grade students and 29 (46.8%) senior-grade students were selected using purposive and convenience sampling techniques. By gender, 23 (37.1%) respondents were male students, whereas 39 (62.9%) respondents were female students. Twenty-seven student respondents (43.5%) were selected from rural schools, whereas 35 (56.5%) students were from urban schools. The mean age of students was 13.03 ± 1.55 years.

Data Collection

The data was collected using a questionnaire. The researchers received help from two postgraduate students to complete the data collection process. The questionnaire used for data collection is called the School Support Services for Students with ADHD Questionnaire (SSSSAQ). It is an 18-item scale that measures the perceived effectiveness of school support services for students with ADHD during career transitions. The respondents are students diagnosed with ADHD. The 5-point Likert-type scale is designed to allow respondents to indicate their level of agreement or perception for each item, with 1 indicating "Not at All" and 5 indicating "Great Extent." Some examples of item statements in the questionnaire include: "To what extent do you find the academic support provided by your school effective for your career transition?", and "To what extent is your school supportive in helping you set realistic career goals??" The SSSSAQ has a good internal consistency reliability, with a Cronbach's alpha of 0.89 in the present research.

Data Analysis

Statistical analysis was conducted using Jeffreys' Amazing Statistics Program software (JASP), version 0.18.3 and Statistical Package for the Social Sciences (SPSS), version 27. JASP is a free and user-friendly statistical software designed to facilitate data analysis (Ashour, 2024). As an open-source application, JASP features an intuitive graphical user interface and employs the R programming language for its analytical processes. It supports a range of advanced analyses, including meta-analysis, network analysis, factor analysis, and structural equation modeling (Panchawagh et al., 2023). In comparison, the Statistical Package for Social Sciences (SPSS) is recognized as one of the pioneering software packages for statistical data analysis (Nwaigwe, 2021). Descriptive statistics was used to summarize the sociodemographic data, while inferential statistics (regression and correlation analysis) were used to analyse the research questions at a .05 significance level. Descriptive statistics encompass both numerical and graphical methods employed to systematically organize, present, and analyze data (Fisher & Marshall, 2009). These techniques serve to summarize data effectively by elucidating the relationships between variables within a sample or population (Kaur et al., 2018). In contrast, inferential statistics facilitate the process of making generalizations about an entire population based on observations derived from a sample (Stapor, 2020), thereby enabling the extraction of statistically significant information.

FINDINGS

Table 1. Mean perspective on the effectiveness of school support services for students with ADHD during career transitioning

Gender	Location	Grade Level	Mean	Std. Deviation	N
Male students	Rural schools	Junior Grades	1.77	.51	6
		Senior Grades	2.94	.00	1
		Total	1.94	.64	7
	Urban schools	Junior Grades	2.27	.39	11
		Senior Grades	2.19	.22	5
		Total	2.24	.34	16
	Total	Junior Grades	2.09	.48	17
		Senior Grades	2.31	.37	6
		Total	2.15	.46	23
Female students	Rural schools	Junior Grades	2.37	.26	8
		Senior Grades	2.44	.31	12
		Total	2.41	.29	20
	Urban schools	Junior Grades	2.08	.65	8
		Senior Grades	2.29	.45	11
		Total	2.20	.54	19
	Total	Junior Grades	2.23	.49	16
		Senior Grades	2.37	.39	23
		Total	2.31	.43	39
Total	Rural schools	Junior Grades	2.11	.48	14
		Senior Grades	2.48	.33	13
		Total	2.29	.45	27
	Urban schools	Junior Grades	2.19	.50	19
		Senior Grades	2.26	.39	16
		Total	2.22	.45	35
	Total	Junior Grades	2.16	.49	33
		Senior Grades	2.36	.38	29
		Total	2.25	.45	62

The mean perspective on the effectiveness of school support services for students with ADHD during career transitioning can be inferred from the overall mean scores presented in Table 1. The total mean score across all students, regardless of gender, location, or grade, is 2.25, with a standard deviation of 0.45. This suggests a low perception of the effectiveness of school support services for students with ADHD during career transitioning.

Table 2. Pearson's correlations among variables

Variables		Pearson's r
Gender -	Location	-.203
Gender -	Grade	.318*
Gender -	SSSSAQ	.174
Location	Grade	-.024
Location	SSSSAQ	-.075
Grade -	SSSSAQ	.225

Table 2 shows a Pearson correlation of .174 between gender and perceived effectiveness (SSSSAQ), which is not significant. The Pearson correlation between location and perceived effectiveness is -.075, as shown in Table 2, which is also non-significant. The Pearson correlation between grade level and perceived effectiveness is .225, which indicates a moderate positive relationship, but it is not statistically significant.

Table 3. Regression analysis of predictors of the perceived effectiveness of school support services among students with ADHD during career transitioning

Model	Unstandardized	Standard Error	T	P	95%CI Lower Upper
H_0 (Intercept)	2.14	.126	17.001	< .001	1.885, 2.388
Gender	.09	.126	.751	.46	-.157, .346
Location	-.05	.116	-.385	.70	-.277, .188
Class Grade	.17	.119	1.425	.16	-.069, .408

Table 3 shows the regression analysis results, indicating that gender does not significantly predict the perceived effectiveness of school support services among students with ADHD during career transitioning, as the p-value is .46 and unstandardized coefficient is .09. The regression analysis shows that school location does not significantly predict perceived effectiveness of school support services among students with ADHD during career transitioning, as the p-value is .70 and unstandardized coefficient is -.05. According to Table 3, the grade level does not significantly predict perceived effectiveness of school support services among students with ADHD during career transitioning, as the p-value is .16 and unstandardized coefficient is .17. Figure 2 shows the relationship between the predictors and the perceived effectiveness of school support services among students with ADHD during career transitioning.

Figure 2. Scatterplot showing the regression model

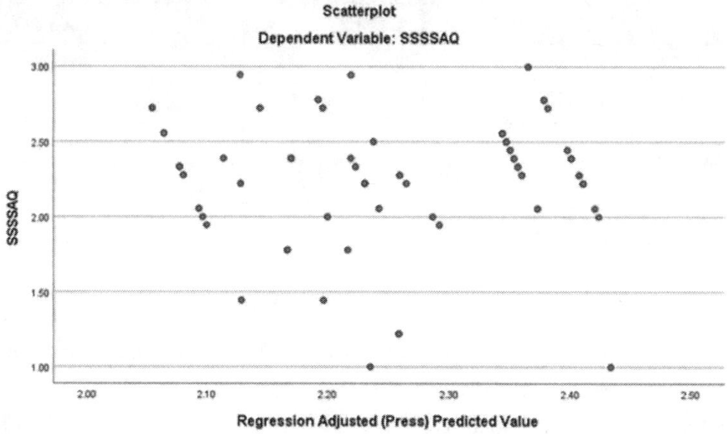

DISCUSSION

This study examined students' perceptions of school support services available for students with ADHD in Abia State, Nigeria. The study found that none of the factors (gender, location, or grade level) significantly predict the perceived effectiveness of school support services among students with ADHD during career transitioning. However, there exists a range of similar and differing perspectives among various authors regarding this issue. For instance, a study conducted by Graczyk et al. (2005) in several urban schools revealed that neither the child's gender nor the subtype of ADHD affected the effectiveness ratings of classroom intervention services. DuPaul et al. (2017) highlighted that while many students utilizing school-based support services, such as coaching, experience academic improvements, those with ADHD show the most substantial increases in grade point average as a result of this support. Furthermore, Zendarski et al. (2020) reported that around 60% of students with ADHD sought educational support during an academic year, with this support being unaffected by factors such as age, gender, ADHD medication use, or socioeconomic status. According to Spiel (2013), students who qualified for services under the Individuals with Disabilities Education Improvement Act demonstrated markedly lower estimated IQ and achievement scores than their ADHD counterparts who were supported by Section 504 or those who did not receive any form of assistance. Schultz and Evans (2012) further clarified that in secondary school settings, students interact with numerous teachers each day, and perceptions of the same student can vary significantly among different teachers. As a result, the data obtained from rating scales may be unclear, depending on which teachers are included in the assessment. Rueger et al. (2008) revealed gender differences in how social support relates to various measures of student adjustment. Regarding the influence of academic accommodations on academic performance, the study by Morris et al. (2023) indicated that women, on average, achieved better academic outcomes. This does not suggest that this support service is more favorable to women; there might be other underlying factors. Tiikkaja and Tindberg (2021) observed that students with ADHD indicated that their conditions adversely affected their school experience, leading to diminished school-related well-being. In other words, there are adverse effects of ADHD; the condition poses a lot of challenges to the individual, and sometimes, the support services available might not be familiar to them or sufficient for them. Arciuli et al. (2019) indicated a notable interaction between disability and gender, with girls who have disabilities reporting the lowest levels of school satisfaction. This effect seemed to be more significantly influenced by the perceived lack of support from teachers than by other factors. Previous research on boys and girls with ADHD, spanning from preschool to adolescence, corroborates that substantial levels of impairment persist (Rucklidge, 2010) regardless of the various support services. Bussing et al. (1998a) noted that factors such as being female, belonging to a minority group, and residing in a rural area were associated with a decreased likelihood of accessing ADHD services within the general health sector. Conversely, the necessity for services among children was a significant predictor of service utilization in both the mental health and informal sectors.

There are rare circumstances where the support service presents problems rather than improving the challenges. O'Callaghan and Sharma (2014) found that students receiving academic accommodations exhibited significantly higher symptoms of ADHD. Bussing et al. (1998b) found that girls receiving special education services were over three times more likely than boys to experience unmet service needs, with factors such as minority status, low income, and health maintenance organization coverage identified as potential risk factors. Rhinehart et al. (2022) found that, after controlling for academic and social skills, female students, those of Hispanic/Latinx descent, and children from households where a language other than English is spoken were less likely to access special education services for ADHD. Locke et al. (2017) identified disparities in service utilization among different racial and ethnic groups, both within and across diagnostic categories, for both in-school and out-of-school services. The authors argued that variations in the utilization of school-based behavioral health services among different racial and ethnic groups highlight the necessity for culturally sensitive outreach and the customization of services to enhance service engagement. Another study utilising a multicomponent function-based intervention demonstrated a reduction in target problem behaviors and an increase in academic engagement in reading, writing, and mathematics among students with ADHD (Cho & Blair, 2017). The findings from the study by Veenman et al. (2018) on the effectiveness of a low-intensive behavioral teacher program indicated that the program had more significant positive effects on older children and those from families with higher educational backgrounds. Conversely, the benefits were less pronounced for children experiencing comorbid conduct or anxiety disorders. Furthermore, the mean perspective indicates a low level of perceived effectiveness of school support services among students with ADHD during career transitioning. This is not surprising as Golson et al. (2022) contended that the journey towards accessing school support services for students with ADHD is intricate, frequently necessitating the involvement of community providers and the advocacy of parents. Bussing et al. (2016) showed that adolescents exhibited a significantly reduced openness to academic interventions in contrast to adult respondents. The study identifies stigma as a major obstacle to the implementation of ADHD interventions, as well as the perception that tailored interventions may lead to unequal treatment. Murray et al. (2014) noted that students who received services exhibited more significant academic and behavioral challenges compared to their peers who did not receive such services. The nature of these services varied according to the type of educational institution, with the highest number of interventions allocated to students in schools dedicated exclusively to individuals with disabilities (Murray et al., 2014). Evans et al. (2009) demonstrated that a significant proportion of middle-school students exhibited enhanced organization of materials, which correlated positively with their academic performance in certain subjects.

Furthermore, DuPaul and Eckert (1997) revealed that school-based intervention services for students with ADHD resulted in behavioral improvements, irrespective of the experimental design utilized. Moreover, Fabiano et al. (2022) indicated no significant differences in ratings or behavioral measures between children with individualized education programs and those without, except in terms of academic achievement, where children in special education scored lower on average. On a positive note, all children showed improvement within the framework of intensive behavioral intervention. According to Miranda et al. (2006), school-based intervention services for ADHD demonstrated effectiveness in the short term, particularly in diminishing disruptive behaviors and enhancing both on-task behavior and academic performance among students with ADHD. Harju-Luukkainen et al. (2018) showed that the perceptions of families regarding the educational support the students received differed depending on several factors, including the extent to which teachers acknowledged the individual needs of students, their knowledge of ADHD, the degree to which families felt their views were considered, and the adequacy of support provided within a multi-professional network.

Field et al. (2013) indicated that students with ADHD who engaged in coaching support demonstrated a statistically significant enhancement in their skill, will, and self-regulation when compared to their peers who did not receive coaching. Pfiffner et al. (2016) revealed that students in schools utilizing a cluster-randomized design received significantly better evaluations from both parents and teachers concerning ADHD symptom severity and organizational functioning, in contrast to those who were provided with traditional services. DuPaul et al. (2017) indicated strategies, which include behavioral interventions, alterations to academic instruction, and initiatives for improving communication between home and school. The support for learning encompasses small group settings, tailored teaching strategies, dedicated educators, and both practical and emotional assistance (Baric et al., 2016). These components collectively reinforce the notion that academic support is intertwined with psychosocial support (Baric et al., 2016). It is essential for each student to comprehend the underlying causes of their challenging behavior, as this understanding is essential for determining the most effective clinical, therapeutic, psychosocial, psycho-educational, or school-based support for their unique situation (Kourkoutas et al., 2018). Those who do not receive appropriate care may suffer from negative impacts on their educational achievements, may become involved in delinquent behavior, may engage in substance use, and may pose risks to the safety of others (Russ, 2016). Martin-Egwuonwu (2022) highlighted that addressing specific challenges in support services could enhance persistence and the overall quality of these services. According to DuPaul and Power (2008), students with ADHD frequently encounter difficulties in their academic pursuits, exhibit challenges in managing their behavior during classroom activities, and often experience strained relationships with both teachers and fellow students. Consequently, it is essential for effective treatment support services to concentrate on enhancing behavioral management, social skills, and academic achievement of students with ADHD. Furthermore, fostering robust collaborations between families and school support services personnel is crucial to providing collaborative and holistic support. While school support strategies such as behavioral interventions and academic resources can significantly mitigate symptoms, relying solely on these strategies is often inadequate. These issues underscore the necessity of assessing and improving engagement in support services across both school and family contexts.

CONCLUSIONS

The low mean perception score of students in this study implies that the current school support services might not be sufficiently meeting the needs of students with ADHD during career transitioning. Schools may need to reevaluate and improve their support strategies to offer more effective support services. Since factors like gender, location, and grade level do not significantly influence perceptions of the effectiveness of school support services, enhancements should be consistently applied across all demographics to ensure fair support. This study, thus, highlights the necessity of improving school support services to better meet the unique career transition needs of students with ADHD. Future research should compare the effectiveness of different forms of support services across various school settings to determine best practices for supporting students with ADHD during career transitioning.

REFERENCES

Akhter, Md. S., & Ferdous, R. (2019). Research in Development Arena: Perspective on Epistemology. *The Social Science Journal*, 22, 34–50.

Arciuli, J., Emerson, E., & Llewellyn, G. (2019). Adolescents' self-report of school satisfaction: The interaction between disability and gender. *School Psychology*, 34(2), 148–158. DOI: 10.1037/spq0000275 PMID: 30284888

Asamoah, M. K. (2014). Re-examination of the limitations associated with correlational research. *Journal of Educational Research and Reviews*, 2(4), 45–52.

Ashour, L. (2024). A review of user-friendly freely-available statistical analysis software for medical researchers and biostatisticians. *Research in Statistics*, 2(1), 2322630. DOI: 10.1080/27684520.2024.2322630

Baltes, S., & Ralph, P. (2022). Sampling in software engineering research: A critical review and guidelines. *Empirical Software Engineering*, 27(4), 94. DOI: 10.1007/s10664-021-10072-8

Baric, B. V., Hellberg, K., Kjellberg, A., & Hemmingsson, H. (2016). Support for learning goes beyond academic support: Voices of students with Asperger's disorder and attention deficit hyperactivity disorder. *Autism*, 20(2), 183–195. DOI: 10.1177/1362361315574582 PMID: 25911093

Bryman, A. (1984). The Debate about Quantitative and Qualitative Research: A Question of Method or Epistemology? *The British Journal of Sociology*, 35(1), 75–92. DOI: 10.2307/590553

Bussing, R., Koro-Ljungberg, M., Gagnon, J. C., Mason, D. M., Ellison, A., Noguchi, K., Garvan, C. W., & Albarracin, D. (2016). Feasibility of School-Based ADHD Interventions: A Mixed-Methods Study of Perceptions of Adolescents and Adults. *Journal of Attention Disorders*, 20(5), 400–413. DOI: 10.1177/1087054713515747 PMID: 24448222

Bussing, R., Zima, B. T., & Belin, T. R. (1998a). Differential access to care for children with ADHD in special education programs. *Psychiatric Services (Washington, D.C.)*, 49(9), 1226–1229. DOI: 10.1176/ps.49.9.1226 PMID: 9735968

Bussing, R., Zima, B. T., Perwien, A. R., Belin, T. R., & Widawski, M. (1998b). Children in special education programs: Attention deficit hyperactivity disorder, use of services, and unmet needs. *American Journal of Public Health*, 88(6), 880–886. DOI: 10.2105/AJPH.88.6.880 PMID: 9618613

Cho, S.-J., & Blair, K.-S. C. (2017). Using a multicomponent function-based intervention to support students with attention deficit hyperactivity disorder. *The Journal of Special Education*, 50(4), 227–238. DOI: 10.1177/0022466916655186

Curtis, E. A., Comiskey, C., & Dempsey, O. (2016). Importance and use of correlational research. *Nurse Researcher*, 23(6), 20–25. DOI: 10.7748/nr.2016.e1382 PMID: 27424963

Denis, C. M. (2012). *Attention Deficit Hyperactivity Disorder and Bronfenbrenner's Ecology of Human Development*. (Doctoral Dissertation, Georgia Southern University). https://digitalcommons.georgiasouthern.edu/etd/64

DuPaul, G., Dahlstrom-Hakki, I., Gormley, M., Fu, Q., Pinho, T., & Banerjee, M. (2017). College Students with ADHD and LD: Effects of Support Services on Academic Performance. *Learning Disabilities Research & Practice*, 32(4), 246–256. Advance online publication. DOI: 10.1111/ldrp.12143

DuPaul, G., & Power, T. J. (2008). Improving School Outcomes for Students With ADHD: Using the Right Strategies in the Context of the Right Relationships. *Journal of Attention Disorders*, 11(5), 519–521. DOI: 10.1177/1087054708314241 PMID: 18258999

DuPaul, G. J., & Eckert, T. L. (1997). The effects of school-based interventions for attention deficit hyperactivity disorder: A meta-analysis. *School Psychology Review*, 26(1), 5–27. DOI: 10.1080/02796015.1997.12085845

DuPaul, G. J., Reid, R., Anastopoulos, A. D., & Power, T. J. (2014). Assessing ADHD symptomatic behaviors and functional impairment in school settings: Impact of student and teacher characteristics. *School Psychology Quarterly*, 29(4), 409–421. DOI: 10.1037/spq0000095 PMID: 25485465

Eseadi, C. (2023). Enhancing Educational and Career Prospects: A Comprehensive Analysis of Institutional Support for Students with Specific Learning Disabilities. *International Journal of Research in Counseling and Education*, 7(1), 1–7.

Eseadi, C., & Diale, B. M. (2024). Institutional Support Services for Career Transitioning of Students With Hearing Impairments: A Mixed-Methods Study. In *Perspectives on Career Transitioning of Students with Hearing Impairments* (pp. 141-172). IGI Global. DOI: 10.4018/979-8-3693-2631-2.ch006

Evans, S. W., Schultz, B. K., White, L. C., Brady, C., Sibley, M. H., & Van Eck, K. (2009). A school-based organization intervention for young adolescents with attention-deficit/hyperactivity disorder. *School Mental Health: A Multidisciplinary Research and Practice Journal, 1*(2), 78–88. DOI: 10.1007/s12310-009-9009-6

Fabiano, G. A., Lupas, K., Merrill, B. M., Schatz, N. K., Piscitello, J., Robertson, E. L., & Pelham, W. E.Jr. (2024). Reconceptualizing the approach to supporting students with attention-deficit/hyperactivity disorder in school settings. *Journal of School Psychology*, 104, 101309. DOI: 10.1016/j.jsp.2024.101309 PMID: 38871418

Fabiano, G. A., Naylor, J., Pelham, W. E.Jr, Gnagy, E. M., Burrows-MacLean, L., Coles, E., Chacko, A., Wymbs, B. T., Walker, K. S., Wymbs, F., Garefino, A., Mazzant, J. R., Sastry, A. L., Tresco, K. E., Waschbusch, D. A., Massetti, G. M., & Waxmonsky, J. (2022). Special Education for Children with ADHD: Services Received and a Comparison to Children with ADHD in General Education. *School Mental Health*, 14(4), 818–830. DOI: 10.1007/s12310-022-09514-5

Field, S., Parker, D. R., Sawilowsky, S., & Rolands, L. (2013). Assessing the Impact of ADHD Coaching Services on University Students' Learning Skills, Self-Regulation, and Well-Being. *Journal of Postsecondary Education and Disability*, 26(1), 67–81.

Fisher, M. J., & Marshall, A. P. (2009). Understanding descriptive statistics. *Australian Critical Care*, 22(2), 93–97. DOI: 10.1016/j.aucc.2008.11.003 PMID: 19150245

Golson, M. E., Roanhorse, T. T., McClain, M. B., Galliher, R. V., & Domenech Rodríguez, M. M. (2022). School-based ADHD services: Perspectives from racially and ethnically minoritized students. *Psychology in the Schools*, 59(4), 726–743. DOI: 10.1002/pits.22640

Graczyk, P. A., Atkins, M. S., Jackson, M. M., Letendre, J. A., Kim-Cohen, J., Baumann, B. L., & Mccoy, J. (2005). Urban Educators' Perceptions of Interventions for Students with Attention Deficit Hyperactivity Disorder: A Preliminary Investigation. *Behavioral Disorders*, 30(2), 95–104. DOI: 10.1177/019874290503000203

Gregg, N. (2009). *Adolescents and Adults with Learning Disabilities and ADHD: Assessment and Accommodation*. Guilford Press.

Grove, Z. (2021). *Perceptions of support among university students diagnosed with Attention-Deficit/Hyperactivity Disorder (ADHD)* (Doctoral dissertation, University of the Witwatersrand).

Harju-Luukkainen, H., Sandberg, E., & Itkonen, T. (2018). Perspectives on Educational Supports: Two Case Studies of Families with School-Aged Children with Attention-Deficit/Hyperactivity Disorder (ADHD). *Journal of the International Association of Special Education*, 18(1), 23–30. http://hdl.handle.net/20.500.12680/4f16c953r

Härkönen, U. (2007). *The Bronfenbrenner ecological systems theory of human development*.Scientific Articles of V International Conference, pp. 1-17.

Hart, K. C., Fabiano, G. A., Evans, S. W., Manos, M. J., Hannah, J. N., & Vujnovic, R. K. (2017). Elementary and middle school teachers' self-reported use of positive behavioral supports for children with ADHD: A national survey. *Journal of Emotional and Behavioral Disorders*, 25(4), 246–256. DOI: 10.1177/1063426616681980

Hassan, D. N. A. (2016). Research Methodology - Research Design. In *Research Design and Methodology*. Intechopen., DOI: 10.5772/intechopen.85731

Howe, K. R. (1988). Against the Quantitative-Qualitative Incompatibility Thesis or Dogmas Die Hard. *Educational Researcher, 17*(8), 10–16. DOI: 10.3102/0013189X017008010

Igboekwe, M. U., & Nwankwo, C. (2011). Geostatistical Correlation of Aquifer Potentials in Abia State, South-Eastern Nigeria. *International Journal of Geosciences*, 2(4), 541–548. DOI: 10.4236/ijg.2011.24057

Jopling, M. (2019). Using quantitative data. In Lambert, M. (Ed.), *Practical Research Methods in Education* (pp. 55–66). Routledge., DOI: 10.4324/9781351188395-6

Kaur, P., Stoltzfus, J., & Yellapu, V. (2018). Descriptive statistics. *International Journal of Academic Medicine*, 4(1), 60–63. DOI: 10.4103/IJAM.IJAM_7_18

Kourkoutas, E., Stavrou, P.-D., & Plexousakis, S. (2018). Teachers' Emotional and Educational Reactions toward Children with Behavioral Problems: Implication for School-Based Counseling Work with Teachers. *Journal of Psychology & Behavioral Science*, 6(2), 2374–2399. DOI: 10.15640/jpbs.v6n2a3

Lasisi, D., Ani, C., Lasebikan, V., Sheikh, L., & Omigbodun, O. (2017). Effect of attention-deficit–hyperactivity-disorder training program on the knowledge and attitudes of primary school teachers in Kaduna, North West Nigeria. *Child and Adolescent Psychiatry and Mental Health*, 11(1), 15. DOI: 10.1186/s13034-017-0153-8 PMID: 28331540

Lau, F. (2017). Methods for Correlational Studies. In *Handbook of eHealth Evaluation: An Evidence-based Approach* [Internet]. University of Victoria., https://www.ncbi.nlm.nih.gov/books/NBK481614/

Locke, J., Kang-Yi, C. D., Pellecchia, M., Marcus, S., Hadley, T., & Mandell, D. S. (2017). Ethnic disparities in school-based behavioral health service use for children with psychiatric disorders. *The Journal of School Health*, 87(1), 47–54. DOI: 10.1111/josh.12469 PMID: 27917490

Loe, I. M., & Feldman, H. M. (2007). Academic and educational outcomes of children with ADHD. *Journal of Pediatric Psychology*, 32(6), 643–654. DOI: 10.1093/jpepsy/jsl054 PMID: 17569716

Martin-Egwuonwu, N. L. (2022). *The Perceptions of Support Services Staff and Their Influence on Students with Learning Disabilities*.(Doctoral Dissertation, Northcentral University).

Miranda, A., Jarque, S., & Tarraga, R. (2006). Interventions in School Settings for Students With ADHD. *Exceptionality*, 14(1), 35–52. DOI: 10.1207/s15327035ex1401_4

Moore, D. A., Russell, A. E., Arnell, S., & Ford, T. J. (2017). Educators' experiences of managing students with ADHD: A qualitative study. *Child: Care, Health and Development*, 43(4), 489–498. DOI: 10.1111/cch.12448 PMID: 28233330

Morris, J., Buchanan, T., Arnold, J., Czerkawski, T., & Congram, B. (2023). The Impact of Gender, Accommodations, and Disability on the Academic Performance of Canadian University Students with LD and/or ADHD. *Learning Disabilities Research & Practice*, 38(4), 296–310. DOI: 10.1111/ldrp.12324

Murray, D. W., Molina, B. S., Glew, K., Houck, P., Greiner, A., Fong, D., Swanson, J., Arnold, L. E., Lerner, M., Hechtman, L., Abikoff, H. B., & Jensen, P. S. (2014). Prevalence and characteristics of school services for high school students with attention-deficit/hyperactivity disorder. *School Mental Health*, 6(4), 264–278. DOI: 10.1007/s12310-014-9128-6 PMID: 25506403

Mytkowicz, P., & Goss, D. (2012). Students' Perceptions of a Postsecondary LD/ADHD Support Program. *Journal of Postsecondary Education and Disability*, 25(4), 345–361.

Norvilitis, J., & Fang, P. (2005). Perceptions of ADHD in China and the United States: A Preliminary Study. *Journal of Attention Disorders*, 9(2), 413–424. DOI: 10.1177/1087054705281123 PMID: 16371664

Nwaigwe, C. (2021). Application of the statistical package for the social sciences (SPSS). In *Educational Research: An African Approach*. Oxford University Press, Southern Africa.

O'Callaghan, P., & Sharma, D. (2014). Severity of symptoms and quality of life in medical students with ADHD. *Journal of Attention Disorders*, 18(8), 654–658. DOI: 10.1177/1087054712445064 PMID: 22582348

Oke, O. J., Adejuyigbe, E. A., Oseni, S. B., & Mosaku, K. S. (2019). Academic Performance of Children with ADHD in Ile Ife, South West, Nigeria. *Journal of Pediatric Neurology*, 17(04), 131–137. DOI: 10.1055/s-0038-1636927

Olatunji, G., Faturoti, O., Jaiyeoba, B., Toluwabori, A. V., Adefusi, T., Olaniyi, P., Aderinto, N., & Abdulbasit, M. O. (2023). Navigating unique challenges and advancing equitable care for children with ADHD in Africa: A review. *Annals of Medicine and Surgery (London)*, 85(10), 4939–4946. DOI: 10.1097/MS9.0000000000001179 PMID: 37811061

Onwuegbuzie, A. J. (2000). Why Can't We All Get along? Towards a Framework for Unifying Research Paradigms. *Education*, 122(3), 518.

Onyeonoro, C. O., Aniemeke, C. N., Ogbenna, D. A., & Onyeonoro, F. N. (2023). Emotional Bonding and Diner's Loyalty to Restaurants in Umuahia, Abia State. *British Journal of Marketing Studies*, 11(5), 44–79. DOI: 10.37745/bjms.13/vol11n54479

Onyishi, N. (2024). Exploring Institutional Support Needs for Career Transitioning among Students with Visual Impairments: A Scoping Review. *International Journal of Home Economics. Hospitality and Allied Research*, 3(1), 139–161. DOI: 10.57012/ijhhr.v3n1.012

Panchawagh, S., Kamath, Y., & Siddiqui, A. (2023). *Simple and intuitive statistical data analysis and teaching for medical students using JASP. TechRxiv*. August 29, 2023. DOI: 10.36227/techrxiv.24046605.v1

Parker, D. R., Hoffman, S. F., Sawilowsky, S., & Rolands, L. (2013). Self-Control in Postsecondary Settings: Students' Perceptions of ADHD College Coaching. *Journal of Attention Disorders*, 17(3), 215–232. DOI: 10.1177/1087054711427561 PMID: 22173150

Pfiffner, L. J., Rooney, M., Haack, L., Villodas, M., Delucchi, K., & McBurnett, K. (2016). A Randomized Controlled Trial of a School-Implemented School–Home Intervention for Attention-Deficit/Hyperactivity Disorder Symptoms and Impairment. *Journal of the American Academy of Child and Adolescent Psychiatry*, 55(9), 762–770. DOI: 10.1016/j.jaac.2016.05.023 PMID: 27566117

Rhinehart, L., Iyer, S., & Haager, D. (2022). Children who receive special education services for ADHD: Early indicators and evidence of disproportionate representation in the Early Childhood Longitudinal Study (ECLS-K: 2011). *Journal of Emotional and Behavioral Disorders*, 30(1), 3–15. DOI: 10.1177/10634266211039757

Rogers, M., Boggia, J., Ogg, J., & Volpe, R. (2015). The Ecology of ADHD in the Schools. *Current Developmental Disorders Reports*, 2(1), 23–29. DOI: 10.1007/s40474-015-0038-6

Rucklidge, J. J. (2010). Gender differences in attention-deficit/hyperactivity disorder. *Psychiatria Clinica*, 33(2), 357–373. DOI: 10.1016/j.psc.2010.01.006 PMID: 20385342

Rueger, S. Y., Malecki, C. K., & Demaray, M. K. (2008). Gender differences in the relationship between perceived social support and student adjustment during early adolescence. *School Psychology Quarterly*, 23(4), 496–514. DOI: 10.1037/1045-3830.23.4.496

Russ, B. R. (2016). *Counselor Preparation and Adolescent Youth: A Study of Clinical Mental Health Counselors*. Western Michigan University.

Schultz, B., & Evans, S. (2012). Sources of Bias in Teacher Ratings of Adolescents with ADHD. *Journal of Educational and Developmental Psychology*, 2(1), 151–162. DOI: 10.5539/jedp.v2n1p151

Sciberras, E., Roos, L. E., & Efron, D. (2009). Review of prospective longitudinal studies of children with ADHD: Mental health, educational, and social outcomes. *Current Attention Disorders Reports*, 1(4), 171–177. DOI: 10.1007/s12618-009-0024-1

Seeram, E. (2019). An Overview of Correlational Research. *Radiologic Technology*, 91(2), 176–179. PMID: 31685592

Somekh, B., & Lewin, C. (2004). Research Methods in the Social Sciences. *Sage (Atlanta, Ga.)*.

Spiel, C. F. (2013). *School-Based Services for Adolescents with ADHD: What is given and to whom?* Ohio University.

Stapor, K. (2020). Descriptive and Inferential Statistics. In Stapor, K. (Ed.), *Introduction to Probabilistic and Statistical Methods with Examples in R* (pp. 63–131). Springer International Publishing., DOI: 10.1007/978-3-030-45799-0_2

Suen, L.-J. W., Huang, H.-M., & Lee, H.-H. (2014). [A comparison of convenience sampling and purposive sampling]. *Hu Li Za Zhi. Journal of Nursing (Luton, England)*, 61(3), 105–111. DOI: 10.6224/JN.61.3.105 PMID: 24899564

Tiikkaja, S., & Tindberg, Y. (2021). Poor school-related well-being among adolescents with disabilities or ADHD. *International Journal of Environmental Research and Public Health*, 19(1), 8. DOI: 10.3390/ijerph19010008 PMID: 35010265

Tongco, M. D. C. (2007). *Purposive Sampling as a Tool for Informant Selection*. http://hdl.handle.net/10125/227

Veenman, B., Luman, M., & Oosterlaan, J. (2018). Moderators Influencing the Effectiveness of a Behavioral Teacher Program. *Frontiers in Psychology*, 9, 298. Advance online publication. DOI: 10.3389/fpsyg.2018.00298 PMID: 29593604

Weyandt, L. L., & DuPaul, G. J. (2008). ADHD in college students: Developmental findings. *Developmental Disabilities Research Reviews*, 14(4), 311–319. DOI: 10.1002/ddrr.38 PMID: 19072759

Wolf, C., Joye, D., Smith, T. W., & Fu, Y. (2016). *The SAGE Handbook of Survey Methodology*. SAGE. DOI: 10.4135/9781473957893

Wolf, L. E., Simkowitz, P., & Carlson, H. (2009). College students with attention-deficit/hyperactivity disorder. *Current Psychiatry Reports*, 11(5), 415–421. DOI: 10.1007/s11920-009-0062-5 PMID: 19785984

Zendarski, N., Sciberras, E., Mensah, F., & Hiscock, H. (2020). Factors associated with educational support in young adolescents with ADHD. *Journal of Attention Disorders*, 24(5), 750–757. DOI: 10.1177/1087054718804351 PMID: 30328744

ADDITIONAL READINGS

Abu-Elfotuh, K., Darwish, A., Elsanhory, H. M., Alharthi, H. H., Hamdan, A. M., Hamdan, A. M., Masoud, R. A. E., Abd El-Rhman, R. H., & Reda, E. (2023). In silico and in vivo analysis of the relationship between ADHD and social isolation in pups rat model: Implication of redox mechanisms, and the neuroprotective impact of Punicalagin. *Life Sciences*, 335, 122252. DOI: 10.1016/j.lfs.2023.122252 PMID: 37935275

Adler, L. A., Faraone, S. V., Sarocco, P., Atkins, N., & Khachatryan, A. (2019). Establishing US norms for the Adult ADHD Self-Report Scale (ASRS-v1. 1) and characterising symptom burden among adults with self-reported ADHD. *International Journal of Clinical Practice*, 73(1), e13260. DOI: 10.1111/ijcp.13260 PMID: 30239073

Al Hamdani, D. (2019, September). The influence of metacognitive awareness skills and attention deficit/hyperactivity disorder (ADHD) on students' achievement. In *Sohar University Proceedings of 5th Teaching & Learning Conference*.

Anastopoulos, A. D., & King, K. A. (2015). A cognitive-behavior therapy and mentoring program for college students with ADHD. *Cognitive and Behavioral Practice*, 22(2), 141–151. DOI: 10.1016/j.cbpra.2014.01.002

Anderson, J., Boyle, C., & Deppeler, J. (2014). The ecology of inclusive education: Reconceptualizing Bronfenbrenner. In *Equality in education: Fairness and Inclusion* (pp. 23–34). Sense Publishers. DOI: 10.1007/978-94-6209-692-9_3

Anderson, N. P., Feldman, J. A., Kolko, D. J., Pilkonis, P. A., & Lindhiem, O. (2022). National norms for the Vanderbilt ADHD diagnostic parent rating scale in children. *Journal of Pediatric Psychology*, 47(6), 652–661. DOI: 10.1093/jpepsy/jsab132 PMID: 34986222

Arnold, L. E., Hodgkins, P., Kahle, J., Madhoo, M., & Kewley, G. (2020). Long-term outcomes of ADHD: Academic achievement and performance. *Journal of Attention Disorders*, 24(1), 73–85. DOI: 10.1177/1087054714566076 PMID: 25583985

Barkley, R. A. (2022). Improving clinical diagnosis using the executive functioning—Self-regulation theory of ADHD. *The ADHD Report*, 30(1), 1–9. DOI: 10.1521/adhd.2022.30.1.1

Basile, A., Toplak, M. E., & Andrade, B. F. (2021). Using metacognitive methods to examine emotion recognition in children with ADHD. *Journal of Attention Disorders*, 25(2), 245–257. DOI: 10.1177/1087054718808602 PMID: 30442038

Berchiatti, M., Ferrer, A., Badenes-Ribera, L., & Longobardi, C. (2022). School adjustments in children with attention deficit hyperactivity disorder (ADHD): Peer relationships, the quality of the student-teacher relationship, and children's academic and behavioral competencies. *Journal of Applied School Psychology*, 38(3), 241–261. DOI: 10.1080/15377903.2021.1941471

Berrezueta-Guzman, S., Kandil, M., Martín-Ruiz, M. L., Pau de la Cruz, I., & Krusche, S. (2024, March). Future of ADHD care: Evaluating the efficacy of ChatGPT in therapy enhancement. [). MDPI.]. *Health Care*, 12(6), 683. PMID: 38540647

Burnette, J. L., Babij, A. D., Oddo, L. E., & Knouse, L. E. (2020). Self-regulation mindsets: Relationship to coping, executive functioning, and ADHD. *Journal of Social and Clinical Psychology*, 39(2), 101–116. DOI: 10.1521/jscp.2020.39.02.101

Butcher, L., & Lane, S. (2024). Neurodivergent (Autism and ADHD) student experiences of access and inclusion in higher education: An ecological systems theory perspective. *Higher Education*, •••, 1–21. DOI: 10.1007/s10734-024-01319-6

Butzbach, M., Fuermaier, A. B., Aschenbrenner, S., Weisbrod, M., Tucha, L., & Tucha, O. (2021). Metacognition in adult ADHD: Subjective and objective perspectives on self-awareness of cognitive functioning. *Journal of Neural Transmission (Vienna, Austria)*, 128(7), 939–955. DOI: 10.1007/s00702-020-02293-w PMID: 33464422

Campbell, A. (2019). *Multi-Professional Collaboration in Addressing Children's Mental Health by Using eHealth Services: An eCAP study survey of early childhood education professionals* (master's thesis, Itä-Suomen yliopisto).

Chaimaha, N., Sriphetcharawut, S., Lersilp, S., & Chinchai, S. (2017). Effectiveness of therapeutic programs for students with ADHD with executive function deficits. *Journal of Occupational Therapy, Schools & Early Intervention*, 10(4), 436–456. DOI: 10.1080/19411243.2017.1359131

Champ, R. E., Adamou, M., & Tolchard, B. (2023). Seeking connection, autonomy, and emotional feedback: A self-determination theory of self-regulation in attention-deficit hyperactivity disorder. *Psychological Review*, 130(3), 569–603. DOI: 10.1037/rev0000398 PMID: 36548057

Chan, T., & Martinussen, R. (2016). Positive illusions? The accuracy of academic self-appraisals in adolescents with ADHD. *Journal of Pediatric Psychology*, 41(7), 799–809. DOI: 10.1093/jpepsy/jsv116 PMID: 26645302

Cheesman, J. E. (2019). *Parenting a child with ADHD: Exploring the experiences of single mothers with ADHD* (Doctoral dissertation, Stellenbosch: Stellenbosch University).

Christensen, J. (2016). A critical reflection of Bronfenbrenner's development ecology model. *Problems of Education in the 21st Century, 69*(1), 22-28.

Christoffersen, M. N. (2023). Overcoming the odds: Does social support make a difference for young people with ADHD symptoms? *Journal of Attention Disorders*, 27(14), 1596–1608. DOI: 10.1177/10870547231188348 PMID: 37470200

Cibrian, F. L., Lakes, K. D., Schuck, S. E., & Hayes, G. R. (2022). The potential for emerging technologies to support self-regulation in children with ADHD: A literature review. *International Journal of Child-Computer Interaction*, 31, 100421. DOI: 10.1016/j.ijcci.2021.100421

Colomer, C., Wiener, J., & Varma, A. (2020). Do adolescents with ADHD have a self-perception bias for their ADHD symptoms and impairment? *Canadian Journal of School Psychology*, 35(4), 238–251. DOI: 10.1177/0829573520936457

Costa, D. D. S., Paula, J. J. D., Alvim-Soares, A. M., Diniz, B. S., Romano-Silva, M. A., Malloy-Diniz, L. F., & Miranda, D. M. D. (2014). ADHD inattentive symptoms mediate the relationship between intelligence and academic performance in children aged 6-14. *Revista Brasileira de Psiquiatria (Sao Paulo, Brazil)*, 36(4), 313–321. DOI: 10.1590/1516-4446-2013-1201 PMID: 25028778

D'Alessio, K. A., & Banerjee, M. (2016). Academic Advising as an Intervention for College Students with ADHD. *Journal of Postsecondary Education and Disability*, 29(2), 109–121.

Dass, P. L. M. (2019). *Attention to retention: Implications of institutional practices of four-year colleges and universities on graduation rates of students with ADHD.* University of North Florida.

De Villiers, Z. (2022). *Grade 1 teachers' experiences of supporting learners with Attention-deficit/Hyperactivity Disorder (ADHD)* (Doctoral dissertation, Cape Peninsula University of Technology).

Delahunt, T., Le Moine, G., & Soan, S. (2021). Challenges of multi-professional working within one English higher education institution: 'we hit a giant': is this a shared experience? *Practice*, 3(1), 58–66. DOI: 10.1080/25783858.2020.1831888

Denis, C. M. (2012). Attention deficit hyperactivity disorder and Bronfenbrenner's Ecology of human development.

Diaz-Garcia, M. E. (2019). *Factors for Parent-Reported ADHD Diagnosis in Hispanic Elementary School-Aged Children.* Walden University.

Dolón-Poza, M., Berrezueta-Guzman, J., & Martín-Ruiz, M. L. (2020, November). Creation of an intelligent system to support the therapy process in children with ADHD. In *Conference on Information and Communication Technologies of Ecuador* (pp. 36-50). Cham: Springer International Publishing. DOI: 10.1007/978-3-030-62833-8_4

Doom, J. R., Georgieff, M. K., & Gunnar, M. R. (2015). Institutional care and iron deficiency increase ADHD symptomology and lower IQ 2.5–5 years post-adoption. *Developmental Science*, 18(3), 484–494. DOI: 10.1111/desc.12223 PMID: 25070881

DuPaul, G. J., Dahlstrom-Hakki, I., Gormley, M. J., Fu, Q., Pinho, T. D., & Banerjee, M. (2017). College students with ADHD and LD: Effects of support services on academic performance. *Learning Disabilities Research & Practice*, 32(4), 246–256. DOI: 10.1111/ldrp.12143

Elmose, M., & Lasgaard, M. (2017). Loneliness and social support in adolescent boys with attention deficit hyperactivity disorder in a special education setting. *Journal of Child and Family Studies*, 26(10), 2900–2907. DOI: 10.1007/s10826-017-0797-2

Enggaard, H., Laugesen, B., DeJonckheere, M., Fetters, M. D., Dalgaard, M. K., Lauritsen, M. B., Zoffmann, V., & Jørgensen, R. (2020). Impact of the guided self-determination intervention among adolescents with co-existing ADHD and medical disorder: A mixed methods study. *Issues in Mental Health Nursing*, 42(1), 87–98. DOI: 10.1080/01612840.2020.1780528 PMID: 32669013

Fabiano, G. A., Naylor, J., Pelham, W. E.Jr, Gnagy, E. M., Burrows-MacLean, L., Coles, E., Chacko, A., Wymbs, B. T., Walker, K. S., Wymbs, F., Garefino, A., Mazzant, J. R., Sastry, A. L., Tresco, K. E., Waschbusch, D. A., Massetti, G. M., & Waxmonsky, J. (2022). Special education for children with ADHD: Services received and a comparison to children with ADHD in general education. *School Mental Health*, 14(4), 818–830. DOI: 10.1007/s12310-022-09514-5

Farmer, J. L., Allsopp, D. H., & Ferron, J. M. (2015). Impact of the personal strengths program on self-determination levels of college students with LD and/or ADHD. *Learning Disability Quarterly*, 38(3), 145–159. DOI: 10.1177/0731948714526998

Franklin, M. S., Mrazek, M. D., Anderson, C. L., Johnston, C., Smallwood, J., Kingstone, A., & Schooler, J. W. (2017). Tracking distraction: The relationship between mind-wandering, meta-awareness, and ADHD symptomatology. *Journal of Attention Disorders*, 21(6), 475–486. DOI: 10.1177/1087054714543494 PMID: 25085650

Freedman, J. E. (2016). An analysis of the discourses on attention deficit hyperactivity disorder (ADHD) in US special education textbooks, with implications for inclusive education. *International Journal of Inclusive Education*, 20(1), 32–51. DOI: 10.1080/13603116.2015.1073375

Fridman, M., Banaschewski, T., Sikirica, V., Quintero, J., & Chen, K. S. (2017). Access to diagnosis, treatment, and supportive services among pharmacotherapy-treated children/adolescents with ADHD in Europe: Data from the Caregiver Perspective on Pediatric ADHD survey. *Neuropsychiatric Disease and Treatment*, 13, 947–958. DOI: 10.2147/NDT.S128752 PMID: 28408828

Frost, N. (2017). From "silo" to "network" profession–a multi-professional future for social work. *Journal of Children's Services*, 12(2-3), 174–183. DOI: 10.1108/JCS-05-2017-0019

Fullen, T., Jones, S. L., Emerson, L. M., & Adamou, M. (2020). Psychological treatments in adult ADHD: A systematic review. *Journal of Psychopathology and Behavioral Assessment*, 42(3), 500–518. DOI: 10.1007/s10862-020-09794-8

Fuller, W. S. (2015). *Teacher knowledge of attention deficit hyperactivity disorder (ADHD) and teacher perceived effectiveness* (Doctoral dissertation, Capella University).

Gallen, C. L., Anguera, J. A., Gerdes, M. R., Simon, A. J., Cañadas, E., & Marco, E. J. (2021). Enhancing neural markers of attention in children with ADHD using digital therapeutics. *PLoS One*, 16(12), e0261981. DOI: 10.1371/journal.pone.0261981 PMID: 34972140

González, R. A., Gudjonsson, G. H., Wells, J., & Young, S. (2016). The role of emotional distress and ADHD on institutional behavioral disturbance and recidivism among offenders. *Journal of Attention Disorders*, 20(4), 368–378. DOI: 10.1177/1087054713493322 PMID: 23893535

Grygiel, P., Humenny, G., Switaj, P., Rebisz, S., & Anczewska, M. (2014). *Between isolation and loneliness: social networks and perceived integration with peers of children diagnosed with ADHD in regular classrooms*. Bulgarian Comparative Education Society.

Gustafsson, B. M., Steinwall, S., & Korhonen, L. (2021). Development of a multi-professional and multi-agency Model, PLUSS (mental health, learning, development, collaboration around pre-school children), to Facilitate Early Detection and Support of Pre-School Children with Neurodevelopmental Difficulties in the Swedish Child Health Care–A Description of the Model and Initial Results.

Harkins, C. M., Handen, B. L., & Mazurek, M. O. (2022). The impact of the comorbidity of ASD and ADHD on social impairment. *Journal of Autism and Developmental Disorders*, 52(6), 2512–2522. DOI: 10.1007/s10803-021-05150-1 PMID: 34181141

Hasewinkel, S. E. (2015). An exploratory case study at Timour Hall Primary School of the perception of parents of children with ADHD concerning their parental challenges and coping strategies.

Heiman, T., Olenik-Shemesh, D., & Eden, S. (2015). Cyberbullying involvement among students with ADHD: Relation to loneliness, self-efficacy and social support. *European Journal of Special Needs Education*, 30(1), 15–29. DOI: 10.1080/08856257.2014.943562

Houghton, S., Lawrence, D., Hunter, S. C., Zadow, C., Kyron, M., Paterson, R., Carroll, A., Christie, R., & Brandtman, M. (2020). Loneliness accounts for the association between diagnosed attention deficit-hyperactivity disorder and symptoms of depression among adolescents. *Journal of Psychopathology and Behavioral Assessment*, 42(2), 237–247. DOI: 10.1007/s10862-020-09791-x

Hulbig, P. R. (2023). *The Pedagogy of Self-Authorship: The Neurocognitive Impact of Science and Metacognition*. Springer Nature. DOI: 10.1007/978-3-031-41436-7

Humphreys, K. L., Gabard-Durnam, L., Goff, B., Telzer, E. H., Flannery, J., Gee, D. G., Park, V., Lee, S. S., & Tottenham, N. (2019). Friendship and social functioning following early institutional rearing: The role of ADHD symptoms. *Development and Psychopathology*, 31(4), 1477–1487. DOI: 10.1017/S0954579418001050 PMID: 30588896

Jones, R. (2021). A phenomenological study of undergraduates with attention deficit hyperactivity disorder and academic library use for research. *New Review of Academic Librarianship*, 27(2), 165–183. DOI: 10.1080/13614533.2020.1731560

Kajka, N. (2019). The influence of metacognitive training on the improvement of working memory in children with ADHD. *Current Problems of Psychiatry*, 20(3), 217–227. DOI: 10.2478/cpp-2019-0015

Karawekpanyawong, N., Wongpakaran, T., Wongpakaran, N., Boonnag, C., Siritikul, S., Chalanunt, S., & Kuntawong, P. (2021). Impact of perceived social support on the relationship between ADHD and depressive symptoms among first year medical students: A structural equation model approach. *Children (Basel, Switzerland)*, 8(5), 401. DOI: 10.3390/children8050401 PMID: 34065767

Kim, M., King, M. D., & Jennings, J. (2019). ADHD remission, inclusive special education, and socioeconomic disparities. *SSM - Population Health*, 8, 100420. DOI: 10.1016/j.ssmph.2019.100420 PMID: 31431914

Kita, Y., & Inoue, Y. (2017). The direct/indirect association of ADHD/ODD symptoms with self-esteem, self-perception, and depression in early adolescents. *Frontiers in Psychiatry*, 8, 137. DOI: 10.3389/fpsyt.2017.00137 PMID: 28824468

Knouse, L. E., & Fleming, A. P. (2016). Applying cognitive-behavioral therapy for ADHD to emerging adults. *Cognitive and Behavioral Practice*, 23(3), 300–315. DOI: 10.1016/j.cbpra.2016.03.008

Kolleck, N. (2023). Trust in cross-sector alliances: Towards a theory of relational trust in multi-professional education networks. *Educational Management Administration & Leadership*, 51(6), 1362–1382. DOI: 10.1177/17411432211043876

Konur, O. (2014). The periodical research on the experiences of the college students with ADHD: A mixed study. *The International Journal of Research in Teacher Education*, 5(3), 12–33.

Krebs, R. J. (2009). Bronfenbrenner's bioecological theory of human development and the process of development of sports talent. *International Journal of Sport Psychology*, 40(1), 108.

Kwan, C., Gitimoghaddam, M., & Collet, J. P. (2020). Effects of social isolation and loneliness in children with neurodevelopmental disabilities: A scoping review. *Brain Sciences*, 10(11), 786. DOI: 10.3390/brainsci10110786 PMID: 33126519

Lake, A. R. (2022). Authorship & Agency: Exploring coaching as a tool for student success.

Laslo-Roth, R., Bareket-Bojmel, L., & Margalit, M. (2022). Loneliness experience during distance learning among college students with ADHD: The mediating role of perceived support and hope. *European Journal of Special Needs Education*, 37(2), 220–234. DOI: 10.1080/08856257.2020.1862339

Lauder, K., McDowall, A., & Tenenbaum, H. R. (2022). A systematic review of interventions to support adults with ADHD at work—Implications from the paucity of context-specific research for theory and practice. *Frontiers in Psychology*, 13, 893469. DOI: 10.3389/fpsyg.2022.893469 PMID: 36072032

Lenartowicz, A., DeSchepper, B., & Simpson, G. V. (2024). Training of Awareness in ADHD: Leveraging Metacognition. *Journal of Psychiatry and Brain Science*, 9(4). PMID: 39493272

Lindstrom, W., Nelson, J. M., & Foels, P. (2015). Postsecondary ADHD documentation requirements: Common practices in the context of clinical issues, legal standards, and empirical findings. *Journal of Attention Disorders*, 19(8), 655–665. DOI: 10.1177/1087054713506262 PMID: 24131894

Luş, M. G., & Erensoy, H. (2020). Metacognitive awareness and executive function in attention deficit/hyperactivity disorder. *Israel Journal of Psychiatry*, 57(2), 42–48.

Malmqvist, J., & Nilholm, C. (2016). The antithesis of inclusion? The emergence and functioning of ADHD special education classes in the Swedish school system. *Emotional & Behavioural Difficulties*, 21(3), 287–300. DOI: 10.1080/13632752.2016.1165978

Martin, A. J. (2014). The role of ADHD in academic adversity: Disentangling ADHD effects from other personal and contextual factors. *School Psychology Quarterly*, 29(4), 395–408. DOI: 10.1037/spq0000069 PMID: 24820011

Mastoras, S. M., Saklofske, D. H., Schwean, V. L., & Climie, E. A. (2018). Social support in children with ADHD: An exploration of resilience. *Journal of Attention Disorders*, 22(8), 712–723. DOI: 10.1177/1087054715611491 PMID: 26515891

Matthews, T., Danese, A., Wertz, J., Ambler, A., Kelly, M., Diver, A., Caspi, A., Moffitt, T. E., & Arseneault, L. (2015). Social isolation and mental health at primary and secondary school entry: A longitudinal cohort study. *Journal of the American Academy of Child and Adolescent Psychiatry*, 54(3), 225–232. DOI: 10.1016/j.jaac.2014.12.008 PMID: 25721188

Meek, F. (2019). *An Investigation of the Student-Teacher Relationship for Children with Attention Deficit/Hyperactivity Disorder: A Developmental Systems Theory Perspective* (Doctoral dissertation, Université d'Ottawa/University of Ottawa).

Meinzer, M. C., Hill, R. M., Pettit, J. W., & Nichols-Lopez, K. A. (2015). Parental support partially accounts for the covariation between ADHD and depressive symptoms in college students. *Journal of Psychopathology and Behavioral Assessment*, 37(2), 247–255. DOI: 10.1007/s10862-014-9449-7

Michael Dass, P. I. (2019). Attention to retention: Implications of institutional practices of four-year colleges and universities on graduation rates of students with ADHD.

Michielsen, M., Comijs, H. C., Aartsen, M. J., Semeijn, E. J., Beekman, A. T., Deeg, D. J., & Kooij, J. S. (2015). The relationships between ADHD and social functioning and participation in older adults in a population-based study. *Journal of Attention Disorders*, 19(5), 368–379. DOI: 10.1177/1087054713515748 PMID: 24378286

Mikami, A. Y., Owens, J. S., Evans, S. W., Hudec, K. L., Kassab, H., Smit, S., Na, J. J., & Khalis, A. (2022). Promoting classroom social and academic functioning among children at risk for ADHD: The MOSAIC program. *Journal of Clinical Child and Adolescent Psychology*, 51(6), 1039–1052. DOI: 10.1080/15374416.2021.1929250 PMID: 34133243

Molina, M. F. (2015). Perceived parenting style and self-perception in children with attention deficit/hyperactivity disorder. *International Journal of Psychological Research*, 8(1), 61–74. DOI: 10.21500/20112084.647

Morrill, M. S. (2018). Special education financing and ADHD medications: A bitter pill to swallow. *Journal of Policy Analysis and Management*, 37(2), 384–402. DOI: 10.1002/pam.22055 PMID: 29693958

Morsink, S., Sonuga-Barke, E., Mies, G., Glorie, N., Lemiere, J., Van der Oord, S., & Danckaerts, M. (2017). What motivates individuals with ADHD? A qualitative analysis from an adolescent's point of view. *European Child & Adolescent Psychiatry*, 26(8), 923–932. DOI: 10.1007/s00787-017-0961-7 PMID: 28233072

Morsink, S., Van der Oord, S., Antrop, I., Danckaerts, M., & Scheres, A. (2022). Studying motivation in ADHD: The role of internal motives and the relevance of self-determination theory. *Journal of Attention Disorders*, 26(8), 1139–1158. DOI: 10.1177/10870547211050948 PMID: 34794343

Ndovela, S. C. (2019). *Contextual barriers in supporting learners with possible ADHD in poverty-stricken areas*. University of Johannesburg.

Nissley-Tsiopinis, J., Normand, S., Mautone, J. A., Fogler, J. M., Featherston, M., & Power, T. J. (2023). Preparing families for evidence-based treatment of ADHD: Development of Bootcamp for ADHD. *Cognitive and Behavioral Practice*, 30(3), 453–470. DOI: 10.1016/j.cbpra.2022.02.022

Pérez-Jorge, D., Pérez-Martín, A., del Carmen Rodríguez-Jiménez, M., Barragán-Medero, F., & Hernández-Torres, A. (2020). Self and hetero-perception and discrimination in attention deficit hyperactivity disorder. *Heliyon*, 6(8), e04504. DOI: 10.1016/j.heliyon.2020.e04504 PMID: 32775742

Pezzica, S., Vezzani, C., & Pinto, G. (2018). Metacognitive knowledge of attention in children with and without ADHD symptoms. *Research in Developmental Disabilities*, 83, 142–152. DOI: 10.1016/j.ridd.2018.08.005 PMID: 30205249

Pfeifer, M. A., Reiter, E. M., Cordero, J. J., & Stanton, J. D. (2021). Inside and out: Factors that support and hinder the self-advocacy of undergraduates with ADHD and/or specific learning disabilities in STEM. *CBE Life Sciences Education*, 20(2), ar17. DOI: 10.1187/cbe.20-06-0107 PMID: 33769838

Pojanapotha, P., Boonnag, C., Siritikul, S., Chalanunt, S., Kuntawong, P., Wongpakaran, N., & Wongpakaran, T. (2021). A helpful family climate moderates the relationship between perceived family support of ADHD symptoms and depression: A conditional process model. *BMC Psychology*, 9(1), 1–8. DOI: 10.1186/s40359-021-00615-5 PMID: 34321085

Ramey, D. M., & Freelin, B. N. (2023). Exploring the relationships between school suspension, ADHD diagnoses, and delinquency across different school punitive and special education climates. *Children and Youth Services Review*, 148, 106849. DOI: 10.1016/j.childyouth.2023.106849

Razani, N., Hilton, J. F., Halpern-Felsher, B. L., Okumura, M. J., Morrell, H. E., & Yen, I. H. (2015). Neighborhood characteristics and ADHD: Results of a national study. *Journal of Attention Disorders*, 19(9), 731–740. DOI: 10.1177/1087054714542002 PMID: 25028386

Reeble, C. J., Lefler, E. K., Abu-Ramadan, T., Bodalski, E. A., & Canu, W. H. (2024). Social support in college students with ADHD symptoms: Quantity beats quality in moderating impairment. *Journal of College Student Mental Health*, 38(3), 519–540. DOI: 10.1080/87568225.2023.2202351

Rhinehart, L., Iyer, S., & Haager, D. (2022). Children who receive special education services for ADHD: Early indicators and evidence of disproportionate representation in the Early Childhood Longitudinal Study (ECLS-K: 2011). *Journal of Emotional and Behavioral Disorders*, 30(1), 3–15. DOI: 10.1177/10634266211039757

Scheithauer, M. C., & Kelley, M. L. (2017). Self-monitoring by college students with ADHD: The impact on academic performance. *Journal of Attention Disorders*, 21(12), 1030–1039. DOI: 10.1177/1087054714553050 PMID: 25319163

Schweikhard, R. (2024). Teaching future educators how to support students with ADHD.

Sedgwick, J. A. (2018). University students with attention deficit hyperactivity disorder (ADHD): A literature review. *Irish Journal of Psychological Medicine*, 35(3), 221–235. DOI: 10.1017/ipm.2017.20 PMID: 30124182

Serrano, J. W., Abu-Ramadan, T. M., Vasko, J. M., Leopold, D. R., Canu, W. H., Willcutt, E. G., & Hartung, C. M. (2023). ADHD and psychological need fulfillment in college students. *Journal of Attention Disorders*, 27(8), 912–924. DOI: 10.1177/10870547231161530 PMID: 36924424

Shiels, K., & Hawk, L. W.Jr. (2010). Self-regulation in ADHD: The role of error processing. *Clinical Psychology Review*, 30(8), 951–961. DOI: 10.1016/j.cpr.2010.06.010 PMID: 20659781

Shogren, K. A., Raley, S. K., Wehmeyer, M. L., Grandfield, E., Jones, J., & Shaw, L. A. (2019). Exploring the relationships among basic psychological needs satisfaction and frustration, agentic engagement, motivation, and self-determination in adolescents with disabilities. *Advances in Neurodevelopmental Disorders*, 3(2), 119–128. DOI: 10.1007/s41252-018-0093-1

Sibley, M. H., Ortiz, M., Gaias, L. M., Reyes, R., Joshi, M., Alexander, D., & Graziano, P. (2021). Top problems of adolescents and young adults with ADHD during the COVID-19 pandemic. *Journal of Psychiatric Research*, 136, 190–197. DOI: 10.1016/j.jpsychires.2021.02.009 PMID: 33610946

Skalski, S., Pochwatko, G., & Balas, R. (2021). Impact of motivation on selected aspects of attention in children with ADHD. *Child Psychiatry and Human Development*, 52(4), 586–595. DOI: 10.1007/s10578-020-01042-0 PMID: 32816140

Slobodin, O. (2023). ADHD in culturally and linguistically diverse children. In *clinical handbooks of ADHD assessment and treatment across the lifespan* (pp. 1-15). Cham: Springer International Publishing. DOI: 10.1007/978-3-031-41709-2_1

Stickley, A., Koyanagi, A., Takahashi, H., Ruchkin, V., & Kamio, Y. (2017). Attention-deficit/hyperactivity disorder symptoms and loneliness among adults in the general population. *Research in Developmental Disabilities*, 62, 115–123. DOI: 10.1016/j.ridd.2017.01.007 PMID: 28131008

Stolzer, J. (2022). ADHD: A bioecological assessment. *Deconstructing ADHD: Mental Disorder or Social Construct*, 3, 179.

Stoutjesdijk, R., Scholte, E. M., & Swaab, H. (2016). Behavioral and academic progress of children displaying substantive ADHD behaviors in special education: A 1-year follow-up. *Journal of Attention Disorders*, 20(1), 21–33. DOI: 10.1177/1087054712474687 PMID: 23382581

Surman, C. B., Biederman, J., Spencer, T., Miller, C. A., Petty, C. R., & Faraone, S. V. (2015). Neuropsychological deficits are not predictive of deficient emotional self-regulation in adults with ADHD. *Journal of Attention Disorders*, 19(12), 1046–1053. DOI: 10.1177/1087054713476548 PMID: 23503813

Tabun, K. (2019). *ADHD college students' self-perceptions of the factors of self-determination theory on their college performance*. Widener University.

Tamm, L., & Nakonezny, P. A. (2015). Metacognitive executive function training for young children with ADHD: A proof-of-concept study. *Attention Deficit and Hyperactivity Disorders*, 7(3), 183–190. DOI: 10.1007/s12402-014-0162-x PMID: 25559877

Taylor, I. (2016). Multi-professional teams and the learning organization. In *Social work, critical reflection and the learning organization* (pp. 75–86). Routledge.

Tegtmejer, T., Hjörne, E., & Säljö, R. (2021). 'The ADHD diagnosis has been thrown out': Exploring the Dilemmas of diagnosing children in a school for all. *International Journal of Inclusive Education*, 25(6), 671–685. DOI: 10.1080/13603116.2019.1569733

Thompson, K. N., Odgers, C. L., Bryan, B. T., Danese, A., Milne, B. J., Strange, L., Matthews, T., & Arseneault, L. (2022). Trajectories of childhood social isolation in a nationally representative cohort: Associations with antecedents and early adulthood outcomes. *JCPP Advances*, 2(2), e12073. DOI: 10.1002/jcv2.12073 PMID: 37431453

Tibu, F., Sheridan, M. A., McLaughlin, K. A., Nelson, C. A., Fox, N. A., & Zeanah, C. H. (2016). Reduced working memory mediates the link between early institutional rearing and symptoms of ADHD at 12 years. *Frontiers in Psychology*, 7, 1850. DOI: 10.3389/fpsyg.2016.01850 PMID: 27933019

Tsampouris, G. (2022). The relationship of metacognitive abilities of students with ADHD with their mathematical competence with the use of ICT's. *EDMETIC*, 11(2), 9–9. DOI: 10.21071/edmetic.v11i2.14569

Ünver, H., Arman, A. R., & Akpunar, Ş. N. (2022). Metacognitive awareness and emotional resilience in children with attention deficit hyperactivity disorder. *Scandinavian Journal of Child and Adolescent Psychiatry and Psychology*, 10(1), 33–39. DOI: 10.2478/sjcapp-2022-0003 PMID: 35799976

Uzuner, F. G., & Sahin, M. (2021). Examining the effect of orienteering on the development of attention, metacognitive awareness and problem-solving skills of primary school students with ADHD. *Journal of Educational Leadership and Policy Studies*.https://files.eric.ed.gov/fulltext/EJ1308451.pdf

Ventouri, E. (2020). ADHD and learning motivations. *OAlib*, 7(8), 1–28. DOI: 10.4236/oalib.1106594

Wilder, S. (2022). *Reading teacher perspectives on classroom behavior and criteria referral for ADHD Testing*. Walden University.

Williams, Y. (2022). Understanding adolescent behavior and victimization of special populations through bronfenbrenner's bioecological theory. In *Victimology: A comprehensive approach to forensic, psychosocial and legal perspectives* (pp. 401–416). Springer International Publishing. DOI: 10.1007/978-3-031-12930-8_18

Wu, I., & Molina, R. M.Jr. (2019). Self-determination of college students with learning and attention challenges. *Journal of Postsecondary Education and Disability*, 32(4), 359–375. DOI: 10.3102/1433236

Zimdars, M. (2022). *An Assessment of ADHD/LD Support in PsyD Programs from the Perspective of Faculty Advisors*. Graduate School of Professional Psychology: Doctoral Papers and Masters Projects. 453. https://digitalcommons.du.edu/capstone_masters/453

KEY TERMS AND DEFINITIONS

Academic Performance: Refers to the extent of achievement or success that a student realizes in their educational pursuits. This performance is generally evaluated through grades, test scores, assignments, projects, and participation in class activities. It reflects a student's grasp of the material, their mastery of subjects, and their ability to apply acquired knowledge and skills. Various elements can affect academic performance, such as motivation, study habits, support from teachers, family background, and the overall learning environment. High academic performance is often correlated with effective learning strategies, diligent effort, and a favorable attitude towards education. Beyond mere grades, academic performance also encompasses critical thinking, problem-solving capabilities, and the development of skills essential for future educational and career opportunities.

Academic Competencies: Refer to the critical knowledge, skills, and abilities necessary for successful engagement in educational settings. These competencies consist of subject-specific expertise, critical thinking, problem-solving, effective communication, and research skills. They also include time management, collaboration, and the ability to transfer knowledge to new contexts. By developing strong academic competencies, students are better equipped to achieve their educational goals, face new challenges, and engage meaningfully in their studies. Educators aim to enhance these competencies through effective teaching strategies, practice, and assessments. By fostering academic competencies, educational institutions prepare students for advanced education, professional careers, and ongoing learning throughout their lives.

Bronfenbrenner's Exosystem: Encompasses the wider social environments and external elements that indirectly affect an individual's development. This includes various institutions or settings in which the individual is not actively involved, yet these factors still exert influence over their life. Examples of such influences are a parent's workplace, community resources, or local governmental policies. If a parent experiences stress at work or lacks adequate support in their job, this can diminish their emotional presence at home, thereby affecting the child's overall well-being. The exosystem highlights the significance of external circumstances and decisions that lie outside an individual's direct control, illustrating how these factors can shape personal experiences and development while underscoring the interconnected nature of various social systems.

Bronfenbrenner's Chronosystem: Pertains to the temporal aspect of an individual's development, which includes the effects of significant life events as well as broader socio-historical transformations. It acknowledges that the timing of personal experiences—such as entering school, experiencing family changes, or relocating—plays a crucial role in shaping individuals' lives. Furthermore, the chronosystem takes into account how societal changes, including technological progress or economic recessions, can influence development over time. For example, the repercussions of a divorce on a child may vary based on the child's age at that moment. The chronosystem emphasizes that development is a fluid process, shaped by the passage of time and evolving circumstances.

Bronfenbrenner's Macrosystem: Represents the most expansive layer of his ecological framework, incorporating the extensive cultural, economic, political, and social contexts that impact an individual's growth. This layer encompasses cultural values, societal norms, ideologies, legal frameworks, and economic structures that define the environment in which individuals exist. The macrosystem illustrates the dominant patterns and beliefs prevalent in a society, including perspectives on education, gender roles, and social policies. For instance, societal beliefs regarding parenting methods or educational aspirations can influence the interactions between families and educational institutions. The macrosystem underscores the crucial influence of broader societal and cultural elements in shaping individuals' experiences, opportunities, and overall development.

Bronfenbrenner's Mesosystem: Describes the interactions and connections among various elements within an individual's microsystem. It includes the relationships that exist between different settings in which a person is directly involved, such as the interactions between family and educational institutions, or between peers and teachers. This mesosystem highlights the impact of these interconnected systems on an individual's development. For example, a constructive relationship between a child's parents and teachers can enhance the child's academic achievements and emotional well-being. On the other hand, conflict between home and school can lead to stress and negatively affect a child's growth. The mesosystem underscores the importance of collaboration and consistency across various areas of influence to cultivate a cohesive and supportive environment.

Bronfenbrenner's Microsystem: Characterized as the immediate environment where an individual interacts and develops. This includes direct relationships and settings such as family, educational institutions, peers, and the neighborhood. These environments significantly influence a person's growth, shaping their beliefs, behaviors, and emotional well-being. In the microsystem, interactions are mutual; individuals are not only influenced by these relationships but also play an active role in shaping them. For instance, a child's relationships with parents, teachers, or friends are fundamental to their microsystem. The nature of these interactions, whether positive or negative, profoundly affects an individual's development and self-concept, highlighting the critical need for nurturing relationships and supportive environments during early developmental phases.

Institutional Support: Refers to the resources, services, and policies that organizations, including schools, universities, and workplaces, provide to promote the well-being and success of their members. Within educational environments, institutional support may manifest as academic advising, counseling services, financial aid, career guidance, and accessibility initiatives. The aim of such support is to establish an inclusive and supportive atmosphere that caters to the needs of students or employees, encourages equity, and assists individuals in achieving their goals. Effective institutional support not only fosters a sense of belonging but also promotes engagement and enhances overall satisfaction and performance. It signifies the organization's commitment to recognizing and addressing the varied challenges and aspirations of its community members.

Self-Authorship: Defined as the ability to independently determine one's beliefs, identity, and relationships, rather than being predominantly shaped by external influences or societal expectations. This involves a critical analysis and integration of a variety of experiences, values, and perspectives to create a coherent self-identity. Individuals who reach the stage of self-authorship are capable of making confident choices, establishing meaningful connections, and effectively managing complex challenges with a clear sense of direction. This developmental process typically begins in the adolescent years and continues into adulthood, as individuals contemplate their values, goals, and beliefs. Self-authorship enhances self-awareness and promotes autonomy, resilience, and authenticity in both personal and professional contexts.

Social Isolation: Refers to a condition in which an individual has limited contact or interaction with others, often resulting in feelings of loneliness, disconnection, and emotional distress. This state can be triggered by various factors, including physical separation, social anxiety, health challenges, or societal barriers. The repercussions of social isolation can adversely affect both mental and physical health, increasing the risk of conditions such as depression, anxiety, and heart-related issues. This issue can impact people of all ages, from children who may feel alienated in school environments to older adults who may experience a decline in social interactions. Addressing social isolation requires the development of supportive social networks, the encouragement of community engagement, and the implementation of inclusive practices that allow individuals to forge and sustain meaningful connections.

Special Education: An individualized instructional strategy specifically designed to cater to the unique learning requirements of students who have disabilities or developmental challenges. It offers tailored support, necessary modifications, and accommodations to ensure that these students can thrive academically, socially, and emotionally. The services provided under special education include specialized teaching techniques, adaptive materials, assistive technology, and related therapies such as speech and occupational therapy. The primary aim is to cultivate an inclusive learning atmosphere where students with diverse needs can realize their full potential. Collaboration among educators, specialists, and families is essential in developing and implementing individualized education programs (IEPs) that define specific learning goals and support strategies for each student.

Self-Determination: Refers to the capacity to make choices and engage in actions that align with one's personal goals, values, and interests. It embodies an individual's autonomy, motivation, and control over their own life. The process of self-determination includes establishing objectives, making informed decisions, and accepting responsibility for their attainment. This principle is fundamental to personal well-being and growth, as it enables individuals to follow meaningful paths and assert their rights. In educational settings, encouraging self-determination among students is crucial for developing self-advocacy skills and enhancing their confidence. This is particularly vital for individuals with disabilities, as fostering self-determination can significantly improve their independence and active participation in their communities.

Self-Regulation: Refers to the capacity to govern one's thoughts, emotions, and actions in a manner that is consistent with personal goals, values, and societal norms. This process entails the ability to identify and manage impulses, cope with stress, maintain focus, and modify responses according to varying circumstances. It is a fundamental component of effective decision-making, goal achievement, and problem resolution, empowering individuals to demonstrate discipline and flexibility. Furthermore, self-regulation is vital for the learning process, as it enables individuals to concentrate, resist distractions, and persevere in the face of difficulties. Cultivating self-regulation skills fosters emotional resilience, encourages constructive social interactions, and enhances overall well-being and success across personal, academic, and professional domains.

Self-Perception: Defined as an individual's awareness and assessment of their own characteristics, including their abilities, personality traits, and overall self-worth. This perception is shaped by a variety of factors, including personal experiences, social interactions, and feedback from others. The manner in which individuals perceive themselves significantly affects their understanding of their strengths and weaknesses, which in turn influences their confidence, motivation, and decision-making capabilities. A positive self-perception is associated with enhanced self-esteem and resilience, while a negative self-perception can lead to self-doubt and anxiety. It is essential to recognize that self-perception is fluid and can change over time as individuals acquire new experiences and insights. Developing a healthy self-perception involves engaging in self-reflection, welcoming constructive feedback, and participating in activities that align with one's personal values and objectives.

Therapeutic Support: Refers to professional aid extended to individuals dealing with emotional, psychological, or behavioral issues. This support is offered through a variety of therapeutic approaches, including individual counseling, group therapy, and family therapy. The goal of therapeutic support is to assist individuals in reflecting on their thoughts and feelings, developing effective coping strategies, and enhancing their mental health and overall well-being. Professionals such as psychologists, counselors, and social workers provide a safe and confidential environment for clients to address concerns such as anxiety, depression, trauma, or relationship problems. Through this support, individuals can cultivate self-awareness, emotional resilience, and personal growth, enabling them to overcome challenges and lead more fulfilling lives.

Metacognitive Awareness: Defined as the recognition and regulation of one's cognitive processes related to learning. It involves an awareness of how one learns, the ability to identify personal strengths and weaknesses, and the application of strategies to improve learning outcomes. This awareness empowers individuals to plan, monitor, and evaluate their cognitive efforts, resulting in enhanced problem-solving and decision-making capabilities. For example, a student with metacognitive awareness may discern that they have difficulty retaining information and thus utilize techniques such as summarization or self-quizzing. The development of metacognitive awareness significantly boosts academic performance, critical thinking, and adaptability, equipping individuals with the skills necessary for more effective engagement with learning tasks.

Multi-Professional Network: Represents a cooperative system where professionals from diverse disciplines unite to confront complex challenges or requirements. In areas such as education, healthcare, or social services, this network encompasses educators, counselors, psychologists, social workers, physicians, and various specialists, all contributing their knowledge and skills. The aim of a multi-professional network is to offer comprehensive support, ensuring that an individual's needs are fulfilled through synchronized and integrated efforts. For instance, in educational settings, a multi-professional network may collaborate to assist a student with special educational needs by merging educational practices, psychological strategies, and social services. This collaborative approach enhances problem-solving, optimizes service delivery, and encourages holistic care and support for individuals and communities.

Norms: The collective expectations, guidelines, or standards that influence the behavior of individuals within a group or society. They determine how people conduct themselves, communicate, and interact, establishing what is regarded as acceptable or unacceptable in various social scenarios. Norms can be classified as formal, such as legal statutes and regulations, or informal, including cultural practices and social conventions. They play a vital role in shaping attitudes, behaviors, and social interactions, thereby contributing to the stability and cohesiveness of communities. Norms are acquired through socialization and can vary significantly across different cultures, societies, and groups. While they offer a framework for behavior, norms can also evolve over time in response to changing values and beliefs. Understanding these norms is essential for individuals to navigate social situations effectively and to foster harmony within groups.

APPENDIX I: STUDY QUESTIONNAIRE

Table 4. School support services for students with ADHD questionnaire (SSSSAQ)

No	Statements	NAA	SE	ME	GE	VGE
1	To what extent do you find the academic support provided by your school effective for your career transition?					
2	To what extent does your school provide career counseling that meets your career transition needs?					
3	To what extent does your school accommodate your ADHD needs during career workshops?					
4	To what extent is the communication between your teachers and career counselors regarding your ADHD effective?					
5	To what extent does your school offer individualised career planning for students with ADHD?					
6	To what extent is your school supportive towards providing ADHD resources for your career transition?					
7	To what extent are the transition programs offered by your school for students with ADHD effective?					
8	To what extent does your school involve parents in career transitioning processes?					
9	How well does your school adapt career materials to be ADHD-friendly?					
10	To what extent is the feedback you receive from career advisors effective in your career transition decision-making?					
11	To what extent does your school provide mentorship opportunities for the career transition of students with ADHD?					
12	How accessible are career services for students with ADHD at your school?					
13	To what extent are the career workshops effective in addressing ADHD-related career challenges?					
14	To what extent are career resources tailored to your interests and needs at your school?					
15	To what extent is your school supportive in helping you set realistic career goals?					
16	To what extent does your school prepare you for job interviews?					
17	To what extent does your school provide information about career opportunities?					
18	To what extent is your school's approach to integrating ADHD accommodations into career planning effective?					

NAA=Not at All, SE=Small Extent, ME=Moderate Extent, GE=Great Extent, VGE=Very Great Extent

APPENDIX II: ADDITIONAL STATISTICS

Table 5. Item-total statistics

No	Statements	Cronbach's Alpha if Item Deleted
1	To what extent do you find the academic support provided by your school effective for your career transition?	.881
2	To what extent does your school provide career counseling that meets your career transition needs?	.882
3	To what extent does your school accommodate your ADHD needs during career workshops?	.884
4	To what extent is the communication between your teachers and career counselors regarding your ADHD effective?	.882
5	To what extent does your school offer individualized career planning for students with ADHD?	.884
6	To what extent is your school supportive towards providing ADHD resources for your career transition?	.881
7	To what extent are the transition programs offered by your school for students with ADHD effective?	.882
8	To what extent does your school involve parents in career transitioning processes?	.881
9	How well does your school adapt career materials to be ADHD-friendly?	.877
10	To what extent is the feedback you receive from career advisors effective in your career transition decision-making?	.880
11	To what extent does your school provide mentorship opportunities for the career transition of students with ADHD?	.884
12	How accessible are career services for students with ADHD at your school?	.884
13	To what extent are the career workshops effective in addressing ADHD-related career challenges?	.887
14	To what extent are career resources tailored to your interests and needs at your school?	.887
15	To what extent is your school supportive in helping you set realistic career goals?	.892
16	To what extent does your school prepare you for job interviews?	.889
17	To what extent does your school provide information about career opportunities?	.890
18	To what extent is your school's approach to integrating ADHD accommodations into career planning effective?	.898

Table 6. Communalities (extraction method: principal component analysis)

No	Statements	Extraction
1	To what extent do you find the academic support provided by your school effective for your career transition?	.882
2	To what extent does your school provide career counseling that meets your career transition needs?	.865
3	To what extent does your school accommodate your ADHD needs during career workshops?	.816
4	To what extent is the communication between your teachers and career counselors regarding your ADHD effective?	.922
5	To what extent does your school offer individualized career planning for students with ADHD?	.818
6	To what extent is your school supportive towards providing ADHD resources for your career transition?	.833
7	To what extent are the transition programs offered by your school for students with ADHD effective?	.773
8	To what extent does your school involve parents in career transitioning processes?	.716
9	How well does your school adapt career materials to be ADHD-friendly?	.836
10	To what extent is the feedback you receive from career advisors effective in your career transition decision-making?	.840
11	To what extent does your school provide mentorship opportunities for the career transition of students with ADHD?	.924
12	How accessible are career services for students with ADHD at your school?	.813
13	To what extent are the career workshops effective in addressing ADHD-related career challenges?	.930
14	To what extent are career resources tailored to your interests and needs at your school?	.824
15	To what extent is your school supportive in helping you set realistic career goals?	.642
16	To what extent does your school prepare you for job interviews?	.805
17	To what extent does your school provide information about career opportunities?	.765
18	To what extent is your school's approach to integrating ADHD accommodations into career planning effective?	.709

Chapter 7
Perspectives on Assessment Tools for Evaluating Students With ADHD During Career Transitioning:
Student Survey

ABSTRACT

This study examined the perceived effectiveness of assessment tools among students with ADHD during career transitioning, with emphasis on how factors such as gender, school location, and grade level influence perceptions among students. This correlational study sampled 88 secondary school students with ADHD. Data was collected using the 14-item Perceived Effectiveness of Assessment Tools for Evaluating Students with ADHD Questionnaire. Results revealed an overall perceived effectiveness score of 2.16, indicating limited perceived effectiveness. It was further found that gender, school location, and grade level did not significantly predict the perceived effectiveness of assessment tools among students with ADHD during career transitioning.

BACKGROUND

Assessment is a process adopted to identify challenges, design programs, evaluate and diagnose students with attention-deficit/hyperactivity disorder (ADHD) and inform them, their parents, and other stakeholders about the students' career transition needs and progress. Madaan et al. (2008) assert that tools designed to

DOI: 10.4018/979-8-3693-2635-0.ch007

assist in the collection and interpretation of information from multiple sources can substantially improve diagnostic assessments and serve as valuable resources for the long-term monitoring of individuals with ADHD. In addition, Langberg et al. (2008) indicated that the ADHD diagnostic process is hindered by multiple factors, including the subjective nature of the diagnosis, the necessity for differential diagnosis in the context of comorbid conditions, and the fluctuating presentation of ADHD symptoms throughout developmental stages. Loh et al. (2022) noted that the insufficient availability of public databases that cover all modalities relevant to ADHD assessment impacts the assessment process. The prevalence rates among students with ADHD can differ due to variations in diagnostic criteria, diverse assessment techniques, and the age differences of the subjects involved (Shin et al., 2001). The perception of the effectiveness of ADHD and its assessment tools may differ owing to the diversity and inconsistencies present in various environments; therefore, an accurate diagnosis necessitates the observation of symptoms in a minimum of two distinct contexts, for instance, at home and in school (Ndukuba et al., 2017). ADHD prevalence rates exhibit significant variation across different nations and regions within a single country, and these differences are additionally shaped by the diagnostic techniques employed (Polanczyk et al., 2007; Salari et al., 2023). There are three distinct types of ADHD that can be identified through diagnosis. In the case of attention-deficit/hyperactivity disorder—predominately inattentive type, individuals exhibit a lack of attention to detail, frequently make careless errors, struggle with organization, and demonstrate difficulties in listening and following instructions accurately. Those diagnosed with attention-deficit/hyperactivity disorder—predominately hyperactive/impulsive type are often characterized by excessive fidgeting, impatience while waiting, an inability to remain seated, and potential disruptive behavior. Lastly, attention-deficit/hyperactivity disorder—combined type presents a mixture of both inattentive and hyperactive/impulsive symptoms (Stargell et al., 2017).

Despite ADHD being a commonly encountered neurodivergent condition, there are numerous controversies surrounding the most effective evaluation tools (Peterson et al., 2024; Sempere-Tortosa et al., 2021). The selection of appropriate assessment and diagnostic tools proves to be challenging due to disparities in the accessibility and quality of available instruments (Fuermaier et al., 2024). The implementation of tools that streamline the collection and interpretation of data from diverse sources in an efficient and evidence-based manner can enhance the diagnostic process (Madaan et al., 2008; Posserud et al., 2014). Furthermore, the adoption of information and communication technology tools is becoming dominant in the assessment of ADHD (Drigas & Tourimpampa, 2014). Enhancing the precision of clinical assessment is crucial to guarantee that individuals who genuinely have ADHD receive timely treatment and support (Peterson et al., 2024). A valid diagnosis and early assessment of ADHD is crucial, as undiagnosed ADHD in adulthood can have severe repercussions (Mörstedt et al., 2015), potentially impeding a student's long-term career prospects. Furthermore, there is an increasing apprehension regarding the possibility that students may simulate symptoms of ADHD to secure academic accommodation and stimulant medications (Jasinski et al., 2011). With the abundance of ADHD-related information available online, contemporary students are likely to be well-informed about symptoms prior to undergoing evaluation (Sollman et al., 2010). The authors further note that this phenomenon may lead to false-positive diagnoses, especially when students are incentivized to present symptoms. There are extensive studies on feigned ADHD, along with various symptom validity assessments (Jachimowicz & Geiselman, 2004; Harrison et al., 2007; Williamson et al., 2014; Berger et al., 2021; Potts et al., 2022). The implications of undetected feigned ADHD are significant, including considerable societal costs associated with unnecessary evaluations and treatments, the inappropriate use of limited medical resources, and a potential hindrance of public trust in the legitimacy of assessment of the disorder and the efficacy of its treatments (Tucha et al., 2015). The utilization of precise measures with strong predictive validity is of paramount importance for the early identification of pathologies such as ADHD (Matson et al., 2009).

As indicated in prior studies, the presence of ADHD symptoms in students presents unique difficulties, thereby necessitating the assessment and diagnosis of ADHD in these individuals (Lefler et al., 2021; Mandah & Mohammed, 2020). Findings suggest that college students lacking a prior ADHD diagnosis are substantially more likely than random chance to successfully mimic ADHD symptoms on rating scales (Fisher, 2006). Lahav et al. (2018) identified significant variations in performance metrics, the length of performance, and the range of strategies utilized in a performance-based diagnostic tool designed to evaluate executive functions in the everyday activities of university students, highlighting differences between students with ADHD and their peers, as well as among genders. Nevertheless, there remains a notable gap in knowledge regarding the optimal assessment and treatment of ADHD behaviors within school environments (Staff, 2022), as well as students' perceptions of ADHD assessment tools in developing regions. Despite the increasing recognition of ADHD and its effects on educational and career outcomes, there seems to be a persistent lack of specialised assessment tools designed for secondary school students with ADHD in Nigeria. This gap is particularly concerning due to the unique cultural, social, and educational contexts that shape the experiences of these students. The issue is further complicated by the reliance on existing assessment tools that are predominantly based on Western models, which may not adequately reflect the cultural nuances, and specific transition needs of Nigerian students with ADHD. Consequently, these tools may not effectively identify the cognitive and behavioral challenges faced by Nigerian students with ADHD, leading to potential misdiagnosis or insufficient support during their career transition. This issue is critical, as effective assessment is essential for creating targeted interventions that can improve academic outcomes and prepare students for their future careers (Eseadi & Diale, 2024).

Furthermore, the absence of reliable assessment tools may hinder teachers, counselors and other school-based professionals in their efforts to provide essential guidance and resources for the successful career transition of students with ADHD. The rationale for this project is rooted in the pressing need to promote culturally appropriate assessment instruments that can accurately assess ADHD among secondary school students in Nigeria. It is recognized that both subjective and objective assessment techniques offer distinct insights into the cognitive functioning of individuals with ADHD, underscoring the necessity of a holistic approach that incorporates feedback from various stakeholders, including students, teachers, and parents (Fuermaier et al., 2015; Lovett & Harrison, 2021). Specifically, this survey seeks to examine the perspectives of students with ADHD on the current assessment tools, aiming to pinpoint deficiencies and opportunities for improvement. Furthermore, addressing ADHD in secondary school students is critical for promoting their long-term success in that undetected and untreated ADHD can result in considerable academic challenges, higher dropout rates, and diminished life satisfaction in individuals (Bhullar et al., 2023; DuPaul et al., 2021; Sjöwall & Thorell, 2022). By concentrating on career transition—a critical phase in a student's educational journey—this study seeks to enhance our understanding of how the perceived effectiveness of assessment tools can impact the career transition of those with ADHD. This research will not only guide educational practices but also contribute to policy dialogues regarding ADHD support in Nigerian schools, ensuring that all students receive the necessary assessment to excel in their future careers. Understanding Nigerian students' perspectives on the effectiveness of assessment tools for ADHD will not only inform the school community about the most effective instruments for future evaluations but may also assist diagnostic and career guidance experts in improving and refining their practices and assessment modalities. Integrating these students' viewpoints into the assessment process can significantly improve the validity and reliability of diagnostic instruments. Utilizing surveys can also assist in confirming whether the constructs evaluated by existing tools resonate with students' actual experiences, ensuring that assessments remain both accurate and relevant. Therefore, this study mainly aims to ascertain perspectives on the assessment tools employed for evaluating Nigerian students with ADHD during their career transition.

Research Objectives

1. To determine the mean perceived effectiveness of assessment tools for evaluating students with ADHD during career transitioning.
2. To ascertain the extent gender predicts the perceived effectiveness of assessment tools for evaluating students with ADHD during career transitioning.
3. To investigate the extent school location predicts the perceived effectiveness of assessment tools for evaluating students with ADHD during career transitioning.
4. To ascertain the extent grade level predicts the perceived effectiveness of assessment tools for evaluating students with ADHD during career transitioning.

Research Questions

1. What is the mean perceived effectiveness of assessment tools for evaluating students with ADHD during career transitioning?
2. To what extent does gender (male and female) predict the perceived effectiveness of assessment tools for evaluating students with ADHD during career transitioning?
3. To what extent does school location (rural and urban) predict the perceived effectiveness of assessment tools for evaluating students with ADHD during career transitioning?
4. To what extent does grade level (junior and senior grades) predict the perceived effectiveness of assessment tools for evaluating students with ADHD during career transitioning?

Theoretical Framework

In this study, we rely on two key theoretical frameworks: the broaden-and-build theory of positive emotions and self-regulation theory. These frameworks are instrumental in offering insights into the assessment tools utilized for evaluating Nigerian students with ADHD during their career transition. The broaden-and-build theory, introduced by Fredrickson (2001), asserts that positive emotions are essential in widening individuals' immediate thought-action repertoires, which in turn facilitate the development of lasting personal resources. This theory suggests that emotions such as joy, interest, and contentment enhance awareness, prompting individuals to investigate new concepts, engage in innovative problem-solving, and foster social relationships. The resulting expansion of thought-action repertoires significantly aids in the cultivation of enduring physical, intellectual, social, and psychological resources. Fredrickson's theory is relevant to our research because cultivating positive emotions in students with ADHD may improve their perceptions of and engagement with assessment tools. When students experience positive emotions, they are more inclined to regard assessment tools not merely as evaluative instruments but as opportunities to explore new career avenues and realize their potential. Johnson et al. (2021) discovered that students who experience positive emotions are better prepared to cope with stressors, such as academic challenges, owing to their enhanced mental and emotional resources. In the context of ADHD, positive emotions could alleviate feelings of frustration or anxiety related to assessments, thereby promoting curiosity and resilience. According to the broaden-and-build theory, positive emotions also play a significant role in helping students establish social connections, which are vital for navigating career transition. Huppert et al. (2004) assert that positive emotions can lead to the creation of personal and social resources by inspiring individuals to seek and cultivate relationships. For students with ADHD, developing positive social connections can offer the necessary support and mentorship to effectively manage career transition. For example, assessment tools that highlight students' strengths and facilitate collaborative feedback can evoke positive emotions, allowing students to view these tools as beneficial partners in their career development rather than as challenges. Thus, the broaden-and-build theory serves as a framework for understanding how assessment tools can be crafted and utilized to foster positive emotions, ultimately improving the career transition process.

The self-regulation theory, which originated from Bandura's Social Cognitive Theory of Self-Regulation (Bandura, 1991), suggests that individuals have the ability to modify their behaviors in reaction to environmental cues instead of following strict guidelines. This adaptability empowers individuals to manage their thoughts, emotions, and actions, facilitating their adjustment to evolving situations (Williams, 2023). In the context of this study, this theory implies that students with ADHD can alter their behaviors and perspectives regarding assessment tools, influenced by their views on the significance and usefulness of these tools. Hall and Fong (2007) expand upon self-regulation theory by highlighting the significance of cognitive processes in influencing behavior. They contend that self-regulation includes various processes, such as establishing goals, tracking progress, and modifying strategies to attain desired results. For students with ADHD, self-regulation may entail understanding the importance of assessment tools, formulating personal objectives for career transitions, and actively utilizing feedback to enhance their career opportunities. Through the adoption of self-regulatory practices, students can improve their capacity to manage the challenges associated with career transitions and make well-informed choices regarding their future trajectories. In this regard, assessment instruments that foster self-reflection, goal establishment, and self-monitoring may prove especially beneficial in facilitating favorable results for students with ADHD. Due to differing socialization experiences and gender-related expectations (Gwyther & Holland, 2012; Tetering et al., 2020), male and female students with ADHD may demonstrate varying self-regulatory strategies, which can shape their views on assessment tools. Thus, gender and school location may be significant predictors of how students evaluate the effectiveness of assessment instruments, consistent with self-regulation theory, which posits that individual characteristics and environmental factors jointly shape students' responses (see Montroy et al., 2016). From this theoretical standpoint, students in higher grade levels are likely to possess enhanced self-awareness and a more defined understanding of their career aspirations, which enables them to evaluate assessment tools more effectively. Conversely, younger students may depend more heavily on external support and feedback while they navigate the process of career transition, and this can impact their evaluation of the effectiveness of assessment tools during this phase (see Figure 1).

Figure 1. Study framework

METHODOLOGY

Ethics Statement

Ethical approval for this study was obtained from the relevant institutional review boards. First, it received approval from the Research Ethics Committee of the Faculty of Education, University of Nigeria, Nigeria. It also received additional ethical approval from the Faculty of Education Research Ethics Committee at the University of Johannesburg, South Africa (Sem 2-2020-057). Informed assent was secured from participants, while written informed consent was obtained from their parents/guardians. We assured confidentiality and clarified participants' right to withdraw from the study at any given time.

Research Design and Approach

This study used a predictive correlational survey research design. A predictive correlational research design identifies the relationships between research variables, allowing for the prediction of existing associations; however, it does not establish causative links (Bloomfield & Fisher, 2019). This design is classified as a non-experimental approach that investigates the relationships among two or more variables within a single group, which can manifest at various levels (Devi, 2022). The correlational research design is deemed suitable for this study due to its inherent characteristics. A predictive correlational research framework was employed to conduct a survey among students regarding their views on assessment tools for evaluating individuals with ADHD during their career transitions. Quantitative research focuses on measurable factors, yielding numerical data that can be statistically analysed through methods such as experimentation, surveys, or questionnaires, particularly within a large, randomly selected population (Petry, 2023). The study adopted a quantitative research approach.

Research Paradigm

The term "paradigm" refers to the scientific belief systems that shape the inquiries, tools, and resolutions that researchers formulate to elucidate phenomena within particular fields, including physics, chemistry, and astronomy (Armstrong, 1999). This study is grounded in the positivist research paradigm. Positivist research maintains that the social world exists independently of human beliefs and actions. It can be described through measurable variables that remain unaffected by the researcher or human experiences (Orlikowski & Baroudi, 1991). The focus of positivist research lies in testing theories to predict and uncover facts (Halaweh, 2012).

Study Area

This research was conducted in Imo State in the South-east zone of Nigeria. The capital city of Imo State, Owerri, is situated in the southeastern part of Nigeria and spans roughly 18,602.38 hectares (Chukwuocha, et al., 2018). Imo State comprises 27 local government areas, categorized into three senatorial districts: Imo East (Owerri zone), Imo West (Orlu zone) and Imo North (Okigwe zone) (Ugo et al., 2024).

Population and Sampling

The study involves 88 students across junior and senior secondary school grades from selected public secondary schools. A total of 45 (51.1%) junior-grade students and 43 (48.9%) senior-grade students were selected using purposive and convenience sampling techniques, which are non-probability sampling methods. The selection mechanism for non-probability samples often relies on specifically designed regression residuals to augment the original dataset by incorporating observations from alternative sources that can be regarded as representative of the target population (Tutz, 2023). Convenience sampling involves gathering data from individuals within the population who are readily available for participation, whereas purposive sampling is utilized when researchers aim to investigate a specific subgroup within the population that possesses characteristics relevant to the research inquiry (FasterCapital, 2024). In qualitative research, sampling is generally purposive, meaning that participants are recruited based on shared experiences pertinent to the research question, or convenience-based, which may consider factors such as accessibility or cost (Denny & Weckesser, 2022). Male students were 32 (36.4%), whereas female students were 56 (63.6%). Participants in rural schools were 41 (46.6%), whereas those in urban schools were 47 (53.4%). The participants' mean age is 13.34 ± 1.46 years.

Data Collection

The data was collected using a questionnaire. The researchers received help from two postgraduate students to complete the data collection process. The questionnaire used for data collection is called the Perceived Effectiveness of Assessment Tools for Evaluating Students with ADHD Questionnaire (PEATESAQ). It is a 14-item scale that measures the perceived effectiveness of assessment tools for evaluating students with ADHD during career transitioning. The respondents are students diagnosed with ADHD. The 5-point Likert-type scale is designed to allow respondents to indicate their level of agreement or perception for each item, with 1 indicating "Strongly disagree" and 5 indicating "Strongly agree." Some examples of item statements in the questionnaire include: "The assessment tools help in identifying career strengths for students with ADHD", and "The feedback from these assessments is useful for planning career transition." The PEATESAQ has a good internal consistency reliability, with a Cronbach's alpha of 0.61 in the present research.

Data Analysis

Statistical analysis was conducted using Jeffreys' Amazing Statistics Program software (JASP), version 0.18.3, and SPSS, version 27. JASP is an open-source statistics package available at no cost, specifically aimed at beginners who wish to navigate analyses through a point-and-click interface, with Bayesian analysis as one of its prominent features (Muenchen, 2019). SPSS, on the other hand, is characterized by its point-and-click operations, serving as a vital tool for performing both fundamental and highly advanced statistical procedures (Mtembenuzeni, 2021). Descriptive statistics was used to summarize the sociodemographic data, while inferential statistics (regression and correlation analysis) were used to analyse the research questions at a .05 significance level. The role of descriptive statistics is to convey or outline the features and characteristics of data, offering quantitative insights via numerical or graphical representations, while inferential statistics are employed to draw conclusions or inferences from the data derived from a smaller population or group (Bradley University, 2020).

FINDINGS

Table 1. Mean perceived effectiveness of assessment tools for evaluating students with ADHD during career transitioning

Gender	School Location	Grade Level	Mean	Std. Deviation	N
Male students	Rural schools	Junior Grades	2.14	.16	4
		Senior Grades	1.87	.53	5
		Total	1.99	.41	9
	Urban schools	Junior Grades	2.10	.24	16
		Senior Grades	2.37	.42	7
		Total	2.18	.32	23
	Total	Junior Grades	2.11	.22	20
		Senior Grades	2.16	.51	12
		Total	2.13	.35	32
Female students	Rural schools	Junior Grades	2.11	.33	12
		Senior Grades	2.22	.27	20
		Total	2.18	.29	32
	Urban schools	Junior Grades	2.07	.25	13
		Senior Grades	2.29	.38	11
		Total	2.17	.33	24
	Total	Junior Grades	2.09	.28	25
		Senior Grades	2.24	.31	31
		Total	2.18	.30	56
Total	Rural schools	Junior Grades	2.12	.29	16
		Senior Grades	2.15	.35	25
		Total	2.14	.32	41
	Urban schools	Junior Grades	2.09	.24	29
		Senior Grades	2.32	.38	18
		Total	2.18	.32	47
	Total	Junior Grades	2.10	.26	45
		Senior Grades	2.22	.37	43
		Total	2.16	.32	88

The mean perceived effectiveness of assessment tools for evaluating students with ADHD during career transitioning is shown in Table 1. The overall mean effectiveness across all students is 2.16, with a standard deviation of .32. The overall average indicates limited perceived effectiveness of assessment tools used for evaluating students with ADHD during career transitioning.

Table 2. Pearson's correlations among study variables

		Pearson's r	P	Lower 95% CI	Upper 95% CI
Gender -	**School Location**	**-.280****	**.008**	**-.462**	**-.075**
Gender -	Grade Level	.172	.109	-.039	.368
Gender -	PEATESAQ	.070	.515	-.141	.276
School Location -	Grade Level	-.226*	.034	-.416	-.018
School Location -	PEATESAQ	.058	.593	-.153	.264
Grade Level -	PEATESAQ	.190	.077	-.020	.384

* p < .05, ** p < .01, *** p < .001

Table 2 shows the Pearson's correlations among the study variables. As shown, there is a significant negative correlation between gender and school location (r =-.280, p<.01), indicating a weak inverse relationship. Also, a significant negative correlation exists between school location and grade level (r =.226, p<.05), suggesting a weak inverse relationship. Other correlations, such as between gender and grade level, and between school location and perceived effectiveness, are not statistically significant.

Table 3. Regression analysis ascertaining whether gender, school location and grade level predict the perceived effectiveness of assessment tools for evaluating students with ADHD during career transitioning

Model		Unstandardized Coefficients		Standardized Coefficients	T	Sig.	95% CI for B	
		B	Std. Error	Beta			Lower Bound	Upper Bound
1	(Constant)	1.767	.217		8.161	.000	1.336	2.198
	Gender	.046	.074	.070	.625	.534	-.101	.193
	School Location	.079	.072	.124	1.099	.275	-.064	.222
	GradeLevel	.131	.070	.206	1.874	.064	-.008	.270

The data in Table 3 suggests that gender does not significantly predict perceived effectiveness, as the regression analysis shows a non-significant p-value (.534) for gender. This indicates that both male and female students perceive the effectiveness of assessment tools similarly. Similarly, school location (rural vs. urban) does not significantly predict perceived effectiveness, with a p-value of .275. This suggests that the location of the school does not have a substantial impact on how students perceive the effectiveness of the assessment tools. Although the p-value for grade level (.064) is closer to the threshold of significance, it is still not statistically significant. This implies that there is no strong evidence to suggest that students in different grade levels (junior vs. senior) perceive the effectiveness differently. Figure 2 illustrates the relationship between the predictor variables and the perceived effectiveness of assessment tools among students with ADHD during career transitioning.

Figure 2. Illustrating the perceived effectiveness of assessment tools for evaluating students with ADHD during career transitioning

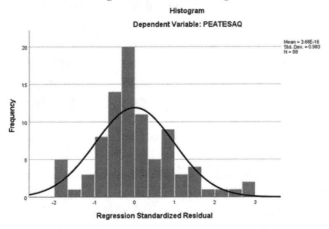

DISCUSSION

This study aimed to examine perspectives on the effectiveness of assessment tools used for evaluating students with ADHD during their career transition. The study found that the overall average indicates limited perceived effectiveness of assessment tools used for evaluating students with ADHD during career transitioning. Student participants in Golson et al. (2022) expressed feelings of indifference or negative emotions regarding the ADHD assessment process, which aligns with our findings. Students expressed that they either did not know about the services offered, decided against using them, or discovered that the services they required were unavailable (Lawrence, 2009). Furthermore, Dvorsky's et al. (2016) analysis of student ratings for ADHD diagnosis suggests that clinical utility analyses of symptoms do not consistently meet acceptable standards for confirming or excluding an ADHD diagnosis. Consequently, this study indicated that self-ratings from students may not be sufficiently reliable or accurate for diagnosing ADHD. Conversely,

Staff (2022) indicated that, in their study, the assessment tools commonly utilized in both school and clinical settings for ADHD diagnosis are valid and beneficial for assessing ADHD behaviours. Drawing from the broaden-and-build theory (Fredrickson, 2001), the effectiveness of these tools can be improved when they generate positive emotional responses from students with ADHD. Assessment tools that are seen as supportive, empowering, and oriented towards personal growth are likely to be regarded as more effective by students, aligning with the theory's principle of enhancing positive emotions and developing lasting resources. Thus, this theory provides a foundation for a potential hypothesis for researchers that assessment tools perceived to encourage positive emotions will likely receive elevated effectiveness ratings from students with ADHD. Notwithstanding these theoretical frameworks, Krumboltz and Worthington (2011) argued that the process of learning is essential for students as it not only aids in the development of employability skills necessary for career transitioning but also cultivates important work habits, values, beliefs, and interests. The authors further posited that career counselors may benefit from adopting a learning-oriented framework by employing assessment tools that facilitate new educational experiences instead of merely correlating existing traits with specific job roles. This approach aims to yield emotional, cognitive, and performance-based outcomes, defining success through the counselees' sustained involvement in learning activities that enhance their quality of life, rather than focusing exclusively on their decisiveness or job compatibility, according to these scholars.

Our study also revealed that gender, school location and grade level did not significantly predict the perceived effectiveness of assessment tools for evaluating students with ADHD during career transitioning. This suggests that students' perceptions of assessment tools remain unaffected by individual factors, including gender, school location, and grade level. Feldman and Reiff (2014) found that the criteria for ADHD diagnosis are centered on behavioral symptoms, as similar characteristics can be found in children and adolescents during typical developmental stages. Various studies (e.g., Hartman et al., 2016; Kieling & Rohde, 2012; Langberg, Epstein, et al., 2008) revealed that ADHD symptoms peak during adolescence, with lower occurrences in early childhood and old age, often resulting in significant dysfunction and morbidity throughout life. Curchack-Lichtin et al. (2014) argued that several ADHD assessment instruments may offer limited diagnostic differentiation before reaching a specific age. It can be inferred that certain ADHD assessment tools may be more effective for specific age groups or grade levels. Lea Holland et al. (1998) identified considerable differences in ADHD symptoms between genders. Findings from Zendarski et al. (2020) demonstrated that students with ADHD exhibited lower social and emotional skills compared to their peers without ADHD, with these skills being influenced by the student's gender. Lee (2008) found that there was a greater prevalence of boys than girls who had been diagnosed with ADHD or were expected to be diagnosed. Skogli et al. (2013) opined that girls may frequently be underdiagnosed due to variations in how the disorder manifests in boys compared to girls. Mowlem et al. (2019) found that various factors may affect the likelihood of girls and boys meeting the diagnostic criteria for ADHD. Slobodin and Davidovitch (2019) argued that while a gender disparity exists in ADHD diagnoses, no significant differences in distractibility levels were observed during assessments. However, a deeper understanding of gender differences could enhance the perceived efficacy of these assessment instruments. Attoe and Climie (2023) indicated the presence of gender disparities in both the rates of diagnosis and the criteria used for diagnosis. The emotional characteristics often attributed to women can impact the diagnosis of ADHD. A woman's gender does not exclusively compromise the perceived effectiveness of assessment tools; instead, individual perceptions influenced by societal norms, traditional beliefs (Song, 2024) or personal experiences may contribute to this issue.

According to Peterson et al. (2024), a reliable and valid diagnosis of ADHD hinges on the assessment conducted by a clinician who possesses substantial expertise in evaluating young individuals, both with and without the condition. This evaluation should be supported by standardized rating scales and insights from various informants across different contexts, including parents, teachers, and the youths involved. Alexopoulou et al. (2019) emphasized that certain technology-based assessment, diagnostic and intervention tools can function in a supportive manner, thereby ensuring optimal outcomes for students. Diale (2022) noted that the implementation of digital assessment tools for students with ADHD was somewhat rated as being useful for this group. Although the study highlighted the efficacy of these digital tools, their adoption remains infrequent, likely due to challenges associated with underdevelopment or the high costs of the required facilities in developing regions. Schools in urban and suburban areas are often favored with access to assessment tools, such as digital assessment technologies, in contrast to their rural counterparts. This points to the fact that when students from rural regions are surveyed, they are likely to base their responses on the less sophisticated assessment tools available to them. Iskandar and Ganesan (2016) indicated that both undergraduate and postgraduate students favored traditional assessment formats over online alternatives. This suggests that ADHD evaluations could be perceived more positively when conducted in a physical format than digital format by students. Also, early diagnosis and identification of ADHD play a crucial role in a student's development and academic achievement, as well as in the impact of their support systems on self-awareness and self-confidence (Pirozzi, 2022). In developing countries, there is currently a significant lack of awareness among the general population, as well as insufficient skills in diagnosis and optimal management (Frank-Briggs, 2011). The implications of this study are the need for further examination of the perception of students on ADHD assessment tools, the identification of effective diagnostic strategies for students diagnosed with ADHD, and the promotion of professional learning communities to enhance collaboration among educators (Garcia, 2013). In practical terms, even when research indicates effectiveness, a perceived lack of acceptability among students can result in reduced adherence and participation, thereby compromising the effectiveness of the services provided (Caporino & Karver, 2012). Nonetheless, in order to identify the most effective ADHD assessment tools, it is essential to take into account additional factors beyond gender, school location, and grade level. Subsequent analyses should take our findings into account and investigate how the reviewed theories can be effectively situated to enhance the understanding of students' perspectives. The limitations of this research stem from its geographical restriction to student participants from Imo State, an area primarily inhabited by the Igbo ethnic group, thereby limiting the applicability of the findings to other geopolitical zones of Nigeria. Furthermore, the study exclusively involved secondary school students, which made it impossible for the researchers to obtain a nuanced understanding of how different educational levels impact the perceived effectiveness of assessment tools for students with ADHD. Gaining an understanding of both secondary and university students' perspectives on the effectiveness of specific ADHD assessment tools can help inform practitioners about effective evaluation methods and assist diagnostic professionals in refining their practices.

CONCLUSIONS

The overall perceived effectiveness of assessment tools used for students with ADHD during career transitioning is limited, with no significant differences based on gender, school location, or grade level. Thus, current assessment tools may not be effectively tailored to meet the diverse needs of students with ADHD during career transitioning. The findings indicate a potential gap in the effectiveness of assessment tools, highlighting the need for more personalized and adaptable tools that can better support students with ADHD during career transitioning. To this end, future research should focus on developing and testing new assessment tools that are more tailored to the unique career transition needs of students with ADHD. These tools should consider individual differences and be adaptable to various educational and career contexts. Further studies should also examine the role of potential factors, such as cultural factors or specific educational interventions, in shaping the perceived effectiveness of these tools among students with ADHD.

REFERENCES

Alexopoulou, A., Batsou, A., & Drigas, A. S. (2019). Effectiveness of Assessment, Diagnostic and Intervention ICT Tools for Children and Adolescents with ADHD. *International Journal of Recent Contributions from Engineering. Science and IT*, 7(3), 51–63. DOI: 10.3991/ijes.v7i3.11178

Armstrong, T. (1999). *ADD/ADHD alternatives in the classroom*. ASCD.

Attoe, D. E., & Climie, E. A. (2023). Miss. Diagnosis: A Systematic Review of ADHD in Adult Women. *Journal of Attention Disorders*, 27(7), 645–657. DOI: 10.1177/10870547231161533 PMID: 36995125

Bandura, A. (1991). Social cognitive theory of self-regulation. *Organizational Behavior and Human Decision Processes*, 50(2), 248–287. DOI: 10.1016/0749-5978(91)90022-L

Berger, C., Lev, A., Braw, Y., Elbaum, T., Wagner, M., & Rassovsky, Y. (2021). Detection of Feigned ADHD Using the MOXO-d-CPT. *Journal of Attention Disorders*, 25(7), 1032–1047. DOI: 10.1177/1087054719864656 PMID: 31364437

Bhullar, A., Kumar, K., & Anand, A. (2023). ADHD and Neuropsychology: Developmental Perspective, Assessment, and Interventions. *Annals of Neurosciences*, 30(1), 5–7. DOI: 10.1177/09727531231171765 PMID: 37313332

Bloomfield, J., & Fisher, M. (2019). Quantitative research design. *JARNA*, 22(2), 27–30. DOI: 10.33235/jarna.22.2.27-30

Bradley University. (2020, February 26). Descriptive Statistics vs. Inferential Statistics. *Bradley University Online*. https://onlinedegrees.bradley.edu/blog/whats-the-difference-between-descriptive-and-inferential-statistics/

Caporino, N. E., & Karver, M. S. (2012). The acceptability of treatments for depression to a community sample of adolescent girls. *Journal of Adolescence*, 35(5), 1237–1245. DOI: 10.1016/j.adolescence.2012.04.007 PMID: 22622004

Chukwuocha, U. M., Okorie, P. C., Iwuoha, G. N., Ibe, S. N., Dozie, I. N., & Nwoke, B. E. (2018). Awareness, perceptions and intent to comply with the prospective malaria vaccine in parts of South Eastern Nigeria. *Malaria Journal*, 17(1), 1–7. DOI: 10.1186/s12936-018-2335-0 PMID: 29720172

Curchack-Lichtin, J. T., Chacko, A., & Halperin, J. M. (2014). Changes in ADHD Symptom Endorsement: Preschool to School Age. *Journal of Abnormal Child Psychology*, 42(6), 993–1004. DOI: 10.1007/s10802-013-9834-9 PMID: 24343794

Denny, E., & Weckesser, A. (2022). How to do qualitative research?: Qualitative research methods. *BJOG*, 129(7), 1166–1167. DOI: 10.1111/1471-0528.17150 PMID: 35430773

Devi, D. B. (2022). Application of correlational research design in nursing and medical research. *Xi'an Shiyou Daxue Xuebao (Ziran Kexue Ban). Journal of Xi'an Shiyou University*, 65(11), 60–69. DOI: 10.17605/OSF.IO/YRZ68

Diale, B. (2022). Digital tools used by teachers for assessing learners with Attention-Deficit/Hyperactivity Disorder (ADHD): Implications for career transitioning. *International Journal of Health Sciences*, •••, 48842–48855. DOI: 10.53730/ijhs.v6nS7.13673

DuPaul, G. J., Gormley, M. J., Anastopoulos, A. D., Weyandt, L. L., Labban, J., Sass, A. J., Busch, C. Z., Franklin, M. K., & Postler, K. B. (2021). Academic Trajectories of College Students with and without ADHD: Predictors of Four-Year Outcomes. *Journal of Clinical Child and Adolescent Psychology: the official journal for the Society of Clinical Child and Adolescent Psychology, American Psychological Association, Division 53*, 50(6), 828–843. DOI: 10.1080/15374416.2020.1867990

Dvorsky, M. R., Langberg, J. M., Molitor, S. J., & Bourchtein, E. (2016). Clinical utility and predictive validity of parent and college student symptom ratings in predicting an ADHD diagnosis. *Journal of Clinical Psychology*, 72(4), 401–418. DOI: 10.1002/jclp.22268 PMID: 26919681

Eseadi, C., & Diale, B. M. (Eds.). (2024). *Perspectives on Career Transitioning of Students with Hearing Impairments*. IGI Global., DOI: 10.4018/979-8-3693-2631-2

FasterCapital. (2024, June 19). *Convenience Sampling: Conveniently Purposed: The Intersection of Convenience and Purposive Sampling* [Online incubator]. FasterCapital. https://fastercapital.com/content/Convenience-Sampling--Conveniently-Purposed--The-Intersection-of-Convenience-and-Purposive-Sampling.html

Feldman, H. M., & Reiff, M. I. (2014). Attention Deficit–Hyperactivity Disorder in Children and Adolescents. *The New England Journal of Medicine*, 370(9), 838–846. DOI: 10.1056/NEJMcp1307215 PMID: 24571756

Fisher, A. B. (2006). *ADHD Rating Scales' Susceptibility to Faking In A College Student Sample* [The Pennsylvania State University]. https://etda.libraries.psu.edu/files/final_submissions/2

Frank-Briggs, A. I. (2011). Attention deficit hyperactivity disorder (ADHD). *Journal of Pediatric Neurology*, 9(03), 291–298. DOI: 10.3233/JPN-2011-0494

Fredrickson, B. L. (2001). The role of positive emotions in positive psychology: The broaden-and-build theory of positive emotions. *The American Psychologist*, 56(3), 218–226. DOI: 10.1037/0003-066X.56.3.218 PMID: 11315248

Fuermaier, A. B. M., Gontijo-Santos Lima, C., & Tucha, O. (2024). Impairment Assessment in Adult ADHD and Related Disorders: Current Opinions From Clinic and Research. *Journal of Attention Disorders*, 28(12), 1529–1541. DOI: 10.1177/10870547241261598 PMID: 38898706

Fuermaier, A. B. M., Tucha, L., Koerts, J., Aschenbrenner, S., Kaunzinger, I., Hauser, J., Weisbrod, M., Lange, K. W., & Tucha, O. (2015). Cognitive impairment in adult ADHD—Perspective matters! *Neuropsychology*, 29(1), 45–58. DOI: 10.1037/neu0000108 PMID: 24933488

Garcia, M. M. (2013). Reaching all learners: A study of teacher's perspectives about cooperative learning and students diagnosed with ADHD. (Doctoral Dissertation, Capella University).

Golson, M. E., Roanhorse, T. T., McClain, M. B., Galliher, R. V., & Domenech Rodríguez, M. M. (2022). School-based ADHD services: Perspectives from racially and ethnically minoritized students. *Psychology in the Schools*, 59(4), 726–743. DOI: 10.1002/pits.22640

Gwyther, H., & Holland, C. (2012). The effect of age, gender and attitudes on self-regulation in driving. *Accident; Analysis and Prevention*, 45, 19–28. DOI: 10.1016/j.aap.2011.11.022 PMID: 22269481

Halaweh, M. (2012). Integration of Grounded Theory and Case Study: An Exemplary Application from E-commerce Security Perception Research. [JITTA]. *Journal of Information Technology Theory and Application*, 13(1), 31–51.

Hall, P. A., & Fong, G. T. (2007). Temporal self-regulation theory: A model for individual health behavior. *Health Psychology Review*, 1(1), 6–52. DOI: 10.1080/17437190701492437

Harrison, A. G., Edwards, M. J., & Parker, K. C. H. (2007). Identifying students faking ADHD: Preliminary findings and strategies for detection. *Archives of Clinical Neuropsychology*, 22(5), 577–588. DOI: 10.1016/j.acn.2007.03.008 PMID: 17507198

Hartman, C. A., Geurts, H. M., Franke, B., Buitelaar, J. K., & Rommelse, N. N. J. (2016). Changing ASD-ADHD symptom co-occurrence across the lifespan with adolescence as crucial time window: Illustrating the need to go beyond childhood. *Neuroscience and Biobehavioral Reviews*, 71, 529–541. DOI: 10.1016/j.neubiorev.2016.09.003 PMID: 27629802

Huppert, F. A., Baylis, N., Keverne, B., & Fredrickson, B. L. (2004). The broaden–and–build theory of positive emotions. *Philosophical Transactions of the Royal Society of London. Series B, Biological Sciences*, 359(1449), 1367–1377. DOI: 10.1098/rstb.2004.1512 PMID: 15347528

Iskandar, N., & Ganesan, N. (2016). Students' Perception Towards the Usage of Online Assessment in University Putra Malaysia Amidst COVID-19 Pandemic. *Journal of Research in Humanities and Social Science*, 9(2), 9–16.

Jachimowicz, G., & Geiselman, R. E. (2004). Comparison of Ease of Falsification of Attention Deficit Hyperactivity Disorder Diagnosis Using Standard Behavioral Rating Scales. *Cognitive Science Online*, 2, 6–20.

Jasinski, L. J., Harp, J. P., Berry, D. T., Shandera-Ochsner, A. L., Mason, L. H., & Ranseen, J. D. (2011). Using symptom validity tests to detect malingered ADHD in college students. *The Clinical Neuropsychologist*, 25(8), 1415–1428. DOI: 10.1080/13854046.2011.630024 PMID: 22084858

Johnson, L. K., Nadler, R., Carswell, J., & Minda, J. P. (2021). Using the Broaden-and-Build Theory to Test a Model of Mindfulness, Affect, and Stress. *Mindfulness*, 12(7), 1696–1707. DOI: 10.1007/s12671-021-01633-5

Kieling, R., & Rohde, L. A. (2012). ADHD in Children and Adults: Diagnosis and Prognosis. In C. Stanford & R. Tannock (Eds.), *Behavioral Neuroscience of Attention Deficit Hyperactivity Disorder and Its Treatment* (pp. 1–16). Springer. DOI: 10.1007/7854_2010_115

Krumboltz, J. D., & Worthington, R. L. (2011). The school-to-work transition from a learning theory perspective. *The Career Development Quarterly*, 47(4), 312–325. DOI: 10.1002/j.2161-0045.1999.tb00740.x

Lahav, O., Ben-Simon, A., Inbar-Weiss, N., & Katz, N. (2018). Weekly Calendar Planning Activity for University Students: Comparison of Individuals With and Without ADHD by Gender. *Journal of Attention Disorders*, 22(4), 368–378. DOI: 10.1177/1087054714564621 PMID: 25555627

Langberg, J. M., Epstein, J. N., Altaye, M., Molina, B. S. G., Arnold, L. E., & Vitiello, B. (2008). The Transition to Middle School is Associated with Changes in the Developmental Trajectory of ADHD Symptomatology in Young Adolescents with ADHD. *Journal of Clinical Child and Adolescent Psychology*, 37(3), 651–663. DOI: 10.1080/15374410802148095 PMID: 18645755

Langberg, J. M., Froehlich, T. E., Loren, R. E., Martin, J. E., & Epstein, J. N. (2008). Assessing children with ADHD in primary care settings. *Expert Review of Neurotherapeutics*, 8(4), 627–641. DOI: 10.1586/14737175.8.4.627 PMID: 18416664

Lawrence, C. N. (2009). *Experiences of community college students with ADHD: A qualitative study in the tradition of phenomenology*. The Graduate College of the University of Nebraska.

Lea Holland, M., Gimpel, G. A., & Merrell, K. W. (1998). Innovations in assessing ADHD: Development, psychometric properties, and factor structure of the ADHD Symptoms Rating Scale (ADHD-SRS). *Journal of Psychopathology and Behavioral Assessment*, 20(4), 307–332. DOI: 10.1023/A:1021915606301

Lee, K. (2008). ADHD in American early schooling: From a cultural psychological perspective. *Early Child Development and Care*, 178(4), 415–439. DOI: 10.1080/03004430701321852

Lefler, E. K., Flory, K., Canu, W. H., Willcutt, E. G., & Hartung, C. M. (2021). Unique considerations in the assessment of ADHD in college students. *Journal of Clinical and Experimental Neuropsychology*, 43(4), 352–369. DOI: 10.1080/13803395.2021.1936462 PMID: 34078248

Loh, H. W., Ooi, C. P., Barua, P. D., Palmer, E. E., Molinari, F., & Acharya, U. R. (2022). Automated detection of ADHD: Current trends and future perspective. *Computers in Biology and Medicine*, 146, 105525. DOI: 10.1016/j.compbiomed.2022.105525 PMID: 35468405

Lovett, B. J., & Harrison, A. G. (2021). Assessing adult ADHD: New research and perspectives. *Journal of Clinical and Experimental Neuropsychology*, 43(4), 333–339. DOI: 10.1080/13803395.2021.1950640 PMID: 34227454

Madaan, V., Daughton, J., Lubberstedt, B., Mattai, A., Vaughan, B. S., & Kratochvil, C. J. (2008). Assessing the efficacy of treatments for ADHD: Overview of methodological issues. *CNS Drugs*, 22(4), 275–290. DOI: 10.2165/00023210-200822040-00002 PMID: 18336058

Mandah, S. N., & Mohammed, J. I. (2020). Curbing Strategies towards Attention Deficit Hyperactivity Disorder (ADHD) Among Senior Secondary School Students in Ikwerre Local Government Area of Rivers State, Nigeria: Implication for Curriculum Planners. *International Journal of Scientific Research in Education*, 13(3), 541–557.

Matson, J. L., Andrasik, F., & Matson, M. L. (Eds.). (2009). *Assessing Childhood Psychopathology and Developmental Disabilities*. Springer., DOI: 10.1007/978-0-387-09528-8

Montroy, J. J., Bowles, R. P., Skibbe, L. E., McClelland, M. M., & Morrison, F. J. (2016). The development of self-regulation across early childhood. *Developmental Psychology*, 52(11), 1744–1762. DOI: 10.1037/dev0000159 PMID: 27709999

Mörstedt, B., Corbisiero, S., Bitto, H., & Stieglitz, R.-D. (2015). Attention-deficit/hyperactivity disorder (ADHD) in adulthood: Concordance and differences between self-and informant perspectives on symptoms and functional impairment. *PLoS One*, 10(11), e0141342. DOI: 10.1371/journal.pone.0141342 PMID: 26529403

Mowlem, F., Agnew-Blais, J., Taylor, E., & Asherson, P. (2019). Do different factors influence whether girls versus boys meet ADHD diagnostic criteria? Sex differences among children with high ADHD symptoms. *Psychiatry Research*, 272, 765–773. DOI: 10.1016/j.psychres.2018.12.128 PMID: 30832197

Mtembenuzeni, A. (2021, February 6). *Best Free Software Alternatives to SPSS for data analysis*. Datafordev. https://datafordev.com/best-free-software-alternatives-to-spss-for-data-analysis/

Muenchen, R. A. (2019, April 9). *A Comparative Review of the JASP Statistical Software*. https://r4stats.com/articles/software-reviews/jasp/

Ndukuba, A., Odinka, P., Muomah, R., Obindo, J., & Omigbodun, O. (2017). ADHD among rural southeastern Nigerian primary school children: Prevalence and psychosocial factors. *Journal of Attention Disorders*, 21(10), 865–871. DOI: 10.1177/1087054714543367 PMID: 25069585

Orlikowski, W. J., & Baroudi, J. J. (1991). Studying Information Technology in Organizations: Research Approaches and Assumptions. *Information Systems Research*, 2(1), 1–28. DOI: 10.1287/isre.2.1.1

Peterson, B. S., Trampush, J., Brown, M., Maglione, M., Bolshakova, M., Rozelle, M., Miles, J., Pakdaman, S., Yagyu, S., Motala, A., & Hempel, S. (2024). Tools for the Diagnosis of ADHD in Children and Adolescents: A Systematic Review. *Pediatrics*, 153(4), e2024065854. DOI: 10.1542/peds.2024-065854 PMID: 38523599

Petry, B. (2023). *Library Guides: Quantitative and Empirical Research vs. Other Types of Research: Quantitative Research*. https://libguides.csusb.edu/c.php?g=234731&p=1557986

Pirozzi, M. (2022). *The Perception of the College Experience for Students with ADHD*.

Polanczyk, G., de Lima, M. S., Horta, B. L., Biederman, J., & Rohde, L. A. (2007). The worldwide prevalence of ADHD: A systematic review and metaregression analysis. *The American Journal of Psychiatry*, 164(6), 942–948. DOI: 10.1176/ajp.2007.164.6.942 PMID: 17541055

Posserud, M.-B., Ullebø, A. K., Plessen, K. J., Stormark, K. M., Gillberg, C., & Lundervold, A. J. (2014). Influence of assessment instrument on ADHD diagnosis. *European Child & Adolescent Psychiatry*, 23(4), 197–205. DOI: 10.1007/s00787-013-0442-6 PMID: 23824470

Potts, H. E., Lewandowski, L. J., & Lovett, B. J. (2022). Identifying feigned ADHD in college students: Comparing the multidimensional ADHD rating scale to established validity measures. *Journal of Attention Disorders*, 26(12), 1622–1630. DOI: 10.1177/10870547221092095 PMID: 35466735

Salari, N., Ghasemi, H., Abdoli, N., Rahmani, A., Shiri, M. H., Hashemian, A. H., Akbari, H., & Mohammadi, M. (2023). The global prevalence of ADHD in children and adolescents: A systematic review and meta-analysis. *Italian Journal of Pediatrics*, 49(1), 48. DOI: 10.1186/s13052-023-01456-1 PMID: 37081447

Sempere-Tortosa, M., Fernández-Carrasco, F., Navarro-Soria, I., & Rizo-Maestre, C. (2021). Movement patterns in students diagnosed with adhd, objective measurement in a natural learning environment. *International Journal of Environmental Research and Public Health*, 18(8), 3870. DOI: 10.3390/ijerph18083870 PMID: 33917074

Shin, M.-S., Cho, S.-C., Hong, K.-E., & Bahn, G.-H. (2001). A preliminary study for the development of the assessment scale for ADHD in adolescents: Reliability and validity for CASS (S). *Journal of the Korean Academy of Child and Adolescent Psychiatry*, 12(2), 218–224. DOI: 10.5765/jkacap.200044 PMID: 33828406

Sjöwall, D., & Thorell, L. B. (2022). Neuropsychological deficits in relation to ADHD symptoms, quality of life, and daily life functioning in young adulthood. *Applied Neuropsychology. Adult*, 29(1), 32–40. DOI: 10.1080/23279095.2019.1704287 PMID: 31881160

Skogli, E. W., Teicher, M. H., Andersen, P. N., Hovik, K. T., & Øie, M. (2013). ADHD in girls and boys – gender differences in co-existing symptoms and executive function measures. *BMC Psychiatry*, 13(1), 298. DOI: 10.1186/1471-244X-13-298 PMID: 24206839

Slobodin, O., & Davidovitch, M. (2019). Gender Differences in Objective and Subjective Measures of ADHD Among Clinic-Referred Children. *Frontiers in Human Neuroscience*, 13, 441. DOI: 10.3389/fnhum.2019.00441 PMID: 31920599

Sollman, M. J., Ranseen, J. D., & Berry, D. T. R. (2010). Detection of feigned ADHD in college students. *Psychological Assessment*, 22(2), 325–335. DOI: 10.1037/a0018857 PMID: 20528060

Song, S. (2024). The Role of Cultural Factors in Attention Deficit Hyperactivity Disorder (ADHD) Diagnosis in Children in Nigeria. *Studies in Psychological Science*, 2(1), 40–47. DOI: 10.56397/SPS.2024.03.05

Staff, A. I. (2022). *Dealing with ADHD at school: Further insight into the assessment and treatment of ADHD behavior in the classroom.* (Doctoral Dissertation, Vrije Universiteit Amsterdam).

Stargell, N. A., Barker, L. A., Kress, V. E., & Bullock, M. L. (2017). Counseling Youth With Attention-Deficit/Hyperactivity Disorder (ADHD). American Counseling Association Practice Briefs, 1-5. The Center for Counseling Practice, Policy, and Research. https://www.counseling.org/docs/default-source/practice-briefs/counseling-youth-with-adhd.pdf

Tetering, M. A. J. V., Laan, A. M. V., Kogel, C. H., Groot, R. H. M., & Jolles, J. (2020). Sex differences in self-regulation in early, middle and late adolescence: A large-scale cross-sectional study. *PLoS One*, 15(1), e0227607. DOI: 10.1371/journal.pone.0227607 PMID: 31929576

Tutz, G. (2023). Probability and non-probability samples: Improving regression modeling by using data from different sources. *Information Sciences*, 621, 424–436. DOI: 10.1016/j.ins.2022.11.032

Ugo, C., Eme, P., Eze, P., Obajaja, H., & Omeili, A.Chinemerem Henry UgoPaul Eze EmePerpetua Ngozi EzeHenry Asusheyi ObajajaAfoma Emmanuela Omeili. (2024). Chemical assessment of the quality of palm oil produced and sold in major markets in Orlu zone in Imo state, Nigeria. *World Journal of Advanced Research and Reviews*, 21(2), 1025–1033. DOI: 10.30574/wjarr.2024.21.2.0529

Williams, K. (2023, November 21). *Self-Regulation Theory | Overview, Components & Strategies—Lesson.* https://study.com/learn/lesson/self-regulation-theory-overview-components-strategies.html

Williamson, K. D., Combs, H. L., Berry, D. T. R., Harp, J. P., Mason, L. H., & Edmundson, M. (2014). Discriminating Among ADHD Alone, ADHD With a Comorbid Psychological Disorder, and Feigned ADHD in a College Sample. *The Clinical Neuropsychologist*, 28(7), 1182–1196. DOI: 10.1080/13854046.2014.956674 PMID: 25225947

Zendarski, N., Haebich, K., Bhide, S., Quek, J., Nicholson, J. M., Jacobs, K. E., Efron, D., & Sciberras, E. (2020). Student–teacher relationship quality in children with and without ADHD: A cross-sectional community based study. *Early Childhood Research Quarterly*, 51, 275–284. DOI: 10.1016/j.ecresq.2019.12.006

ADDITIONAL READINGS

Adamou, M., Fullen, T., & Jones, S. L. (2020). EEG for diagnosis of adult ADHD: A systematic review with narrative analysis. *Frontiers in Psychiatry*, 11, 871. DOI: 10.3389/fpsyt.2020.00871 PMID: 33192633

Ainsworth, B., Cahalin, L., Buman, M., & Ross, R. (2015). The current state of physical activity assessment tools. *Progress in Cardiovascular Diseases*, 57(4), 387–395. DOI: 10.1016/j.pcad.2014.10.005 PMID: 25446555

Alexopoulou, A., Batsou, A., & Drigas, A. S. (2019). Effectiveness of assessment, diagnostic and intervention ict tools for children and adolescents with ADHD. *Int. J. Recent Contributions Eng. Sci. IT*, 7(3), 51–63. DOI: 10.3991/ijes.v7i3.11178

Alghamdi, N., den Heijer, A., & de Jonge, H. (2017). Assessment tools' indicators for sustainability in universities: An analytical overview. *International Journal of Sustainability in Higher Education*, 18(1), 84–115. DOI: 10.1108/IJSHE-04-2015-0071

Alshuraidah, A., & Storch, N. (2019). Investigating a collaborative approach to peer feedback. *ELT Journal*, 73(2), 166–174. DOI: 10.1093/elt/ccy057

Ameen, R. F. M., Mourshed, M., & Li, H. (2015). A critical review of environmental assessment tools for sustainable urban design. *Environmental Impact Assessment Review*, 55, 110–125. DOI: 10.1016/j.eiar.2015.07.006

Antshel, K. M., Zhang-James, Y., Wagner, K. E., Ledesma, A., & Faraone, S. V. (2016). An update on the comorbidity of ADHD and ASD: A focus on clinical management. *Expert Review of Neurotherapeutics*, 16(3), 279–293. DOI: 10.1586/14737175.2016.1146591 PMID: 26807870

Baker, D., & Scanlon, D. (2016). Student perspectives on academic accommodations. *Exceptionality*, 24(2), 93–108. DOI: 10.1080/09362835.2015.1064411

Bélanger, S. A., Andrews, D., Gray, C., & Korczak, D. (2018). ADHD in children and youth: Part 1—Etiology, diagnosis, and comorbidity. *Pediatrics' & child health*, 23(7), 447-453.

Belchior, P., Holmes, M., Bier, N., Bottari, C., Mazer, B., Robert, A., & Kaur, N. (2015). Performance-based tools for assessing functional performance in individuals with mild cognitive impairment.

Bilotta, G. S., Milner, A. M., & Boyd, I. L. (2014). Quality assessment tools for evidence from environmental science. *Environmental Evidence*, 3(1), 1–14. DOI: 10.1186/2047-2382-3-14

Condra, M., Dineen, M., Gills, H., Jack-Davies, A., & Condra, E. (2015). Academic accommodations for postsecondary students with mental health disabilities in Ontario, Canada: A review of the literature and reflections on emerging issues. *Journal of Postsecondary Education and Disability*, 28(3), 277–291.

Cremone, A., Lugo-Candelas, C. I., Harvey, E. A., McDermott, J. M., & Spencer, R. M. (2018). Positive emotional attention bias in young children with symptoms of ADHD. *Child Neuropsychology*, 24(8), 1137–1145. DOI: 10.1080/09297049.2018.1426743 PMID: 29347861

Diener, E., Thapa, S., & Tay, L. (2020). Positive emotions at work. *Annual Review of Organizational Psychology and Organizational Behavior*, 7(1), 451–477. DOI: 10.1146/annurev-orgpsych-012119-044908

Drigas, A., & Tourimpampa, A. (2014). Processes and ICT Tools for ADHD Assessment, Intervention and Attention Training. *International Journal of Emerging Technologies in Learning*, 9(6), 20. DOI: 10.3991/ijet.v9i6.4001

Du Rietz, E., Kuja-Halkola, R., Brikell, I., Jangmo, A., Sariaslan, A., Lichtenstein, P., Kuntsi, J., & Larsson, H. (2017). Predictive validity of parent-and self-rated ADHD symptoms in adolescence on adverse socioeconomic and health outcomes. *European Child & Adolescent Psychiatry*, 26(7), 857–867. DOI: 10.1007/s00787-017-0957-3 PMID: 28185096

Dvorsky, M. R., Langberg, J. M., Molitor, S. J., & Bourchtein, E. (2016). Clinical utility and predictive validity of parent and college student symptom ratings in predicting an ADHD diagnosis. *Journal of Clinical Psychology*, 72(4), 401–418. DOI: 10.1002/jclp.22268 PMID: 26919681

Edwards, M., Poed, S., Al-Nawab, H., & Penna, O. (2022). Academic accommodation for university students living with disabilities and the potential of universal design to address their needs. *Higher Education*, 84(4), 779–799. DOI: 10.1007/s10734-021-00800-w PMID: 35079174

Florell, D., & Strait, A. (2020). Academic accommodation and modifications. In *The clinical guide to assessment and treatment of childhood learning and attention problems* (pp. 125–147). Academic Press. DOI: 10.1016/B978-0-12-815755-8.00006-X

Fuermaier, A., Tucha, L., Koerts, J., Aschenbrenner, S., Kaunzinger, I., Hauser, J., Weisbrod, M., Lange, K. W., & Tucha, O. (2015). Cognitive impairment in adult ADHD—Perspective matters! *Neuropsychology*, 29(1), 45–58. DOI: 10.1037/neu0000108 PMID: 24933488

Goh, P. K., Lee, C. A., Martel, M. M., Karalunas, S. L., & Nigg, J. T. (2020). Subgroups of childhood ADHD based on temperament traits and cognition: Concurrent and predictive validity. *Journal of Abnormal Child Psychology*, 48(10), 1251–1264. DOI: 10.1007/s10802-020-00668-x PMID: 32666315

Gregório Hertz, P., Müller, M., Barra, S., Turner, D., Rettenberger, M., & Retz, W. (2022). The predictive and incremental validity of ADHD beyond the VRAG-R in a high-risk sample of young offenders. *European Archives of Psychiatry and Clinical Neuroscience*, 272(8), 1469–1479. DOI: 10.1007/s00406-021-01352-x PMID: 34860261

Hanachi, H., Mechefske, C., Liu, J., Banerjee, A., & Chen, Y. (2018). Performance-based gas turbine health monitoring, diagnostics, and prognostics: A survey. *IEEE Transactions on Reliability*, 67(3), 1340–1363. DOI: 10.1109/TR.2018.2822702

Harrison, A. G., & Armstrong, I. (2022). Accommodation decision-making for post-secondary students with ADHD: Treating the able as disabled. *Psychological Injury and Law*, 15(4), 367–384. DOI: 10.1007/s12207-022-09461-1 PMID: 36068830

Harrison, J. R., Evans, S. W., Baran, A., Khondker, F., Press, K., Noel, D., Wasserman, S., Belmonte, C., & Mohlmann, M. (2020). Comparison of accommodations and interventions for youth with ADHD: A randomized controlled trial. *Journal of School Psychology*, 80, 15–36. DOI: 10.1016/j.jsp.2020.05.001 PMID: 32540088

Hsiao, F., Zeiser, S., Nuss, D., & Hatschek, K. (2018). Developing effective academic accommodation in higher education: A collaborative decision-making process. *International Journal of Music Education*, 36(2), 244–258. DOI: 10.1177/0255761417729545

Instanes, J. T., Klungsøyr, K., Halmøy, A., Fasmer, O. B., & Haavik, J. (2018). Adult ADHD and comorbid somatic disease: A systematic literature review. *Journal of Attention Disorders*, 22(3), 203–228. DOI: 10.1177/1087054716669589 PMID: 27664125

Katzman, M. A., Bilkey, T. S., Chokka, P. R., Fallu, A., & Klassen, L. J. (2017). Adult ADHD and comorbid disorders: Clinical implications of a dimensional approach. *BMC Psychiatry*, 17(1), 1–15. DOI: 10.1186/s12888-017-1463-3 PMID: 28830387

Khaleghi, A., Birgani, P. M., Fooladi, M. F., & Mohammadi, M. R. (2020). Applicable features of electroencephalogram for ADHD diagnosis. *Research on Biomedical Engineering*, 36(1), 1–11. DOI: 10.1007/s42600-019-00036-9

Klekociuk, S. Z., Summers, J. J., Vickers, J. C., & Summers, M. J. (2014). Reducing false positive diagnoses in mild cognitive impairment: The importance of comprehensive neuropsychological assessment. *European Journal of Neurology*, 21(10), 1330–e83. DOI: 10.1111/ene.12488 PMID: 24943259

Krtek, A., Malinakova, K., Rudnicka, R. K., Pesoutova, M., Zovincova, V., Meier, Z., Tavel, P., & Trnka, R. (2022). Ambivalent bonds, positive and negative emotions, and expectations in teachers' perceptions of relationship with their students with ADHD. *International Journal of Qualitative Studies on Health and Well-being*, 17(1), 2088456. DOI: 10.1080/17482631.2022.2088456 PMID: 35711126

Kuhl, C. K., Keulers, A., Strobel, K., Schneider, H., Gaisa, N., & Schrading, S. (2018). Not all false positive diagnoses are equal: On the prognostic implications of false-positive diagnoses made in breast MRI versus in mammography/digital tomosynthesis screening. *Breast Cancer Research*, 20(1), 1–9. DOI: 10.1186/s13058-018-0937-7 PMID: 29426360

Langberg, J. M., Smith, Z. R., Dvorsky, M. R., Molitor, S. J., Bourchtein, E., Eddy, L. D., Eadeh, H.-M., & Oddo, L. E. (2018). Factor structure and predictive validity of a homework motivation measure for use with middle school students with attention-deficit/hyperactivity disorder (ADHD). *School Psychology Quarterly*, 33(3), 390–398. DOI: 10.1037/spq0000219 PMID: 28857587

Lefler, E. K., Alacha, H. F., Weed, B. M., Reeble, C. J., & Garner, A. M. (2023). Professor and peer perceptions of requests for academic accommodations in college: An examination of ADHD and specific learning disorder. *Psychological Reports*, •••, 00332941231156821. DOI: 10.1177/00332941231156821 PMID: 36792310

Lemay-Gaulin, M. (2022). Efficacy and perceptions of academic accommodations for university students with ADHD.

Lenartowicz, A., & Loo, S. K. (2014). Use of EEG to diagnose ADHD. *Current Psychiatry Reports*, 16(11), 1–11. DOI: 10.1007/s11920-014-0498-0 PMID: 25234074

Lerchenfeldt, S., Mi, M., & Eng, M. (2019). The utilization of peer feedback during collaborative learning in undergraduate medical education: A systematic review. *BMC Medical Education*, 19(1), 1–10. DOI: 10.1186/s12909-019-1755-z PMID: 31443705

Libutzki, B., Ludwig, S., May, M., Jacobsen, R. H., Reif, A., & Hartman, C. A. (2019). Direct medical costs of ADHD and its comorbid conditions on basis of claims data analysis. *European Psychiatry*, 58, 38–44. DOI: 10.1016/j.eurpsy.2019.01.019 PMID: 30802682

Loh, H. W., Ooi, C. P., Barua, P. D., Palmer, E. E., Molinari, F., & Acharya, U. R. (2022). Automated detection of ADHD: Current trends and future perspective. *Computers in Biology and Medicine*, 146, 105525. DOI: 10.1016/j.compbiomed.2022.105525 PMID: 35468405

Lovett, B. J., & Nelson, J. M. (2021). Systematic review: Educational accommodations for children and adolescents with attention-deficit/hyperactivity disorder. *Journal of the American Academy of Child and Adolescent Psychiatry*, 60(4), 448–457. DOI: 10.1016/j.jaac.2020.07.891 PMID: 32745597

Mårland, C., Lichtenstein, P., Degl'Innocenti, A., Larson, T., Råstam, M., Anckarsäter, H., Gillberg, C., Nilsson, T., & Lundström, S. (2017). The autism–tics, ADHD and other comorbidities inventory (A-TAC): Previous and predictive validity. *BMC Psychiatry*, 17(1), 1–8. DOI: 10.1186/s12888-017-1563-0 PMID: 29246205

Martel, M. M., Goh, P. K., Lee, C. A., Karalunas, S. L., & Nigg, J. T. (2021). Longitudinal ADHD symptom networks in childhood and adolescence: Key symptoms, stability, and predictive validity. *Journal of Abnormal Psychology*, 130(5), 562. DOI: 10.1037/abn0000661 PMID: 34472891

Massey, G., & Brändli, B. (2016). Collaborative feedback flows and how we can learn from them: Investigating a synergetic learning experience in translator education. *Towards authentic experiential learning in Translator Education*, 43, 177-199.

McKay, E., Cornish, K., & Kirk, H. (2023). Impairments in emotion recognition and positive emotion regulation predict social difficulties in adolescents with ADHD. *Clinical Child Psychology and Psychiatry*, 28(3), 895–908. DOI: 10.1177/13591045221141770 PMID: 36440882

McQuade, J. D., Taubin, D., & Mordy, A. E. (2024). Positive Emotion Dysregulation and Social Impairments in Adolescents with and without ADHD. *Research on Child and Adolescent Psychopathology*, •••, 1–13. DOI: 10.1007/s10802-024-01237-2 PMID: 39180616

Mitchell, P., Reinap, M., Moat, K., & Kuchenmüller, T. (2023). An ethical analysis of policy dialogues. *Health Research Policy and Systems*, 21(1), 13. DOI: 10.1186/s12961-023-00962-2 PMID: 36707839

Mohammadi, M. R., Zarafshan, H., Khaleghi, A., Ahmadi, N., Hooshyari, Z., Mostafavi, S. A., Ahmadi, A., Alavi, S.-S., Shakiba, A., & Salmanian, M. (2021). Prevalence of ADHD and its comorbidities in a population-based sample. *Journal of Attention Disorders*, 25(8), 1058–1067. DOI: 10.1177/1087054719886372 PMID: 31833803

Moore, Z. E., & Patton, D. (2019). Risk assessment tools for the prevention of pressure ulcers. *Cochrane Database of Systematic Reviews*, 2019(1), 1. DOI: 10.1002/14651858.CD006471.pub4 PMID: 30702158

Morris, J., Buchanan, T., Arnold, J., Czerkawski, T., & Congram, B. (2023). The impact of gender, accommodations, and disability on the academic performance of Canadian university students with LD and/or ADHD. *Learning Disabilities Research & Practice*, 38(4), 296–310. DOI: 10.1111/ldrp.12324

Mwisongo, A., Nabyonga-Orem, J., Yao, T., & Dovlo, D. (2016). The role of power in health policy dialogues: Lessons from African countries. *BMC Health Services Research*, 16(S4), 337–346. DOI: 10.1186/s12913-016-1456-9 PMID: 27454227

Newark, P. E., Elsässer, M., & Stieglitz, R.-D. (2016). Self-Esteem, Self-Efficacy, and Resources in Adults With ADHD. *Journal of Attention Disorders*, 20(3), 279–290. DOI: 10.1177/1087054712459561 PMID: 23074301

Overgaard, K. R., Oerbeck, B., Friis, S., Pripp, A. H., Aase, H., & Zeiner, P. (2021). Predictive validity of attention-deficit/hyperactivity disorder from ages 3 to 5 Years. *European Child & Adolescent Psychiatry*, •••, 1–10. PMID: 33677627

Parsons, J., McColl, M. A., Martin, A. K., & Rynard, D. W. (2021). Accommodation and academic performance: First-year university students with disabilities. *Canadian Journal of Higher Education*, 51(1), 41–56. DOI: 10.47678/cjhe.vi0.188985

Piñeiro-Dieguez, B., Balanzá-Martínez, V., García-García, P., & Soler-López, B. (2016). Psychiatric comorbidity at the time of diagnosis in adults with ADHD: The CAT Study. *Journal of Attention Disorders*, 20(12), 1066–1075. DOI: 10.1177/1087054713518240 PMID: 24464326

Posserud, M. B., Ullebø, A. K., Plessen, K. J., Stormark, K. M., Gillberg, C., & Lundervold, A. J. (2014). Influence of assessment instrument on ADHD diagnosis. *European Child & Adolescent Psychiatry*, 23(4), 197–205. DOI: 10.1007/s00787-013-0442-6 PMID: 23824470

Power, V., Van De Ven, P., Nelson, J., & Clifford, A. M. (2014). Predicting falls in community-dwelling older adults: A systematic review of task performance-based assessment tools. *Physiotherapy Practice and Research*, 35(1), 3–15. DOI: 10.3233/PPR-130027

Power, V., Van De Ven, P., Nelson, J., & Clifford, A. M. (2014). Predicting falls in community-dwelling older adults: A systematic review of task performance-based assessment tools. *Physiotherapy Practice and Research*, 35(1), 3–15. DOI: 10.3233/PPR-130027

Pritchard, A. E., Koriakin, T., Carey, L., Bellows, A., Jacobson, L., & Mahone, E. M. (2016). Academic testing accommodations for ADHD: Do they help? *Learning Disabilities (Pittsburgh, Pa.)*, 21(2), 67–78. DOI: 10.18666/LDMJ-2016-V21-I2-7414 PMID: 28503058

Quon, J. S., Moosavi, B., Khanna, M., Flood, T. A., Lim, C. S., & Schieda, N. (2015). False positive and false negative diagnoses of prostate cancer at multi-parametric prostate MRI in active surveillance. *Insights Into Imaging*, 6(4), 449–463. DOI: 10.1007/s13244-015-0411-3 PMID: 26002487

Reale, L., Bartoli, B., Cartabia, M., Zanetti, M., Costantino, M. A., Canevini, M. P., Termine, C., & Bonati, M. (2017). Comorbidity prevalence and treatment outcome in children and adolescents with ADHD. *European Child & Adolescent Psychiatry*, 26(12), 1443–1457. DOI: 10.1007/s00787-017-1005-z PMID: 28527021

Rogers, M., & Tannock, R. (2018). Are classrooms meeting the basic psychological needs of children with ADHD symptoms? A self-determination theory perspective. *Journal of Attention Disorders*, 22(14), 1354–1360. DOI: 10.1177/1087054713508926 PMID: 24327276

Sharifi, A., & Murayama, A. (2013). A critical review of seven selected neighborhood sustainability assessment tools. *Environmental Impact Assessment Review*, 38, 73–87. DOI: 10.1016/j.eiar.2012.06.006

Sridhar, C., Bhat, S., Acharya, U. R., Adeli, H., & Bairy, G. M. (2017). Diagnosis of attention deficit hyperactivity disorder using imaging and signal processing techniques. *Computers in Biology and Medicine*, 88, 93–99. DOI: 10.1016/j.compbiomed.2017.07.009 PMID: 28709145

Tahan, M., Tsoutsanis, E., Muhammad, M., & Karim, Z. A. (2017). Performance-based health monitoring, diagnostics and prognostics for condition-based maintenance of gas turbines: A review. *Applied Energy*, 198, 122–144. DOI: 10.1016/j.apenergy.2017.04.048

Tan, J. S., & Chen, W. (2022). Peer feedback to support collaborative knowledge improvement: What kind of feedback feed-forward? *Computers & Education*, 187, 104467. DOI: 10.1016/j.compedu.2022.104467

Weis, R., Hombosky, M. L., Schafer, K. K., Shulman, D., & Tull, J. K. (2021). Accommodation decision-making for postsecondary students with ADHD: Implications for neuropsychologists. *Journal of Clinical and Experimental Neuropsychology*, 43(4), 370–383. DOI: 10.1080/13803395.2021.1918645 PMID: 33899673

Whiting, P., Wolff, R., Mallett, S., Simera, I., & Savović, J. (2017). A proposed framework for developing quality assessment tools. *Systematic Reviews*, 6(1), 1–9. DOI: 10.1186/s13643-017-0604-6 PMID: 29041953

Wilder, D. A., Cymbal, D., & Echeverria, F. (2024). Performance diagnostic assessment. In *Behavior Safety and Clinical Practice in Intellectual and Developmental Disabilities* (pp. 17–35). Springer Nature Switzerland. DOI: 10.1007/978-3-031-54923-6_2

Yaghoobi Karimu, R., & Azadi, S. (2018). Diagnosing the ADHD using a mixture of expert fuzzy models. *International Journal of Fuzzy Systems*, 20(4), 1282–1296. DOI: 10.1007/s40815-016-0285-7

Zhang, Z. (2022). Promoting student engagement with feedback: Insights from collaborative pedagogy and teacher feedback. *Assessment & Evaluation in Higher Education*, 47(4), 540–555. DOI: 10.1080/02602938.2021.1933900

KEY TERMS AND DEFINITIONS

Academic Accommodation: Refers to the modifications and support systems established for students with disabilities or special needs, aimed at ensuring equitable access to educational opportunities. These adjustments are designed to eliminate obstacles to learning, enabling students to showcase their knowledge and abilities alongside their classmates. Typical examples of such accommodations include additional time for examinations, preferred seating arrangements, adjusted assignments, the use of assistive technologies, and the provision of lecture notes prior to class. These accommodations are tailored to meet the individual requirements of each student, which are typically identified through a comprehensive evaluation process. The primary objective is not to change academic standards but to create an equitable environment that fosters fairness and inclusivity within educational settings. By adopting academic accommodations, educational institutions enhance student success and cultivate a more just and supportive learning atmosphere.

Assessment Tools: Refer to the various methods, instruments, or strategies employed to measure, evaluate, and analyze an individual's knowledge, skills, abilities, or behaviors. These tools may take the form of tests, questionnaires, observation checklists, interviews, or standardized assessments. Within educational environments, they serve to assess student learning and academic advancement. In the field of psychology, these tools are utilized to evaluate mental health, cognitive functioning, or personality characteristics. The primary objective of assessment tools is to collect objective and reliable data that can inform decision-making, facilitate interventions, or monitor development. Effective assessment tools are characterized by their validity, reliability, and alignment with the specific context or purpose. They are essential in identifying strengths and areas needing improvement, thereby guiding personalized support and enhancing outcomes across various domains.

Clinical Assessment: Represents a methodical procedure utilized by healthcare professionals to obtain detailed information about an individual's psychological, emotional, or physical health status. Its primary goal is to identify symptoms, assess their implications, and develop a diagnosis or treatment plan. This process includes conducting interviews, making observations, and administering standardized tests or questionnaires. Through this approach, clinicians can better understand the client's background, current situation, and the fundamental factors contributing to their difficulties. An effective clinical assessment is vital for ensuring accurate diagnoses, crafting personalized treatment strategies, and tracking progress. It demands not only technical proficiency but also the ability to empathize and engage in active listening to cultivate trust and extract valuable insights.

Comorbid Conditions: Refer to the simultaneous existence of two or more disorders or diseases in a single individual. These conditions may be interconnected, potentially worsening each other, or they may be entirely separate. In medical and psychological contexts, the presence of comorbidity often complicates the processes of diagnosis, treatment, and overall management. For example, an individual with ADHD may concurrently experience anxiety or depression, which necessitates a comprehensive approach to address all existing issues. Comorbid conditions are frequently observed in both physical and mental health sectors, requiring integrated and personalized treatment plans. Understanding the concept of comorbidity is vital, as it impacts the severity of symptoms, the efficacy of interventions, and the overall quality of life for the individual. Addressing comorbid conditions involves thorough evaluation and collaboration among healthcare providers to ensure comprehensive care and improved patient outcomes.

Collaborative Feedback: Refers to a systematic approach in which individuals engage collectively to give, receive, and contemplate feedback aimed at enhancing performance, comprehension, or results. This process prioritizes transparent communication, mutual respect, and a collective sense of accountability during the feedback exchange. In both educational and professional contexts, collaborative feedback entails peers, mentors, or team members providing constructive observations while appreciating varied viewpoints. Such an approach cultivates a nurturing learning atmosphere, encourages self-assessment, and strengthens critical thinking skills. It promotes active involvement, as both the feedback provider and recipient play a role in refining concepts, recognizing strengths, and addressing areas for improvement. The overarching objective is to establish a culture of ongoing enhancement and shared knowledge, wherein feedback serves as a collaborative instrument for development.

Diagnostic Techniques: Refer to the various methodologies and tools that healthcare professionals utilize to identify and analyze medical or psychological conditions. These techniques typically consist of a combination of clinical interviews, physical examinations, laboratory tests, imaging scans (such as MRIs), and standardized assessments. In the field of mental health, diagnostic techniques may involve psychological evaluations, behavioral observations, and structured interviews to assess symptoms and their impact on daily activities. The primary purpose of these techniques is to collect comprehensive information that aids in making precise diagnoses and guiding treatment options. The dependability of diagnostic techniques is essential for differentiating between similar conditions, understanding the severity of symptoms, and uncovering underlying issues. An accurate diagnosis is crucial for facilitating effective interventions, providing focused care, and enhancing patient outcomes.

False-Positive Diagnoses: When a diagnostic test or evaluation mistakenly indicates that an individual has a condition or disorder that they do not possess. Such misdiagnoses can result in unnecessary treatments, heightened anxiety, and social stigma for the affected individual. In both medical and psychological settings, false positives may stem from flawed testing methods, unclear diagnostic criteria, or human error. For instance, diagnosing a child with ADHD without sufficient evidence may lead to inappropriate treatment strategies. To mitigate false positives, it is essential to implement stringent diagnostic standards, meticulously interpret assessment outcomes, and consider various sources of information. Tackling this issue is vital for enhancing diagnostic precision, ensuring the effectiveness of interventions, and safeguarding individuals from the adverse effects of erroneous diagnoses.

Performance-Based Diagnostic Tools: Evaluations designed to assess an individual's abilities, skills, or knowledge through tasks that replicate real-life scenarios. In contrast to conventional written tests, these tools necessitate that individuals exhibit specific competencies or behaviors in practical settings. For instance, in the field of education, performance-based assessments may encompass oral presentations, hands-on examinations, or project-oriented evaluations. In psychology, such tools might include role-playing activities, observational assessments, or simulations aimed at understanding social skills, executive functioning, or behavioral reactions. By evaluating individuals in dynamic and authentic environments, performance-based diagnostic tools offer a more holistic view of their capabilities. They play a crucial role in identifying strengths, diagnosing challenges, and informing tailored interventions or training programs.

Positive Emotions: Feelings that contribute to enhanced well-being, resilience, and personal growth, ultimately leading to greater happiness. They include emotions like joy, gratitude, hope, love, pride, and inspiration. Experiencing these emotions enables individuals to build psychological resilience, strengthen social connections, and improve their overall physical and mental health. Positive emotions broaden one's perspective, facilitating creative problem-solving and adaptive responses to challenges. Furthermore, they can counterbalance negative emotions, reducing stress and promoting a sense of well-being. By practicing gratitude journaling, mindfulness, or engaging in acts of kindness, individuals can cultivate positive emotions, resulting in higher life satisfaction and improved emotional regulation.

Policy Dialogues: An organized discussion among various stakeholders, such as policymakers, specialists, community representatives, and other pertinent groups, with the objective of addressing particular issues and formulating effective policies. These dialogues serve as a forum for the exchange of evidence, viewpoints, and experiences, thereby enhancing the decision-making process. They are structured to promote collaborative problem-solving, transparency, and inclusivity in the development of policies. Through these dialogues, stakeholders can identify key priorities, reach consensus, and investigate practical solutions to intricate challenges in sectors such as education, healthcare, and social services. By encouraging open communication and fostering mutual understanding, policy dialogues play a crucial role in the creation of well-informed, equitable, and sustainable policies that cater to the needs and interests of all involved parties.

Predictive Validity: Defined as the degree to which a test or measurement can accurately forecast future performance or outcomes. It evaluates the effectiveness of a specific assessment tool, such as a standardized test, aptitude assessment, or psychological evaluation, in predicting an individual's success or behavior within a particular context. For instance, the predictive validity of a college entrance examination reflects the correlation between test scores and students' subsequent academic performance in higher education. A high level of predictive validity indicates that the test serves as a dependable foundation for making informed decisions or predictions regarding future achievements or behaviors. This concept holds significant importance in fields such as education and psychology, where precise forecasting is essential for guiding decision-making, interventions, and policy development.

Psychological Resources: The internal strengths, capabilities, and coping mechanisms that individuals rely on to manage challenges, stress, and adversity. These resources encompass resilience, self-efficacy, optimism, emotional regulation, and a sense of purpose. They play a crucial role in helping individuals maintain mental well-being, adapt to changing circumstances, and pursue personal growth. Additionally, psychological resources support the formation of positive relationships, promote constructive approaches to problem-solving, and facilitate recovery from setbacks. Influenced by personal experiences, social support, and ongoing development, these resources can be cultivated through practices such as mindfulness, therapy, and self-reflection. By fostering these resources, individuals can enhance their mental health, emotional stability, and overall satisfaction in life, empowering them to succeed in various areas.

Social Resources: Refer to the support, connections, and relationships that individuals maintain within their social networks, which consist of family, friends, colleagues, and community members. These resources deliver emotional, informational, and practical assistance, aiding individuals in overcoming challenges, making decisions, and achieving their aspirations. They are crucial for enhancing mental health, resilience, and well-being by providing companionship, advice, and concrete support during difficult times. Additionally, social resources help cultivate a sense of belonging, alleviate feelings of isolation, and bolster individuals' ability to cope with stress. Strong social resources promote trust, collaboration, and reciprocity within communities, thereby creating a nurturing environment where individuals can thrive both personally and socially.

Stimulant Medications: A group of drugs that are often prescribed for the management of attention-deficit/hyperactivity disorder (ADHD) and certain sleep disorders, such as narcolepsy. Examples of these medications include methylphenidate (Ritalin) and various amphetamine-based products (Adderall). These agents operate by enhancing the levels of particular neurotransmitters in the brain, especially dopamine and norepinephrine. This increase aids in improving concentration, attention span, and impulse control among individuals with ADHD. While stimulant medications are effective in controlling symptoms, boosting cognitive performance, and enhancing everyday functioning and academic success, they require careful oversight due to the risk of side effects, including increased heart rate, decreased appetite, and disturbances in sleep patterns. Physicians often adjust dosages to align with the specific needs of each patient, aiming to optimize benefits while minimizing risks.

Stressors: Refer to both external and internal influences that elicit a physical, emotional, or psychological response, often resulting in stress. External stressors may include significant life events or changes, such as financial hardships, job-related pressures, or interpersonal conflicts. Internal stressors, on the other hand, originate from an individual's own thoughts, beliefs, or perceptions, such as feelings of inadequacy or fear of failure. These stressors can be acute, arising from sudden crises, or chronic, stemming from persistent health issues or ongoing workplace demands. While some stressors can drive positive transformation, excessive or unmanaged stressors can have detrimental effects on mental and physical health. Therefore, recognizing and managing stressors through coping mechanisms, support systems, and self-care routines is vital for sustaining well-being and resilience.

APPENDIX I: STUDY QUESTIONNAIRE

Table 4. Perceived effectiveness of assessment tools for evaluating students with ADHD questionnaire (PEATESAQ)

No	Statements	SD	D	UD	D	SD
1	The assessment tools help in identifying career strengths for students with ADHD.					
2	The tools provide clear insights into the challenges faced by students with ADHD during career transitions.					
3	The assessments are tailored to the specific needs of students with ADHD.					
4	The feedback from these assessments is useful for planning career transition.					
5	The tools effectively measure the impact of ADHD on career decision-making.					
6	The assessments are easy for students with ADHD to understand and complete.					
7	The results from these tools are reliable and consistent.					
8	The assessments help in setting realistic career goals for students with ADHD.					
9	The tools are comprehensive in evaluating all relevant aspects of career readiness.					
10	The assessments help in improving self-awareness among students with ADHD.					
11	The tools facilitate better communication between students with ADHD and career counselors.					
12	The assessments are adaptable to different career fields.					
13	The tools are effective in reducing anxiety about career transitions for students with ADHD.					
14	The assessment process respects the individuality of each student with ADHD.					

SD=Strongly Disagree, D=Disagree, UD=Undecided, A=Agree, SA=Strongly Agree

APPENDIX II: ADDITIONAL STATISTICS

Table 5. Item-total statistics

No	Statements	Cronbach's Alpha if Item Deleted
1	The assessment tools help in identifying career strengths for students with ADHD.	.586
2	The tools provide clear insights into the challenges faced by students with ADHD during career transitions.	.607
3	The assessments are tailored to the specific needs of students with ADHD.	.606
4	The feedback from these assessments is useful for planning career transition.	.589
5	The tools effectively measure the impact of ADHD on career decision-making.	.585
6	The assessments are easy for students with ADHD to understand and complete.	.560
7	The results from these tools are reliable and consistent.	.595
8	The assessments help in setting realistic career goals for students with ADHD.	.589
9	The tools are comprehensive in evaluating all relevant aspects of career readiness.	.604
10	The assessments help in improving self-awareness among students with ADHD.	.603
11	The tools facilitate better communication between students with ADHD and career counselors.	.618
12	The assessments are adaptable to different career fields.	.599
13	The tools are effective in reducing anxiety about career transitions for students with ADHD.	.596
14	The assessment process respects the individuality of each student with ADHD.	.593

Table 6. Communalities (extraction method: principal component analysis)

No	Statements	Extraction
1	The assessment tools help in identifying career strengths for students with ADHD.	.832
2	The tools provide clear insights into the challenges faced by students with ADHD during career transitions.	.710
3	The assessments are tailored to the specific needs of students with ADHD.	.812
4	The feedback from these assessments is useful for planning career transition.	.817
5	The tools effectively measure the impact of ADHD on career decision-making.	.875
6	The assessments are easy for students with ADHD to understand and complete.	.722
7	The results from these tools are reliable and consistent.	.845
8	The assessments help in setting realistic career goals for students with ADHD.	.691
9	The tools are comprehensive in evaluating all relevant aspects of career readiness.	.744
10	The assessments help in improving self-awareness among students with ADHD.	.710

No	Statements	Extraction
11	The tools facilitate better communication between students with ADHD and career counselors.	.758
12	The assessments are adaptable to different career fields.	.788
13	The tools are effective in reducing anxiety about career transitions for students with ADHD.	.812
14	The assessment process respects the individuality of each student with ADHD.	.773

Chapter 8
Exploring Career Counseling Models and Services for Students With ADHD:
Counselors' Perspectives

ABSTRACT

This study aimed at examining the perspectives held by inclusive secondary school counselors regarding the use of career counseling models and services for students with ADHD during career transitioning. The researchers made use of a cross-sectional survey design that was principally quantitative and involved 39 school counselors. Moderate overall perceptions about the effectiveness of career counseling models and services emerged from the findings, with no statistically significant differences across gender, experience or location. This implies that demographic factors under consideration did not significantly influence how counselors see the use or application of career counseling models and services in supporting students with ADHD during career transitioning.

BACKGROUND

There has been a surge in interest regarding career development, a phenomenon that can be linked to the economic trends of globalization and the acknowledged necessity to mitigate social inequalities (AVD Group, 2023; Benjamin et al., 2011; Brown, 2008; IMF Staff, 2008; Pan, 2005). Globalization has significantly increased competition in the employment sector, requiring individuals to compete not just within their local markets but also on a global scale (AVD Group, 2023; Jackie,

DOI: 10.4018/979-8-3693-2635-0.ch008

2023). This evolution highlights the importance of improving qualifications and skill sets to enable individuals to stand out in a saturated job market (IMF Staff, 2008). As economies grow more interconnected, there is a rising demand for specialized skills, especially within the technology and service industries (AVD Group, 2023). Employers are now placing greater emphasis on both technical proficiency and soft skills, including effective communication and cultural competence (Jackie, 2023). Furthermore, the advent of remote work has broadened career possibilities beyond geographical constraints, enabling job seekers to seek opportunities that resonate with their career goals without being restricted by location (Jackie, 2023). Nevertheless, current global competition may result in wage stagnation, particularly affecting low-skilled workers and marginalized groups, as companies strive to reduce expenses (AVD Group, 2023). This situation accentuates the critical need for individuals to pursue education and training that provides them with sought-after skills. Career counseling serves as a valuable resource for individuals seeking to recognize and cultivate specialized skills that are sought after in the global job market (Lika et al., 2022). Career development services offer customized guidance that corresponds with personal career aspirations and current market dynamics. Through career counseling services, individuals can gain a deeper understanding of international job markets, enabling them to recognize potential opportunities and the qualifications needed to attain them (Eseadi & Diale, 2024). Career counseling services prioritize inclusivity, guaranteeing that underrepresented communities, including those with disabilities, can access career development resources (Gibson, 2017). This approach can alleviate social disparities by offering assistance for skill enhancement and facilitating access to employment opportunities. Unfortunately, career engagement for young individuals with disabilities remains lower than those of their non-disabled peers (Newman et al., 2009), presenting distinct challenges for professionals striving to deliver high-quality transition services (Luft, 2015). A pertinent example is students with attention-deficit/hyperactivity disorder (ADHD). Students with ADHD generally achieve lower grade point averages, take a longer time to finish their studies, and show a greater propensity to drop out than their counterparts without ADHD (Canu et al., 2021) alongside a range of diminished learning abilities and substantial necessities (Taymans & West, 2001). These students often face social stigmas associated with their condition, often relegating them to a state of perceived inferiority and a false sense of normalcy imposed by societal expectations (Furtick Jr, 2005). Consequently, these students experience subpar postsecondary outcomes, which may stem from inadequate career development services (Altantawy, 2016). Such services can include career counseling (Stevenson et al., 2021).

According to Ihuoma (2021), counseling services emphasize the overall development of the students by addressing the psycho-social, intellectual, emotional, and physical factors in relation to their environment. School-based career counseling plays a crucial role in personal development by assisting students examine a variety of career options and making educated decisions about their professional trajectories (Gomez, 2024). The primary aim of career counseling is to support clients in enhancing their career decision-making processes (Gati, 1991). School career counseling service is a key factor in promoting student satisfaction (Nie & Zarei, 2023). School counselors are responsible for providing a variety of career counseling models and services. It is essential for school counselors and their clients to be familiar with the different counseling models available, as this knowledge enables counselors to select the most appropriate method for each student. Counseling models are generally classified into six categories: humanistic, cognitive, behavioral, psychoanalytic, constructionist, and systemic, each providing a distinct perspective on the human experience (Axinte, 2014; Main, 2023;). Notable counseling models include cognitive behavioral theory (Bertoni, 2024), trait and factor theory (Dianti et al., 2022), social learning theory (Yunus et al., 2024), psychodynamic theory, person-centred theory (Gray, 2009), interpersonal counseling, mindfulness-based counseling, rational-emotive behavioral theory, narrative counseling, and creative approaches (Lonczak, 2020). School counselors dedicate the majority of their time to providing counseling services to students (Hannor-Walker et al., 2022; Ugwoke et al., 2015). Furthermore, the integration of constructivist-narrative models in career counseling is important (Kaliris & Issari, 2022), particularly for students with learning disorders such as ADHD. The challenges associated with ADHD have placed considerable pressure on counselors, who are facing an increasing demand for their services (Shankar & Ip, 2018). This situation, coupled with the difficulties in managing students with ADHD, may prompt some counselors to reconsider their professional paths.

Counseling services within Nigerian schools have been undergoing progressive reforms, shifting from a position-services model to a holistic program model rooted in the principles of human growth and development, according to Ihuoma (2021). The author highlighted that Nigeria, as a nation, is also undergoing considerable changes in occupational, social, and economic structures, in pursuit of sustainable development goals. Bella – Awusah et al. (2022) stressed the necessity for national policies that would guide the training and practice of school counselors, thereby enhancing the quality and effectiveness of counseling services offered to students in Nigerian schools. It is pertinent for school counselors to understand the specific needs and experiences of college students with ADHD (Huegel, 2015) to implement effective career counseling services tailored to these individuals. Furthermore, understanding the perspectives of these counselors regarding the available ADHD career counseling models and services is crucial for identifying the most suitable career options for these students and informing future practices to address the challenges faced by students with ADHD during career transition. Carlson and Kees

(2013) revealed that while school counselors generally exhibit confidence in their counseling abilities and feel at ease addressing common student issues, they express discomfort when it comes to supporting students diagnosed with disabilities. Among the counseling services offered are individual and group counseling, consultation, referral, and crisis counseling (DeBose, 2008). Services such as individualized counseling have been linked to significant increases in earnings for individuals with disabilities (Tremblay et al., 2006). Holistic understanding of the experiences and perceptions of school counselors can enable the facilitation of more tailored training experiences which can lead to the cultivation of more capable and ready professional counselors to assist children and adolescents in this context (Walsh, 2012). Career counseling can enhance diversity, thereby ensuring that the support process is accessible and dependable for individuals with special educational needs (Chen, 2021) including students with ADHD. Engaging in career counseling training enables students to delve into a specialized area of both professional and personal interest; this specialization can significantly benefit their career trajectories (Grenawalt et al., 2020). Although there is a growing awareness of ADHD and the impact of counseling services on the career transition of students with this condition, research focusing on the perspectives of Nigerian school counselors concerning the efficacy of career counseling models and services designed for students with ADHD during career transition remains scarce. A significant number of counselors may not possess the requisite training, facilities, and resources to tackle the specific transition challenges encountered by these students, resulting in a generalized approach that fails to accommodate their individual career transition needs (*see*Eleke, 2023; Ohunene, et al., 2021). The cultural understanding of ADHD in Nigeria can play a significant role in shaping the perspectives of school counselors, which can hinder their ability to engage effectively with students who have this condition. This issue can be compounded by the dearth of culturally-sensitive career counseling models and services that include ADHD-specific approaches, leaving students without appropriate career support during career transition. As a result, it is imperative to investigate how Nigerian school counselors perceive the counseling models and services available for assisting students with ADHD. Such an assessment can uncover barriers to effective counseling services and inform the development of more relevant models and services that are consistent with the career transition needs of students with ADHD. The aim of this research is to examine the perspectives of counselors on the career counseling models and services for students with ADHD in Edo state, Nigeria.

Research Objectives

1. To assess the overall mean perspective of inclusive secondary school counselors regarding the use of career counseling models and services in supporting the career transition of students with ADHD.
2. To examine gender differences in the perspectives of inclusive secondary school counselors regarding the use of career counseling models and services in supporting the career transitioning of students with ADHD.
3. To determine how the perspectives of inclusive secondary school counselors regarding the use of career counseling models and services in supporting the career transitioning of students with ADHD vary based on years of professional experience.
4. To investigate whether rural and urban inclusive secondary school counselors have differing perspectives on the use of career counseling models and services in supporting the career transitioning of students with ADHD.

Research Questions

1. What is the overall mean perspective of inclusive secondary school counselors regarding the use of career counseling models and services in supporting the career transitioning of students with ADHD?
2. Do gender differences exist in the perspectives of inclusive secondary school counselors regarding the use of career counseling models and services in supporting the career transitioning of students with ADHD?
3. How well do the perspectives of inclusive secondary school counselors regarding the use of career counseling models and services in supporting the career transitioning of students with ADHD vary based on years of professional experience?
4. Do rural and urban inclusive secondary school counselors have differing perspectives on the use of career counseling models and services in supporting the career transitioning of students with ADHD?

Theoretical Framework

Social Cognitive Career Theory (SCCT), formulated by Lent and colleagues (1994), extends the principles of Albert Bandura's social cognitive theory to elucidate the processes through which individuals cultivate career interests, make decisions regarding education and occupation, and attain success in their professional lives. This theory highlights the interaction between cognitive components—such as beliefs in self-efficacy and expectations of outcomes—and environmental factors, including social support systems and obstacles, in influencing career development

(Drucker, 2012; Lent et al., 1994). The application of this theory to the views of secondary school counselors on career counseling models and services for students with ADHD in Nigeria facilitates a deeper understanding of how these models and services are interpreted and tailored by counselors to cater to the distinct career transition needs of these students. This theoretical approach is particularly pertinent in Nigeria, where differences in educational resources, counselor training, and societal norms may affect the perceived success of career counseling services for students with ADHD. The theory can help shed light on the extent of perspectives held by counselors, particularly regarding how their beliefs about self-efficacy and anticipated outcomes can shape their counseling practice (Lent et al., 1998). Counselors who exhibit a strong belief in their ability to foster positive career results (high self-efficacy) may show a more favorable outlook on career counseling models and services. In contrast, those with diminished self-efficacy may harbor doubts about the efficacy of these models and services, especially when confronted with the specific challenges that ADHD presents. Utilizing this theoretical framework allows for an examination of how counselors' expectations of outcomes affect their application of particular counseling models and rendering of counseling services. Counselors who expect favorable outcomes from certain counseling models and services are likely to be more committed to them and adept at customizing these models and services to address the unique career transition needs of students with ADHD. On the other hand, those who are less confident in the models' and services' effectiveness may adopt a more reserved or critical stance. Gender can shape the perceptions that school counselors hold regarding the career models and services they adopt. Within the Nigerian context, gender roles may impact male and female school counselors in distinct ways, resulting in different degrees of involvement with particular counseling models and services. Female counselors may place a greater emphasis on the emotional and relational aspects within counseling models and service delivery in comparison to their male counterparts. Counselors who possess greater experience tend to have a wider array of counseling strategies at their disposal and may have tailored traditional models to better suit individual needs. Conversely, less experienced counselors might depend more on established counseling frameworks, which they may regard with either admiration or doubt, influenced by their recent training and experiences. Counselors in rural and urban settings function within unique social, cultural, and institutional frameworks that shape their perspectives on career counseling approaches for students with ADHD. For example, rural counselors might encounter constraints related to resources and training opportunities, potentially causing them to perceive existing models as less relevant or effective in their particular context. Conversely, urban counselors are likely to benefit from a wider array of specialized resources and training, which may bolster their confidence in the effective application of these models. Therefore, this theory is crucial for clarifying counselors' perceptions of career counseling models and services available to students with ADHD in Nigeria.

METHODOLOGY

Ethics Statement

Ethical approval for this study was obtained from the relevant institutional review boards. First, it received approval from the Research Ethics Committee of the Faculty of Education, University of Nigeria, Nigeria. It also received additional ethical approval from the Faculty of Education Research Ethics Committee at the University of Johannesburg, South Africa (Sem 2-2020-057). Informed consent was secured from participants. We assured confidentiality and clarified participants' right to withdraw from the study at any given time.

Research Design and Approach

The application of survey research is instrumental in addressing significant topics (Van der Stede, 2014). Thus, our study adopted a cross-sectional survey design. This type of research involves gathering data from a variety of individuals within a timeframe, enabling the observation of variables without interference (Thomas, 2020). The term "cross-sectional" reflects the fact that the data regarding variables X and Y is captured at one specific time point (Olsen & St. George, 2006). These studies are observational in nature, providing insights into the characteristics of a population and laying the groundwork for future, more comprehensive research (Wang & Cheng, 2020). The cross-sectional survey design was selected for this study due to its advantageous features. The study adopted a quantitative research approach. A framework based on this design was implemented to survey counselors about their perspectives on career counseling models and services for students diagnosed with ADHD. A quantitative research approach was employed, which aims to enhance objectivity, reliability, and generalizability of results, with a focus on predictive outcomes (Harwell, 2011).

Research Paradigm

A research paradigm serves to articulate one's understanding of reality and the means by which knowledge can be interpreted (Lynette, 2024). There are about four distinct research paradigms: positivism, realism, critical theory, and interpretivism (Keong et al., 2023). This study is grounded in the positivist research paradigm.

The positivist approach asserts the existence of a singular, objective reality that can be known and accurately described by individuals (Proofed, 2023). The application of positivism involves the formulation of significant research questions, the identification of critical variables, the collection of measurements from participants regarding these variables, and the analysis of data to uncover causal relationships between them (Kincheloe & Tobin, 2009).

Study Area

Covering a total land area of 923,768 square kilometres, Nigeria is recognized as the 14th largest country in Africa, divided into six geopolitical zones: North West, North East, North Central, South West, South East, and South (Abubakar, 2017). This research was conducted in Edo State, located in South-south region of Nigeria. Edo State is primarily home to Edo (Bini) speaking communities (John-Abebe, 2023). The state consists of eighteen local government areas and is divided into three senatorial districts: Edo North, Edo Central, and Edo South (Magnus & Eseigbe, 2012).

Population and Sampling

The selection of sampling methods is primarily determined by the objective of the study and the research questions it seeks to address (Boeri & Lamonica, 2015). Sampling techniques can be classified into two main types: probability and non-probability sampling. The latter allows researchers to make generalizations about their findings when the sampling approach is implemented thoughtfully (Moniruzzaman Sarker & Al-Muaalemi, 2022). In this study, we utilized purposive and convenience sampling techniques, both of which are categorized as non-probability sampling methods. The study involves inclusive secondary school counselors in public secondary schools. A total of 39 inclusive secondary school counselors were selected using purposive and convenience sampling techniques. Convenience sampling focuses on selecting participants who are easily accessible and willing to take part in the research (Teddlie & Yu, 2007), while purposive sampling, known as judgment sampling, serves to effectively narrow down the potential participant pool (Thomas, 2022). The sample size included 13 (33.3%) male counselors and 26 (66.7%) female counselors; 17 (43.6%) early career counselors and 22 (56.4%) experienced counselors; 21 (53.8%) rural school counselors and 18 (46.2%) urban school counselors. Participants' mean age is 40.13 ± 6.36 years.

Data Collection

The data was collected using a questionnaire. The researchers received help from two postgraduate students to complete the data collection process. The questionnaire used for data collection is called the Counselors' Perspectives on Career Counseling Models and Services for Students with ADHD (CPCCMSSAQ). It is a 12-item scale, with response options ranging from Not at All (1) to Great Extent (4) that measures counselors' perspectives regarding the use of career counseling models and services in supporting the career transitioning of students with ADHD. Higher scores indicate a positive perspective and great extent of the use of career counselling models and services. Examples of item statements in the questionnaire include: " To what extent do you feel knowledgeable about career counseling techniques and their impact on the career transition of students with ADHD?", " To what extent do you utilize specific career counseling models and techniques to support students with ADHD during their career transition?" and "To what extent do you feel that you have received adequate training and resources to provide career counseling services for students with ADHD?". The CPCCMSSAQ has a good internal consistency reliability, with a Cronbach's alpha of 0.93 in the present research.

Data Analysis

A statistical model serves the dual purpose of describing sample data and making inferences about the population from which the sample originates (Denis, 2018). The statistical analysis was performed utilizing the Statistical Package for the Social Sciences (SPSS), version 27. This software, developed by IBM, is designed for data management, criminal investigations, multivariate analysis, advanced analytics, and business intelligence (Murugan & Govindarajan, 2023). Researchers utilize SPSS to aid in the comprehension and interpretation of research outcomes (Arkkelin, 2014), ensuring that findings are accessible to readers. The application of this statistical package significantly minimizes errors in data analysis, presentation, and interpretation of research results among students (Sampson et al., 2023). Descriptive statistics was used to summarize the sociodemographic data, while univariate analysis was used to analyse the research questions at a .05 significance level. Descriptive statistics offer comprehensive insights into the data and assist in addressing inquiries related to the dataset through the three measures of central tendency: mean, median, and mode (Abu-Bader, 2021). The univariate analysis is a type of analysis that focuses solely on a single variable within a dataset (Kapil, 2022).

FINDINGS

Table 1. Mean perspective of inclusive secondary school counselors regarding the use of career counseling models and services in supporting the career transitioning of students with ADHD

Gender	Professional Experience	School Location	Mean	SD	N
Male counselors	Early career counsellors	Rural counselors	2.13	.06	2
		Urban counselors	2.31	.39	4
		Total	2.25	.32	6
	Experienced counsellors	Rural counselors	1.96	.06	2
		Urban counselors	2.23	.26	5
		Total	2.15	.25	7
	Total	Rural counselors	2.04	.11	4
		Urban counselors	2.27	.31	9
		Total	2.19	.28	13
Female counselors	Early career counsellors	Rural counselors	2.26	.11	6
		Urban counselors	2.03	.32	5
		Total	2.16	.25	11
	Experienced counsellors	Rural counselors	2.45	.67	11
		Urban counselors	2.17	.24	4
		Total	2.37	.59	15
	Total	Rural counselors	2.38	.54	17
		Urban counselors	2.09	.27	9
		Total	2.28	.48	26
Total	Early career counsellors	Rural counselors	2.23	.12	8
		Urban counselors	2.16	.36	9
		Total	2.19	.27	17
	Experienced counsellors	Rural counselors	2.37	.64	13
		Urban counselors	2.20	.24	9
		Total	2.30	.51	22
	Total	Rural counselors	2.32	.51	21
		Urban counselors	2.18	.29	18
		Total	2.25	.42	39

The overall mean perspective of inclusive secondary school counselors regarding the use of career counseling models and services in supporting the career transitioning of students with ADHD is 2.25 with a standard deviation of 0.42, as seen in Table 1. This value represents the average view of all counselors regardless of gender, experience, or location, which can be interpreted as being a moderate perspective regarding the use of career counseling models and services in supporting the career transitioning of students with ADHD.

Figure 1. Mean perspective of inclusive secondary school counselors regarding the use of career counseling models and services in supporting the career transitioning of students with ADHD of early career school counselors across gender and school location

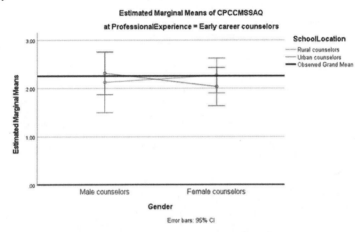

Figure 1 shows the mean perspectives of early career counselors across gender and location, highlighting minor differences but overall consistency in perspectives.

Figure 2. Mean perspective of inclusive secondary school counselors regarding the use of career counseling models and services in supporting the career transitioning of students with ADHD of experienced school counselors across gender and school location

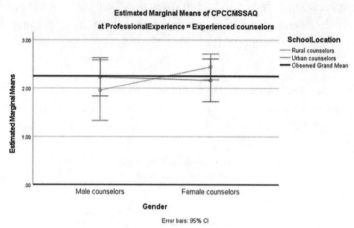

Figure 2 illustrates the perspectives of experienced counselors, showing similar patterns with no significant deviations across gender and location.

Table 2. Univariate analysis of differences in the perspectives of inclusive secondary school counselors regarding the use of career counseling models and services in supporting the career transitioning of students with ADHD

Source	Type III Sum of Squares	Df	Mean Square	F	Sig.
Corrected Model	.908a	7	.130	.685	.68
Intercept	142.592	1	142.592	753.175	<.001
Gender	.037	1	.037	.194	.66
ProfessionalExperience	.002	1	.002	.012	.91
SchoolLocation	.001	1	.001	.006	.94
Gender * ProfessionalExperience	.147	1	.147	.774	.39
Gender * SchoolLocation	.439	1	.439	2.319	.14
ProfessionalExperience * SchoolLocation	.001	1	.001	.003	.95
Gender * ProfessionalExperience * SchoolLocation	.009	1	.009	.046	.83
Error	5.869	31	.189		

continued on following page

Table 2. Continued

Source	Type III Sum of Squares	Df	Mean Square	F	Sig.
Total	204.965	39			
Corrected Total	6.777	38			

The univariate analysis in Table 2 shows that the effect of gender on perspectives of inclusive secondary school counselors regarding the use of career counseling models and services in supporting the career transitioning of students with ADHD is not statistically significant (F =.194, p=.66), indicating that gender differences in perspectives are not meaningful. Table 2 further shows that professional experience does not significantly affect the perspectives of inclusive secondary school counselors regarding the use of career counseling models and services in supporting the career transitioning of students with ADHD (F=.012, p=.91), suggesting that years of experience do not lead to significant differences in perspectives. Table 2 also indicates that school location does not significantly influence perspectives of inclusive secondary school counselors regarding the use of career counseling models and services in supporting the career transitioning of students with ADHD (F=.006, p=.94). Therefore, there is no significant difference between rural and urban counselors' perspectives regarding the use of career counseling models and services in supporting the career transitioning of students with ADHD.

DISCUSSION

This study examined the perspectives of counselors on the career counseling models and services for students with ADHD in Nigeria. The study revealed that school counselors held a moderate viewpoint concerning the use of career counseling models and services to support students with ADHD in their career transitioning. In line with this, Balcı (2023) highlighted that counselors' perceptions included positive metaphors related to the counseling profession and the ethics of career counseling. Furthermore, Ahmed and Sajjad (2014) revealed that professional counselors displayed a positive disposition towards career counseling, emphasizing its significant role in fostering an individual's confidence regarding their skills and in shaping a value system for their professional endeavors. Hidayat (2017) explained that the application of a cognitive-behavioral counseling model for students with ADHD by their counselors demonstrated positive outcomes for these students. In another study, counselors characterized the career counseling services as limited and suggested that the perspectives of the counselees should be explored to enhance the effectiveness of these services and models (Kivlighan Jr et al., 1987). DeBose

(2008) revealed that counselors expressed uncertainty regarding the effectiveness of certain counseling services for these students. In a previous study, counselors were found to be showing a diminishing interest in the field of career development (Hackett, 1993). The implementation of service delivery can be influenced by the level of training received (Parikh-Foxx et al., 2020; Powers & Boes, 2013). Also, it has been argued that current career counseling practices are failing to adequately communicate relevant job characteristics to prospective job seekers and students (Carpenter et al., 2018). A prior study showed that school counselors acknowledged spending a significant portion of their time on activities consistent with the ASCA Model (Buchanan, 2011). Career counselors perceived that clients often displayed a lack of commitment and held unrealistic expectations regarding the career counseling process and the role of the counselor (Lim, 2005) suggesting that while the models and services were deemed reliable, students' expectations were not aligned with reality. Despite the availability of career counseling services for students, there is a pressing need for ongoing professional development and training (Cartan, 2016). In the same vein, we would like to reiterate that career counseling models and services are designed for use in supporting and guiding students in navigating their career paths, making it crucial to understand how counselors perceive these models and services. If the principles of social learning theory are embraced, for instance, students with ADHD are likely to achieve greater success. This is because counselors will be more inclined to consider alternative factors that may contribute to the ineffectiveness of career counseling models and services rather than attributing it solely to the models themselves, thereby seeking ways to improve their efficacy.

This study indicates that gender, experience, and school location did not result in any significant difference in the perspectives of inclusive secondary school counselors regarding the application of career counseling models and services to assist students with ADHD during their career transitioning. However, Babins (2016) revealed that gender plays a considerable role in shaping school counselors' self-efficacy regarding the services they provide to students. Ahrons (1976) showed that counselors' perceptions of vocational roles varied by gender, adhering to traditional views of women's roles. Likewise, it was found that men, according to Rochlen and O'Brien (2002), preferred a more directive approach to career counseling as opposed to a contextual and emotionally oriented one. Gutman et al. (2019) examined the role of occupational therapy as a supplementary approach to counseling, and the findings indicated that women with ADHD who participated in the intervention reported improved performance and greater satisfaction with their chosen occupational roles. It is crucial to recognize that there are instances where factors beyond their gender shape an individual's perspective. It is essential to acknowledge that as rational beings, our perceptions are often informed by logical reasoning that considers various factors beyond gender. While Perdrix et al. (2012) did not take into account the counselors' years of experience, it highlighted that a client or student's age emerged as a crucial factor in long-term effectiveness, with younger clients exhibiting a more pronounced difficulty in career decision-making. Lent et al. (2003) showed that the number of years of experience significantly influenced school counselors' self-efficacy, particularly concerning specific aspects of the counselor activity self-efficacy scales. Payne III (2020) demonstrated that counselors with dual licenses possessed significant experiential knowledge concerning the mental health needs of youth. It is essential to differentiate between having dual licenses and possessing experience, as an individual with a single license may have more years of experience than another with multiple licenses. A national survey indicated that the use of college counseling services differed significantly according to the size of the school rather than its location (The Association for University and College Counseling Center Directors, 2021). The school environment plays a crucial role in the variability of school counselors' functions, as well as in the increased engagement and efficacy of their services (McLean, 2006). Furthermore, research requiring school counselors to deliver career counseling services revealed that they encountered obstacles in grasping the career needs of students (Winkelman, 2018). Another study indicated that gender has a significant impact on the role self-efficacy of school counselors (Babins, 2016). Future studies should take into account the perspectives of counselors with dual or more licenses, in comparison to those with one. Also, different interpretations may emerge if subsequent researchers employ an alternative methodology, such as a mixed-methods approach and a larger sample size that includes an equal number of male and female participants.

CONCLUSIONS

The study sheds light on how inclusive secondary school counselors perceive the use of career counseling models and services in supporting students with ADHD during career transitioning. It shows that factors such as gender, years of experience, and school location do not have a significant impact on counselors' perspectives. Given that counselors typically have moderate views on the use of career counseling models and services in supporting students with ADHD during career transitioning, there is a need to further improve their perceptions through ongoing professional development programs.

REFERENCES

Abu-Bader, S. H. (2021). *Using Statistical Methods in Social Science Research: With a Complete SPSS Guide*. Oxford University Press.

Abubakar, I. R. (2017). Access to Sanitation Facilities among Nigerian Households: Determinants and Sustainability Implications. *Sustainability (Basel)*, 547(4), 547. Advance online publication. DOI: 10.3390/su9040547

Ahmed, S., & Sajjad, M. (2014). Career Selection Behavior: Individual Perceptions and Counseling Effectiveness for Career Roles. *Journal of Basic and Applied Scientific Research*, 4(2), 289–300.

Ahrons, C. R. (1976). Counselors' perceptions of career images of women. *Journal of Vocational Behavior*, 8(2), 197–207. DOI: 10.1016/0001-8791(76)90021-X

Altantawy, M. (2016). *Perceptions of rehabilitation professionals regarding career development services for transition youth with disabilities*. (Doctoral Dissertation, Michigan State University). https://d.lib.msu.edu/etd/4480

Arkkelin, D. (2014). *Using SPSS to Understand Research and Data Analysis. Psychology Curricular Materials 1*. Valparaiso University., https://scholar.valpo.edu/psych_oer/1

Axinte, R. (2014). The school counselor: Competencies in a constructivist model of counseling for career development. *Procedia: Social and Behavioral Sciences*, 142, 255–259. DOI: 10.1016/j.sbspro.2014.08.290

Babins, S. B. (2016). *From the trenches to the field: Practicing high school counselors' perceived self-efficacy regarding role (s) and responsibilities pertaining to students' mental health needs*. (Doctoral Dissertation, Temple University).

Balcı, S. (2023). Importance Of Ethics For Counseling Profession: Metaphorical Perceptions Of Candidate Counselors. *Elektronik Sosyal Bilimler Dergisi*, 22(88), 2099–2116. DOI: 10.17755/esosder.1309789

Bella - Awusah. T., Oyewole, G., Falaye, A., & Omigbodun, O. (2022). Adolescents' Perceptions of School Counselling in Ibadan, Nigeria. *Journal of School-Based Counseling Policy and Evaluation*, 4(1), 26-34. https://doi.org/https://doi.org/10.25774/qge2-1z94

Benjamin, B. A., Gati, I., & Braunstein-Bercovitz, H. (2011). Career development in Israel: Characteristics, services and challenges. *Career Planning and Adult Development Journal*, 27(1), 20–38.

Bertoni, B. (2024, April 26). *Counseling Theories and Approaches: Understanding Different Modalities*. (Keiser University). https://www.keiseruniversity.edu/counseling-theories-and-approaches-understanding-different-modalities/

Boeri, M., & Lamonica, A. K. (2015). Sampling designs and issues in qualitative criminology. In *The Routledge Handbook of Qualitative Criminology*. Routledge., DOI: 10.4324/9780203074701-12

Brown, V. (2008). Going global–does career development need to think bigger to support the most disadvantaged? *Perspectives in Education*, 26(3), 101–107.

Buchanan, D. K. (2011). *A comparative analysis of school counselors' and school principals' perceptions of school counselors' activities*.(Doctoral Dissertation, University of Tennessee). https://trace.tennessee.edu/utk_graddiss/1170

Canu, W. H., Stevens, A. E., Ranson, L., Lefler, E. K., LaCount, P., Serrano, J. W., Willcutt, E., & Hartung, C. M. (2021). College readiness: Differences between first-year undergraduates with and without ADHD. *Journal of Learning Disabilities*, 54(6), 403–411. DOI: 10.1177/0022219420972693 PMID: 33238816

Carlson, L. A., & Kees, N. L. (2013). Mental health services in public schools: A preliminary study of school counselor perceptions. *Professional School Counseling*, 16(4), 211–221. DOI: 10.1177/2156759X150160401

Carpenter, D., Young, D. K., & McLeod Michele, A. (2018). IT career counseling: Are occupational congruence and the job characteristics model effective at predicting IT job satisfaction? *Journal of Information Systems Education*, 29(4), 225–238.

Cartan, M. E. (2016). *A descriptive study of perceptions of high school guidance counselors of the factors that affect delivery of career counseling and career development opportunities to students*.(Doctoral Dissertation, University of La Verne).

Chen, C. P. (2021). Career counselling university students with learning disabilities. *British Journal of Guidance & Counselling*, 49(1), 44–56. DOI: 10.1080/03069885.2020.1811205

DeBose, T. C. (2008). *School-based mental-health services in Georgia: The school counselor's perspective*. (Dissertation, Capella University).

Denis, D. J. (2018). *SPSS Data Analysis for Univariate, Bivariate, and Multivariate Statistics*. John Wiley & Sons. DOI: 10.1002/9781119465775

Dianti, T. M., Iswari, M., & Daharnis. (2022). Implementation of trait and factor theory in improving career planning for class xii students of SMA N 4 Sungai Penuh in the new normal era. *Literasi Nusantara*, 2(2), Article 2.

Drucker, M. V. (2012). *Attention deficit hyperactivity disorder and career ideation: An application of hope theory and social cognitive career theory.* (Masters Thesis, Smith College, Northampton, MA). https://scholarworks.smith.edu/theses/905

Eleke, E. M. (2023). Challenges and Opportunities in Counsellor Education in Nigeria: A Comprehensive Analysis. *International Journal for Innovation Education and Research*, 11(2), 218–224.

Eseadi, C., & Diale, B. M. (Eds.). (2024). *Perspectives on Career Transitioning of Students with Hearing Impairments.* IGI Global., DOI: 10.4018/979-8-3693-2631-2

Furtick, J., Jr. (2005). *The impact of labeling on African American males diagnosed with attention deficit disorder (ADD) and attention deficit hyperactive disorder (ADHD): A social work perspective.* (Doctoral Dissertation, The Union Institute and University, Ohio).

Gati, I. (1991). Career counselors' perception of the structure of vocational interests. *Journal of Counseling Psychology*, 38(2), 175–181. DOI: 10.1037/0022-0167.38.2.175

Gibson, S. (2017). *Counseling College Students with Attention-Deficit/Hyperactivity Disorder (ADHD): A Consensual Qualitative Research (CQR) Study Examining the Experiences of College Counselors* (Doctoral dissertation, Ohio University).

Gomez, A. (2024, June 4). *15 Types of Counseling You Should Know About* [Our Lady of the Lake University]. https://www.ollusa.edu/blog/types-of-counseling.html

Gray, G. B. (2009). *Career decision making for male students with Attention Deficit Hyperactivity Disorder: A model of critical factors aiding in transitional efforts.* (Doctoral Dissertation, Western Michigan University). https://scholarworks.wmich.edu/dissertations/663

Grenawalt, T. A., Degeneffe, C. E., & Kesselmayer, R. F. (2020). Perceived Career Impacts From Specialized Instruction in Cognitive Disabilities: A Phenomenological Study. *Rehabilitation Research, Policy, and Education*, 34(4), 235–249. Advance online publication. DOI: 10.1891/RE-19-34

Group, A. V. D. (2023. December 4). The Impact of Globalization on Career Choices. https://www.linkedin.com/pulse/impact-globalization-career-choices-avdgroup-vappc/

Gutman, S., Balasubramanian, S., Herzog, M., Kim, E., Swirnow, H., Retig, Y., & Wolff, S. (2019). Effectiveness of a Tailored Intervention for Women With ADHD and ADHD Symptoms: A Randomized Controlled Study. *The American Journal of Occupational Therapy, 73*(4_Supplement_1), 7311520394p1-7311520394p1. DOI: 10.5014/ajot.2020.033316

Hackett, G. (1993). Career counseling and psychotherapy: False dichotomies and recommended remedies. *Journal of Career Assessment*, 1(2), 105–117. DOI: 10.1177/106907279300100201

Hannor-Walker, T., Pincus, R., Wright, L. S., Rock, W., Money-Brady, J., & Bohecker, L. (2022). School counselors and administrators agree: Time and testing are barriers. *International Journal of Education Policy and Leadership*, 18(2), 36–53. DOI: 10.22230/ijepl.2022v18n2a1243

Harwell, M. (2011). Research Design in Qualitative/Quantitative/Mixed Methods. In C. Conrad & R. Serlin, *The SAGE Handbook for Research in Education: Pursuing Ideas as the Keystone of Exemplary Inquiry* (pp. 147–164). SAGE Publications. DOI: 10.4135/9781483351377.n11

Hidayat, H. (2017). Cognitive-Behavioral Counseling Model to Optimize Cognitive Potentiality and Adaptive Behavior of Attention Deficite Hyperactivity Disorders (ADHD) Students: *1st International Conference on Educational Sciences*, 954–958. DOI: 10.5220/0007051509540958

Huegel, J. (2015). *Supporting College Students with ADHD*. (Master's Thesis, Winona State University). https://openriver.winona.edu/counseloreducationcapstones/32

Ihuoma, C. P. (2021). Developing A School-Based Counselling Programme in Nigerian Schools in the 21st Century. *Benin Journal of Educational Studies*, 27(1), 170–184.

Jackie, C. H. F. (2023, December 26). Globalization's Impact on Economic Development: Unveiling the Effects. https://www.linkedin.com/pulse/globalizations-impact-economic-development-unveiling-dr--9sj9c/

John-Abebe, R. (2023). Influence of geographical location on maternal mortality in southern senatorial district of Edo state, Nigeria. *Port Harcourt Journal of the Social Sciences*, 10(2), 202–220.

Kaliris, A., & Issari, P. (2022). Exploring Narrative Ideas in Career Counseling. *Open Journal of Social Sciences*, 10(2), 2. Advance online publication. DOI: 10.4236/jss.2022.102026

Kapil, A. R. (2022, July 11). What is Univariate Analysis? *Blogs & Updates on Data Science, Business Analytics, AI Machine Learning*. https://www.analytixlabs.co.in/blog/univariate-analysis/

Keong, Y., Md Husin, M., & Kamarudin, S. (2023). Understanding Research Paradigms: A Scientific Guide. *Journal of Contemporary Issues in Business and Government*, 27, 2021. DOI: 10.47750/cibg.2021.27.02.588

Kincheloe, J. L., & Tobin, K. (2009). The much exaggerated death of positivism. *Cultural Studies of Science Education*, 4(3), 513–528. DOI: 10.1007/s11422-009-9178-5

Kivlighan, D. M.Jr, Johnsen, B., & Fretz, B. (1987). Participant's perception of change mechanisms in career counseling groups: The role of emotional components in career problem solving. *Journal of Career Development*, 14(1), 35–44. DOI: 10.1177/089484538701400104

Lent, R. W., Brown, S. D., & Hackett, G. (1994). Toward a unifying social cognitive theory of career and academic interest, choice, and performance. *Journal of Vocational Behavior*, 45(1), 79–122. DOI: 10.1006/jvbe.1994.1027

Lent, R. W., Hackett, G., & Brown, S. D. (1998). Extending social cognitive theory to counselor training: Problems and prospects. *The Counseling Psychologist*, 26(2), 295–306. DOI: 10.1177/0011000098262005

Lent, R. W., Hill, C. E., & Hoffman, M. A. (2003). Development and validation of the counselor activity self-efficacy scales. *Journal of Counseling Psychology*, 50(1), 97–108. DOI: 10.1037/0022-0167.50.1.97

Lika, Iswari, M., & Daharnis. (2022). Implementation of career guidance in improving career planning skills in students in senior high school: Array. *Literasi Nusantara*, 2(2), 655–665.

Lim, R. B. (2005). *Career counselling services: Client expectations and provider perceptions*. (Doctoral Dissertation, Queensland University of Technology).

Lonczak, H. S. (2020, April 3). *12 Popular Counseling Approaches to Consider*. PositivePsychology.Com. https://positivepsychology.com/popular-counseling-approaches/

Luft, P. (2015). Transition services for DHH adolescents and young adults with disabilities: Challenges and theoretical frameworks. *American Annals of the Deaf*, 160(4), 395–414. DOI: 10.1353/aad.2015.0028 PMID: 26497077

Lynette, P. (2024, February 10). *Demystifying research paradigms.* https://www.lynettepretorius.com/the_scholars_way_blog/demystifying-research-paradigms/

Magnus, O., & Eseigbe, J. (2012). Categorization of Urban Centres in Edo State, Nigeria. *IOSR Journal of Business and Management*, 3(6), 19–25. DOI: 10.9790/487X-0361925

Main, P. (2023, July 17). *Counselling Theories.* Structural Learning. https://www.structural-learning.com/post/counselling-theories

Maree, J. G., & Warnock, K. (2023). Teachers' Perceptions of how Attention-Deficit/Hyperactivity Disorder May Influence Learners' Career Choices. *South African Journal of Higher Education*, 37(4), 205–224. DOI: 10.20853/37-4-5732

McLean, K. M. (2006). *School counselors' perceptions of their changing roles and responsibilities.* (Master's Dissertation, University of Wisconsin-Stout).

Murugan, K., & Govindarajan, B. (2023). Statistical Package for the Social Science. *International Journal of Business and Economics Research*, 8, 616–618.

Newman, L., Wagner, M., Cameto, R., & Knokey, A.-M. (2009). The Post-High School Outcomes of Youth With Disabilities up to 4 Years After High School: A Report From the National Longitudinal Transition Study-2 (NLTS2). NCSER 2009-3017. *National Center for Special Education Research.* https://files.eric.ed.gov/fulltext/ED505448.pdf

Nie, Z., & Zarei, H. (2023). A cross-cultural study on the career counseling service ecosystem: Implications for higher education marketing. *Journal of Marketing for Higher Education*, 0(0), 1–27. DOI: 10.1080/08841241.2023.2242805

Ohunene, L. A., Audu, B. C., & Jacob, O. N. (2021). Challenges facing counsellors in Nigerian public primary schools and way forward. *Middle European Scientific Bulletin*, 17, 301–310.

Olsen, C., & St. George, D. M. M. (2006). *Cross-Sectional Study Design and Data Analysis.* College Entrance Examination Board., http://cdn.physioblasts.org/f/public/1355667773_1_FT0_4297_module_05.pdf

Pan, E. T.-S. (2005). Globalization and Your Career. *The Bent of Tau Beta Pi*, 31-33. https://www.tbp.org/pubs/Features/Sp05Pan.pdf

Parikh-Foxx, S., Martinez, R., Baker, S. B., & Olsen, J. (2020). Self-efficacy for enhancing students' career and college readiness: A survey of professional school counselors. *Journal of Counseling and Development*, 98(2), 183–192. DOI: 10.1002/jcad.12312

Payne, D. S., III. (2020). *Continuing the Evolution: Examining the Experiences, Perceptions, and Practices of Dually Licensed Counselors Working with Children and Adolescents with Mental Health Concerns.* (Doctoral Dissertation, North Carolina State University).

Perdrix, S., Stauffer, S., Masdonati, J., Massoudi, K., & Rossier, J. (2012). Effectiveness of career counseling: A one-year follow-up. *Journal of Vocational Behavior*, 80(2), 565–578. DOI: 10.1016/j.jvb.2011.08.011

Powers, P., & Boes, S. R. (2013). Steps toward Understanding: Teacher Perceptions of the School Counselor Role. *Georgia School Counselors Association Journal*, 20(1), n1.

Proofed. (2023, January 22). The Four Types of Research Paradigms: A Comprehensive Guide | Proofed's Writing Tips. *Proofed.* https://proofed.com/writing-tips/the-four-types-of-research-paradigms-a-comprehensive-guide/

Rochlen, A. B., & O'Brien, K. M. (2002). The relation of male gender role conflict and attitudes toward career counseling to interest in and preferences for different career counseling styles. *Psychology of Men & Masculinity*, 3(1), 9–21. DOI: 10.1037/1524-9220.3.1.9

Sampson, A. S., Mutiu, B. M., & Udoh, A. U. (2023). Utilisation of Statistical Packages for Data Analysis among Post-Graduate Students in Universities in Rivers State. *Journal of Education in Developing Areas*, 31(2), 352–366.

Moniruzzaman Sarker, & AL-Muaalemi, M. A. (2022). Sampling Techniques for Quantitative Research. In M. R. Islam, N. A. Khan, & R. Baikady (Eds.), *Principles of Social Research Methodology* (pp. 221–234). Springer Nature. DOI: 10.1007/978-981-19-5441-2_15

Shankar, J., & Ip, C. (2018). Community college counselors' experiences and challenges with postsecondary students with mental health disorders. In *Health and Academic Achievement.* IntechOpen., DOI: 10.5772/intechopen.75661

Staff, I. M. F. (2008, May). Globalization: A Brief Overview. https://www.imf.org/external/np/exr/ib/2008/053008.htm

Stevenson, B. J., Gorman, J. A., Crossman, D. M., & Mueller, L. (2021). Providing career development services to veterans: Perceived need, acceptability, and demand. *Rehabilitation Counseling Bulletin*, 64(2), 97–107. DOI: 10.1177/0034355220914737

Taymans, J. M., & West, L. L. (2001). *Selecting a College for Students with Learning Disabilities or Attention Deficit Hyperactivity Disorder (ADHD).* ERIC Clearinghouse on Disabilities and Gifted Education Arlington VA.

Teddlie, C., & Yu, F. (2007). Mixed Methods Sampling: A Typology With Examples. *Journal of Mixed Methods Research*, 1(1), 77–100. DOI: 10.1177/1558689806292430

The Association for University and College Counseling Center Directors. (2021). *The AUCCCD Annual Survey Report Public Survey*. The Association for University and College Counseling Center Directors (AUCCCD). https://www.aucccd.org/assets/2020-21%20Annual%20Survey%20Report%20Public%20Survey.pdf

Thomas, B. (2022). *The Role of Purposive Sampling Technique as a Tool for Informal Choices in a Social Sciences in Research Methods. Just Agriculture Multidisciplinary e-Newsletter, 2(5), 1-8.*

Thomas, L. (2020, May 8). *Cross-Sectional Study | Definition, Uses & Examples*. Scribbr. https://www.scribbr.com/methodology/cross-sectional-study/

Tremblay, T., Smith, J., Xie, H., & Drake, R. E. (2006). Effect of benefits counseling services on employment outcomes for people with psychiatric disabilities. *Psychiatric Services (Washington, D.C.)*, 57(6), 816–821. DOI: 10.1176/ps.2006.57.6.816 PMID: 16754758

Ugwoke, S. C., Eseadi, C., Ugwuanyi, L. T., & Ikechukwu-Ilomuanya, A. B. (2015). Extending the role of guidance counselors to address quality assurance in inclusive schools in Nigeria. *Buletin Teknologi Tanaman*, 12, 265–271.

Van der Stede, W. A. (2014). A manipulationist view of causality in cross-sectional survey research. *Accounting, Organizations and Society*, 39(7), 567–574. DOI: 10.1016/j.aos.2013.12.001

Walsh, M. E. (2012). *The Experiences of Professional Counselors Who Exhibit Exceptional Practice with Children and Adolescents in Nonschool Settings*. (Doctoral Dissertation, Georgia State University). DOI: 10.57709/2781509

Wang, X., & Cheng, Z. (2020). Cross-Sectional Studies: Strengths, Weaknesses, and Recommendations. *Chest*, 158(1, Supplement), S65–S71. DOI: 10.1016/j.chest.2020.03.012 PMID: 32658654

Winkelman, L. B. (2018). *University career counselors' perceptions of counseling international students*. (Doctoral Dissertation, Texas Tech University). https://hdl.handle.net/2346/82695

Yunus, M. N., Zainudin, Z. N., Mohamad Yusop, Y., Wan Othman, W. N., Engku Kamarudin, E. M., & Anuar, M. (2024). Understanding Career Decision-Making: Influencing Factors and Application of Krumboltz's Social Learning Theory. *International Journal of Academic Research in Business & Social Sciences*, 14(7), 36–51. DOI: 10.6007/IJARBSS/v14-i7/21562

ADDITIONAL READINGS

Abuse, S. (2016). Mental Health Services. *Key substance uses and mental health indicators in the United States: Results from the*.

Alhadi, S., Supriyanto, A., & Dina, D. A. M. (2016). Media in guidance and counseling services: A tool and innovation for school counselors. *SCHOULID: Indonesian Journal of School Counseling*, 1(1), 6–11. DOI: 10.23916/schoulid.v1i1.35.6-11

Altmann, S., Falk, A., Jäger, S., & Zimmermann, F. (2018). Learning about job search: A field experiment with job seekers in Germany. *Journal of Public Economics*, 164, 33–49. DOI: 10.1016/j.jpubeco.2018.05.003

Alum, E. U., Obeagu, E. I., Ugwu, O. P., Samson, A. O., Adepoju, A. O., & Amusa, M. O. (2023). Inclusion of nutritional counseling and mental health services in HIV/AIDS management: A paradigm shift. *Medicine*, 102(41), e35673. DOI: 10.1097/MD.0000000000035673 PMID: 37832059

American Occupational Therapy Association. (2020). Occupational therapy practice framework: Domain et process: Vol. 74. *No. 7412410010*. American Occupational Therapy Association.

Antshel, K. M. (2018). Attention deficit/hyperactivity disorder (ADHD) and entrepreneurship. *The Academy of Management Perspectives*, 32(2), 243–265. DOI: 10.5465/amp.2016.0144

Araujo, E. A., Pfiffner, L., & Haack, L. M. (2017). Emotional, social and cultural experiences of Latino children with ADHD symptoms and their families. *Journal of Child and Family Studies*, 26(12), 3512–3524. DOI: 10.1007/s10826-017-0842-1

Ardi, Z., Putra, M. R. M., & Ifdil, I. (2017). Ethics and legal issues in online counseling services: Counseling principles analysis. *Jurnal Psikologi Pendidikan Dan Konseling: Jurnal Kajian Psikologi Pendidikan Dan Bimbingan Konseling*, 3(2), 15. DOI: 10.26858/jpkk.v0i0.3657

Arrogi, A., Schotte, A., Bogaerts, A., Boen, F., & Seghers, J. (2017). Short-and long-term effectiveness of a three-month individualized need-supportive physical activity counseling intervention at the workplace. *BMC Public Health*, 17(1), 1–20. DOI: 10.1186/s12889-016-3965-1 PMID: 28069016

Arulmani, G., Bakshi, A. J., Leong, F. T., & Watts, A. G. (2014). *Handbook of career development. International Perspectives*. Springer. DOI: 10.1007/978-1-4614-9460-7

Astuti, L. P. (2021). The role of guidance and counseling services in individual counseling during the covid-19 pandemic. *International Journal of Applied Guidance and Counseling*, 2(1), 25–30. DOI: 10.26486/ijagc.v2i1.1592

Avery, C., Howell, J. S., & Page, L. (2014). *A Review of the Role of College Counseling, Coaching, and Mentoring on Students' Postsecondary Outcomes. Research Brief.* College Board.

Baluku, M. M., Mugabi, E. N., Nansamba, J., Matagi, L., Onderi, P., & Otto, K. (2021). Psychological capital and career outcomes among final year university students: The mediating role of career engagement and perceived employability. *International Journal of Applied Positive Psychology*, 6(1), 55–80. DOI: 10.1007/s41042-020-00040-w

Bharti, T., & Rangnekar, S. (2019). Optimism and career engagement in employees: An empirical test. *International Journal of Business Excellence*, 19(3), 429–446. DOI: 10.1504/IJBEX.2019.102834

Bolognese, M. A., Franco, C. B., Ferrari, A., Bennemann, R. M., Lopes, S. M. A., Bertolini, S. M., Júnior, N. N., & Branco, B. H. M. (2020). Group nutrition counseling or individualized prescription for women with obesity. A clinical trial. *Frontiers in Public Health*, 8, 127. DOI: 10.3389/fpubh.2020.00127 PMID: 32426316

Caolo, J. L. (2014). *The Relationship Between Age of Diagnosis and the Occurrence of Dysfunctional Career Thoughts Among College Students With ADHD* (Order No. 10595068). Available from ProQuest Dissertations & Theses Global. (1906301920). https://www.proquest.com/dissertations-theses/relationship-between-age-diagnosis-occurrence/docview/1906301920/se-2

Cardoso, P., & Sales, C. M. (2019). Individualized career counseling outcome assessment: A case study using the personal questionnaire. *The Career Development Quarterly*, 67(1), 21–31. DOI: 10.1002/cdq.12160

Carroll, L. J., Finelli, C. J., & DesJardins, S. L. (2022, February). *Academic success of college students with ADHD: the first year of college. In 2022 ASEE CoNECD (Collaborative Network for Engineering & Computing Diversity) Conference.* American Society of Engineering Education.

Case-Smith, J., & O'Brien, J. C. (2013). *Occupational therapy for children-E-Book.* Elsevier Health Sciences.

Castilhos, R. B., Dolbec, P. Y., & Veresiu, E. (2017). Introducing a spatial perspective to analyze market dynamics. *Marketing Theory*, 17(1), 9–29. DOI: 10.1177/1470593116657915

Chen, L., Mittendorfer-Rutz, E., Björkenstam, E., Rahman, S., Gustafsson, K., Kjeldgård, L., Ekselius, L., Taipale, H., Tanskanen, A., & Helgesson, M. (2024). Labour market integration among young adults diagnosed with attention-deficit/hyperactivity disorder (ADHD) at working age. *Psychological Medicine*, 54(1), 148–158. DOI: 10.1017/S003329172300096X PMID: 37185065

Chen, W., Epstein, A., Toner, M., Murphy, N., Rudaizky, D., & Downs, J. (2023). Enabling successful life engagement in young people with ADHD: New components beyond adult models of recovery. *Disability and Rehabilitation*, 45(14), 2288–2300. DOI: 10.1080/09638288.2022.2087763 PMID: 35944517

Christiansen, C. H., Bass, J., & Baum, C. M. (2024). *Occupational therapy: Performance, participation, and well-being*. Taylor & Francis. DOI: 10.4324/9781003522997

Chronis-Tuscano, A., Wang, C. H., Strickland, J., Almirall, D., & Stein, M. A. (2016). Personalized treatment of mothers with ADHD and their young at-risk children: A SMART pilot. *Journal of Clinical Child and Adolescent Psychology*, 45(4), 510–521. DOI: 10.1080/15374416.2015.1102069 PMID: 26799502

Cole, M. B., & Tufano, R. (2024). *Applied theories in occupational therapy: A practical approach*. Taylor & Francis. DOI: 10.4324/9781003522591

Crawford, B. (2014). How to Help Counselees with Psychoactive Medications. *Journal of Biblical Counseling*, 28(2).

D'Alessio, K. A., & Banerjee, M. (2016). Academic Advising as an Intervention for College Students with ADHD. *Journal of Postsecondary Education and Disability*, 29(2), 109–121.

Dastbaaz, A., Yeganehfarzand, S. H., Azkhosh, M., Shoaee, F., & Salehi, M. (2014). The effect of group counseling.

Daswati, D., Wirawan, H., Hattab, S., Salam, R., & Iskandar, A. S. (2022). The effect of psychological capital on performance through the role of career engagement: Evidence from Indonesian public organizations. *Cogent Social Sciences*, 8(1), 2012971. DOI: 10.1080/23311886.2021.2012971

Derefinko, K. J., Hayden, A., Sibley, M. H., Duvall, J., Milich, R., & Lorch, E. P. (2014). A story mapping intervention to improve narrative comprehension deficits in adolescents with ADHD. *School Mental Health*, 6(4), 251–263. DOI: 10.1007/s12310-014-9127-7 PMID: 25436018

Dillahunt, T. R., Bose, N., Diwan, S., & Chen-Phang, A. (2016, June). Designing for disadvantaged job seekers: Insights from early investigations. In *Proceedings of the 2016 ACM Conference on Designing Interactive Systems* (pp. 905-910). DOI: 10.1145/2901790.2901865

Dipeolu, A., Hargrave, S., & Storlie, C. A. (2015). Enhancing ADHD and LD Diagnostic Accuracy Using Career Instruments. *Journal of Career Development*, 42(1), 19–32. DOI: 10.1177/0894845314521691

Dipeolu, A., Hargrave, S., Tineo, Y. A. C., Longoria, A., & Escalante, M. (2023). Dysfunctional career thoughts and peer relationships in adolescents with ADHD. *International Journal for Educational and Vocational Guidance*, •••, 1–17. DOI: 10.1007/s10775-023-09612-z

Emadian, S. O., Bahrami, H., Hassanzadeh, R., & Banijamali, S. (2016). Effects of narrative therapy and computer-assisted cognitive rehabilitation on the reduction of ADHD symptoms in children. *Majallah-i Danishgah-i Ulum-i Pizishki-i Babul*, 18(6), 28–34.

Fall, K. A., Holden, J. M., & Marquis, A. (2017). *Theoretical models of counseling and psychotherapy*. Routledge. DOI: 10.4324/9781315733531

Farmakopoulou, I., Metaxa, A., & Theodoratou, M. (2024). Examining Challenges and Evaluating Supportive Counseling Approaches for Students with Attention Deficit Hyperactivity Disorder (ADHD). *European Psychiatry*, 67(S1), S689–S689. DOI: 10.1192/j.eurpsy.2024.1433

Flores, M. F. (2019). Understanding the challenges of remote working and its impact to workers. [IJBMM]. *International Journal of Business Marketing and Management*, 4(11), 40–44.

Flurentin, E., & Santoso, D. B. (2017, September). Cultural study of counselors and counselees in counseling. In *9th international conference for science educators and teachers (ICSET 2017)* (pp. 1106-1113). Atlantis Press. DOI: 10.2991/icset-17.2017.180

Francis, P. C., & Horn, A. S. (2017). Mental health issues and counseling services in US higher education: An overview of recent research and recommended practices. *Higher Education Policy*, 30(2), 263–277. DOI: 10.1057/s41307-016-0036-2

Galanti, T., Guidetti, G., Mazzei, E., Zappalà, S., & Toscano, F. (2021). Work from home during the COVID-19 outbreak: The impact on employees' remote work productivity, engagement, and stress. *Journal of Occupational and Environmental Medicine*, 63(7), e426–e432. DOI: 10.1097/JOM.0000000000002236 PMID: 33883531

Gerdes, A. C., Kapke, T. L., Grace, M., & Castro, A. (2021). Feasibility, acceptability, and preliminary outcomes of a culturally adapted evidence-based treatment for Latino youth with ADHD. *Journal of Attention Disorders*, 25(3), 432–447. DOI: 10.1177/1087054718821729 PMID: 30667285

Golos, A., Mor, R., Fisher, O., & Finkelstein, A. (2021). Clinicians' views on the need for cultural adaptation of intervention for children with ADHD from the ultraorthodox community. *Occupational Therapy International*, 2021(1), 5564364. DOI: 10.1155/2021/5564364 PMID: 34121956

Haack, L. M., Gerdes, A. C., Lawton, K. E., & Schneider, B. W. (2016). Understanding and measuring functional impairment in diverse children with ADHD: Development of the ADHD-FX scale with an at-risk, community sample. *Journal of Attention Disorders*, 20(6), 487–500. DOI: 10.1177/1087054714527791 PMID: 24695438

Hidayat, H. (2018). Cognitive-behavioral counseling model to optimize cognitive potentiality and adaptive behavior of attention deficit hyperactivity disorders (ADHD) students.

Hirschi, A., Freund, P. A., & Herrmann, A. (2014). The career engagement scale: Development and validation of a measure of proactive career behaviors. *Journal of Career Assessment*, 22(4), 575–594. DOI: 10.1177/1069072713514813

Hirschi, A., & Froidevaux, A. (2019). Career counseling. In *The Routledge Companion to Career Studies* (pp. 331–345). Routledge. DOI: 10.4324/9781315674704-24

Hirschi, A., & Jaensch, V. K. (2015). Narcissism and career success: Occupational self-efficacy and career engagement as mediators. *Personality and Individual Differences*, 77, 205–208. DOI: 10.1016/j.paid.2015.01.002

Hodkinson, A., Zhou, A., Johnson, J., Geraghty, K., Riley, R., Zhou, A., Panagopoulou, E., Chew-Graham, C. A., Peters, D., Esmail, A., & Panagioti, M. (2022). Associations of physician burnout with career engagement and quality of patient care: Systematic review and meta-analysis. *BMJ (Clinical Research Ed.)*, •••, 378. DOI: 10.1136/bmj-2022-070442 PMID: 36104064

Holm-Hadulla, R. M., & Koutsoukou-Argyraki, A. (2015). Mental health of students in a globalized world: Prevalence of complaints and disorders, methods and effectiveness of counseling, structure of mental health services for students. *Mental Health & Prevention*, 3(1-2), 1–4. DOI: 10.1016/j.mhp.2015.04.003

Hwang, B., Bennett, R., & Beauchemin, J. (2014). International students' utilization of counseling services. *College Student Journal*, 48(3), 347–354.

Jones, D. A., Willness, C. R., & Madey, S. (2014). Why are job seekers attracted by corporate social performance? Experimental and field tests of three signal-based mechanisms. *Academy of Management Journal*, 57(2), 383–404. DOI: 10.5465/amj.2011.0848

Kapke, T. L., Grace, M. A., Castro, A., & Gerdes, A. C. (2019). Examining Latino family participation in treatment for childhood ADHD: The role of parental cultural factors and perceptions. *Child & Family Behavior Therapy*, 41(2), 84–109. DOI: 10.1080/07317107.2019.1599260

Karibwende, F., Niyonsenga, J., Biracyaza, E., Nyirinkwaya, S., Hitayezu, I., Sebatukura, G. S., Ntete, J. M., & Mutabaruka, J. (2023). Efficacy of narrative therapy for orphan and abandoned children with anxiety and attention deficit and hyperactivity disorders in Rwanda: A randomized controlled trial. *Journal of Behavior Therapy and Experimental Psychiatry*, 78, 101802. DOI: 10.1016/j.jbtep.2022.101802 PMID: 36435544

Kim, B., Jang, S. H., Jung, S. H., Lee, B. H., Puig, A., & Lee, S. M. (2014). A moderated mediation model of planned happenstance skills, career engagement, career decision self-efficacy, and career decision certainty. *The Career Development Quarterly*, 62(1), 56–69. DOI: 10.1002/j.2161-0045.2014.00070.x

Lachenmeier, H. (2023). Transition: Growing up with ADHD: Adolescence, career choice, education and further training. In *ADHD and success at work: How to turn supposed shortcomings into strengths* (pp. 125–162). Springer International Publishing. DOI: 10.1007/978-3-031-13437-1_9

Lasky, A. K., Weisner, T. S., Jensen, P. S., Hinshaw, S. P., Hechtman, L., Arnold, L. E., & Swanson, J. M. (2016). ADHD in context: Young adults' reports of the impact of occupational environment on the manifestation of ADHD. *Social Science & Medicine*, 161, 160–168. DOI: 10.1016/j.socscimed.2016.06.003 PMID: 27299978

Lauen, D. L., Fuller, S., Barrett, N., & Janda, L. (2017). Early colleges at scale: Impacts on secondary and postsecondary outcomes. *American Journal of Education*, 123(4), 523–551. DOI: 10.1086/692664

Law, M., Baum, C. M., & Dunn, W. (2024). *Measuring occupational performance: Supporting best practice in occupational therapy*. Taylor & Francis. DOI: 10.4324/9781003525042

Lawton, K. E., Gerdes, A. C., Haack, L. M., & Schneider, B. (2014). Acculturation, cultural values, and Latino parental beliefs about the etiology of ADHD. *Administration and Policy in Mental Health*, 41(2), 189–204. DOI: 10.1007/s10488-012-0447-3 PMID: 23224619

Li, W., Yang, Y., Liu, Z. H., Zhao, Y. J., Zhang, Q., Zhang, L., Cheung, T., & Xiang, Y. T. (2020). Progression of mental health services during the COVID-19 outbreak in China. *International Journal of Biological Sciences*, 16(10), 1732–1738. DOI: 10.7150/ijbs.45120 PMID: 32226291

Lyhne, C. N., Pedersen, P., Nielsen, C. V., & Bjerrum, M. B. (2021). Needs for occupational assistance among young adults with ADHD to deal with executive impairments and promote occupational participation–a qualitative study. *Nordic Journal of Psychiatry*, 75(5), 362–369. DOI: 10.1080/08039488.2020.1862911 PMID: 33380255

Mack, W. (2017). Taking Counselee Inventory: Collecting Data.". *Counseling: How to Counsel Biblically*, 131-46.

Major, A. (2016). *Sources of self-efficacy, self-efficacy for self-regulated learning, and student engagement in adolescents with ADHD* (Order No. 10192925). Available from ProQuest Central; ProQuest Dissertations & Theses Global. (1884789717). https://www.proquest.com/dissertations-theses/sources-self-efficacy-regulated-learning-student/docview/1884789717/se-2

McColl, M. A., Law, M. C., & Debra, S. (2024). *Theoretical basis of occupational therapy*. Taylor & Francis.

McIlveen, P., & Perera, H. N. (2016). Career Optimism Mediates the Effect of Personality on Teachers' Career Engagement. *Journal of Career Assessment*, 24(4), 623–636. DOI: 10.1177/1069072715616059

Michael, R., Zakai-Mashiach, M., & Shavit, P. (2024). Future career expectations of college students-the contribution of disability status, self-advocacy, self-efficacy, and support. *European Journal of Special Needs Education*, ●●●, 1–18. DOI: 10.1080/08856257.2024.2323251

Michelsen, G., Slettebø, T., & Moser, I. B. (2017). Introduction of Cognitive Support Technologies (CST) for job seekers.

Morningstar, M. E., Trainor, A. A., & Murray, A. (2015). Examining outcomes associated with adult life engagement for young adults with high incidence disabilities. *Journal of Vocational Rehabilitation*, 43(3), 195–208. DOI: 10.3233/JVR-150769

Mullen, P. R., & Lambie, G. W. (2016). The contribution of school counselors' self-efficacy to their programmatic service delivery. *Psychology in the Schools*, 53(3), 306–320. DOI: 10.1002/pits.21899

Nagata, M., Nagata, T., Inoue, A., Mori, K., & Matsuda, S. (2019). Effect modification by attention deficit hyperactivity disorder (ADHD) symptoms on the association of psychosocial work environments with psychological distress and work engagement. *Frontiers in Psychiatry*, 10, 166. DOI: 10.3389/fpsyt.2019.00166 PMID: 30971966

Nasamran, A., Witmer, S. E., & Los, J. E. (2017). Exploring predictors of postsecondary outcomes for students with autism spectrum disorder. *Education and Training in Autism and Developmental Disabilities*, 52(4), 343–356.

Nice, M. L., Kolbert, J. B., Joseph, M., Crothers, L. M., Hilts, D., & Kratsa, K. (2020). School counselors' self-efficacy in knowledge of the college process. *Professional School Counseling, 24*(1), 2156759X20976374.

Nilforooshan, P., & Salimi, S. (2016). Career adaptability as a mediator between personality and career engagement. *Journal of Vocational Behavior*, 94, 1–10. DOI: 10.1016/j.jvb.2016.02.010

Nkosi, R. R. (2022). *Parent-teacher collaboration in mapping career transitioning of youth diagnosed with ADHD* (Order No. 30360447). Available from ProQuest Dissertations & Theses Global. (2800161558). https://www.proquest.com/dissertations-theses/parent-teacher-collaboration-mapping-career/docview/2800161558/se-2

O'brien, J. C. (2017). *Introduction to occupational therapy-E-Book*. Elsevier Health Sciences.

Ozimek, A. (2020). The future of remote work. *Available at SSRN* 3638597.

Panahifar, S., & Nouriani, J. M. (2021). The effectiveness of narrative therapy on behavioral maladaptation and psychological health of children with ADHD in Kerman.

Pandang, A. (2020). The implementation of narrative counseling to improve students' self-concept. *Jurnal Psikologi Pendidikan dan Konseling, 6*(2), 26-34.

Park, S. (2019). *ADHD, high ability, or both: The paths to young adulthood career outcomes* (Order No. 13808231). Available from ProQuest Central; ProQuest Dissertations & Theses Global. (2307147075). https://www.proquest.com/dissertations-theses/adhd-high-ability-both-paths-young-adulthood/docview/2307147075/se-2

Park, S., Foley-Nicpon, M., & Mahatmya, D. (2024). Young adult career outcomes for adolescents with adhd, high ability, or twice-exceptionality. *Journal for the Education of the Gifted*, 47(3), 237–265. DOI: 10.1177/01623532241258759

Patel, P. C., Rietveld, C. A., & Verheul, I. (2021). Attention deficit hyperactivity disorder (adhd) and earnings in later-life self-employment. *Entrepreneurship Theory and Practice*, 45(1), 43–63. DOI: 10.1177/1042258719888641

Patton, W., & McMahon, M. (2014). *Career development and systems theory: Connecting theory and practice* (Vol. 2). Springer. DOI: 10.1007/978-94-6209-635-6

Pendleton, H. M., & Schultz-Krohn, W. (2017). *Pedretti's Occupational therapybook: Practice skills for physical dysfunction.* Elsevier Health Sciences.

Perry, J., Parikh, S., Vazquez, M., Saunders, R., Bolin, S., & Dameron, M. L. (2020). School counselor self-efficacy in advocating for self: How prepared are we? *The Journal of Counselor Preparation and Supervisor*, 13(4), 5.

Pham, A. V. (2015). Understanding ADHD from a biopsychosocial-cultural framework: A case study. *Contemporary School Psychology*, 19(1), 54–62. DOI: 10.1007/s40688-014-0038-2

Philipsen, A., Jans, T., Graf, E., Matthies, S., Borel, P., Colla, M., & van Elst, L. T. (2015). Effects of group psychotherapy, individual counseling, methylphenidate, and placebo in the treatment of adult attention-deficit/hyperactivity disorder: A randomized clinical trial. *JAMA Psychiatry*, 72(12), 1199–1210. DOI: 10.1001/jamapsychiatry.2015.2146 PMID: 26536057

Pickerell, D. A., & Borgen, R. A. (2023). *Optimizing career engagement.* Cognella.

Popovici, V., & Popovici, A. L. (2020). Remote work revolution: Current opportunities and challenges for organizations. *Ovidius Univ. Ann. Econ. Sci. Ser*, 20(1), 468–472.

Prevatt, F., Osborn, D., & Coffman, T. P. (2015). Utility of the barkley deficits in executive functioning scale (BDEFS) for career planning in college students with ADHD. *Career Planning and Adult Development Journal*, •••, 69–79.

Ravasco, P. (2015). Nutritional approaches in cancer: Relevance of individualized counseling and supplementation. *Nutrition (Burbank, Los Angeles County, Calif.)*, 31(4), 603–604. DOI: 10.1016/j.nut.2014.12.001 PMID: 25770326

Rice, M. S., Tomlin, G., & Stein, F. (2024). *Clinical research in occupational therapy.* Routledge.

Robbins, R. (2017). The untapped potential of the ADHD employee in the workplace. *Cogent Business & Management*, 4(1), 1271384. DOI: 10.1080/23311975.2016.1271384

Royal, C., Wade, W., & Nickel, H. (2015). Career development and vocational behavior of adults with attention-deficit/hyperactivity disorder [ADHD]. *Career Planning and Adult Development Journal*, 31(4), 54–63.

Ruiz, M. T., Rodrigues, E. D. C., da Silva, K. E. P. O., de Resende, C. V., Cavalcanti, M. C., Dos Santos, L. M., Wernet, M., Gomes, A. L. M., Christoffel, M. M., Raponi, M. B. G., da Silva, J. A., de Oliveira, J. F., Contim, D., & Linares, A. M. (2023). Effectiveness of individualized counseling on the duration of exclusive breastfeeding: Study protocol for a multicenter, randomized, parallel, and open clinical trial. *Trials*, 24(1), 455. DOI: 10.1186/s13063-023-07490-y PMID: 37454111

Rushton, S., Giallo, R., & Efron, D. (2020). ADHD and emotional engagement with school in the primary years: Investigating the role of student–teacher relationships. *The British Journal of Educational Psychology*, 90(S1), 193–209. DOI: 10.1111/bjep.12316 PMID: 31654412

Sanders, C., Welfare, L. E., & Culver, S. (2017). Career Counseling in Middle Schools: A Study of School Counselor Self-Efficacy. *The Professional Counselor*, 7(3), 238–250. DOI: 10.15241/cs.7.3.238

Savickas, M. (2019). *Career counseling*. American Psychological Association.

Savickas, M. L. (2015). Career counseling paradigms: Guiding, developing, and designing.

Schultz, B. K., Evans, S. W., Schultz, B. K., & Evans, S. W. (2015). Counseling Adolescents with ADHD. *A Practical Guide to Implementing School-Based Interventions for Adolescents with ADHD*, 61-86.

Shabanpour, A., & Mohammadyfar, M. A., TalePesand, S., & Rezaei, A. M. (2017). Comparison of the effectiveness of three methods of cognitive-behavioral therapy (individual counseling, group counseling and parent education) on reduction of ADHD syndrome. *Eurasian Journal of Biosciences*, 11(1).

Shahidullah, J. D., Carlson, J. S., Haggerty, D., & Lancaster, B. M. (2018). Integrated care models for ADHD in children and adolescents: A systematic review. *Families, Systems & Health*, 36(2), 233–247. DOI: 10.1037/fsh0000356 PMID: 29902040

Slobodin, O., & Crunelle, C. L. (2019). Mini review: Socio-cultural influences on the link between ADHD and SUD. *Frontiers in Public Health*, 7, 173. DOI: 10.3389/fpubh.2019.00173 PMID: 31294015

Slobodin, O., & Masalha, R. (2020). Challenges in ADHD care for ethnic minority children: A review of the current literature. *Transcultural Psychiatry*, 57(3), 468–483. DOI: 10.1177/1363461520902885 PMID: 32233772

Sou, E. K., Yuen, M., & Chen, G. (2022). Career adaptability as a mediator between social capital and career engagement. *The Career Development Quarterly*, 70(1), 2–15. DOI: 10.1002/cdq.12289

Syharat, C., Hain, A., & Zaghi, E., A. (2020, June). Diversifying the engineering pipeline through early engagement of Neurodiverse learners. In *2020 ASEE Virtual Annual Conference*. DOI: 10.18260/1-2--34470

Tang, A. (2020). The impact of school counseling supervision on practicing school counselors' self-efficacy in building a comprehensive school counseling program. *Professional School Counseling, 23*(1), 2156759X20947723.

Tucker, R., Zuo, L., Marino, L. D., Lowman, G. H., & Sleptsov, A. (2021). ADHD and entrepreneurship: Beyond person-entrepreneurship fit. *Journal of Business Venturing Insights*, 15, e00219. DOI: 10.1016/j.jbvi.2020.e00219

Turpin, M. J., Garcia, J., & Iwama, M. K. (2023). *Using Occupational Therapy Models in Practice E-Book: Using Occupational Therapy Models in Practice E-Book*. Elsevier Health Sciences.

Upadyaya, K., & Salmela-Aro, K. (2015). Development of early vocational behavior: Parallel associations between career engagement and satisfaction. *Journal of Vocational Behavior*, 90, 66–74. DOI: 10.1016/j.jvb.2015.07.008

Van der Oord, S., Boyer, B. E., Van dyck, L., Mackay, K. J., De Meyer, H., & Baeyens, D. (2020). A Randomized Controlled Study of a Cognitive Behavioral Planning Intervention for College Students With ADHD: An Effectiveness Study in Student Counseling Services in Flanders. *Journal of Attention Disorders*, 24(6), 849–862. DOI: 10.1177/1087054718787033 PMID: 29998770

Varrasi, S., Boccaccio, F. M., Guerrera, C. S., Platania, G. A., Pirrone, C., & Castellano, S. (2022). Schooling and occupational outcomes in adults with ADHD: Predictors of success and support strategies for effective learning. *Education Sciences*, 13(1), 37. DOI: 10.3390/educsci13010037

Wanberg, C. R., Ali, A. A., & Csillag, B. (2020). Job seeking: The process and experience of looking for a job. *Annual Review of Organizational Psychology and Organizational Behavior*, 7(1), 315–337. DOI: 10.1146/annurev-orgpsych-012119-044939

Warnock, K. (2022). *Teachers' Experiences of How Attention-deficit/hyperactivity Disorder Influences Learners' Career Choices* (Order No. 30700024). Available from ProQuest Dissertations & Theses Global. (2890696971). https://www.proquest.com/dissertations-theses/teachers-experiences-how-attention-deficit/docview/2890696971/se-2DOI: 10.25403/UPresearchdata.21610653

Wells, R. S., Manly, C. A., Kommers, S., & Kimball, E. (2019). Narrowed gaps and persistent challenges: Examining rural-nonrural disparities in postsecondary outcomes over time. *American Journal of Education*, 126(1), 1–31. DOI: 10.1086/705498

Yang, L., Holtz, D., Jaffe, S., Suri, S., Sinha, S., Weston, J., Joyce, C., Shah, N., Sherman, K., Hecht, B., & Teevan, J. (2022). The effects of remote work on collaboration among information workers. *Nature Human Behaviour*, 6(1), 43–54. DOI: 10.1038/s41562-021-01196-4 PMID: 34504299

Zendarski, N., Sciberras, E., Mensah, F., & Hiscock, H. (2017). Early high school engagement in students with attention/deficit hyperactivity disorder. *The British Journal of Educational Psychology*, 87(2), 127–145. DOI: 10.1111/bjep.12140 PMID: 28054712

KEY TERMS AND DEFINITIONS

Career Aspirations: Refer to the hopes, goals, and ambitions that individuals have concerning their professional lives. These aspirations are shaped by a combination of personal interests, values, experiences, and external influences, including family, mentors, and societal expectations. They provide essential guidance and motivation, enabling individuals to set long-term objectives and plan their career paths effectively. For example, a person who aspires to be a doctor may focus on acquiring the necessary education, skills, and experiences to reach this goal. As individuals progress in their careers, their aspirations may evolve in response to new insights, opportunities, or challenges. Understanding and clearly articulating one's career aspirations is vital for making informed decisions, seeking growth opportunities, and achieving a meaningful and satisfying professional life.

Career Counseling: A professional service aimed at guiding individuals in the exploration of their career interests, values, skills, and goals, thereby enabling them to make informed choices about their future. Career counselors utilize assessments, facilitate discussions, and apply various guidance techniques to help clients understand their strengths, identify potential career avenues, and develop actionable plans. This process involves examining various options, establishing realistic goals, refining job-search strategies, and addressing career-related challenges such as transitions or dissatisfaction. Career counseling is particularly beneficial for students, job seekers, and individuals contemplating a career change. It provides clarity, enhances self-confidence, and assists individuals in aligning their career decisions with their personal values and aspirations, ultimately contributing to increased career satisfaction and success.

Career Development: Refers to the ongoing process of managing and enhancing one's professional journey and growth. It involves acquiring the necessary knowledge, skills, and experiences that assist individuals in exploring career possibilities, setting objectives, and making informed decisions regarding their career trajectories. Career development encompasses various activities, including education, training, mentorship, job experiences, and networking, all aimed at achieving professional goals and adapting to fluctuations in the job market. This process is inherently non-linear and dynamic, as individuals regularly reassess their aspirations and adjust their strategies in response to changing interests, opportunities, and life situations. The roles of employers, educators, and counselors are essential in this context, as they provide the guidance, resources, and opportunities necessary to foster growth and adaptability in an ever-evolving professional landscape.

Cultural Competence: Refers to the capacity to comprehend, appreciate, and engage effectively with individuals from various cultural backgrounds. This skill entails acknowledging the impact of culture on beliefs, behaviors, values, and communication methods, and adjusting one's approach as necessary. Achieving cultural competence necessitates an awareness of personal biases, a commitment to continuous learning, and a dedication to inclusivity and sensitivity. It is particularly vital in professional domains such as healthcare, education, and social services, where practitioners must take cultural differences into account to offer equitable and respectful assistance. By fostering cultural competence, both individuals and organizations can cultivate trust, minimize misunderstandings, and encourage inclusive environments that celebrate diversity, ultimately leading to more effective and meaningful interactions with people from diverse backgrounds.

Career Engagement: The degree of enthusiasm, commitment, and participation an individual exhibits towards their professional journey. It includes a proactive approach to career advancement, ongoing education, and the active pursuit of professional objectives. Individuals who are engaged take responsibility for their career trajectories, actively seeking avenues for personal growth, skill enhancement, and significant contributions. This level of engagement is associated with increased job satisfaction, enhanced performance, and a profound sense of purpose in one's work life. It necessitates the alignment of personal interests, values, and strengths with career decisions, thereby fostering a positive cycle of motivation and success. Employers and career advisors are crucial in promoting career engagement by creating supportive environments, offering career advice, and facilitating opportunities for progression.

Counseling Services: Refer to the professional guidance provided to individuals or groups aimed at helping them confront personal, emotional, psychological, or social issues. These services are rendered by trained counselors or therapists who utilize a range of methodologies, including talk therapy, cognitive-behavioral therapy, and solution-focused strategies, to assist clients. Counseling can address a variety of concerns, such as anxiety, depression, relationship challenges, career issues, and stress management. The intention is to create a safe and non-judgmental atmosphere where clients can delve into their emotions, acquire insights, and develop effective coping strategies. The overarching goal of counseling services are to enhance mental wellness, promote self-awareness, and facilitate personal growth, empowering individuals to lead healthier and more fulfilling lives.

Counseling Models: Serve as organized frameworks that aid counselors in assisting clients to investigate, comprehend, and address their issues. These models furnish both theoretical insights and practical approaches for dealing with a variety of concerns, such as mental health difficulties, career paths, and relationship dynamics. Prominent counseling models include Cognitive-Behavioral Therapy (CBT), which seeks to change harmful thought patterns; Person-Centered Therapy, which focuses on empathy and the independence of the client; and Solution-Focused Therapy, which aims at specific outcomes. The application of these models allows practitioners to maintain a consistent and effective approach in their work, utilizing validated techniques and principles. The choice of the most suitable model is based on the unique needs, objectives, and situations of the client, thereby enabling the counselor to provide customized and meaningful support that enhances well-being and personal growth.

Counselees: Refer to individuals who seek guidance, support, or therapeutic assistance from a counselor or mentor. These individuals often look for help with a variety of personal, academic, career, or social-emotional challenges. By engaging with counselors, counselees are able to explore their thoughts, feelings, and behaviors, thereby gaining insights and strategies to address difficulties or fulfill their aspirations. The relationship between counselors and counselees is founded on trust, empathy, and open communication. The objective of effective counseling is to empower counselees to make informed decisions, enhance their self-awareness, and develop effective problem-solving skills. Counselees may be students, employees, or individuals in any context where guidance and personal development are necessary for improving well-being or achieving success.

Individualized Counseling: A customized therapeutic approach that aligns interventions and support with the specific needs, aspirations, and circumstances of each client. Unlike traditional methods, this approach prioritizes an in-depth understanding of the client's background, values, and challenges, which aids in formulating a personalized plan. This flexibility allows the counselor to draw from various counseling models and adapt techniques to ensure they resonate with the client's experiences. Such a framework nurtures a more significant counselor-client relationship, providing clients with a safe and empathetic space to explore their thoughts and emotions. The overarching objective of individualized counseling is to enhance self-awareness, encourage personal development, and strengthen problem-solving skills, thus empowering clients to make informed decisions and pursue their personal and professional ambitions.

Job Seekers: Individuals who are in the process of seeking employment opportunities. This category encompasses recent graduates, those making a career transition, and individuals re-entering the workforce. Engaging in a range of activities, job seekers conduct research on companies, network with professionals, prepare their resumes, and participate in interviews to obtain positions that correspond with their skills, interests, and career ambitions. The effectiveness of a job seeker's efforts can be affected by various factors, including the current job market, relevant experience, qualifications, and the strategies employed during the job search. Many job seekers take advantage of online job boards, social media, and professional networks to discover suitable job openings. A successful job search necessitates a proactive mindset, adaptability, and resilience, along with a solid understanding of one's strengths and career goals.

Narrative Counseling: A therapeutic method designed to assist individuals in comprehending and reconstructing their personal narratives to discover meaning, purpose, and a sense of empowerment. This approach is founded on the premise that individuals shape their identities and experiences through storytelling, which in turn affects their self-perception and the challenges they face. In this counseling process, the counselor collaborates with the client to examine, deconstruct, and rewrite their narratives, emphasizing strengths, accomplishments, and positive transformations. This journey enables clients to acquire fresh insights, enhance their resilience, and formulate more empowering stories. Narrative counseling is frequently employed to tackle personal and professional challenges, guiding individuals to redefine their experiences and envision new avenues for growth and satisfaction.

Market Dynamics: Involve the various forces and factors that impact the behavior, trends, and alterations within a market. These dynamics consist of fluctuations in supply and demand, changes in pricing, consumer preferences, technological innovations, competitive landscapes, and regulatory frameworks. They play a pivotal role in shaping how businesses operate, adapt, and devise strategies to stay competitive and responsive to market shifts. A thorough understanding of market dynamics allows businesses and policymakers to predict changes, make informed choices, and identify avenues for growth or risk reduction. In the context of career planning, these dynamics are vital in influencing job availability, the skills required, and future opportunities, thus affecting individuals' career paths and professional development.

Occupational Therapy (OT): A specialized field within healthcare dedicated to assisting individuals across the lifespan in attaining autonomy and enhancing their overall quality of life through engaging in meaningful activities, referred to as "occupations." Occupational therapists collaborate with clients facing physical, cognitive, emotional, or developmental obstacles that hinder their capacity to carry out daily functions. These functions may encompass self-care, professional responsibilities, educational tasks, or recreational activities. By employing tailored interventions, adaptive strategies, and therapeutic exercises, occupational therapists strive to improve clients' functional skills, foster skill acquisition, and encourage active participation in daily life. The practice of OT is comprehensive, taking into account not only the physical abilities of the individual but also their surroundings and emotional health, thereby facilitating the achievement of personal goals and the pursuit of a fulfilling life.

Postsecondary Outcomes: Refer to the achievements and results that individuals attain after they have completed their high school or secondary education. These outcomes cover a variety of domains, including enrollment in higher education, graduation rates, job prospects, vocational training, and personal development. Successful postsecondary outcomes reflect effective transitions into college, technical programs, or the workforce, indicating an individual's preparedness for adult responsibilities. Several factors influence these outcomes, such as academic preparation, career planning, access to resources, and social-emotional skills. Schools, educators, and counselors work diligently to prepare students for favorable postsecondary outcomes by providing the necessary guidance, support, and skills to navigate challenges and achieve their educational and career objectives.

Professional Development: Refers to the continuous effort to acquire new skills, knowledge, and experiences that facilitate career progression and enhance workplace effectiveness. This includes a variety of activities such as attending training sessions, pursuing further education, participating in workshops, engaging in networking, and obtaining relevant certifications. Professional development is essential for adapting to the evolving demands of the job market, keeping abreast of industry developments, and improving overall job performance. Employers often advocate for professional development as a means to encourage employee growth, enhance job satisfaction, and develop a competent workforce. For individuals, involvement in professional development leads to career advancement, personal enrichment, and the ability to contribute effectively to their respective fields.

Remote Work: Represents a flexible employment model that enables individuals to carry out their professional responsibilities from locations beyond the conventional office setting, often from their residences or other distant sites. This working arrangement utilizes digital tools, communication technologies, and cloud-based systems to ensure ongoing connectivity, collaboration, and efficiency. The rise of remote work can be attributed to advancements in technology. This approach offers advantages such as improved work-life balance, decreased travel time, and greater independence. Nevertheless, it also poses challenges, including the need for effective communication, time management, and the risk of social isolation. Organizations that implement remote work strategies strive to foster a supportive environment, supply necessary digital resources, and promote flexibility.

School Counselors' Self-Efficacy: Defined as the belief in their own capability to successfully carry out counseling tasks and respond to the academic, career, and social-emotional requirements of students. A high level of self-efficacy allows counselors to approach the planning and implementation of interventions with confidence, assist students in their decision-making processes, and effectively manage challenges encountered in educational settings. This feeling of competence affects how counselors set their goals, balance their workloads, and interact with students, faculty, and parents. Various factors, including training, experience, and a nurturing work environment, significantly enhance counselors' self-efficacy. When counselors feel empowered and assured in their abilities, they are more likely to offer thorough and proactive services, which in turn fosters a supportive school climate and encourages student success.

APPENDIX I: STUDY QUESTIONNAIRE

Table 3. Counselors' perspectives on career counseling models and services for students with ADHD questionnaire (CPCCMSSAQ)

No	Statements	NAA	SE	ME	GE	VGE
1	To what extent do you feel knowledgeable about career counseling techniques and their impact on the career transition of students with ADHD?					
2	To what extent do you utilize specific career counseling models and techniques to support students with ADHD during their career transition?					
3	To what extent do you feel that you have received adequate training and resources to provide career counseling services for students with ADHD?					
4	How reliable do you find current career counseling models in addressing the needs of students with ADHD?					
5	To what extent do you collaborate with educators to provide counseling services that supports the career transition of students with ADHD?					
6	To what extent do you involve parents in the career counseling process for students with ADHD?					
7	To what extent do you use technology-based tools and resources in career counseling for students with ADHD?					
8	To what extent do you often create individualized career plans for students with ADHD?					
9	To what extent do you seek feedback from students with ADHD to evaluate and improve your counseling services?					
10	To what extent are you aware of career opportunities that are well-suited for individuals with ADHD?					
11	To what extent do you experience challenges in providing career counseling services to students with ADHD?					
12	To what extent do you engage in professional development activities to enhance your skills in counseling students with ADHD?					

NAA=Not at All, SE=Small Extent, ME=Moderate Extent, GE=Great Extent, VGE=Very Great Extent

APPENDIX II: ADDITIONAL STATISTICS

Table 4. Item-total statistics

No	Statements	Cronbach's Alpha if Item Deleted
1	To what extent do you feel knowledgeable about career counseling techniques and their impact on the career transition of students with ADHD?	.924
2	To what extent do you utilize specific career counseling models and techniques to support students with ADHD during their career transition?	.922
3	To what extent do you feel that you have received adequate training and resources to provide career counseling services for students with ADHD?	.921
4	How reliable do you find current career counseling models in addressing the needs of students with ADHD?	.924
5	To what extent do you collaborate with educators to provide counseling services that supports the career transition of students with ADHD?	.921
6	To what extent do you involve parents in the career counseling process for students with ADHD?	.920
7	To what extent do you use technology-based tools and resources in career counseling for students with ADHD?	.921
8	To what extent do you often create individualized career plans for students with ADHD?	.921
9	To what extent do you seek feedback from students with ADHD to evaluate and improve your counseling services?	.924
10	To what extent are you aware of career opportunities that are well-suited for individuals with ADHD?	.921
11	To what extent do you experience challenges in providing career counseling services to students with ADHD?	.920
12	To what extent do you engage in professional development activities to enhance your skills in counseling students with ADHD?	.921

Table 5. Communalities (extraction method: principal component analysis)

	Statements	Extraction
1	To what extent do you feel knowledgeable about career counseling techniques and their impact on the career transition of students with ADHD?	.755
2	To what extent do you utilize specific career counseling models and techniques to support students with ADHD during their career transition?	.868
3	To what extent do you feel that you have received adequate training and resources to provide career counseling services for students with ADHD?	.879
4	How reliable do you find current career counseling models in addressing the needs of students with ADHD?	.866
5	To what extent do you collaborate with educators to provide counseling services that supports the career transition of students with ADHD?	.941
6	To what extent do you involve parents in the career counseling process for students with ADHD?	.876
7	To what extent do you use technology-based tools and resources in career counseling for students with ADHD?	.987
8	To what extent do you often create individualized career plans for students with ADHD?	.879
9	To what extent do you seek feedback from students with ADHD to evaluate and improve your counseling services?	.866
10	To what extent are you aware of career opportunities that are well-suited for individuals with ADHD?	.941
11	To what extent do you experience challenges in providing career counseling services to students with ADHD?	.876
12	To what extent do you engage in professional development activities to enhance your skills in counseling students with ADHD?	.987

Chapter 9
Examining Barriers to Career Transition of Students With ADHD:
Teachers and Parents' Perspectives

ABSTRACT

The study investigates the differing perspectives of teachers and parents on the barriers to career transition for students with ADHD. A survey design was adopted for this research. A total of 28 secondary school teachers and 28 parents were selected using purposive and convenience sampling techniques. The findings revealed that teachers perceive greater barriers to career transition for students with ADHD compared to parents. Both groups exhibit strong perceptions of barriers, with teachers showing a higher mean score compared to parents. This difference is statistically significant. However, when considering gender and location, no significant differences are observed in the perspectives of either group. The study underscores the need for career transition programs to address specific concerns of both teachers and parents to better support students with ADHD.

BACKGROUND

Students with attention-deficit/hyperactivity disorder (ADHD) often experience a range of obstacles that can adversely impact their academic and professional development, and the process of moving from school to employment can be extended due to their condition (Kingsley, 2024). ADHD is a neurodevelopmental condition marked by difficulties in executive functioning (Ogrodnik et al., 2023). The

DOI: 10.4018/979-8-3693-2635-0.ch009

presence of ADHD is linked to several economic obstacles, including diminished yearly income, increased reliance on government support, and an elevated likelihood of homelessness (Gordon & Fabiano, 2019). Long-standing societal beliefs and stereotypes about people with disabilities may continue to exist despite the existence of legal protections (Atoyebi, 2024). Discrimination, both at school and in the world of work, frequently manifests in nuanced forms, complicating efforts to recognize and confront it. According to the findings of Muller et al. (2012), various factors contribute to the stigma surrounding ADHD. Key factors include the public's uncertainty about the reliability and validity of ADHD diagnoses and the associated assessment methods. The perceived dangerousness of individuals with ADHD, as well as socio-demographic characteristics such as the age, gender, and ethnicity of both the respondent and the diagnosed individual, are also significant. Moreover, the stigma attached to ADHD treatment, particularly public skepticism regarding ADHD medications and the sharing of diagnostic and medication statuses, further exacerbates this issue (Muller et al., 2012). Thus, students with disabilities frequently need to exert effort beyond their capabilities to attain success in higher education and to gain access to significant employment opportunities (Goodall et al., 2022). Similarly, Samosh et al., (2024) observed that individuals with ADHD are at an increased risk of being unemployed, underemployed, and experiencing poverty compared to individuals without the disorder. As these individuals grow older, the difficulties associated with ADHD can evolve into complications in their career paths (Dipeolu et al., 2011). The developmental-contextual framework of career development posits that individuals construct their career trajectories by engaging with complex systems, such as family and educational environments, which are simultaneously influenced by their personal attributes, including levels of achievement and abilities (Vondracek et al., 2019). According to Bella-Awusah et al. (2022), barriers to seeking school counseling services include negative beliefs and past experiences with the counseling process, along with a tendency to rely on significant others for support. The authors found that students sought counselors who possessed personal qualities that would promote supportive interpersonal relationships. Furthermore, there was a clear desire among students for the inclusion of peers in the counseling process. Individuals with ADHD often lack access to career exploration activities that could assist them in making fulfilling career choices (Harris, 2016). The majority of interactions between parents and teachers concerning these students are usually influenced by the repercussions of ADHD on their academic journeys and career prospects (Nkosi, 2022). Furthermore, teachers significantly impact the educational and social development of students with special educational needs within an inclusive school setting (Efthymiou & Kington, 2017). They are charged with the responsibility of recognizing behaviors that are consistent with the disorder (Petruzzi, 2005) as well as educating these students. On the other hand, parents are crucial in the support system for their child with ADHD (Janssens et al., 2023), and their perspectives are equally important as those of the teachers involved in the student's education. Support from parents can facilitate a successful transition to college, while a robust parent-child relationship may enhance the equilibrium between independence and assistance that is essential during this period of adjustment (Stevens et al., 2023).

Parents act as advocates for students with ADHD, who are often regarded by most teachers and classmates as disruptive, disrespectful, and lacking in achievement (Peterson-Malen, 2013). Furthermore, most teachers assert that parents significantly influence the career decisions of students with ADHD (Maree & Warnock, 2023). In certain instances, some teachers may attribute the disruptive behaviors exhibited by students with ADHD to parental influence while also recognizing the complex nature of ADHD itself (Gwernan-Jones et al., 2015). Parents often express concerns regarding the obstacles that hinder the evaluation of evidence-based solutions and shared decision-making for children with ADHD (Fiks et al., 2011). Among the barriers faced are unequal access to Individualised Education Plans, a lack of policy frameworks to facilitate formal transition planning (Doyle et al., 2017), insufficient engagement from parents (Martin, 2017), negative attitudes from some professionals (Matheson et al., 2013), inability to task switch (Gillette, 2023), parents' limited availability due to time constraints (Dreyer et al., 2010), the severity of a child's challenges, the perceived acceptability of an intervention (Stagg, 2010), insufficient awareness, limited availability of mental health services, challenges within the educational system, economic barriers, and cultural practices (Olatunji et al., 2023). Families encounter numerous attitudinal and structural obstacles, including financial burdens, accessibility issues, stigma, and low self-efficacy in implementing necessary changes (Baweja et al., 2021). Warnock (2022) indicated that teachers identified various factors that directly impact the career decisions of students with ADHD. These factors include a reluctance to pursue higher education, financial limitations associated with attending tertiary institutions, and issues related to self-confidence and self-efficacy. This author further reported that the teachers noted that the use of medication for ADHD could affect the career choices of these students in both beneficial and detrimental ways. Furthermore, parents and potential employers were recognized as having a significant influence on the career paths of students with ADHD, with the symptoms of inattentive ADHD often leading them to opt for entrepreneurial careers.

According to prior research by Sibley et al. (2014), reports from parents and teachers indicated that students with ADHD encountered significant academic difficulties in numerous daily tasks, with the most common issues being related to time management and planning, and that the diverse academic difficulties faced by adolescents with ADHD necessitate a thorough evaluation before initiating treatment.

Those who pursue or are referred to counseling for ADHD typically exhibit behaviors such as restlessness, an inability to remain seated, or challenges in engaging in quiet play (Stargell et al., 2017). They often face difficulties with short-term memory, struggle to adhere to instructions, encounter obstacles in finishing assigned tasks, frequently shift their attention from one activity to another before completing them and may find it hard to redirect their focus when engaged in activities they find enjoyable (American Psychological Association, 2013). Park (2019) identified both common and distinct pathways influencing the career outcomes of individuals with ADHD, high ability, or a combination of both. These pathways were associated with various factors, including parental education, expectations regarding education from parents, family income, attachment to school, symptoms of depression and anxiety, educational aspirations, high school grade point average, and enrollment in post-secondary education, all of which were analyzed in relation to perceived social class, occupational status, and the achievement of career goals. Bussing et al. (2003) showed that African American parents were less inclined to associate the school system with the identification of ADHD issues. They exhibited fewer concerns regarding ADHD-related challenges within the educational environment and demonstrated a lower preference for school-based interventions compared to their Caucasian counterparts, indicating a possible disconnection from the school system. These concerns notwithstanding, addressing the potential career transition challenges that students with ADHD experience during their career transition is crucial in that such challenges may stem from family dynamics, school environments, or personal factors.

It is important to consider how parents and teachers view such challenges. This will ensure effective transition planning, which plays a crucial role in maintaining treatment continuity, fostering adherence to therapeutic recommendations, and aiding in adapting to new life situations, thereby preventing adverse educational, vocational, and social outcomes (Robb & Findling, 2013). In light of the increasing research on ADHD and its influence on the career transition of students, there remains a significant gap in understanding the perceived barriers that students with ADHD encounter in the Nigerian school context. The insights of Nigerian schoolteachers and parents are important in this context, as they can illuminate the current career transition challenges of these students. Most existing studies on this issue have been centered on the Global North. The present study aims to bridge this gap by investigating the barriers to career transition from the perspectives of Nigerian schoolteachers and parents, thereby contributing to a more holistic understanding of the issue. Examining the perspectives of Nigerian parents and schoolteachers on the challenges that students with ADHD face in their career transition will provide valuable information to the school-based career transition planning team to enable them to decide on what might be the most effective strategies for facilitating students' career transition. Thus, this study aims to assess the perspectives of Nigerian teachers and parents concerning the barriers to career transition of students with ADHD.

Research Objectives

1. To ascertain teachers' and parents' overall mean perspectives on the barriers to career transition of students with ADHD.
2. To determine the extent to which teachers and parents differ in their perspectives on the barriers to career transition of students with ADHD.
3. To determine the extent to which teachers and parents differ in their perspectives on the barriers to career transition of students with ADHD by gender.
4. To determine the extent to which teachers and parents differ in their perspectives on the barriers to career transition of students with ADHD by place of residence.

Research Questions

1. What are teachers' and parents' overall mean perspectives on the barriers to career transition of students with ADHD?
2. To what extent do teachers and parents differ in their perspectives on the barriers to career transition of students with ADHD?
3. To what extent do teachers and parents differ in their perspectives on the barriers to career transition of students with ADHD by gender?
4. To what extent do teachers and parents differ in their perspectives on the barriers to career transition of students with ADHD by place of residence?

Theoretical Framework

In this research, we have incorporated Bandura's self-efficacy theory alongside social constructionism to analyze the perspectives of parents and teachers regarding the obstacles faced in the career transition of students with ADHD. The self-efficacy theory proposed by Bandura in 1977 is essential for understanding how personal beliefs regarding one's abilities can greatly affect performance in various fields. Bandura identifies four main mechanisms that contribute to the formation of self-efficacy: achievements in performance, learning through observation, encouragement from others, and emotional states (Bandura, 1977; Lippke, 2020). These mechanisms are instrumental in influencing an individual's motivation, resilience, and capacity to tackle challenges. The impact of performance outcomes, whether favorable or unfavorable, plays a crucial role in shaping self-efficacy beliefs. Students with ADHD who experience success in their academic or personal endeavors are more inclined to cultivate a robust sense of self-efficacy. In contrast, consistent failures or adverse feedback can diminish self-confidence (Lopez-Garrido, 2023), posing a considerable hindrance to their career transition. The concept of vicarious experiences suggests that watching the successes and failures of others, particularly individuals in similar situations, can shape one's beliefs about self-efficacy. For students with ADHD, the observation of peers and significant others navigating career transition—whether successfully or with challenges—can either strengthen or weaken their confidence in their own skills. Thus, the influence of teachers and parents is vital, as they model behaviors that promote healthy self-perception and resilience (Artino, 2012). Encouragement and constructive feedback from teachers, parents, and peers, as forms of verbal persuasion, are essential in developing a belief in one's capabilities. For students with ADHD, this verbal support and motivational reinforcement can help counter feelings of inadequacy, thus removing perceived hindrances to career transition. The relationship between emotional arousal and self-efficacy is well-documented, with emotional states like anxiety and excitement exerting a significant influence (Lopez-Garrido, 2023). Students with ADHD often face heightened stress and anxiety, which can hinder their academic performance. Nonetheless, with appropriate support from teachers and parents, these students can learn to effectively manage their emotional responses, promoting a smoother transition into their future careers.

Alongside self-efficacy, social constructionism offers an additional viewpoint by examining the influence of societal and cultural elements on perceptions. This theory asserts that realities, encompassing views on abilities and constraints, are formed through social and cultural exchanges (Andrews, 2012; Mallon, 2024). Within this context, the challenges encountered by students with ADHD during career transition are not merely a result of personal characteristics or diagnoses; they are also shaped by societal norms and stereotypes. The application of social constructionism in this study seeks to reveal the ways in which parents and educators, through their interactions and common beliefs, establish a collective understanding of ADHD that can either promote or impede career transition. For instance, if a particular culture or community predominantly perceives ADHD as a major barrier, such a viewpoint can influence the attitudes of both teachers and parents, potentially constraining the career transition of students. Conversely, a socially constructed belief that embraces neurodiversity may lead to more favorable career transition outcomes by diminishing stigma and fostering adaptive strategies. By examining the perspectives of both teachers and parents, we can better understand the impact of self-efficacy beliefs and socially constructed views of ADHD on perceptions of barriers to career transitions. Those who consider ADHD to be a manageable issue or who have confidence in the students' potential and available resources are likely to perceive fewer obstacles. Teachers, shaped by their educational backgrounds, may have differing expectations and attitudes when compared to parents. The self-efficacy theory may account for these differences by examining the levels of encouragement and reinforcement provided by each group. Moreover, social constructionism can offer insights into possible variations by investigating how the roles of teachers and parents foster distinct social constructions of ADHD, resulting in a range of perspectives on the challenges associated with career transition. The two theoretical frameworks can aid in understanding the gender-based variations in perceptions. Social constructionism can provide a lens through which to analyze how gender norms shape perceptions of career transition challenges for students with ADHD. Meanwhile, self-efficacy theory can assess whether parents and teachers possess gender-specific self-efficacy beliefs about students with ADHD in the context of career transition. These variations may impact how teachers and parents view the career transition process for male and female students with ADHD. Social constructionism can enhance our understanding of how cultural distinctions between urban and rural contexts influence the perceptions of teachers and parents concerning the obstacles faced by students with ADHD during career transition. Variations in community attitudes and resources, determined by location, may significantly shape the perspectives of teachers and parents on the career transition challenges encountered by these students (see Figure).

Figure 1. Framework of the study

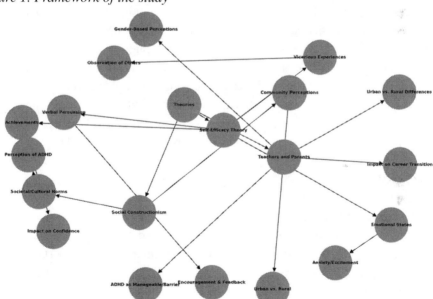

METHODOLOGY

Ethics Statement

Ethical approval for this study was obtained from the relevant institutional review boards. First, it received approval from the Research Ethics Committee of the Faculty of Education, University of Nigeria, Nigeria. It also received additional ethical approval from the Faculty of Education Research Ethics Committee at the University of Johannesburg, South Africa (Sem 2-2020-057). Informed consent was secured from participants. We assured confidentiality and clarified participants' right to withdraw from the study at any given time.

Research Design and Approach

This study used a survey research design. The use of survey methodology has gained significant traction as a favoured strategy for investigating environmental sustainability in the realm of small businesses (Roxas & Lindsay, 2012). Surveys utilize various data collection techniques, such as questionnaires (Addington-Hall, 2007). They can differ significantly in terms of timing regarding when or how often they are conducted and in their administration methods, which dictate how they are presented to participants. Surveys may be classified as either cross-sectional or longitudinal in nature (Sheppard, 2020). The methods of survey research encompass a range of formats, including online surveys, in-person interviews, focus groups, panel sampling, telephone surveys, mail-in surveys, and kiosk surveys (Vasiliou, 2024). However, our research specifically employed a quantitative approach. In contrast, qualitative research focuses on gathering insights related to lived experiences, emotions, or behaviors, enabling researchers to better comprehend intricate concepts, social interactions, or cultural phenomena (Research Guides, 2024).

Research Paradigm

This study is grounded in the positivist research paradigm. Grasping the principles of positivism is essential for researchers who seek to enhance scientific knowledge through systematic, quantifiable, and verifiable approaches (Robertson, 2024). However, it has been observed that positivist researchers often exhibit a degree of subjectivity in their practices (Shook, 1993). Positivists assert the existence of a singular reality that can be quantified and understood, leading them to favor quantitative methodologies for its measurement (Salma, 2015).

Study Area

This research was conducted in Cross River State in the South-South zone of Nigeria. The capital of Cross River State is Calabar (Okon et al., 2017). This city is positioned between the longitudes of 8°18'1" and 8°25'E, and the latitudes of 4°50'N and 5°67'N, covering an area of 157.65 square kilometers (Bassey et al., 2020).

Population and Sampling

The careful selection of populations and the implementation of a strategic sampling approach in research are essential for improving the reliability and relevance of research findings (Hossan et al., 2023). The study involves schoolteachers and parents of students with ADHD in public secondary schools. A total of 28 secondary school teachers and 28 were selected using purposive and convenience sampling techniques. Participants' age is 35.48±5.89years. Techniques such as purposive and convenience sampling are categorized as non-probability sampling methods and do not adhere to a scientific basis (Shukla, 2020). Convenience sampling involves selecting participants based on their immediate availability, which can help alleviate numerous research-related limitations (Taherdoost, 2016). Purposive sampling, often referred to as judgmental, selective, or subjective sampling, is based on the researcher's assessment in choosing the units to be studied, which may include individuals, cases, organizations, events, or data (Rai & Thapa, 2015). Male respondents were 23, while female respondents were 33. Rural residents were 30, while urban residents were 26.

Data Collection

The data was collected using a questionnaire. The researchers received help from two postgraduate students to complete the data collection process. The questionnaire used for data collection is called the Teachers' and Parents' Perspectives on the Barriers to Career Transition of Students with ADHD Questionnaire (TPPBCTSAQ). It is a 21-item scale, with response options ranging from Strongly disagree (1) to Strongly Agree (5). This scale measures teachers' and parents' perspectives on the barriers to career transition of students with ADHD. Higher scores indicate a great extent of agreement to each item statement. Some examples of item statements in the questionnaire include: "There is a lack of resources tailored to career transition for students with ADHD" and "Students with ADHD have limited access to career mentorship programs?" The TPPBCTSAQ has good internal consistency reliability, with a Cronbach's alpha of 0.92 in the present research.

Data Analysis

A statistical analysis was conducted using Statistical Package for the Social Sciences (SPSS), version 27. SPSS is a tool developed by IBM which is predominantly employed for conducting statistical analyses on data (Pedamkar, 2024). This computer program serves a diverse array of research purposes, enabling users to analyze data and construct models grounded in statistical principles (Green, 2023). Descriptive statistics was used to summarize the sociodemographic data, while univariate analysis was used to analyse the research questions at a .05 significance level. Descriptive statistics play a crucial role in summarizing and elucidating fundamental characteristics of a quantitative dataset, thereby facilitating a clearer understanding of the overall structure of the data (Jansen, 2023). Univariate analysis focuses on providing insights regarding a single variable (Clark, 2021).

FINDINGS

Table 1. Teachers' and parents' overall mean perspectives on the barriers to career transition of students with ADHD

Group	Gender	Location	Mean	Std. Deviation	N
Schoolteachers	Male respondents	Rural residents	4.42	.32	6
		Urban residents	4.39	.30	4
		Total	4.41	.29	10
	Female respondents	Rural residents	4.30	.29	6
		Urban residents	4.30	.41	12
		Total	4.30	.36	18
	Total	Rural residents	4.36	.29	12
		Urban residents	4.32	.38	16
		Total	4.34	.34	28

continued on following page

Table 1. Continued

Group	Gender	Location	Mean	Std. Deviation	N
Parents	Male respondents	Rural residents	4.19	.39	9
		Urban residents	4.23	.60	4
		Total	4.19	.44	13
	Female respondents	Rural residents	4.07	.39	9
		Urban residents	3.94	.19	6
		Total	4.02	.33	15
	Total	Rural residents	4.13	.39	18
		Urban residents	4.06	.40	10
		Total	4.10	.39	28
Total	Male respondents	Rural residents	4.28	.37	15
		Urban residents	4.31	.45	8
		Total	4.29	.39	23
	Female respondents	Rural residents	4.16	.37	15
		Urban residents	4.18	.38	18
		Total	4.17	.37	33
	Total	Rural residents	4.22	.37	30
		Urban residents	4.22	.40	26
		Total	4.22	.38	56

Table 1 shows that male teachers have a slightly higher mean perspective (Mean = 4.41) on the barriers to career transition for students with ADHD compared to female teachers (Mean = 4.30). There is a minor difference between rural (Mean = 4.36) and urban teachers (Mean = 4.32). Male parents also have a slightly higher mean perspective (Mean = 4.19) compared to female parents (Mean = 4.02). The difference between rural (Mean = 4.13) and urban parents (Mean = 4.06) is minimal. The mean perspectives of both groups combined show little variation between rural and urban respondents (Mean = 4.22 for both). Schoolteachers had an overall mean perspective score of $4.34\pm.34$ while parents of students with ADHD had an overall mean perspective of $4.10\pm.39$. These results further imply that both teachers and parents have a strong perception of barriers to career transition for students with ADHD.

Figure 2. Teachers' overall mean perspectives on the barriers to career transition of students with ADHD by gender and location

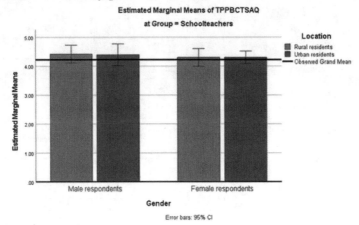

Figure 2 shows that both male and female teachers have high mean scores, indicating a strong perception of barriers to career transition for students with ADHD. The error bars representing the 95% confidence interval suggest that there is a slight overlap between rural and urban teachers, indicating no significant difference by location.

Figure 3. Parents' overall mean perspectives on the barriers to career transition of students with ADHD by gender and location

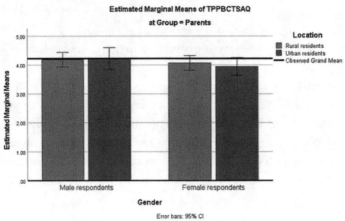

Figure 3 shows parents' mean scores, with female parents showing slightly lower scores than male parents. The error bars also overlap significantly, indicating no substantial difference in perspectives based on location.

Table 2. Univariate analysis of difference in extent to which teachers and parents differ in their perspectives on the barriers to career transition of students with ADHD

Source	Type III Sum of Squares	Df	Mean Square	F	Sig.
Corrected Model	1.153ª	7	.165	1.166	.34
Intercept	877.199	1	877.199	6209.637	<.001
Group	.754	1	.754	5.336	.03
Gender	.284	1	.284	2.007	.16
Location	.009	1	.009	.067	.79
Group * Gender	.027	1	.027	.191	.66
Group * Location	.002	1	.002	.017	.89
Gender * Location	.014	1	.014	.103	.75
Group * Gender * Location	.029	1	.029	.202	.66
Error	6.781	48	.141		
Total	1005.719	56			
Corrected Total	7.934	55			

The univariate analysis in Table 2 reveals that there is a statistically significant difference between teachers and parents in their perspectives on the barriers to career transition for students with ADHD (F =5.336, p=.025). Also, there are no significant differences based on gender (F=2.007, p=.16) or location (F =.067, p=.79). No significant interactions were found between group and gender, group and location, or gender and location regarding teachers' and parents' mean perspectives on the barriers to career transition of students with ADHD.

DISCUSSION

This study sought to examine and compare the perspectives of parents and teachers on the barriers to career transition of students with ADHD in Nigeria. The study showed that both teachers and parents have a strong perception of barriers to the career transition of students with ADHD. Teachers perceived greater barriers than parents when it comes to the career transition of students with ADHD. On the other hand, Efron et al. (2016) demonstrated that parents of students with ADHD identified obstacles such as a lack of adequate understanding of ADHD among teachers and insufficient resources within schools to address these students' needs. The authors emphasized the necessity for schools to acquire additional resources and for teachers to receive enhanced training to foster positive experiences and outcomes for students with ADHD. According to a recent study, it appears that the way teachers perceive their students with ADHD has a substantial impact on the overall performance and achievements of these individuals (Akdağ, 2023). Furthermore, Ward et al. (2021) pointed out that teachers frequently feel unprepared to support the needs of their students, which poses a barrier to their career advancement. Lawson et al. (2022) noted that teachers possess a limited understanding of the obstacles that hinder the success of students with ADHD, leading to infrequent application of available classroom interventions. According to Vitanza (2014), teachers consider students with ADHD to be more challenging to handle. In terms of parents, Maree and Warnock (2023) contended that parents play a crucial role in shaping the career paths of students with ADHD. Janssens et al. (2023) opined that parents of students with ADHD will exhibit differing abilities to assume designated roles of caring and may gradually reduce their involvement as their children transition into adulthood. Price et al. (2019) also indicated that parents report unfavorable experiences concerning the quality of the information provided about their children's transitions. Effective communication of information to parents and caregivers regarding the expectations during the transition of students with ADHD is essential (Price et al., 2019). Wood (2012) found that the evaluations of students with ADHD by both parents and teachers did not show a significant correlation, nor were there notable differences in the ratings and perceptions provided by parents and teachers. Furthermore, Marete (2020) stressed the necessity for teachers to maintain a positive attitude towards the transition preparedness of students entering the workforce. Ghanizadeh et al. (2009) found that there was no significant variation in the attitudes of teachers towards different types of ADHD, whether disclosed or undisclosed. Consequently, the authors emphasized that enhancing teachers' knowledge about ADHD is a crucial initial step in addressing ADHD in students.

The perceptions of teachers and parents did not significantly differ by gender or location. In contrast, Lawrence et al. (2017) revealed that teachers' perceptions are indeed affected by gender. Their approaches to managing ADHD in the classroom were primarily based on anecdotal experiences, and they often grappled with feelings of guilt and apprehension while attempting to reconcile the needs of their students with the educational system and family-related issues. Li et al. (2022) aimed at understanding the perspectives of parents and teachers regarding students with ADHD and indicated that the gender of the children influenced the view of the parents. Gordon and Fabiano (2019) demonstrated a decrease in occupational attainment, revealed diminished job performance, and faced heightened job instability, and these barriers remained largely consistent irrespective of gender. According to Ugwu et al. (2016), parental residential location and occupation often play a crucial role in shaping how much they are able to support students' educational outcomes. Abdullah and Ibrahim (2021) noted that parental participation in supporting career transition for students with disabilities is more pronounced in suburban schools than in urban ones. As a result, the study indicated that parents in suburban environments face fewer hurdles in facilitating these transitions compared to those in urban areas. According to the findings by Gwernan-Jones et al. (2015), the presence of high-quality relationships between parents and teachers was observed to be rare, with mothers expressing feelings of being marginalized and facing criticism. Their results were in alignment with prior research concerning parental experiences, yet they also highlight unique sources of conflict, particularly stemming from parental attribution of blame for students' disruptive conduct and the complex perceptions surrounding the concept of ADHD. According to the findings of Gordon and Fabiano (2019), individuals with a background of ADHD faced more significant educational difficulties and were less likely to complete their education than those without such a history. It is important, therefore, for parents and teachers to ensure that students with ADHD who are transitioning to a career or education have a clear understanding of their strengths and weaknesses. It is important for these students to choose a career path that enhances their strengths and mitigates their weaknesses. For example, those who are prone to distraction might find it beneficial to engage in a field that holds significant interest for them. Furthermore, many individuals with ADHD thrive in positions that require physical engagement (AccessComputing, 2024). In terms of limitations, the small sample size limits our study. The geographical scope was confined to participants from Cross River State, which restricts the generalizability of the findings to other culturally diverse regions of Nigeria. Furthermore, the study involved only the parents and teachers of the students, overlooking other family members and school professionals who may have some form of relationship with the students. This oversight suggests that a more holistic understanding of the various barriers to career transition of students with ADHD could have been achieved had other individuals been included. It is crucial to recognize these limitations in future research. Overall, there is an urgent need for further studies that involve larger sample sizes across various regions to identify the barriers to the career transition of Nigerian students with ADHD.

CONCLUSION

The study showed a significant difference between teachers' and parents' perspectives on barriers to career transition for students with ADHD. Teachers perceived greater barriers than parents when it comes to the career transition of students with

ADHD. It is important for career transition programs to take into account the specific concerns of both teachers and parents. This could involve providing additional resources for them to better support students with ADHD during career transition. The school transition plans should consider the viewpoints of both teachers and parents in order to create a more supportive and inclusive context for students with ADHD during career transition. There is also a need for increased awareness and training for both teachers and parents to learn effective ways of facilitating career transition for students with ADHD.

REFERENCES

Abdullah, N., & Ibrahim, R. (2021). Parents Involvement in Implementation of Career Transition for Students with Learning Disabilities from a Teacher's Perspective in Malaysia. *International Journal of Academic Research in Business & Social Sciences*, 11(8), 1047–1059. DOI: 10.6007/IJARBSS/v11-i8/10418

AccessComputing. (2024). *What issues should a student with AD/HD consider when planning for the transition from high school to college or a career?* https://www.washington.edu/accesscomputing/what-issues-should-student-adhd-consider-when-planning-transition-high-school-college-or-career

Addington-Hall, J. M. (2007). Survey research: Methods of data collection, questionnaire design and piloting. In J. M. Addington-Hall, E. Bruera, I. J. Higginson, & S. Payne (Eds.), *Research Methods in Palliative Care* (p. 0). Oxford University Press. DOI: 10.1093/acprof:oso/9780198530251.003.0005

American Psychiatric Association. (2013). *Diagnostic and statistical manual of mental disorders* (5th ed.). Author.

Andrews, T. (2012). What is Social Constructionism? *The Grounded Theory Review*, 11(1). https://groundedtheoryreview.com/2012/06/01/what-is-social-constructionism/

Artino, A. R.Jr. (2012). Academic self-efficacy: From educational theory to instructional practice. *Perspectives on Medical Education*, 1(2), 76–85. DOI: 10.1007/S40037-012-0012-5 PMID: 23316462

Atoyebi, O. M. (2024, July 22). *An Appraisal of the Discrimination Against Persons with Disabilities (Prohibition) Act 2019—Omaplex Law Firm*. https://omaplex.com.ng/an-appraisal-of-the-discrimination-against-persons-with-disabilities-prohibition-act-2019/#post-3499-footnote-ref-1

Bandura, A. (1977). Self-efficacy: Towards a Unifying Theory of Behavioral Change. *Psychological Review*, 84(2), 191–213. DOI: 10.1037/0033-295X.84.2.191 PMID: 847061

Bassey, S. I., Amba, N. E., & Eteng, S. U. (2020). Assessment of domestic solid waste transportation to approved dumpsite in Calabar, Nigeria. *International Journal of Research and Sustainable Development*, 7(3), 165–185.

Baweja, R., Soutullo, C. A., & Waxmonsky, J. G. (2021). Review of barriers and interventions to promote treatment engagement for pediatric attention deficit hyperactivity disorder care. *World Journal of Psychiatry*, 11(12), 1206–1227. DOI: 10.5498/wjp.v11.i12.1206 PMID: 35070771

Bella-Awusah, T., Oyewole, G., Falaye, A., & Omigbodun, O. (2022). Adolescents' Perceptions of School Counselling in Ibadan, Nigeria. *Journal of School-Based Counseling Policy and Evaluation*, 4(1), 26–34. https://doi.org/https://doi.org/10.25774/qge2-1z94

Bussing, R., Gary, F. A., Mills, T. L., & Garvan, C. W. (2003). Parental explanatory models of ADHD: Gender and cultural variations. *Social Psychiatry and Psychiatric Epidemiology*, 38(10), 563–575. DOI: 10.1007/s00127-003-0674-8 PMID: 14564385

Clark, R. (2021). *Univariate Analysis*. https://pressbooks.ric.edu/socialdataanalysis/chapter/univariateanalysis/

Dipeolu, A., Sniatecki, J. L., & Lalin, M. (2011, October 1). Career Development Keys to Post-School Transition Success for Students with ADHD. https://www.ncda.org/aws/NCDA/pt/sd/news_article/50250/_self/layout_ccmsearch/true

Doyle, A., Mc Guckin, C., & Shevlin, M. (2017). 'Close the door on your way out': Parent perspectives on supported transition planning for young people with Special Educational Needs and Disabilities in Ireland. *Journal of Research in Special Educational Needs*, 17(4), 274–281. DOI: 10.1111/1471-3802.12385

Dreyer, A. S., O'Laughlin, L., Moore, J., & Milam, Z. (2010). Parental adherence to clinical recommendations in an ADHD evaluation clinic. *Journal of Clinical Psychology*, 66(10), 1101–1120. DOI: 10.1002/jclp.20718 PMID: 20578185

Efron, D., Sciberras, E., & Hassell, P. (2008). Are Schools Meeting the Needs of Students with ADHD? *Australasian Journal of Special Education*, 32(2), 187–198. DOI: 10.1017/S1030011200025847

Efthymiou, E., & Kington, A. (2017). The development of inclusive learning relationships in mainstream settings: A multimodal perspective. *Cogent Education*, 4(1), 1304015. DOI: 10.1080/2331186X.2017.1304015

Fiks, A. G., Hughes, C. C., Gafen, A., Guevara, J. P., & Barg, F. K. (2011). Contrasting parents' and pediatricians' perspectives on shared decision-making in ADHD. *Pediatrics*, 127(1), e188–e196. DOI: 10.1542/peds.2010-1510 PMID: 21172996

Ghanizadeh, A., Fallahi, M., & Akhondzadeh, S. (2009). Disclosure of attention deficit hyperactivity disorder and its effect on rejection of students by teachers. *Iranian Journal of Medical Sciences*, 34(4), 259–264.

Gillette, H. (2023, October 26). *ADHD and Task Switching: 10 Tips for Improvement*. Healthline. https://www.healthline.com/health/adhd/task-switching-adhd

Goodall, G., Mjøen, O. M., Witsø, A. E., Horghagen, S., & Kvam, L. (2022). Barriers and Facilitators in the Transition From Higher Education to Employment for Students With Disabilities: A Rapid Systematic Review. *Frontiers in Education*, 7, 882066. Advance online publication. DOI: 10.3389/feduc.2022.882066

Gordon, C. T., & Fabiano, G. A. (2019). The Transition of Youth with ADHD into the Workforce: Review and Future Directions. *Clinical Child and Family Psychology Review*, 22(3), 316–347. DOI: 10.1007/s10567-019-00274-4 PMID: 30725305

Green, M. (2023). SPSS software: What are the uses of SPSS? *Fynzo*. https://www.fynzo.com/blog/spss-software/

Gwernan-Jones, R., Moore, D., Garside, R., Richardson, M., Thompson-Coon, J., Rogers, M., Cooper, P., Stein, K., & Ford, T. (2015). ADHD, parent perspectives and parent-teacher relationships: Grounds for conflict. *British Journal of Special Education*, 42(3), 279–300. DOI: 10.1111/1467-8578.12087

Harris, A. N. (2016). *Perceived barriers to career self-exploration for adults with learning disabilities.*(Doctoral Dissertation, Boston College, Lynch School of Education).

Hossan, D., Mansor, Z., & Jaharuddin, N. (2023). Research Population and Sampling in Quantitative Study. *International Journal of Business and Technopreneurship*, 13(3), 209–222. DOI: 10.58915/ijbt.v13i3.263

Jansen, D. (2023, October). What Is Descriptive Statistics: Full Explainer With Examples. *Grad Coach*. https://gradcoach.com/descriptive-statistics/

Janssens, A., Blake, S., Eke, H., Price, A., & Ford, T. (2023). Parenting roles for young people with attention-deficit/hyperactivity disorder transitioning to adult services. *Developmental Medicine and Child Neurology*, 65(1), 136–144. DOI: 10.1111/dmcn.15320 PMID: 35723621

Kingsley, E. (2024, April 1). Grow Up Already! Why It Takes So Long to Mature. *ADDitude Magazine.*https://www.additudemag.com/grow-up-already-why-it-takes-so-long-to-mature/

Lawrence, K., Dawson, R., & McCormick, J. (2017). Teachers' Experiences With and Perceptions of Students With Attention Deficit/hyperactivity Disorder. *Journal of Pediatric Nursing*, 36, 141–148. DOI: 10.1016/j.pedn.2017.06.010 PMID: 28888495

Lawson, G. M., Owens, J. S., Mandell, D. S., Tavlin, S., Rufe, S., So, A., & Power, T. J. (2022). Barriers and Facilitators to Teachers' Use of Behavioral Classroom Interventions. *School Mental Health*, 14(4), 844–862. DOI: 10.1007/s12310-022-09524-3 PMID: 35669254

Li, H.-H., Wang, T.-T., Dong, H.-Y., Liu, Y.-Q., & Jia, F.-Y. (2022). Screening of ADHD symptoms in primary school students and investigation of parental awareness of ADHD and its influencing factors: A cross-sectional study. *Frontiers in Psychology*, 13, 1070848. Advance online publication. DOI: 10.3389/fpsyg.2022.1070848 PMID: 36619017

Lippke, S. (2020). Self-Efficacy Expectation. In Zeigler-Hill, V., & Shackelford, T. K. (Eds.), *Encyclopedia of Personality and Individual Differences* (pp. 4719–4722). Springer., DOI: 10.1007/978-3-319-24612-3_1166

Lopez-Garrido, G. (2023, July 10). *Self-Efficacy: Bandura's Theory of Motivation in Psychology*. https://www.simplypsychology.org/self-efficacy.html

Mallon, R. (2024). Naturalistic Approaches to Social Construction. In E. N. Zalta & U. Nodelman (Eds.), *The Stanford Encyclopedia of Philosophy* (Summer 2024). Metaphysics Research Lab, Stanford University. https://plato.stanford.edu/archives/sum2024/entries/social-construction-naturalistic/

Maree, J. G., & Warnock, K. (2023). Teachers' perceptions of how attention-deficit/hyperactivity disorder may influence learners' career choices. *South African Journal of Higher Education*, 37(4). Advance online publication. DOI: 10.20853/37-4-5732

Marete, L. M. (2020). *Teachers' Perception of Transition Preparedness by Learners with Physical Disabilities towards Employment: Joytown, Joyland and Mombasa Special Secondary Schools, Kenya*. (Doctoral Dissertation, Kenyatta University).

Martin, D. M. (2017). School Counselors' Perceptions of Family Systems Perspectives. *The Family Journal (Alexandria, Va.)*, 25(3), 271–277. DOI: 10.1177/1066480717711109

Matheson, L., Asherson, P., Wong, I. C. K., Hodgkins, P., Setyawan, J., Sasane, R., & Clifford, S. (2013). Adult ADHD patient experiences of impairment, service provision and clinical management in England: A qualitative study. *BMC Health Services Research*, 13(1), 184. DOI: 10.1186/1472-6963-13-184 PMID: 23692803

Mueller, A. K., Fuermaier, A. B., Koerts, J., & Tucha, L. (2012). Stigma in attention deficit hyperactivity disorder. *Attention Deficit and Hyperactivity Disorders*, 4(3), 101–114. DOI: 10.1007/s12402-012-0085-3 PMID: 22773377

Nkosi, R. R. (2022). *Parent-Teacher Collaboration in Mapping Career Transitioning of Youth Diagnosed with ADHD.* (Master's Dissertation, University of Johannesburg, South Africa). Handle: https://hdl.handle.net/10210/502275

Ogrodnik, M., Karsan, S., Malamis, B., Kwan, M., Fenesi, B., & Heisz, J. J. (2023). Exploring Barriers and Facilitators to Physical Activity in Adults with ADHD: A Qualitative Investigation. *Journal of Developmental and Physical Disabilities*, 36(2), 307–327. DOI: 10.1007/s10882-023-09908-6 PMID: 37361454

Okon, I. E., Njoku, C. G., Ikelegu, M. E., & Awhen, V. O. (2017, June). *Residential Housing in Calabar, Cross River State, Nigeria: An Appraisal of Choices, Quality and Affordability.* 1st Geography and Environmental Science World Environmental Science World Environment Day Conference, University of Calabar, Calabar, Cross River State, Nigeria.

Olatunji, G., Faturoti, O., Jaiyeoba, B., Toluwabori, A. V., Adefusi, T., Olaniyi, P., Aderinto, N., & Abdulbasit, M. O. (2023). Navigating unique challenges and advancing equitable care for children with ADHD in Africa: A review. *Annals of Medicine and Surgery (London)*, 85(10), 4939–4946. DOI: 10.1097/MS9.0000000000001179 PMID: 37811061

Park, S. (2019). *ADHD, high ability, or both: The paths to young adulthood career outcomes.* (Doctoral Dissertation, University of Iowa). DOI: 10.17077/etd.s43m-3gfi

Pedamkar, P. (2024). What is SPSS? *Educab Blog.* https://www.educba.com/what-is-spss/

Peterson-Malen, M. (2013). *Phenomenological Study of the Experience of Parent Advocates of Students Diagnosed with ADHD.* (Doctoral Dissertation, University of Minnesota).

Petruzzi, L. (2005). *Attention deficit disorder: Family physicians' perspective on diagnosis and treatment.* (Doctoral Dissertation, University of Saint Thomas, Minnesota).

Price, A., Mitchell, S., Janssens, A., Eke, H., Ford, T., & Newlove-Delgado, T. (2022). In transition with attention deficit hyperactivity disorder (ADHD): Children's services clinicians' perspectives on the role of information in healthcare transitions for young people with ADHD. *BMC Psychiatry*, 22(1), 1. Advance online publication. DOI: 10.1186/s12888-022-03813-6 PMID: 35397599

Rai, N., & Thapa, B. (2015). *A study on purposive sampling method in research.* Kathmandu School of Law. Nepal., https://www.academia.edu/28087388/A_STUDY_ON_PURPOSIVE_SAMPLING_METHOD_IN_RESEARCH

Research Guides. (2024, August 19). *Research Methods: What are research methods?* https://libguides.newcastle.edu.au/researchmethods/home

Robb, A., & Findling, R. L. (2013). Challenges in the Transition of Care for Adolescents with Attention-Deficit/Hyperactivity Disorder. *Postgraduate Medicine*, 125(4), 131–140. DOI: 10.3810/pgm.2013.07.2685 PMID: 23933901

Robertson, P. (2024, September 11). *Positivism Philosophy in Research Methods | Research Paradigm*. https://bestdissertationwriter.com/positivism-philosophy-in-research/

Roxas, B., & Lindsay, V. (2012). Social Desirability Bias in Survey Research on Sustainable Development in Small Firms: An Exploratory Analysis of Survey Mode Effect. *Business Strategy and the Environment*, 21(4), 223–235. DOI: 10.1002/bse.730

Salma, P. (2015, July 15). *The research paradigm—Methodology, epistemology and ontology—Explained in simple language*. https://salmapatel.co.uk/academia/the-research-paradigm-methodology-epistemology-and-ontology-explained-in-simple-language/

Samosh, D., Lilius, J., & Atwood, K. (2024). ADHD and Career Success: Barriers, Facilitators, and Future Research Directions. In Patton, E., & Santuzzi, A. M. (Eds.), *Neurodiversity and Work: Employment, Identity, and Support Networks for Neurominorities* (pp. 257–281). Springer Nature Switzerland., DOI: 10.1007/978-3-031-55072-0_12

Sheppard, V. (2020). *Research Methods for the Social Sciences: An Introduction*. PressBooks. https://pressbooks.bccampus.ca/jibcresearchmethods/

Shook, M. (1993). *Mixed paradigms: Combining participatory and positivist research methods : Guyanese case studies*. (Master's Thesis, Saint Mary's University, Halifax, NS, Canada). https://library2.smu.ca/xmlui/handle/01/22412

Shukla, S. (2020). *Concept of population and sample*. Conference on How to Write a Research Paper at Indore, M. P., India. https://www.researchgate.net/publication/346426707_CONCEPT_OF_POPULATION_AND_SAMPLE

Sibley, M. H., Altszuler, A. R., Morrow, A. S., & Merrill, B. M. (2014). Mapping the academic problem behaviors of adolescents with ADHD. *School Psychology Quarterly*, 29(4), 422–437. DOI: 10.1037/spq0000071 PMID: 24933215

Stagg, A. M. (2010). *Barriers to Attention-Deficit/Hyperactivity Disorder Intervention Implementation in the Public School Setting*. (Doctoral Dissertation, Indiana State University). http://hdl.handle.net/10484/1180

Stargell, N. A., Barker, L. A., Kress, V. E., & Bullock, M. L. (2017). Counseling Youth With Attention-Deficit/Hyperactivity Disorder (ADHD). American Counseling Association Practice Briefs, 1-5. The Center for Counseling Practice, Policy, and Research. https://www.counseling.org/docs/default-source/practice-briefs/counseling-youth-with-adhd.pdf

Stevens, A. E., Lefler, E. K., Serrano, J. W., & Hartung, C. M. (2023). Transitioning to college with ADHD: A qualitative examination of parental support and the renegotiation of the parent-child relationship. *Current Psychology (New Brunswick, N.J.)*, 43(4), 3134–3149. DOI: 10.1007/s12144-023-04525-0 PMID: 37359679

Taherdoost, H. (2016). Sampling Methods in Research Methodology; How to Choose a Sampling Technique for Research. SSRN *Electronic Journal* 5(2),18-27. DOI: 10.2139/ssrn.3205035

Ugwu, G. C., Ifelunni, C. O., Eseadi, C., Eze, C., & Onuorah, A. (●●●). Influence of Socio-Economic Factors on Parental Expenditure on Children's Education at the Nursery School Level in Delta State, Nigeria. *European Journal of Scientific Research*, 141(3), 264–285.

Vasiliou, C. (2024, October 10). *7 Types of Survey Research Methods & When to Use Them. Woorise Blog.* https://woorise.com/blog/types-of-survey-research-methods-when-to-use-them

Vitanza, B. S. (2014). *Attention-Deficit Hyperactivity Disorder: Teachers' Perceptions and Acceptability of Interventions.* (Doctoral Dissertation, Philadelphia College of Osteopathic Medicine).https://digitalcommons.pcom.edu/psychology_dissertations/315/

Vondracek, F. W., Lerner, R. M., & Schulenberg, J. E. (2019). *Career Development: A Life-span Developmental Approach.* Routledge., DOI: 10.4324/9781315792705

Ward, R. J., Kovshoff, H., & Kreppner, J. (2021). School staff perspectives on ADHD and training: Understanding the needs and views of UK primary staff. *Emotional & Behavioural Difficulties*, 26(3), 306–321. DOI: 10.1080/13632752.2021.1965342

Warnock, K. (2022). *Teachers' experiences of how Attention-Deficit/Hyperactivity Disorder influences learners' career.* (Master's Dissertation, University of Pretoria South Africa).

Wood, S. C. (2012). Examining Parent and Teacher Perceptions of Behaviors Exhibited by Gifted Students Referred for ADHD Diagnosis Using the Conners 3 (An Exploratory Study). *Roeper Review*, 34(3), 194–204. DOI: 10.1080/02783193.2012.686426

ADDITIONAL READINGS

Alhefdhi, H., Alshehri, N., Al Zomia, A., Lahiq, L., Hussain, A., Alaskari, A., Alasiri, W., Alqarni, A., Asiri, F., Alqahtani, A., Asiri, M., & Alhifthy, E. (2024). Exploring quality of life, discrimination, and knowledge of parents of ADHD children in Saudi Arabia: A cross-sectional study. *Medicine*, 103(24), e38102. DOI: 10.1097/MD.0000000000038102 PMID: 38875372

Bassuk, E. L. (2017). The homelessness problem. In *Housing the homeless* (pp. 253–261). Routledge. DOI: 10.4324/9780203789728-18

Climie, E. A., & Mitchell, K. (2017). Parent-child relationship and behavior problems in children with ADHD. *International Journal of Developmental Disabilities*, 63(1), 27–35. DOI: 10.1080/20473869.2015.1112498

D'Agati, E., Curatolo, P., & Mazzone, L. (2019). Comorbidity between ADHD and anxiety disorders across the lifespan. *International Journal of Psychiatry in Clinical Practice*, 23(4), 238–244. DOI: 10.1080/13651501.2019.1628277 PMID: 31232613

De Meyer, H., Beckers, T., Tripp, G., & van Der Oord, S. (2019). Deficits in conditional discrimination learning in children with adhd are independent of delay aversion and working memory. *Journal of Clinical Medicine*, 8(9), 1381. DOI: 10.3390/jcm8091381 PMID: 31484457

Duncan, G. J., Magnuson, K., & Votruba-Drzal, E. (2014). Boosting family income to promote child development. *The Future of Children*, 24(1), 99–120. DOI: 10.1353/foc.2014.0008 PMID: 25518705

Figueiredo, T., Lima, G., Erthal, P., Martins, R., Corção, P., Leonel, M., Ayrão, V., Fortes, D., & Mattos, P. (2020). Mind-wandering, depression, anxiety and ADHD: Disentangling the relationship. *Psychiatry Research*, 285, 112798. DOI: 10.1016/j.psychres.2020.112798 PMID: 31991281

Fuermaier, A., Tucha, L., Butzbach, M., Weisbrod, M., Aschenbrenner, S., & Tucha, O. (2021). ADHD at the workplace: ADHD symptoms, diagnostic status, and work-related functioning. *Journal of Neural Transmission (Vienna, Austria)*, 128(7), 1021–1031. DOI: 10.1007/s00702-021-02309-z PMID: 33528652

Gair, S. L., Brown, H. R., Kang, S., Grabell, A. S., & Harvey, E. A. (2021). Early development of comorbidity between symptoms of ADHD and anxiety. *Research on Child and Adolescent Psychopathology*, 49(3), 311–323. DOI: 10.1007/s10802-020-00724-6 PMID: 33404952

Grafström, J., & Aasma, S. (2021). Breaking circular economy barriers. *Journal of Cleaner Production*, 292, 126002. DOI: 10.1016/j.jclepro.2021.126002

Guo, X., & He, L. (2014, November). ADHD discrimination based on social network. In *2014 International Conference on Cloud Computing and Big Data* (pp. 55-61). IEEE. DOI: 10.1109/CCBD.2014.38

Haratsis, J. M., Hood, M., & Creed, P. A. (2015). Career goals in young adults: Personal resources, goal appraisals, attitudes, and goal management strategies. *Journal of Career Development*, 42(5), 431–445. DOI: 10.1177/0894845315572019

Huang, J., Mauche, N., Ahlers, E., Bogatsch, H., Böhme, P., Ethofer, T., Fallgatter, A. J., Gallinat, J., Hegerl, U., Heuser, I., Hoffmann, K., Kittel-Schneider, S., Reif, A., Schöttle, D., Unterecker, S., & Strauß, M. (2024). The impact of emotional dysregulation and comorbid depressive symptoms on clinical features, brain arousal, and treatment response in adults with ADHD. *Frontiers in Psychiatry*, 14, 1294314. DOI: 10.3389/fpsyt.2023.1294314 PMID: 38250266

Ismail, M., & Lu, H. S. (2014). Cultural values and career goals of the millennial generation: An integrated conceptual framework. *Journal of International Management Studies*, 9(1), 38–49.

Jarrett, M. A., Wolff, J. C., Davis, T. E. III, Cowart, M. J., & Ollendick, T. H. (2016). Characteristics of Children With ADHD and Comorbid Anxiety. *Journal of Attention Disorders*, 20(7), 636–644. DOI: 10.1177/1087054712452914 PMID: 22863769

Jiang, Z., Newman, A., Le, H., Presbitero, A., & Zheng, C. (2019). Career exploration: A review and future research agenda. *Journal of Vocational Behavior*, 110, 338–356. DOI: 10.1016/j.jvb.2018.08.008

Johnston, C., & Chronis-Tuscano, A. (2015). Families and ADHD.

Kim, S., & Rim, H. (2024). The role of public skepticism and distrust in the process of CSR communication. *International Journal of Business Communication*, 61(2), 198–218. DOI: 10.1177/2329488419866888

Kleine, A. K., Schmitt, A., & Wisse, B. (2021). Students' career exploration: A meta-analysis. *Journal of Vocational Behavior*, 131, 103645. DOI: 10.1016/j.jvb.2021.103645

Lewandowsky, S., Mann, M. E., Brown, N. J., & Friedman, H. (2016). Science and the public: Debate, denial, and skepticism. *Journal of Social and Political Psychology*, 4(2), 537–553. DOI: 10.5964/jspp.v4i2.604

Lim, N. (2016). Cultural differences in emotion: Differences in emotional arousal level between the East and the West. *Integrative Medicine Research*, 5(2), 105–109. DOI: 10.1016/j.imr.2016.03.004 PMID: 28462104

Llanes, E., Blacher, J., Stavropoulos, K., & Eisenhower, A. (2020). Parent and teacher reports of comorbid anxiety and ADHD symptoms in children with ASD. *Journal of Autism and Developmental Disorders*, 50(5), 1520–1531. DOI: 10.1007/s10803-018-3701-z PMID: 30062398

Maree, J. G., & Warnock, K. (2023). Teachers' Perceptions of how Attention-Deficit/Hyperactivity Disorder May Influence Learners' Career Choices. *South African Journal of Higher Education*, 37(4), 205–224. DOI: 10.20853/37-4-5732

Markel, C., & Wiener, J. (2014). Attribution processes in parent–adolescent conflict in families of adolescents with and without ADHD. *Canadian Journal of Behavioral Science/Revue Anadienne des sciences du Comportment, 46*(1), 40.

Martella, D., Aldunate, N., Fuentes, L. J., & Sánchez-Pérez, N. (2020). Arousal and executive alterations in attention deficit hyperactivity disorder (ADHD). *Frontiers in Psychology*, 11, 1991. DOI: 10.3389/fpsyg.2020.01991 PMID: 32903419

McVey, A. J., Schiltz, H. K., Haendel, A. D., Dolan, B. K., Willar, K. S., Pleiss, S. S., Karst, J. S., Carlson, M., Krueger, W., Murphy, C. C., Casnar, C. L., Yund, B., & Van Hecke, A. V. (2018). Social difficulties in youth with autism with and without anxiety and ADHD symptoms. *Autism Research*, 11(12), 1679–1689. DOI: 10.1002/aur.2039 PMID: 30475451

Mesra, B. (2018). Factors That Influencing Households Income and Its Contribution On Family Income In Hamparan Perak Sub-District, Deli Serdang Regency, North. *Int. J. Civ. Eng. Technol*, 9(10), 461–469.

Morrissey, T. W., Hutchison, L., & Winsler, A. (2014). Family income, school attendance, and academic achievement in elementary school. *Developmental Psychology*, 50(3), 741–753. DOI: 10.1037/a0033848 PMID: 23914750

Nemteanu, M. S., Dinu, V., & Dabija, D. C. (2021). Job insecurity, job instability, and job satisfaction in the context of the COVID-19 pandemic. *Journal of Competitiveness*, (2).

Noble, K. G., Houston, S. M., Brito, N. H., Bartsch, H., Kan, E., Kuperman, J. M., Akshoomoff, N., Amaral, D. G., Bloss, C. S., Libiger, O., Schork, N. J., Murray, S. S., Casey, B. J., Chang, L., Ernst, T. M., Frazier, J. A., Gruen, J. R., Kennedy, D. N., Van Zijl, P., & Sowell, E. R. (2015). Family income, parental education and brain structure in children and adolescents. *Nature Neuroscience*, 18(5), 773–778. DOI: 10.1038/nn.3983 PMID: 25821911

Pliszka, S. R. (2019). ADHD and anxiety: Clinical implications. *Journal of Attention Disorders*, 23(3), 203–205. DOI: 10.1177/1087054718817365 PMID: 30791800

Powell, V., Riglin, L., Ng-Knight, T., Frederickson, N., Woolf, K., McManus, C., Collishaw, S., Shelton, K., Thapar, A., & Rice, F. (2021). Investigating friendship difficulties in the pathway from ADHD to depressive symptoms. Can parent–child relationships compensate? *Research on Child and Adolescent Psychopathology*, 49(8), 1031–1041. DOI: 10.1007/s10802-021-00798-w PMID: 33655375

Prevatt, F., Dehili, V., Taylor, N., & Marshall, D. (2015). Anxiety in College Students With ADHD: Relationship to Cognitive Functioning. *Journal of Attention Disorders*, 19(3), 222–230. DOI: 10.1177/1087054712457037 PMID: 22930788

Qureshi, M. N. I., Oh, J., Min, B., Jo, H. J., & Lee, B. (2017). Multi-modal, multi-measure, and multi-class discrimination of ADHD with hierarchical feature extraction and extreme learning machine using structural and functional brain MRI. *Frontiers in Human Neuroscience*, 11, 157. PMID: 28420972

Ravenhill, M. (2016). *The culture of homelessness*. Routledge. DOI: 10.4324/9781315615240

Reimherr, F. W., Marchant, B. K., Gift, T. E., & Steans, T. A. (2017). ADHD and anxiety: Clinical significance and treatment implications. *Current Psychiatry Reports*, 19(12), 1–10. DOI: 10.1007/s11920-017-0859-6 PMID: 29152677

Riglin, L., Leppert, B., Dardani, C., Thapar, A. K., Rice, F., O'Donovan, M. C., Davey Smith, G., Stergiakouli, E., Tilling, K., & Thapar, A. (2021). ADHD and depression: Investigating a causal explanation. *Psychological Medicine*, 51(11), 1890–1897. DOI: 10.1017/S0033291720000665 PMID: 32249726

Robbins, L. (2017). *The great depression*. Routledge. DOI: 10.4324/9781315132327

Romero-Ayuso, D., Maciver, D., Richmond, J., Jorquera-Cabrera, S., Garra-Palud, L., Zabala-Baños, C., Toledano-González, A., & Triviño-Juárez, J. M. (2020). Tactile discrimination, praxis and cognitive impulsivity in adhd children: A cross-sectional study. *International Journal of Environmental Research and Public Health*, 17(6), 1897. DOI: 10.3390/ijerph17061897 PMID: 32183331

Shushakova, A., Ohrmann, P., & Pedersen, A. (2018). Exploring deficient emotion regulation in adult ADHD: Electrophysiological evidence. *European Archives of Psychiatry and Clinical Neuroscience*, 268(4), 359–371. DOI: 10.1007/s00406-017-0826-6 PMID: 28770370

Simmons, J. A., & Antshel, K. M. (2021, June). Bullying and depression in youth with ADHD: A systematic review. []. Springer US.]. *Child and Youth Care Forum*, 50(3), 379–414. DOI: 10.1007/s10566-020-09586-x

Smith, K., & De Torres, I. (2014). A world of depression. *Nature*, 515(181), 10–1038. PMID: 25391942

Speerforck, S., Hertel, J., Stolzenburg, S., Grabe, H. J., Carta, M. G., Angermeyer, M. C., & Schomerus, G. (2021). Attention deficit hyperactivity disorder in children and adults: A population survey on public beliefs. *Journal of Attention Disorders*, 25(6), 783–793. DOI: 10.1177/1087054719855691 PMID: 31271090

Spolaore, E., & Wacziarg, R. (2014). Long-term barriers to economic development. In *Handbook of economic growth* (Vol. 2, pp. 121–176). Elsevier.

Tien, Y. M., Chen, V. C. H., Lo, T. S., Hsu, C. F., Gossop, M., & Huang, K. Y. (2019). Deficits in auditory sensory discrimination among children with attention-deficit/hyperactivity disorder. *European Child & Adolescent Psychiatry*, 28(5), 645–653. DOI: 10.1007/s00787-018-1228-7 PMID: 30229307

Tsang, T. W., Kohn, M. R., Efron, D., Clarke, S. D., Clark, C. R., Lamb, C., & Williams, L. M. (2015). Anxiety in young people with ADHD: Clinical and self-report outcomes. *Journal of Attention Disorders*, 19(1), 18–26. DOI: 10.1177/1087054712446830 PMID: 22713359

Williamson, K. D., Combs, H. L., Berry, D. T., Harp, J. P., Mason, L. H., & Edmundson, M. (2014). Discriminating among ADHD alone, ADHD with a comorbid psychological disorder, and feigned ADHD in a college sample. *The Clinical Neuropsychologist*, 28(7), 1182–1196. DOI: 10.1080/13854046.2014.956674 PMID: 25225947

Wong, I. Y., Hawes, D. J., Clarke, S., Kohn, M. R., & Dar-Nimrod, I. (2018). Perceptions of ADHD among diagnosed children and their parents: A systematic review using the common-sense model of illness representations. *Clinical Child and Family Psychology Review*, 21(1), 57–93. DOI: 10.1007/s10567-017-0245-2 PMID: 29079900

KEY TERMS AND DEFINITIONS

Anxiety: Defined as a psychological condition characterized by intense worry, fear, or apprehension regarding future occurrences or scenarios. Although it is a natural reaction to stress, it can develop into a disorder when it hinders daily life. Anxiety disorders can take multiple forms, including generalized anxiety disorder, social anxiety disorder, panic disorder, and specific phobias. Common manifestations include feelings of restlessness, rapid heart rate, difficulty in concentrating, muscle tension, and avoidance of anxiety-provoking situations. Triggers for anxiety may include stress, traumatic experiences, or biological factors. Treatment options typically consist of cognitive-behavioral therapy (CBT), relaxation techniques, lifestyle adjustments, and medication. Managing anxiety effectively involves identifying its triggers, developing constructive coping mechanisms, and seeking support to enhance mental health and resilience.

Career Choices: Refer to the selections individuals make regarding their professional journeys, which are influenced by their personal interests, values, competencies, and external factors such as job market conditions or family expectations. The process of making these choices involves evaluating various options, considering the advantages and disadvantages, and reflecting on long-term objectives and potential opportunities. Such decisions are vital as they significantly impact an individual's work life, job satisfaction, and personal fulfillment. As individuals gain new experiences, adapt to changes in their interests, or respond to market fluctuations, their career choices may evolve. Effective decision-making in this realm requires a strong sense of self-awareness, diligent research, and a willingness to take risks and pursue new opportunities.

Career Exploration: A comprehensive process that involves researching, understanding, and assessing various career options to find a suitable path that aligns with an individual's interests, values, skills, and aspirations. This process requires the collection of detailed information about different professions, job roles, necessary qualifications, and work environments, enabling individuals to make informed career choices. Activities that may be part of career exploration include job shadowing, internships, informational interviews, career assessments, and consultations with mentors or career advisors. The ultimate goal is to assist individuals in discovering their passions, strengths, and potential career avenues. Effective career exploration not only helps in identifying appropriate opportunities but also cultivates self-awareness and encourages proactive planning for future professional advancement and satisfaction.

Career Goals: Defined as the specific aims or ambitions that individuals pursue within their professional lives. These objectives provide essential guidance and motivation, shaping the decisions and actions taken in one's career. Career goals may be short-term, such as acquiring a new competency or receiving a promotion, or long-term, including aspirations like becoming a manager or starting a successful business. Establishing well-defined career goals enables individuals to direct their efforts effectively, assess their progress, and make educated choices regarding education, training, and employment opportunities. Realizing these goals demands strategic planning, resilience, and the flexibility to navigate challenges while embracing new possibilities. Well-articulated career goals foster a sense of purpose and fulfillment in one's professional path.

Depression: A mental health condition marked by enduring feelings of sadness, despair, and a diminished interest in activities that were once enjoyable. It influences an individual's thoughts, emotions, and overall functioning, often resulting in both emotional and physical challenges. Typical symptoms of depression encompass alterations in appetite, sleep irregularities, fatigue, difficulties with concentration, and pervasive feelings of worthlessness. The origins of depression can be diverse, encompassing genetic, biological, psychological, and environmental influences. Stressful life events, trauma, or chronic stress can act as catalysts for this condition. Given its severity, depression necessitates professional intervention, which may include therapy, medication, or modifications to one's lifestyle. Effectively addressing depression requires a comprehensive understanding of its root causes and the implementation of suitable strategies to foster well-being and recovery.

Economic Barriers: Defined as financial obstacles that hinder individuals or groups from obtaining vital resources, services, and opportunities. These challenges encompass factors such as low income, unemployment, insufficient affordable housing, inadequate healthcare, and restricted access to quality education. Marginalized communities are particularly affected by these economic barriers, resulting in significant disparities in social mobility, health outcomes, and overall well-being. Such barriers limit individuals' capacity to invest in their futures, pursue higher education, or attain financial stability. To effectively address economic barriers, systemic initiatives are necessary, including job creation, equitable wages, accessible healthcare, and policies that ensure equal educational opportunities. Overcoming these barriers is essential for mitigating inequality, enhancing quality of life, and promoting inclusive growth within society.

Emotional Arousal: Refers to the increased emotional and physiological states that occur in response to both internal and external stimuli. This process involves the activation of the nervous system, which can lead to physical changes such as an increased heart rate, sweating, or muscle tension, as well as emotional reactions that may include excitement, fear, anger, or happiness. The impact of emotional arousal is significant, influencing how individuals perceive situations, respond to challenges, and make decisions. While elevated emotional arousal can enhance concentration and alertness in certain contexts, such as competitive sports, it may also lead to impulsive behavior or stress in high-pressure scenarios. To manage emotional arousal effectively, individuals should identify their emotional triggers, practice relaxation techniques, and develop coping strategies to maintain emotional balance and regulate their responses in challenging situations.

Family Income: The total earnings generated by all individuals within a household, which includes wages, salaries, investment returns, pensions, and government aid. This metric serves as a crucial indicator of a family's financial health, impacting their ability to secure essential resources such as food, housing, healthcare, and education. Additionally, family income plays a significant role in determining lifestyle choices, personal development opportunities, and overall financial security. A lower family income can present economic obstacles, resulting in difficulties such as restricted access to quality education, healthcare services, and leisure activities. Conversely, a higher family income typically offers greater security and enhances prospects for upward mobility. Analyzing family income is vital for policymakers and organizations focused on mitigating social disparities and assisting families in achieving economic stability and overall well-being.

Homelessness: Denotes the lack of stable, safe, and adequate housing. Individuals or families facing homelessness may reside in temporary shelters, on the streets, in vehicles, or in unstable living conditions with friends or relatives. Various factors contribute to homelessness, including economic challenges, unemployment, mental health disorders, substance dependency, domestic abuse, and insufficient affordable housing. This complex social issue significantly affects physical and mental health, educational access, and social interactions. Those who are homeless often experience stigma, which hinders their ability to secure necessary resources and assistance. To effectively combat homelessness, a multifaceted approach is essential, incorporating affordable housing solutions, mental health services, job creation, and social support systems aimed at fostering stability and improving quality of life.

Job Instability: Refers to the lack of security and uncertainty surrounding one's employment, often manifested through temporary contracts, frequent job changes, or the risk of losing one's job. This instability can be attributed to various factors, including economic downturns, corporate restructuring, shifts in industry requirements, or a limited number of job opportunities. The ramifications of job instability can result in financial and emotional distress for employees, negatively influencing their job satisfaction, motivation, and overall well-being. It can also lead to feelings of insecurity and anxiety, making future planning difficult. To combat job instability, it is vital to enhance employability through skill development, pursue stable job opportunities, and establish policies that aid workers in transitioning between jobs or adapting to the changing labor market.

Job Performance: Defined as the degree to which an individual effectively executes their assigned duties and responsibilities. This encompasses the quality, efficiency, and consistency of the output, alongside the employee's capability to meet established expectations, deadlines, and objectives. Various factors that impact job performance include the individual's skills, motivation levels, the work environment, and the support received from supervisors or peers. High levels of job performance are typically linked to a robust work ethic, proficient time management, and a proactive mindset. Such performance is vital for an organization's success and may result in recognition, promotions, or opportunities for career progression. Employers evaluate job performance through assessments, feedback mechanisms, and performance indicators to pinpoint strengths, identify areas needing improvement, and explore avenues for professional development.

Parental Attribution: Refers to the perceptions and rationalizations that parents form regarding their child's actions, accomplishments, or difficulties. It reflects how parents interpret their child's behavior, skills, and results, influenced by factors such as effort, talent, luck, or external circumstances. These attributions have a profound effect on parenting styles, expectations, and the support parents offer their children. For example, if parents believe that their child's academic success stems from hard work, they may be inclined to provide praise focused on effort, while attributing success to inherent ability could lead to alternative forms of encouragement. Thus, parental attributions are instrumental in shaping a child's self-esteem, motivation, and self-concept, highlighting the importance of maintaining balanced and supportive perspectives to promote healthy growth and resilience.

Parent-Child Relationship: Constitutes the emotional and social connection between a parent and their offspring, marked by affection, care, communication, and support. This bond plays a crucial role in shaping a child's emotional growth, self-worth, behavior, and social abilities. A constructive parent-child relationship is characterized by open dialogue, mutual respect, and active participation in the child's life. Parents who offer consistent support, warmth, and guidance create a secure attachment, thereby enhancing the child's psychological health and resilience. Conversely, negative interactions, neglect, or excessively authoritarian parenting styles can result in emotional turmoil, behavioral challenges, or inadequate social development. Fostering a healthy parent-child relationship necessitates empathy, effective communication, and the establishment of appropriate boundaries to promote the child's development and overall well-being.

Public Skepticism: Refers to the prevalent doubt, distrust, or disbelief that individuals may exhibit towards information, policies, institutions, or figures in authority. This skepticism often emerges from a lack of transparency, misinformation, historical failures, or inconsistencies in communication. It can manifest in various contexts, such as governmental decisions, scientific conclusions, media reports, or corporate practices. While skepticism can foster critical thinking and demand accountability, an excessive degree of distrust may lead to cynicism, disengagement, or the spread of conspiracy theories. To establish public trust, it is crucial to prioritize clear communication, transparency, evidence-based information, and accountability from leaders and organizations. Effectively addressing public skepticism is vital for promoting informed public discourse and enhancing social cohesion.

Time Management: Refers to the capacity to strategically plan, prioritize, and allocate time in a manner that facilitates the completion of tasks and the attainment of objectives. This process encompasses the establishment of clear goals, the organization of activities, and the reduction of distractions to enhance overall productivity. Proficient time management skills enable individuals to balance their various responsibilities, alleviate stress, and improve efficiency. Essential techniques include the development of schedules, the division of tasks into smaller, manageable components, and the implementation of deadlines. Mastery of time management is crucial across academic, professional, and personal domains, allowing individuals to fulfill their commitments and pursue long-term aspirations. Effective time management cultivates discipline, self-regulation, and the capacity to navigate competing demands, ultimately contributing to increased success and fulfillment in multiple areas of life.

APPENDIX I: STUDY QUESTIONNAIRE

Table 3. Teachers' and parents' perspectives on the barriers to career transition of students with ADHD questionnaire (TPPBCTSAQ)

No	Statements	SD	D	UD	A	SA
1	Students with ADHD face difficulties in maintaining focus during career counseling sessions.					
2	ADHD symptoms hinder students' ability to explore different career options.					
3	There is a lack of resources tailored to career transition for students with ADHD.					
4	Teachers and parents are not adequately trained to support the career transition of students with ADHD.					
5	Students with ADHD struggle with time management, and this is affecting their career transition.					
6	Most school environments are not conducive to the career transition of students with ADHD.					
7	Students with ADHD have limited access to career mentorship programs.					
8	ADHD impacts students' ability to set realistic career goals.					
9	There is a stigma associated with ADHD that affects career opportunities.					
10	Students with ADHD have difficulty developing the necessary social skills for career success.					
11	Career transition programs do not accommodate the unique needs of students with ADHD.					
12	Parents of students with ADHD are not well-informed about career transition options.					
13	Students with ADHD experience anxiety about career transitions.					
14	ADHD affects students' ability to complete necessary career transition tasks.					
15	There is insufficient collaboration between schools and external career support services.					
16	Students with ADHD lack the self-advocacy skills needed for career transitions.					
17	The transition from school to work is daunting for students with ADHD.					
18	ADHD impacts students' ability to engage in career exploration activities.					
19	Teachers and parents have limited awareness of effective career transition strategies for ADHD.					
20	Students with ADHD face challenges in adapting to new work environments.					
21	ADHD symptoms interfere with students' ability to make informed career decisions.					

SD=Strongly Disagree, D=Disagree, UD=Undecided, A=Agree, SA=Strongly Agree

APPENDIX II: ADDITIONAL STATISTICS

Table 4. Item-total statistics

No	Statements	Cronbach's Alpha if Item Deleted
1	Students with ADHD face difficulties in maintaining focus during career counseling sessions.	.925
2	ADHD symptoms hinder students' ability to explore different career options.	.912
3	There is a lack of resources tailored to career transition for students with ADHD.	.903
4	Teachers and parents are not adequately trained to support the career transition of students with ADHD.	.908
5	Students with ADHD struggle with time management, and this is affecting their career transition.	.912
6	Most school environments are not conducive to the career transition of students with ADHD.	.925
7	Students with ADHD have limited access to career mentorship programs.	.912
8	ADHD impacts students' ability to set realistic career goals.	.903
9	There is a stigma associated with ADHD that affects career opportunities.	.908
10	Students with ADHD have difficulty developing the necessary social skills for career success.	.912
11	Career transition programs do not accommodate the unique needs of students with ADHD.	.925
12	Parents of students with ADHD are not well-informed about career transition options.	.912
13	Students with ADHD experience anxiety about career transitions.	.903
14	ADHD affects students' ability to complete necessary career transition tasks.	.908
15	There is insufficient collaboration between schools and external career support services.	.912
16	Students with ADHD lack the self-advocacy skills needed for career transitions.	.912
17	The transition from school to work is daunting for students with ADHD.	.912
18	ADHD impacts students' ability to engage in career exploration activities.	.903
19	Teachers and parents have limited awareness of effective career transition strategies for ADHD.	.908
20	Students with ADHD face challenges in adapting to new work environments.	.903
21	ADHD symptoms interfere with students' ability to make informed career decisions.	.908

Table 5. Communalities (extraction method: principal component analysis)

No	Statements	Extraction
1	Students with ADHD face difficulties in maintaining focus during career counseling sessions.	.994
2	ADHD symptoms hinder students' ability to explore different career options.	.942
3	There is a lack of resources tailored to career transition for students with ADHD.	.966
4	Teachers and parents are not adequately trained to support the career transition of students with ADHD.	.997
5	Students with ADHD struggle with time management, and this is affecting their career transition.	.993
6	Most school environments are not conducive to the career transition of students with ADHD.	.994
7	Students with ADHD have limited access to career mentorship programs.	.942
8	ADHD impacts students' ability to set realistic career goals.	.966
9	There is a stigma associated with ADHD that affects career opportunities.	.997
10	Students with ADHD have difficulty developing the necessary social skills for career success.	.993
11	Career transition programs do not accommodate the unique needs of students with ADHD.	.994
12	Parents of students with ADHD are not well-informed about career transition options.	.942
13	Students with ADHD experience anxiety about career transitions.	.966
14	ADHD affects students' ability to complete necessary career transition tasks.	.997
15	There is insufficient collaboration between schools and external career support services.	.993
16	Students with ADHD lack the self-advocacy skills needed for career transitions.	.993
17	The transition from school to work is daunting for students with ADHD.	.993
18	ADHD impacts students' ability to engage in career exploration activities.	.966
19	Teachers and parents have limited awareness of effective career transition strategies for ADHD.	.997
20	Students with ADHD face challenges in adapting to new work environments.	.966
21	ADHD symptoms interfere with students' ability to make informed career decisions.	.997

Chapter 10
Determining Solutions to Challenges in the Career Transition of Students With ADHD:
Teachers' and Parents' Perspectives

ABSTRACT

This study investigated the perspectives of school teachers and parents on possible solutions for addressing challenges faced by students with ADHD during career transition. The study employed a survey design and quantitative research approach to survey a total of 56 respondents. The findings reveal that both groups hold strong and positive views on solutions, with teachers generally exhibiting more favorable perspectives than parents. Although rural respondents tend to have slightly higher mean scores than urban ones, these differences are not statistically significant. This research emphasizes the necessity of incorporating the perspectives of teachers and parents to develop proactive strategies that can aid in addressing challenges in the career transition of students with ADHD.

BACKGROUND

The long-lasting repercussions of attention-deficit/hyperactivity disorder (ADHD) on students continue well after their schooling, impacting their career transition and subsequent professional achievements. Teachers and parents are instrumental in the process of career transition (Maree & Warnock, 2023), but their

DOI: 10.4018/979-8-3693-2635-0.ch010

level of knowledge and support can further surmount or complicate the challenges of students with ADHD during career transition. Exploring the potential solutions to surmount obstacles faced by students with ADHD during career transition is crucial for improving their employment prospects. Tartakovsky (2012) pointed out that the key to success lies in identifying and utilizing tools and techniques specifically designed for students with ADHD, rather than applying those intended for their non-ADHD counterparts. Watson et al. (2023) observed that employers often prioritize attributes such as exceptional focus, meticulous attention to detail, speed, and organizational skills, which can be particularly challenging for individuals with ADHD. Rashidian (2024) argued that ADHD presents certain advantages, such as hyperfocus, creativity, and innovative thinking, which can be beneficial in various contexts. Therefore, it is prudent to consider career paths that utilize these strengths, including project management, entrepreneurship, or roles in fast-paced settings (Twanna, 2024). Enlightened Minds (2024) observed that, although many studies concentrate on addressing the challenges associated with the disorder, there is merit in investigating the positive aspects that can benefit students with ADHD in their career decisions and improve their contributions in professional settings. It is crucial to recognize that ADHD symptoms can significantly influence career development efforts, as well as clients' perceptions and attitudes towards their professional paths, necessitating tailored strategies for individuals with ADHD (Dickson, 2022). Furthermore, those diagnosed with ADHD frequently require support that is attuned to neurodiversity to alleviate the challenges they face and to strengthen the factors that aid in their transition process (Tang et al., 2024). Among the potential solutions are counseling services (Dipeolu et al., 2011), career coaching (Rapson, 2021), behavioral coaching (Martinig, 2023), brain-based psychotherapeutic interventions (Nadeau, 2005), advancements in medication (Ivey, 2022), career development initiatives that include advocacy and disclosure (Crook & McDowall, 2023; Enlightened Minds, 2024), self-awareness and self-reflection (Magill, 2024), proactive parental involvement (Young et al., 2011; Price et al., 2019), family aid (Mesfin & Habtamu, 2024), positive behavior reinforcement strategies (Fabiano et al., 2021), the establishment of strong teacher-student relationships, the incorporation of shared decision-making (Baweja et al., 2021), and strategic planning and effective policy execution (Australasian ADHD Professionals Association, 2022). As noted by Smith (2024), medication may assist certain individuals in alleviating the symptoms of ADHD; however, it is important to recognize that it does not serve as a cure and is not the sole remedy available. When prescribed, it should be administered alongside other therapeutic interventions or self-help methods. Bracken (2022) advocated for a more compassionate and non-judgmental approach to student engagement, acknowledging that disruptive behaviors may arise from factors such as boredom, frustration, or other deeper issues rather than the intention to cause disruption. This perspective emphasizes the importance of recognizing each student's unique strengths and challenges, allowing for the adaptation of teaching methods to better suit their academic and career transition needs. Also, the development of personalized plans is recommended, which entails establishing specific goals and tasks collaboratively with the student. This process may include organizing materials, engaging in focused work sessions followed by breaks, and utilizing graphic organizers to enhance task structure. Such strategies empower students, fostering a sense of ownership and agency in their learning journey and career transition process.

Umar et al. (2018) reported that in Nigeria, the identified subtypes of ADHD include inattentive, hyperactive-impulsive, and combined, with a male-to-female ratio of 1.4:1. The study revealed a significant correlation between ADHD and paternal substance use, maternal substance use and lower maternal education levels. In addition, poor handwriting quality and diminished global functioning were significantly linked to ADHD among adolescents. Thus, it is important that solutions are tailored to accommodate the individual needs of students with ADHD. Students with ADHD thrive in structured environments, which educational institutions can offer to enhance their concentration. Resources such as behavioral coaching, dedicated applications like Inflow, and additional support systems can significantly assist in fostering organization and motivation, enabling students to more effectively manage their academic duties (Martinig, 2023). While some individuals benefit from roles with a structured schedule that aids their concentration, others excel in dynamic positions that allow them to leverage their adaptability (APM Group, 2020). Also, an individual with ADHD may find a more subdued office position intellectually engaging, whereas another may excel in a dynamic retail environment; in both scenarios, they can contribute significantly to their workplace (Centre for ADHD Awareness Canada, 2023). Certain managers may exhibit greater receptiveness towards employees with ADHD, influenced by the increasing awareness surrounding the condition, particularly when they have personal connections to it within their families (Olsen & Turits, 2022). This development is one of the positive results stemming from enhanced awareness of ADHD. The implementation of tailored solutions can significantly reduce the stress levels of their parents and foster a sense of pride among teachers and other professionals. Here, we would like to emphasize that both teachers and parents play a key role in the career transition of students with ADHD. According to Song et al. (2022), the involvement of parents and teachers in offering career-related support is vital for enhancing the career development of students. Teachers engage with the academic and behavioral concerns of students on a regular basis (Hosseinnia et al., 2024). They stress the importance of interventions aimed at mitigating the long-term effects of ADHD on students' career decisions, asserting that parents have a significant role to play in this process (Maree & Warnock, 2023). Fabiano et al. (2021) pointed out that the involvement of fathers may hold significant value for students with ADHD, highlighting the importance of both parents' involvement. There is also a need to recognize the experiences and views of parents and formulate a suitable evidence-based approach for ADHD that includes psychological counseling or a combination of interventions, avoiding reliance on medication alone (Alqahtani, 2017). According to Moore et al. (2017), it is essential to take into account several factors, such as attitudes towards ADHD, the interpersonal relationships of students with ADHD, and the treatments they receive before establishing classroom strategies. The views of teachers are relevant in this regard.

The significant influence of both teachers and parents in facilitating career transition is well acknowledged; however, there exists a scarcity of research in the Nigerian context regarding their perceptions of potential solutions to the career transition challenges encountered by students with ADHD. A lack of insight into their perspectives may hinder the effectiveness of interventions and resources aimed at supporting these students in their career transition. Ndukuba et al. (2015) argued that perception may be influenced by the differences and inconsistencies that exist across various contexts. These authors further stressed that this is specifically critical in African rural regions where the educational levels and attitudes of teachers are often quite distinct from those of the parents. According to Adewuya and Famuyiwa (2007), the significant prevalence of ADHD in Nigeria necessitates the development of strategies to ensure the early identification and referral of affected children for holistic evaluation and treatment. The teachers often feel that their educational backgrounds and the duration of their teaching careers do not correspond to an enhancement of their collective knowledge regarding ADHD (Ojionuka, 2016). To effectively tackle the existing challenges, it is crucial to investigate the perspectives of these teachers and parents concerning the potential solutions for addressing the career transition difficulties faced by students with ADHD. Our research is of paramount importance for several reasons. It seeks to fill a critical void in the existing literature by examining the perspectives of Nigerian school teachers and parents on the solutions to the career transition challenges encountered by students with ADHD. The results will lead to significant insight into the factors that shape these perceptions, which is particularly important in our sociocultural context, where awareness and support for students with ADHD are often limited. By pinpointing the solutions recognized by teachers and parents, this study will enhance our understanding of potential strategies to assist students with ADHD in Nigerian school settings during their career transition. This study will also provide practical implications for inclusion in the formulation of career transition policies and practices within the Nigerian school system. By unveiling the solution-focused perspectives of both teachers and parents, policymakers can be better positioned to design programs and interventions that would rectify misunderstandings related to ADHD and equip teachers, schools and parents with the necessary competencies to assist these students effectively during the career transition process. Moreover, the insights derived from this research can influence strategies for enhancing teacher and parental involvement, thereby creating a more nurturing environment at home and in school settings that support the career transition of students with ADHD. To this end, the aim of this research, therefore, is to examine the perspective of Nigerian school teachers and parents regarding the various solutions to surmount the challenges in the career transition of students with ADHD.

Research Objectives

1. To ascertain mean perspectives from teachers and parents regarding solutions to challenges in the career transition of students with ADHD.
2. To determine the extent to which teachers and parents differ in their perspectives regarding solutions to challenges in the career transition of students with ADHD.
3. To determine the extent to which teachers and parents differ in their perspectives regarding solutions to challenges in the career transition of students with ADHD by gender.
4. To determine the extent to which teachers and parents differ in their perspectives regarding solutions to challenges in the career transition of students with ADHD by place of residence.

Research Questions

1. What are teachers' and parents' overall mean perspectives regarding solutions to challenges in the career transition of students with ADHD?
2. To what extent do teachers and parents differ in their perspectives regarding solutions to challenges in the career transition of students with ADHD?
3. To what extent do teachers and parents differ in their perspectives regarding solutions to challenges in the career transition of students with ADHD by gender?
4. To what extent do teachers and parents differ in their perspectives regarding solutions to challenges in the career transition of students with ADHD by place of residence?

Theoretical Framework

The application of psychological theory perspectives, such as positive psychology framework, can provide useful insights into the perspectives of teachers and parents regarding potential solutions to the challenges faced by students with

ADHD during their career transition. Positive Psychology highlights the importance of individual strengths, well-being, and the conditions that facilitate personal flourishing. This viewpoint is essential when considering the support of students with ADHD during their career transition, as it emphasizes their potential strengths rather than their limitations. According to Hefferon and Boniwell (2011), Positive Psychology revolves around themes such as happiness, personal growth, creativity, and the resilience of both individuals and communities. For students with ADHD, a positive psychological perspective suggests that teachers and parents can play a pivotal role in creating environments that enhance these students' unique skills and talents, rather than focusing exclusively on their challenges. The broaden-and-build theory proposed by Fredrickson (2001) within the framework of Positive Psychology suggests that the experience of positive emotions expands an individual's immediate thought-action repertoire, which, over time, fosters the development of enduring personal resources. This theory is particularly applicable in educational environments because by promoting positive emotions through supportive and inclusive practices, teachers and parents can aid students with ADHD in building resilience, confidence, and motivation. By concentrating on achievements, celebrating small victories, and creating structured yet flexible learning settings, self-efficacy can be enhanced, and adaptive strategies for career-related tasks can be cultivated. Utilizing the Positive Psychology framework in this way can help shift the perspectives of teachers and parents from a deficit-focused understanding of ADHD to a strengths-based approach that highlights creativity, perseverance, and empathy—qualities often associated with individuals diagnosed with ADHD. The importance of Positive Psychology in connection with the aims of this study is apparent, as it establishes a framework for understanding the various perspectives on the career transition of students with ADHD. For example, by exploring how teachers and parents assess the potential strategies that focus on well-being, studies can reveal common trends in current career transition support for students with ADHD in Nigeria. Moreover, the emphasis on strengths-based interventions in Positive Psychology highlights the opportunities for development and achievement, enabling teachers and parents to perceive ADHD not as a hindrance, but rather as an alternative approach to tasks and social interactions. This viewpoint is crucial for cultivating inclusive educational and professional settings where students with ADHD are motivated to pursue roles that capitalize on their distinctive abilities. Through this theoretical lens, the study aims to contribute practical recommendations that empower students with ADHD to navigate career transition successfully and fulfill their potential (see Figure 1).

Figure 1. Study framework

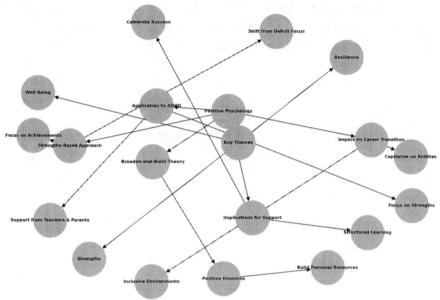

METHODOLOGY

Ethics Statement

Ethical approval for this study was obtained from the relevant institutional review boards. First, it received approval from the Research Ethics Committee of the Faculty of Education, University of Nigeria, Nigeria. It also received additional ethical approval from the Faculty of Education Research Ethics Committee at the University of Johannesburg, South Africa (Sem 2-2020-057). Informed consent was secured from participants. We assured confidentiality and clarified participants' right to withdraw from the study at any given time.

Research Design and Approach

This study used a survey research design. Survey research is a methodology employed by researchers to gather significant data from a designated population (Testbook, 2024). Surveys can be categorized into two main types: questionnaires completed by respondents, and interviews, which are conducted by an interviewer based on the responses provided by the participant (Trochim, 2024). The authors add that the primary aim of survey design is to enhance accuracy while adhering to constraints related to cost and timeliness. Likewise, the survey budget must consider other essential objectives such as relevance, accessibility, interpretability, comparability, coherence, and completeness, all of which are vital for ensuring the survey's overall effectiveness (Biemer, 2010). Surveys may be conducted as one-time events or as ongoing studies, and they can be quantitative or qualitative in nature. They can be administered online, in person, through mail-in forms, or via telephone calls within a brief timeframe (Harappa, 2021). The study adopted a quantitative research approach. Quantitative approach serves as a robust method for those seeking to collect empirical data on their subject matter through the application of statistical models and mathematical analysis, allowing researchers to assess their hypotheses (Adam, 2024).

Research Paradigm

This study is grounded in the positivist research paradigm. Positivism constitutes a research paradigm characterized by a commitment to 'scientific' inquiry, aiming to explore, validate, and forecast consistent patterns of behaviour, theories or hypotheses (Geoffjordan, 2019). It emphasizes an evidence-based understanding of reality that can be interpreted through mathematical frameworks (Keyter, 2016). The positivist paradigm often aligns with methodologies found in the natural sciences and is capable of elucidating the regularities of human social behavior in a universal and causal manner (Kirana, 2021).

Study Area

This research was conducted in Cross River State in the South-South zone of Nigeria. Cross River State has Calabar as its capital and is divided into 18 local government areas, which include Abi, Akamkpa, Akpabuyo, Bakassi, Bekwara, Biase, Boki, Calabar Municipal, Calabar South, Etung, Ikom, Obanliku, Obubra, Obudu, Odukpani, Ogoja, Yakurr, and Yala (Commonwealth Parliamentary Association Africa Region, 2019). The state is adjacent to Benue, Ebonyi, and Akwa-Ibom, and it also shares an international boundary with the Republic of Cameroon (Okedu et al., 2020).

Population and Sampling

The term "population" refers to the entirety of individuals, items, or observations that are the focus of a study, whereas a "sample" denotes a specific subset selected for analysis, which aids researchers in deriving meaningful conclusions about the larger group based on the sample's attributes (Simplilearn, 2021). The study involves school teachers and parents of students with ADHD in public secondary schools. A total of 28 secondary school teachers and 28 were selected using purposive and convenience sampling techniques. Purposive and convenience sampling are both non-probability sampling methods that enable researchers to selectively choose participants (Enago Academy, 2019). Purposeful sampling is particularly prevalent in qualitative research, as it facilitates the identification and selection of cases that provide rich information pertinent to the phenomenon of interest (Palinkas et al., 2015). On the other hand, convenience sampling is characterized by the selection of individuals based on their availability and ease of access to the researcher, rather than through a random selection process that ensures equal opportunity for all members of the population (JoHo, 2019). In terms of residential location, 53.6% of the respondents were residing in rural areas, whereas 46.4% were residing in urban areas. In terms of gender, 41.1% of the respondents were males, whereas 58.9% were females.

Data Collection

The data was collected using a questionnaire. The researchers received help from two postgraduate students to complete the data collection process. The questionnaire used for data collection is called the Teachers' and Parents' Perspectives on the Solutions to Challenges in the Career Transition of Students with ADHD Questionnaire (TPPSCCTSAQ). It is a 25-item scale, with response options ranging from Strongly Disagree (1) to Strongly Agree (5). This scale measures teachers' and parents' perspectives regarding solutions to challenges in the career transition of students with ADHD. Higher scores indicate a great extent of agreement to each item statement. Some examples of item statements in the questionnaire include: "Teachers should receive adequate training to support students with ADHD in career transitions.", and "Schools should offer workshops for parents on supporting career transitions for students with ADHD." The TPPSCCTSAQ has a good internal consistency reliability, with a Cronbach's alpha of .64 in the present research.

Data Analysis

Statistical analysis was conducted using Jeffreys' Amazing Statistics Program software (JASP), version 0.18.3. The software known as Jeffreys' Amazing Statistics Program (JASP), version 0.18.3, is named in honor of the Bayesian pioneer Sir Harold Jeffreys (Adam, 2023). This software allows researchers to utilize the advantages of the Bayesian framework for hypothesis testing and effective parameter estimation (Marsman & Wagenmakers, 2017). Descriptive statistics was used to summarize the sociodemographic data, while univariate analysis was used to analyse the research questions at a .05 significance level. Descriptive statistics are concerned with outlining the observable features of a dataset, whether it pertains to a population or a sample (Hillier, 2021). This branch of statistics encompasses various types of variables, including nominal, ordinal, interval, and ratio, as well as measures of frequency, central tendency, dispersion/variation, and position (Kaur, 2018). Univariate analysis focuses on examining a single variable to extract, define, summarize, and analyze the underlying patterns within the data (Khushi, 2021).

FINDINGS

Table 1. Teachers' and parents' overall mean perspectives regarding solutions to challenges in the career transition of students with ADHD

Group	Gender	Location	Mean	Std. Deviation	N
School teachers	Male respondents	Rural residents	4.49	.14	6
		Urban residents	4.32	.26	4
		Total	4.42	.20	10
	Female respondents	Rural residents	4.42	.12	6
		Urban residents	4.27	.22	12
		Total	4.32	.20	18
	Total	Rural residents	4.45	.13	12
		Urban residents	4.28	.22	16
		Total	4.35	.20	28

continued on following page

Table 1. Continued

Group	Gender	Location	Mean	Std. Deviation	N
Parents	Male respondents	Rural residents	4.31	.14	9
		Urban residents	4.24	.16	4
		Total	4.29	.14	13
	Female respondents	Rural residents	4.17	.19	9
		Urban residents	4.19	.17	6
		Total	4.18	.17	15
	Total	Rural residents	4.24	.18	18
		Urban residents	4.21	.16	10
		Total	4.23	.17	28
Total	Male respondents	Rural residents	4.38	.16	15
		Urban residents	4.28	.21	8
		Total	4.35	.18	23
	Female respondents	Rural residents	4.27	.20	15
		Urban residents	4.24	.20	18
		Total	4.25	.19	33
	Total	Rural residents	4.33	.19	30
		Urban residents	4.25	.20	26
		Total	4.29	.19	56

Table 1 shows that teachers in rural areas have a mean perspective score of 4.45 with a standard deviation of .13. Teachers in urban areas have a mean perspective score of 4.28 with a standard deviation of .22. The mean score for male teachers is 4.42 for rural and 4.32 for urban residents. The mean score for female teachers is 4.42 for rural and 4.27 for urban residents. The overall mean score for teachers is 4.35 with a standard deviation of .20. Parents in rural areas have a mean perspective score of 4.24 with a standard deviation of .18. Parents in urban areas have a mean perspective score of 4.21 with a standard deviation of .16. The mean score for male parents is 4.31 for rural and 4.24 for urban residents. The mean score for female parents is 4.17 for rural and 4.19 for urban residents. The overall mean score for parents is 4.23 with a standard deviation of .17. These results further imply that both teachers and parents have strong and positive perspectives regarding solutions to challenges in the career transition of students with ADHD.

Figure 2. Teachers' overall mean perspectives regarding solutions to challenges in the career transition of students with ADHD by gender and location

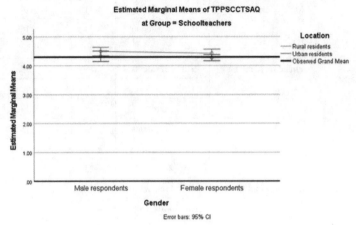

Figure 2 illustrates that both male and female teachers in rural areas have slightly higher mean scores compared to those in urban areas. The difference in mean scores between genders is minimal in perspectives regarding solutions to challenges in the career transition of students with ADHD.

Figure 3. Parents' overall mean perspectives regarding solutions to challenges in the career transition of students with ADHD by gender and location

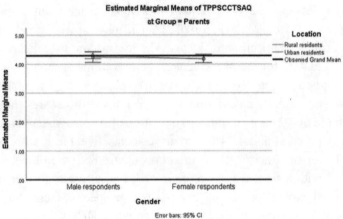

Figure 3 shows that male parents have slightly higher mean scores than female parents, with rural residents having slightly higher scores than urban residents in their perspectives regarding solutions to challenges in the career transition of students with ADHD.

Table 2. Univariate analysis of difference in the extent teachers and parents differ in their perspectives regarding solutions to challenges in the career transition of students with ADHD

Source	Type III Sum of Squares	Df	Mean Square	F	Sig.
Corrected Model	.545ᵃ	7	.078	2.393	.035
Intercept	906.755	1	906.755	27844.616	<.001
Group	.258	1	.258	7.912	.007
Gender	.073	1	.073	2.244	.14
Location	.103	1	.103	3.162	.08
Group * Gender	.004	1	.004	.112	.74
Group * Location	.057	1	.057	1.757	.19
Gender * Location	.009	1	.009	.279	.60
Group * Gender * Location	.005	1	.005	.159	.69
Error	1.563	48	.033		
Total	1033.768	56			
Corrected Total	2.109	55			

The univariate analysis in Table 2 assesses the extent of differences in perspectives between teachers and parents. The analysis shows a significant difference between teachers and parents (F=7.912, p=.007), indicating that teachers and parents have statistically different perspectives on the solutions to challenges in the career transition of students with ADHD. There are no significant differences based on gender (F=2.244, p=.14) or location (F=3.162, p=.08), nor are there significant interactions between group and gender, group and location, or gender and location in the extent of teachers' and parents' perspectives regarding solutions to challenges in the career transition of students with ADHD.

DISCUSSION

This study examined the perspectives of teachers and parents regarding solutions to challenges in the career transition of students with ADHD. Specifically, it explored the overall mean perspectives and differences based on gender and location.

The study found that both school teachers and parents of students with ADHD have strong and positive perspectives regarding solutions to challenges in the career transition of students with ADHD, with teachers typically showing more favorable perspectives than parents. It has been observed that parents and teachers interpret the symptoms of ADHD in distinct ways (Li et al., 2022). The unique perspectives of parents and teachers are crucial in the career transition process of students with ADHD. Dryer et al. (2012) observed a significant level of positive agreement between parents and professionals, including teachers, regarding the effectiveness of different treatment approaches for ADHD, which is consistent with our findings. In contrast, Bradshaw and Kamal (2013) highlighted a different finding, revealing that teachers possess limited knowledge about the disorder, which correlates with their understanding of necessary interventions. Bolinger et al. (2020) demonstrated that a teacher's knowledge of ADHD significantly influences their teaching practices, thereby impacting their capacity to provide essential support. Furthermore, it has been recognized that parents also play a vital role in the lives of their children with ADHD (Janssens et al., 2023). Nevertheless, Condo et al. (2022) noted that the level of parental involvement in the outcomes for students with ADHD is somewhat restricted, with mixed findings suggesting a positive correlation between parental engagement and academic performance. Although this does not specifically address career transitions, it emphasizes the considerable impact that parental involvement can have on the success of students with ADHD. Hosseinnia et al. (2024) emphasized that equipping parents and teachers with training and effective strategies to improve their awareness, attitudes, and practices can lead to a reduction in ADHD symptoms. Although teachers predominantly maintained a positive perspective on students with ADHD, they indicated a desire for robust interventions to help manage the challenges it creates (Mulholland et al., 2023). West et al. (2005) indicated that the awareness of ADHD treatment among teachers and parents is generally insufficient, with parents showing a significantly greater understanding than their teacher counterparts. This difference may stem from the informal dynamics present in parent-child relationships, as opposed to the formal relationships teachers have with their students. Bied et al. (2017) showed that both parents and teachers demonstrated moderate to good diagnostic accuracy regarding ADHD diagnoses. In this context, similar consensus will likely merge concerning solutions for career transition challenges for students with ADHD. Ghanizadeh et al. (2009) found that teachers exhibited similar beliefs concerning treatment and its advantages for students with ADHD; however, the authors contended that this uniformity in the teachers' views on the necessity and benefits of treatment suggests a deficiency in their understanding of ADHD.

Some explanations for our study's findings may stem from the fact that teachers undergo formal and professional training to support these students (Mohammed et al., 2023; Zentall & Javorsky, 2007; Brown, 2024), which facilitates the implementation of various solutions, leading to a more positive perspective on the career transition solutions for these students. Furthermore, teachers accumulate professional experience (Anderson et al., 2012) and encounter numerous students with ADHD throughout their careers, thereby enhancing their understanding of potential solutions and increasing their agreement on the efficacy of solutions in aiding career transition. In contrast, parents may lack comparable experience in this area. This is why Fabiano and Pyle (2019) advocated for parent training as a supportive intervention. Moreover, Shen et al. (2021) indicated that parent-teacher training positively influences the outcomes for students with ADHD. While rural teachers and parents tend to have slightly higher mean scores than their urban counterparts, these differences are not statistically significant. On the contrary, in an effort to analyze the views of teachers, parents, and other stakeholders on ADHD treatment, the findings from Bussing et al. (2012) suggested that while the interventions were perceived as both acceptable and valuable, there was no significant relationship with socio-demographic factors. Kyser et al. (2021) indicated that urban educational institutions tend to have a higher number of certified teachers who have undergone more integrated training programs, in contrast to rural schools, which have fewer teachers. Furthermore, schools in urban areas with limited resources often encounter additional challenges that complicate access to ADHD interventions (Shippen et al., 2022). There is a noted discrepancy in the reports of ADHD symptoms between parents and teachers, which may vary according to the socioeconomic status of a child (Lawson et al., 2017). The disparities in the teacher-parent ratio may contribute to the findings; had there been an equal distribution of teachers and parents, the outcomes of our study might reflect more favourable results for both groups. It is vital to appreciate the unique insights of families from various backgrounds in order to fully comprehend ethnic and racial views as well as to create ecologically suitable and family-centred interventions for family members diagnosed with ADHD (Paidipati et al., 2017). The difference in perspectives between teachers and parents highlights the need for collaborative approaches that consider both perspectives in developing proactive transition programs and policy-driven solutions to career transition challenges for students with ADHD. Establishing strong relationships between parents and teachers is often a complex endeavor, especially when it comes to creating interventions to address students' emotional, social, and behavioral difficulties (Gwernan-Jones et al., 2015). Dor and Shmuel-Nir (2023) emphasized that effective collaboration between teachers and parents is fundamental to the successful and consistent application of behavior-management programs in both home and academic contexts. Ongoing dialogue and cooperation between parents and teachers are vital. This engagement can encompass discussions regarding the student's strengths, the formulation of common goals, and the execution of cohesive strategies both at home and in the educational environment to foster the student's behavioral and academic success. Bracken (2022) recognizes that some students may feel disengaged or insufficiently challenged, and therefore advocates for the introduction of enrichment activities to sustain their interest. Such activities should correspond with the students' personal interests, which can enhance their motivation and focus. Furthermore, imparting self-management techniques to students with ADHD is of paramount importance. This includes approaches for managing frustration, such as employing Play-Doh to channel anger, coping with anxiety through deep breathing exercises and positive self-talk, and segmenting extensive tasks into smaller, achievable parts. In a Nigerian professional environment, individuals diagnosed with ADHD may find it advantageous to reveal their condition and request accommodations in accordance with protective legislation such as the Discrimination Against Persons with Disabilities (Prohibition) Act 2019 (Federal Republic of Nigeria, 2019). Employers can promote inclusivity by designing roles that cater to the distinct abilities and requirements of those with ADHD, including positions that emphasize interpersonal interactions or require dynamic activities. Fostering self-acceptance is of utmost importance. Interacting with peers who also experience ADHD, whether through online discussions or support groups, can help mitigate feelings of isolation and anxiety during the career transition process. These supportive communities encourage a sense of belonging and empowerment, leading to enhanced self-acceptance for individuals with ADHD. Characteristics such as impulsivity may correlate with heightened creativity, and numerous individuals with ADHD exhibit significant empathy (Martinig, 2023). Acknowledging and utilizing these strengths can be beneficial in professions that demand brainstorming, interpersonal abilities, or emotional intelligence, thereby transforming ADHD into a valuable asset in appropriate settings. Overall, it is essential to involve various stakeholders in order to address current challenges, reinforce existing support systems, and initiate new strategies aimed at improving career transition outcomes for students with ADHD within the Nigerian context.

CONCLUSIONS

The study demonstrated that both teachers and parents have strong and positive perspectives on the solutions to challenges in the career transition of students with ADHD, with teachers typically showing more favorable perspectives than parents. While rural respondents generally have slightly higher mean scores compared to their urban counterparts, these differences are not statistically significant. Thus, the study highlights the need for proactive strategies that consider the distinct perspectives of teachers and parents in combating the career transition challenges of students with ADHD. The significant difference between teachers and parents indicates a need for strategies that bridge these gaps to enhance parent-teacher collaboration in supporting the career transition of students with ADHD. Schools and policymakers should consider these differences when designing transition programs and support systems for students with ADHD, ensuring that both their teachers and parents are actively involved, and their perspectives are valued. Future research should explore strategies to bridge the differences in perspectives and enhance collaborative efforts among parents and teachers of students with ADHD.

REFERENCES

Adam, A.-K. (2023). The Impact of Work Culture and Job Satisfaction with Drivers: Total Effect Regression Test Using JASP. *Journal of Organizational Behavior Research, 8*(2–2023), Article 2–2023. DOI: 10.51847/uLuZQg6qAu

Adam, R. (2024, August 1). *10 Quantitative Research Advantages & Disadvantages- Helpful.* https://helpfull.com/blog/10-advantages-disadvantages-of-quantitative-research

Adewuya, A. O., & Famuyiwa, O. O. (2007). Attention deficit hyperactivity disorder among Nigerian primary school children: Prevalence and co-morbid conditions. *European Child & Adolescent Psychiatry*, 16(1), 10–15. DOI: 10.1007/s00787-006-0569-9 PMID: 17136303

Alqahtani, M. M. J. (2017). How do parents view psychological assessment and intervention for their children with ADHD in Saudi Arabia? *Asia Pacific Journal of Counselling and Psychotherapy*, 8(1), 41–52. DOI: 10.1080/21507686.2016.1260612

Anderson, D. L., Watt, S. E., Noble, W., & Shanley, D. C. (2012). Knowledge of attention deficit hyperactivity disorder (ADHD) and attitudes toward teaching children with ADHD: THE role of teaching experience. *Psychology in the Schools*, 49(6), 511–525. DOI: 10.1002/pits.21617

Australasian ADHD Professionals Association. (2022, July 30). *Transition ADHD patient care- Australian ADHD Clinical Practice Guideline.* https://adhdguideline.aadpa.com.au/treatment-and-support/transitions/

Baweja, R., Soutullo, C. A., & Waxmonsky, J. G. (2021). Review of barriers and interventions to promote treatment engagement for pediatric attention deficit hyperactivity disorder care. *World Journal of Psychiatry*, 11(12), 1206–1227. DOI: 10.5498/wjp.v11.i12.1206 PMID: 35070771

Bied, A., Biederman, J., & Faraone, S. (2017). Parent-based diagnosis of ADHD is as accurate as a teacher-based diagnosis of ADHD. *Postgraduate Medicine*, 129(3), 375–381. DOI: 10.1080/00325481.2017.1288064 PMID: 28271921

Biemer, P. P. (2010). Total Survey Error: Design, Implementation, and Evaluation. *Public Opinion Quarterly*, 74(5), 817–848. DOI: 10.1093/poq/nfq058

Bolinger, S. J., Mucherah, D. W., & Markelz, D. A. M. (2020). Teacher Knowledge of Attention-Deficit/Hyperactivity Disorder and Classroom Management. *The Journal of Special Education Apprenticeship*, 9(1). Advance online publication. DOI: 10.58729/2167-3454.1098

Bracken, A. (2022, March 18). *Parenting Changed My Perspective on "ADHD."* Mad In America. https://www.madinamerica.com/2022/03/parenting-changed-my-perspective-on-adhd/

Bradshaw, L., & Kamal, M. (2013). Teacher knowledge, training and acceptance of students with ADHD in their classrooms: Qatar case study. *Near and Middle Eastern Journal of Research in Education, 2013*, 5. DOI: 10.5339/nmejre.2013.5

Brown, R. (2024). Effects of Professional Development on Secondary School Teachers' Self-Efficacy, Knowledge, and Attitudes About ADHD. *Theses and Dissertations*. https://scholarsarchive.byu.edu/etd/10412

Bussing, R., Koro-Ljungberg, M., Noguchi, K., Mason, D., Mayerson, G., & Garvan, C. W. (2012). Willingness to use ADHD treatments: A mixed methods study of perceptions by adolescents, parents, health professionals and teachers. *Social Science & Medicine*, 74(1), 92–100. DOI: 10.1016/j.socscimed.2011.10.009 PMID: 22133584

Centre for ADHD Awareness Canada. (2023, May 24). *Finding a Career You Love When You Have ADHD - CADDAC*. Https://Caddac.Ca/. https://caddac.ca/finding-a-career-you-love-when-you-have-adhd/

Chowdhury, S. A. (2024). Developing a Sustainable Education Protocol for Children with Attention Deficit Hyperactivity Disorder (adhd) in the Context of Developing Country. *Journal of Science of Learning and Innovations*, 1(1), 90–106. https://brill.com/view/journals/jsli/1/1/article-p90_006.xml. DOI: 10.1163/29497736-bja00005

Condo, J. S., Chan, E. S. M., & Kofler, M. J. (2022). Examining the Effects of ADHD Symptoms and Parental Involvement on Children's Academic Achievement. *Research in Developmental Disabilities*, 122, 104156. DOI: 10.1016/j.ridd.2021.104156 PMID: 35007980

Crook, T., & McDowall, A. (2023). Paradoxical career strengths and successes of ADHD adults: An evolving narrative. *Journal of Work-Applied Management*, 16(1), 112–126. DOI: 10.1108/JWAM-05-2023-0048

Dickson, H. (2022, April 1). *Tailoring Career Development Practices for Clients with ADHD*. https://www.ncda.org/aws/NCDA/pt/sd/news_article/430859/_PARENT/CC_layout_details/false

Dipeolu, A., Sniatecki, J. L., & Lalin, M. (2011, October 1). Career Development Keys to Post-School Transition Success for Students with ADHD. *Career Convergence Web Magazine*.

Dor, A., & Shmuel-Nir, O. (2023). Teachers as a Source of Support: Perceptions of Parents of Children With ADHD During COVID-19 Distance Learning. *Educational Practice and Theory*, 45(2), 5–18. DOI: 10.7459/ept/45.2.02

Dryer, R., Kiernan, M. J., & Tyson, G. A. (2012). Parental and Professional Beliefs on the Treatment and Management of ADHD. *Journal of Attention Disorders*, 16(5), 398–405. DOI: 10.1177/1087054710392540 PMID: 21490177

Enago Academy. E. (2019, March 21). The Importance of Sampling Methods in Research Design. *Enago Academy*. https://www.enago.com/academy/the-importance-of-sampling-methods-in-research-design/

Enlightened Minds. (2024). ADHD in the Workplace: Navigating Challenges In Your Career. https://enlightenedminds.co.uk/adhd-in-the-workplace-navigating-challenges-in-your-career/

Fabiano, G. A., & Pyle, K. (2019). Best Practices in School Mental Health for Attention-Deficit/Hyperactivity Disorder: A Framework for Intervention. *School Mental Health*, 11(1), 72–91. DOI: 10.1007/s12310-018-9267-2

Fabiano, G. A., Schatz, N. K., Aloe, A. M., Pelham, W. E.Jr, Smyth, A. C., Zhao, X., Merrill, B. M., Macphee, F., Ramos, M., Hong, N., Altszuler, A., Ward, L., Rodgers, D. B., Liu, Z., Karatoprak Ersen, R., & Coxe, S. (2021). Comprehensive Meta-Analysis of Attention-Deficit/Hyperactivity Disorder Psychosocial Treatments Investigated Within Between Group Studies. *Review of Educational Research*, 91(5), 718–760. DOI: 10.3102/00346543211025092

Fabiano, G. A., Schatz, N. K., Lupas, K., Gordon, C., Hayes, T., Tower, D., Soto, T. S., Macphee, F., Pelham, W. E.Jr, & Hulme, K. (2021). A school-based parenting program for children with attention-deficit/hyperactivity disorder: Impact on paternal caregivers. *Journal of School Psychology*, 86, 133–150. DOI: 10.1016/j.jsp.2021.04.002 PMID: 34051909

Federal Republic of Nigeria. (2019). Discrimination Against Persons with Disabilities (Prohibition) Act 2019. https://archive.gazettes.africa/archive/ng/2019/ng-government-gazette-supplement-dated-2019-01-21-no-10.pdf

Fredrickson, B. L. (2001). The Role of Positive Emotions in Positive Psychology. *The American Psychologist*, 56(3), 218–226. DOI: 10.1037/0003-066X.56.3.218 PMID: 11315248

Geoffjordan. (2019, October 30). Positivist and Constructivist Paradigms. *What Do You Think You're Doing?* https://applingtesol.wordpress.com/2019/10/30/positivist-and-constructivist-paradigms/

Ghanizadeh, A., Fallahi, M., & Akhondzadeh, S. (2009). Disclosure of attention deficit hyperactivity disorder and its effect on rejection of students by teachers. *Iranian Journal of Medical Sciences*, 34(4), 259–264.

Group, A. P. M. (2020, December 17). *How to get and keep a job if you're living with ADHD | Expert Advice*. APM AU. https://apm.net.au/job-seekers/resources/how-to-get-and-keep-a-job-if-you-re-living-with-ad

Gwernan-Jones, R., Moore, D. A., Garside, R., Richardson, M., Thompson-Coon, J., Rogers, M., Cooper, P., Stein, K., & Ford, T. (2015). ADHD, parent perspectives and parent–teacher relationships: Grounds for conflict. *British Journal of Special Education*, 42(3), 279–300. DOI: 10.1111/1467-8578.12087

Harappa. (2021, September 27). Survey Research: Types And Examples. *Harappa*. https://harappa.education/harappa-diaries/survey-research

Hefferon, K., & Boniwell, I. (2011). *Positive psychology: Theory, research and applications* (Vol. 1). McGraw-Hill, Open Univ. Press.

Hillier, W. (2021, April 13). *Descriptive vs Inferential Statistics Explained*. https://careerfoundry.com/en/blog/data-analytics/inferential-vs-descriptive-statistics/

Ivey, A. G. (2022, July 11). *Common Workplace ADHD Problems and How to Fix Them*. WebMD. https://www.webmd.com/add-adhd/common-adhd-workplace-problems

Janssens, A., Blake, S., Eke, H., Price, A., & Ford, T. (2023). Parenting roles for young people with attention-deficit/hyperactivity disorder transitioning to adult services. *Developmental Medicine and Child Neurology*, 65(1), 136–144. DOI: 10.1111/dmcn.15320 PMID: 35723621

JoHo. (2019). *What is a convenience sample? | WorldSupporter* [Development Organisation]. WorldSupporter. Retrieved September 24, 2024, from https://www.worldsupporter.org/en/tip/66638-what-convenience-sample

Kauffman, J. M., Ahrbeck, B., Anastasiou, D., Badar, J., Crockett, J. B., Felder, M., Hallahan, D. P., Hornby, G., Lopes, J., Pullen, P. C., & Smith, C. R. (2023). Parents' and Educators' Perspectives on Inclusion of Students with Disabilities. In *Research for Inclusive Quality Education* (pp. 205–217). Springer., DOI: 10.1007/978-981-16-5908-9_16

Kaur, P., Stoltzfus, J., & Yellapu, V. (2018). Descriptive statistics. *International Journal of Academic Medicine*, 4(1), 60. DOI: 10.4103/IJAM.IJAM_7_18

Keyter, A. (2016, October 13). Research Methods: Positivism v.s. Post-positivism. *RePrac | Resource Practitioners*. https://reprac.co.nz/research-methods-positivism-v-s-post-positivism/

Khushi. (2021, April 19). Exploratory Analysis: Using Univariate, Bivariate, & Multivariate Analysis Techniques. *Analytics Vidhya*. https://www.analyticsvidhya.com/blog/2021/04/exploratory-analysis-using-univariate-bivariate-and-multivariate-analysis-techniques/

Kirana. (2021, April 19). *Positivism: Dominant Paradigm in Accounting and Business Research*. FEB UGM. https://feb.ugm.ac.id/en/news/3228-positivism-dominant-paradigm-in-accounting-and-business-research

Kyser, C., Youngs, S., Nelson, A., & Monaghan, T. (2021). Transitioning From High School Students to Aspiring Future Rural Educators: Promising Practices to Fuel the Rural Teacher Pipeline. *Journal of Educational Research and Innovation*, 9(1). https://digscholarship.unco.edu/jeri/vol9/iss1/5

Lawson, G. M., Nissley-Tsiopinis, J., Nahmias, A., McConaughy, S. H., & Eiraldi, R. (2017). Do Parent and Teacher Report of ADHD Symptoms in Children Differ by SES and Racial Status? *Journal of Psychopathology and Behavioral Assessment*, 39(3), 426–440. DOI: 10.1007/s10862-017-9591-0

Li, H.-H., Wang, T.-T., Dong, H.-Y., Liu, Y.-Q., & Jia, F.-Y. (2022). Screening of ADHD symptoms in primary school students and investigation of parental awareness of ADHD and its influencing factors: A cross-sectional study. *Frontiers in Psychology*, 13, 1070848. DOI: 10.3389/fpsyg.2022.1070848 PMID: 36619017

Magill, C. (2024, May 24). ADHD Coach Explains—Why We Job Hop (and what to do about it). *It's ADHD Friendly*. https://itsadhdfriendly.com/adhd-job-hopping/

Maree, J. G., & Warnock, K. (2023). Teachers' perceptions of how attention-deficit/hyperactivity disorder may influence learners' career choices. *South African Journal of Higher Education*, 37(4), 205–224. DOI: 10.20853/37-4-5732

Marsman, M., & Wagenmakers, E.-J. (2017). Bayesian benefits with JASP. *European Journal of Developmental Psychology*, 14(5), 545–555. DOI: 10.1080/17405629.2016.1259614

Martinig, E. (2023, January 16). *How a career change at 30 and adult ADHD led me to my passion*. The Career Changers. https://thecareerchangers.com/adult-adhd/

Mesfin, W., & Habtamu, K. (2024). Challenges and coping mechanisms of parents of children with attention deficit hyperactivity disorder in Addis Ababa, Ethiopia: A qualitative study. *BMC Psychology*, 12(1), 354. DOI: 10.1186/s40359-024-01828-0 PMID: 38886856

Mohammed, M., Bella-Awusah, T., Adedokun, B., Lagunju, I., & Ani, C. (2023). Effectiveness of a training programme on the knowledge and perception of Attention-Deficit Hyperactivity Disorder among primary school teachers in Kano, Nigeria. *International Journal of Mental Health*, •••, 1–15. DOI: 10.1080/00207411.2023.2253397

Moore, D. A., Russell, A. E., Arnell, S., & Ford, T. J. (2017). Educators' experiences of managing students with ADHD: A qualitative study. *Child: Care, Health and Development*, 43(4), 489–498. DOI: 10.1111/cch.12448 PMID: 28233330

Mulholland, S., Cumming, T. M., & Lee, J. (2023). Accurately Assessing Teacher ADHD-Specific Attitudes Using the Scale for ADHD-Specific Attitudes. *Journal of Attention Disorders*, 27(5), 554–568. DOI: 10.1177/10870547231153938 PMID: 36843350

Nadeau, K. (2005). Career choices and workplace challenges for individuals with ADHD. *Journal of Clinical Psychology*, 61(5), 549–563. DOI: 10.1002/jclp.20119 PMID: 15723424

Ndukuba, A. C., Ibekwe, R. C., Odinka, P. C., Muomah, R. C., Igwe, M. N., Obindo, J. T., & Omigbodun, O. (2015). Symptoms of Attention Deficit Hyperactivity Disorder (ADHD) Among Rural Primary School Children in Southeastern Nigeria: Comparison of School and Home Settings. *Nigerian Journal of Paediatrics*, 42(4), 329–334. DOI: 10.4314/njp.v42i4.9

Ojionuka, A. N. (2016). *Nigerian Educators' Attention-Deficit Hyperactivity Disorder Knowledge and Classroom Behavior Management Practices*. (Doctoral Dissertation, Walden University). https://scholarworks.waldenu.edu/dissertations/2224

Okedu, K. E., Uhunmwangho, R., & Odje, M. (2020). Harnessing the potential of small hydropower in Cross River state of Southern Nigeria. *Sustainable Energy Technologies and Assessments*, 37, 100617. DOI: 10.1016/j.seta.2019.100617

Olsen, H. B., & Turits, M. (2022, December 12). *The silent struggles of workers with ADHD*. https://www.bbc.com/worklife/article/20221209-the-silent-struggles-of-workers-with-adhd

Paidipati, C. P., Brawner, B., Eiraldi, R., & Deatrick, J. A. (2017). Parent and Family Processes Related to ADHD Management in Ethnically Diverse Youth. *Journal of the American Psychiatric Nurses Association*, 23(2), 90–112. DOI: 10.1177/1078390316687023 PMID: 28076687

Palinkas, L. A., Horwitz, S. M., Green, C. A., Wisdom, J. P., Duan, N., & Hoagwood, K. (2015). Purposeful sampling for qualitative data collection and analysis in mixed method implementation research. *Administration and Policy in Mental Health*, 42(5), 533–544. DOI: 10.1007/s10488-013-0528-y PMID: 24193818

Parker, D. R., & Benedict, K. B. (2002). Assessment and Intervention: Promoting Successful Transitions for College Students with ADHD. *Assessment for Effective Intervention*, 27(3), 3–24. DOI: 10.1177/073724770202700302

Price, A., Newlove-Delgado, T., Eke, H., Paul, M., Young, S., Ford, T., & Janssens, A. (2019). In transition with ADHD: The role of information, in facilitating or impeding young people's transition into adult services. *BMC Psychiatry*, 19(1), 404. DOI: 10.1186/s12888-019-2284-3 PMID: 31847827

Rapson, S. (2021, August 26). *Does ADHD Affect Your Career? Four strategies to navigate job transitions*. Unconventional Org. https://www.unconventionalorganisation.com/post/does-adhd-affect-your-career-four-strategies-to-navigate-job-transitions

Rashidian, C. (2024, April 30). *Navigating Career Transitions with ADHD: Insights and Strategies*. https://www.linkedin.com/pulse/navigating-career-transitions-adhd-insights-rashidian-pcac-pcc-zehyc

Shen, L., Wang, C., Tian, Y., Chen, J., Wang, Y., & Yu, G. (2021). Effects of Parent-Teacher Training on Academic Performance and Parental Anxiety in School-Aged Children With Attention-Deficit/Hyperactivity Disorder: A Cluster Randomized Controlled Trial in Shanghai, China. *Frontiers in Psychology*, 12, 733450. DOI: 10.3389/fpsyg.2021.733450 PMID: 34955960

Shippen, N., Horn, S. R., Triece, P., Chronis-Tuscano, A., & Meinzer, M. C. (2022). Understanding ADHD in Black Adolescents in Urban Schools: A Qualitative Examination of Factors that Influence ADHD Presentation, Coping Strategies, and Access to Care. *Evidence-Based Practice in Child and Adolescent Mental Health*, 7(2), 213–229. DOI: 10.1080/23794925.2021.2013140 PMID: 35602172

Simplilearn. (2021, July 27). *Difference Between Population And Sample*. Simplilearn.Com. https://www.simplilearn.com/tutorials/machine-learning-tutorial/population-vs-sample

Smith, M. (2024, September 25). *Tips for Managing Adult ADHD*. HelpGuide.org. https://www.helpguide.org/mental-health/adhd/managing-adult-adhd

Song, Y., Mu, F., Zhang, J., & Fu, M. (2022). The Relationships Between Career-Related Emotional Support From Parents and Teachers and Career Adaptability. *Frontiers in Psychology*, 13, 823333. DOI: 10.3389/fpsyg.2022.823333 PMID: 36619048

Tang, K., Hill, E., Pellicano, E., Thompson, C., & Myers, B. (2024). Barriers to and enablers of the transition from child and adolescent to adult mental health services for autistic young people and/or those with attention deficit hyperactivity disorder: Protocol for a scoping review. *BMJ Open*, 14(8), e083373. DOI: 10.1136/bmjopen-2023-083373 PMID: 39153772

Tartakovsky, M. M. S. (2012). Experts Share Solutions to Their ADHD Obstacles [Coach Training and ADHD Education]. *ADDCA Blog*. https://addca.com/adhd-coach-training/ADHD-Blog-Details/experts_share_solutions_to_their_adhd_obstacles/

Testbook. (2024, January 6). *Survey Method of Research | Meaning & Classification: UPSC Notes*. Testbook. https://testbook.com/ias-preparation/survey-method-of-research

Trochim, W. M. K. (2024). *Types of Surveys*. https://conjointly.com/kb/types-of-surveys/

Twanna, C. (2024, July 1). *Thriving With ADHD: Career Coaching For Black Women Leaders*. https://twannacarter.com/thrive-with-adhd-career-coaching-for-black-women/

Umar, M. U., Obindo, J. T., & Omigbodun, O. O. (2018). Prevalence and Correlates of ADHD Among Adolescent Students in Nigeria. *Journal of Attention Disorders*, 22(2), 116–126. DOI: 10.1177/1087054715594456 PMID: 26220786

Verheul, I., Block, J., Burmeister-Lamp, K., Thurik, R., Tiemeier, H., & Turturea, R. (2015). ADHD-like behavior and entrepreneurial intentions. *Small Business Economics*, 45(1), 85–101. DOI: 10.1007/s11187-015-9642-4

Watson, S., Bonvissuto, D., Schmidt, N., & Gopal, A. (2023, December 26). *ADHD in the Workplace*. WebMD. https://www.webmd.com/add-adhd/adhd-in-the-workplace

West, J., Taylor, M., Houghton, S., & Hudyma, S. (2005). A Comparison of Teachers' and Parents' Knowledge and Beliefs About Attention-Deficit/Hyperactivity Disorder(ADHD). *School Psychology International*, 26(2), 192–208. DOI: 10.1177/0143034305052913

Young, S., Murphy, C. M., & Coghill, D. (2011). Avoiding the "twilight zone": Recommendations for the transition of services from adolescence to adulthood for young people with ADHD. *BMC Psychiatry*, 11(1), 174. DOI: 10.1186/1471-244X-11-174 PMID: 22051192

Zentall, S. S., & Javorsky, J. (2007). Professional Development for Teachers of Students with ADHD and Characteristics of ADHD. *Behavioral Disorders*, 32(2), 78–93. DOI: 10.1177/019874290703200202

ADDITIONAL READINGS

Anthony, D. R., Gordon, S., Gucciardi, D. F., & Dawson, B. (2018). Adapting a behavioral coaching framework for mental toughness development. *Journal of Sport Psychology in Action*, 9(1), 32–50. DOI: 10.1080/21520704.2017.1323058

Armstrong, T. (2015). The myth of the normal brain: Embracing neurodiversity. *AMA Journal of Ethics*, 17(4), 348–352. DOI: 10.1001/journalofethics.2015.17.4.msoc1-1504 PMID: 25901703

Austin, R. D., & Pisano, G. P. (2017). Neurodiversity as a competitive advantage. *Harvard Business Review*, 95(3), 96–103.

Backman, C., Chartrand, J., Crick, M., Devey Burry, R., Dingwall, O., & Shea, B. (2021). Effectiveness of person-and family-centred care transition interventions on patient-oriented outcomes: A systematic review. *Nursing Open*, 8(2), 721–754. DOI: 10.1002/nop2.677 PMID: 33570290

Baron-Cohen, S. (2017). Editorial Perspective: Neurodiversity–a revolutionary concept for autism and psychiatry. *Journal of Child Psychology and Psychiatry, and Allied Disciplines*, 58(6), 744–747. DOI: 10.1111/jcpp.12703 PMID: 28524462

Boeckmans, L. (2021). *Spotlighting strengths: An exploration of character strengths interventions and the impact for young people with ADHD* (Doctoral dissertation, University of Southampton).

Cammisuli, D. M., & Castelnuovo, G. (2023). Neuroscience-based psychotherapy: A position paper. *Frontiers in Psychology*, 14, 1101044. DOI: 10.3389/fpsyg.2023.1101044 PMID: 36860785

Carrick, H., & Randle-Phillips, C. (2018). Solution-focused approaches in the context of people with intellectual disabilities: A critical review. *Journal of Mental Health Research in Intellectual Disabilities*, 11(1), 30–53. DOI: 10.1080/19315864.2017.1390711

Chang, G. (2020). Maternal substance use: Consequences, identification, and interventions. *Alcohol Research : Current Reviews*, 40(2), arcr.v40.2.06. DOI: 10.35946/arcr.v40.2.06 PMID: 32612898

Chung, S., Williams, A., Owens, E., McBurnett, K., Hinshaw, S. P., & Pfiffner, L. J. (2024). Parental cognitions, treatment engagement, and child outcomes of ADHD behavioral treatment among Asian American families. *Research on Child and Adolescent Psychopathology*, 52(3), 325–337. DOI: 10.1007/s10802-023-01139-9 PMID: 37861939

Clarke, A. T., Marshall, S. A., Mautone, J. A., Soffer, S. L., Jones, H. A., Costigan, T. E., Patterson, A., Jawad, A. F., & Power, T. J. (2015). Parent attendance and homework adherence predict response to a family–school intervention for children with ADHD. *Journal of Clinical Child and Adolescent Psychology*, 44(1), 58–67. DOI: 10.1080/15374416.2013.794697 PMID: 23688140

Deek, H., Hamilton, S., Brown, N., Inglis, S. C., Digiacomo, M., Newton, P. J., Noureddine, S., MacDonald, P. S., & Davidson, P. M.FAMILY Project Investigators. (2016). Family-centered approaches to healthcare interventions in chronic diseases in adults: A quantitative systematic review. *Journal of Advanced Nursing*, 72(5), 968–979. DOI: 10.1111/jan.12885 PMID: 26751971

Ding, X., Zhu, L., Zhang, R., Wang, L., Wang, T. T., & Latour, J. M. (2019). Effects of family-centred care interventions on preterm infants and parents in neonatal intensive care units: A systematic review and meta-analysis of randomised controlled trials. *Australian Critical Care*, 32(1), 63–75. DOI: 10.1016/j.aucc.2018.10.007 PMID: 30554939

DuPaul, G. J., Kern, L., Belk, G., Custer, B., Daffner, M., Hatfield, A., & Peek, D. (2018). Face-to-face versus online behavioral parent training for young children at risk for ADHD: treatment engagement and outcomes. *Journal of Clinical Child & Adolescent Psychology, 47*(sup1), S369-S383.

Dwyer, P. (2022). The neurodiversity approach (es): What are they and what do they mean for researchers? *Human Development*, 66(2), 73–92. DOI: 10.1159/000523723 PMID: 36158596

Espinet, S. D., Motz, M., Jeong, J. J., Jenkins, J. M., & Pepler, D. (2016). 'Breaking the Cycle' of maternal substance use through relationships: A comparison of integrated approaches. *Addiction Research and Theory*, 24(5), 375–388. DOI: 10.3109/16066359.2016.1140148

Field, T. A., Jones, L. K., & Russell-Chapin, L. A. (Eds.). (2017). *Neurocounseling: Brain-based clinical approaches*. John Wiley & Sons. DOI: 10.1002/9781119375487

Friedman, L. M., Dvorsky, M. R., McBurnett, K., & Pfiffner, L. J. (2020). Do parents' ADHD symptoms affect treatment for their children? The impact of parental ADHD on adherence to behavioral parent training for childhood ADHD. *Journal of Abnormal Child Psychology*, 48(11), 1425–1437. DOI: 10.1007/s10802-020-00672-1 PMID: 32813210

Goodall, J. (2017). *Narrowing the achievement gap: Parental engagement with children's learning*. Routledge. DOI: 10.4324/9781315672465

Goodall, J., & Montgomery, C. (2023). Parental involvement to parental engagement: A continuum. *Mapping the Field*, 158-169.

Govindan, P. (2024). *Unlocking Potential: A Strength-Based Curriculum for Understanding ADHD in the Home-School Partnership* (Doctoral dissertation, California State University, Northridge).

Hasan, A. (2024). 6000 Parental engagement in parent training ADHD behavior program.

Hetzel, A. (2024). How Positive Deviance in High-Achieving Adults with ADHD can inform Strength-Based Coaching and Life Design to Complement Traditional ADHD Management (extended version). *Available at SSRN 4986555*. DOI: 10.2139/ssrn.4985832

Hinojosa, M. S., Hinojosa, R., & Nguyen, J. (2020). Shared decision making and treatment for minority children with ADHD. *Journal of Transcultural Nursing*, 31(2), 135–143. DOI: 10.1177/1043659619853021 PMID: 31156057

Hser, Y. I., Lanza, H. I., Li, L., Kahn, E., Evans, E., & Schulte, M. (2015). Maternal mental health and children's internalizing and externalizing behaviors: Beyond maternal substance use disorders. *Journal of Child and Family Studies*, 24(3), 638–648. DOI: 10.1007/s10826-013-9874-3 PMID: 25750503

Jarlenski, M., Krans, E. E., Chen, Q., Rothenberger, S. D., Cartus, A., Zivin, K., & Bodnar, L. M. (2020). Substance use disorders and risk of severe maternal morbidity in the United States. *Drug and Alcohol Dependence*, 216, 108236. DOI: 10.1016/j.drugalcdep.2020.108236 PMID: 32846369

Karakaya, D., & Özgür, G. (2019). Effect of a solution-focused approach on self-efficacy and self-esteem in Turkish adolescents with attention-deficit/hyperactivity disorder. *Journal of Psychosocial Nursing and Mental Health Services*, 57(11), 45–55. DOI: 10.3928/02793695-20190708-01 PMID: 31305949

Lipstein, E. A., Lindly, O. J., Anixt, J. S., Britto, M. T., & Zuckerman, K. E. (2016). Shared decision making in the care of children with developmental and behavioral disorders. *Maternal and Child Health Journal*, 20(3), 665–673. DOI: 10.1007/s10995-015-1866-z PMID: 26518006

Matanova, V., Kostova, Z., & Kolev, M. (2018). Brain-based treatment—A new approach or a well-forgotten old one? *Journal of Evaluation in Clinical Practice*, 24(4), 859–863. DOI: 10.1111/jep.12915 PMID: 29691958

Mayer, S. E., Kalil, A., Oreopoulos, P., & Gallegos, S. (2015). Using behavioral insights to increase parental engagement. *The Journal of Human Resources*, 5(4), 4.

McCarthy, E., & Guerin, S. (2022). Family-centered care in early intervention: A systematic review of the processes and outcomes of family-centered care and impacting factors. *Child: Care, Health and Development*, 48(1), 1–32. DOI: 10.1111/cch.12901 PMID: 34324725

McGovern, R., Bogowicz, P., Meader, N., Kaner, E., Alderson, H., Craig, D., Geijer-Simpson, E., Jackson, K., Muir, C., Salonen, D., Smart, D., & Newham, J. J. (2023). The association between maternal and paternal substance use and child substance use, internalizing and externalizing problems: A systematic review and meta-analysis. *Addiction (Abingdon, England)*, 118(5), 804–818. DOI: 10.1111/add.16127 PMID: 36607011

McQueen, K. A., Murphy-Oikonen, J., & Desaulniers, L. (2015). Maternal substance uses and neonatal abstinence syndrome: A descriptive study. *Maternal and Child Health Journal*, 19(8), 1756–1765. DOI: 10.1007/s10995-015-1689-y PMID: 25656717

Miller, C. L., Jelinkova, K., Charabin, E. C., & Climie, E. A. (2024). Parent and Child-Reported Strengths of Children With ADHD. *Canadian Journal of School Psychology*, 39(1), 3–28. DOI: 10.1177/08295735231225261

Miller, R. (2016). Neuro-education: Integrating brain-based psychoeducation into clinical practice. *Journal of Mental Health Counseling*, 38(2), 103–115. DOI: 10.17744/mehc.38.2.02

Mitchell, M. L., Coyer, F., Kean, S., Stone, R., Murfield, J., & Dwan, T. (2016). Patient, family-centred care interventions within the adult ICU setting: An integrative review. *Australian Critical Care*, 29(4), 179–193. DOI: 10.1016/j.aucc.2016.08.002 PMID: 27592540

Moss, R. A. (2014). Brain-based views on psychotherapy integration. *New Therapist*, 6.

Moss, R. A. (2015). Psychotherapy integration from a brain-based perspective: Clinical biopsychology. In *Continuing education course offered through Health Forum Online. Available from:*www. healthforumonline. com

Nelson, T. S. (2018). *Solution-focused brief therapy with families*. Routledge. DOI: 10.4324/9781351011778

Ogg, J. A., Rogers, M. A., & Volpe, R. J. (2020). Child ADHD symptoms and parent involvement in education. *Journal of Child and Family Studies*, 29(12), 3586–3595. DOI: 10.1007/s10826-020-01834-x

Phiri, P. G., Chan, C. W., & Wong, C. L. (2020). The scope of family-centered care practices, and the facilitators and barriers to implementation of family-centered care for hospitalized children and their families in developing countries: An integrative review. *Journal of Pediatric Nursing*, 55, 10–28. DOI: 10.1016/j.pedn.2020.05.018 PMID: 32629368

Ratiu, L., David, O. A., & Baban, A. (2016). Developing managerial skills through coaching: Efficacy of a cognitive-behavioral coaching program. *Journal of Rational-Emotive & Cognitive-Behavior Therapy*, 34(4), 244–266. DOI: 10.1007/s10942-016-0256-9

Rosqvist, H. B., Chown, N., & Stenning, A. (2020). *Neurodiversity studies*. Routledge. DOI: 10.4324/9780429322297

Ruisch, I. H., Dietrich, A., Glennon, J. C., Buitelaar, J. K., & Hoekstra, P. J. (2018). Maternal substance use during pregnancy and offspring conduct problems: A meta-analysis. *Neuroscience and Biobehavioral Reviews*, 84, 325–336. DOI: 10.1016/j.neubiorev.2017.08.014 PMID: 28847489

Schrevel, S. J., Dedding, C., & Broerse, J. E. (2016). Why do adults with ADHD choose strength-based coaching over public mental health care? A qualitative case study from the Netherlands. *SAGE Open*, 6(3), 2158244016662498. DOI: 10.1177/2158244016662498

Spencer, A. E., Sikov, J., Loubeau, J. K., Zolli, N., Baul, T., Rabin, M., Hasan, S., Rosen, K., Buonocore, O., Lejeune, J., Dayal, R., Fortuna, L., Borba, C., & Silverstein, M. (2021). Six stages of engagement in ADHD treatment described by diverse, urban parents. *Pediatrics*, 148(4), e2021051261. DOI: 10.1542/peds.2021-051261 PMID: 34531290

Valentine, K. D., Lipstein, E. A., Vo, H., Cosenza, C., Barry, M. J., & Sepucha, K. (2022). Pediatric caregiver version of the shared decision-making process scale: Validity and reliability for ADHD treatment decisions. *Academic Pediatrics*, 22(8), 1503–1509. DOI: 10.1016/j.acap.2022.07.014 PMID: 35907446

Walker, N. (2014). Neurodiversity: Some basic terms & definitions.

Walter, J. K., Hwang, J., & Fiks, A. G. (2018). Pragmatic strategies for shared decision-making. *Pediatrics*, 142(Supplement_3), S157–S162. DOI: 10.1542/peds.2018-0516F PMID: 30385622

Waters, A. C., & Mayberg, H. S. (2017). Brain-based biomarkers for the treatment of depression: Evolution of an idea. *Journal of the International Neuropsychological Society*, 23(9-10), 870–880. DOI: 10.1017/S1355617717000881 PMID: 29198278

KEY TERMS AND DEFINITIONS

Behavioral Coaching: An organized methodology designed to assist individuals in fostering positive behaviors, skills, and attitudes essential for accomplishing their personal or professional objectives. Coaches engage with clients to identify particular behaviors that require enhancement, establish explicit goals, and formulate actionable plans for transformation. This coaching approach prioritizes the cultivation of self-awareness, accountability, and self-regulation, utilizing strategies such as feedback, reinforcement, and goal-setting. It is often applied in contexts such as leadership training, performance improvement, career development, and lifestyle adjustments. The coach provides essential guidance, support, and motivation, aiding clients in overcoming challenges and enhancing their confidence in achieving their desired results. The primary objective is to empower individuals to effectuate sustainable behavioral changes that contribute to personal growth and achievement.

Brain-Based Psychotherapeutic Interventions: Represent a category of therapeutic strategies that merge insights from brain functioning, neurobiology, and the mind-body relationship to effectively address mental health concerns. These interventions are based on a thorough understanding of how the brain manages emotions, stress, trauma, and behavioral patterns. Various techniques may be employed, including mindfulness practices, neurofeedback, Eye Movement Desensitization and Reprocessing (EMDR), and cognitive-behavioral approaches, all aimed at regulating the nervous system and fostering neuroplasticity. The ultimate aim is to support clients in developing healthier emotional responses, enhancing their resilience, and facilitating positive changes in behavior. By drawing on the principles of brain function and neurobiology, these interventions offer a scientifically validated framework for therapy, assisting clients in reshaping maladaptive patterns and forging new pathways toward recovery and well-being.

Employers: Refer to individuals, organizations, or entities that recruit and compensate individuals for performing designated tasks or roles within a business or institution. They are tasked with managing the workforce, providing salaries or wages, and ensuring that employees have access to the necessary resources and support to execute their responsibilities effectively. Employers are pivotal in defining organizational goals, policies, and expectations while promoting a productive and positive workplace culture. Furthermore, they bear legal responsibilities, such as ensuring fair compensation, complying with labor laws, and providing employee benefits. Proficient employers prioritize the well-being of their employees, support professional advancement, and foster inclusive workplaces, thereby enhancing job satisfaction, productivity, and the overall success of the organization.

Entrepreneurship: Defined as the process of initiating, developing, and managing a new business venture with the objective of generating profit, solving specific issues, or fulfilling market requirements. Entrepreneurs are skilled at spotting opportunities, innovating products or services, and taking calculated risks to bring their ideas to fruition. This endeavor involves securing necessary resources, crafting a robust business plan, and overcoming challenges within a competitive environment. Important qualities for entrepreneurs include creativity, resilience, adaptability, and strategic insight. The significance of entrepreneurship is evident in its contribution to economic expansion, job creation, and technological innovation by introducing new solutions, businesses, and sectors.

Family-Centered Interventions: Therapeutic methodologies that involve the participation of the entire family in addressing various challenges, promoting well-being, and cultivating healthy relationships. These interventions recognize the pivotal role that family dynamics, communication patterns, and support systems play in shaping an individual's development and behavior. The focus of family-centered interventions is to enhance familial ties, improve communication, and equip family members with the skills necessary to effectively manage conflicts and stressors. In environments such as mental health, education, or healthcare, these interventions strive to create a nurturing setting where all family members engage in problem-solving and decision-making. Techniques utilized may include family therapy, parental training, and collaborative goal-setting, with the overarching aim of empowering families to work in unison towards favorable outcomes for all individuals involved.

Maternal Substance Use: Refers to the intake or misuse of drugs or alcohol by a mother, whether during pregnancy or at other times. When a mother engages in substance use while pregnant, it can pose significant risks to the developing fetus, leading to issues such as low birth weight, premature delivery, or developmental disorders like Fetal Alcohol Spectrum Disorders (FASD). Following birth, a mother's substance use may impair her ability to provide stable care, which can negatively influence the child's emotional, cognitive, and social development. As a result, children may encounter neglect, challenges in forming secure attachments, or unstable living conditions, which can increase their risk of emotional or behavioral difficulties. Effectively addressing maternal substance use requires a comprehensive support system that includes addiction treatment, prenatal care, counseling, and family interventions aimed at promoting recovery, maternal health, and the healthy development of the child.

Motivation: The driving force, whether internal or external, that compels individuals to take action, pursue their ambitions, and maintain their efforts toward achieving those ambitions. It is a fundamental element in shaping behavior, influencing decisions, and determining the persistence with which a person works toward a specific goal. Motivation can be intrinsic, originating from personal interests, values, or a sense of satisfaction, or extrinsic, motivated by rewards, recognition, or external pressures. A strong sense of motivation results in heightened productivity, creativity, and resilience in overcoming challenges. Understanding the sources of motivation for individuals or teams is crucial for setting meaningful goals, providing support, and nurturing a positive environment. Motivation plays a vital role in education, the workplace, sports, and daily life, as it fuels passion, determination, and achievement.

Neurodiversity: A principle that acknowledges and appreciates the inherent variations in human brain function and cognitive processes. It asserts that neurological differences, including autism, ADHD, dyslexia, and similar conditions, should not be viewed as disorders requiring treatment, but rather as distinctive elements of human diversity. The neurodiversity movement promotes the perspective that these differences are valuable and essential components of human identity, advocating for inclusivity and acceptance. It challenges the conventional medical approach that categorizes neurodevelopmental conditions as deficits, instead focusing on individual strengths and unique viewpoints. Embracing neurodiversity entails fostering supportive environments, offering necessary accommodations, and cultivating respect for diverse cognitive experiences. This methodology encourages equality, diminishes stigma, and inspires individuals to recognize and celebrate their unique abilities and contributions to society.

Parental Engagement: Signifies the active participation of parents in their child's educational experience, development, and overall well-being. This involvement includes engaging in school functions, supporting educational activities at home, attending parent-teacher conferences, and maintaining dialogue with educators. Such engagement not only enhances the parent-child relationship but also boosts academic success and fosters social-emotional development. When parents are involved, children are more inclined to be motivated, self-assured, and successful in their studies. Schools and communities can encourage parental engagement by creating inclusive opportunities for parents to collaborate, offer feedback, and assist in their child's growth. Effective parental engagement is built on trust, transparent communication, and a mutual commitment to the child's holistic development.

Paternal Substance Use: Refers to the use or abuse of drugs or alcohol by a father or father figure. This issue can have considerable repercussions on the family's well-being, especially concerning the development of children and the overall family dynamics. The presence of paternal substance use may result in financial instability, emotional neglect, and strained relationships among family members. Furthermore, it can increase the risk of children facing behavioral, emotional, or substance-related problems due to genetic predispositions or exposure to negative role models. Addressing this issue often requires a multifaceted approach, which includes substance abuse treatment, counseling, and family support services. The goal of effective interventions is to restore healthy family functioning, strengthen the bond between father and child, and foster positive behavioral changes.

Project Management: The systematic approach of planning, organizing, and supervising tasks and resources to accomplish specific objectives within a predetermined timeline and budget. This discipline involves the coordination of diverse activities, risk management, and the assurance that project goals are achieved effectively. The responsibilities of a project manager include defining the project scope, establishing clear milestones, allocating resources appropriately, monitoring progress, and addressing any challenges that may arise. Successful project management necessitates robust leadership, effective communication, and adept problem-solving skills to synchronize team efforts and keep focus on essential deliverables. It is extensively applied across various sectors to implement projects such as product development, infrastructure projects, research endeavors, or business initiatives. The primary aim of project management is to achieve successful results while fulfilling stakeholder expectations and upholding quality standards.

Self-Acceptance: Refers to the capacity to fully embrace oneself, recognizing both personal strengths and weaknesses, as well as imperfections, without succumbing to excessive self-criticism or judgment. This process entails cultivating a realistic perception of one's identity and accepting these characteristics unconditionally, rather than aspiring to an unattainable ideal. The practice of self-acceptance contributes to a positive self-image, emotional resilience, and inner tranquility, empowering individuals to transcend negative self-views and concentrate on personal development. It is essential for fostering self-esteem and overall well-being, as it nurtures self-compassion, alleviates anxiety, and encourages a life of authenticity. The journey toward self-acceptance requires confronting negative beliefs, viewing setbacks as opportunities for growth, and celebrating one's individuality. This foundation allows individuals to form more meaningful relationships, pursue their ambitions with confidence, and live in alignment with their true selves.

Shared Decision-Making: A joint approach in which individuals or groups, including professionals and stakeholders, collaborate to make well-informed choices. In various settings such as education, healthcare, or community initiatives, this process involves engaging key participants—like students, patients, families, or colleagues—in the decision-making journey. This method values the input of all contributors, fostering mutual understanding, respect, and shared accountability for the outcomes. By merging professional expertise with individual preferences and values, Shared Decision-Making enables decisions that resonate with the interests and well-being of all stakeholders. It encourages open communication, transparency, and active involvement, leading to decisions that are better informed and more readily accepted, thus reinforcing trust and commitment within teams, families, or communities.

Solution-Focused Perspectives: Prioritize the identification and enhancement of an individual's inherent strengths and resources to devise practical solutions for current difficulties. Instead of extensively exploring past issues or underlying causes, this methodology emphasizes the visualization of positive outcomes and the implementation of small, attainable steps toward those goals. Such perspectives are frequently applied in brief therapeutic frameworks, such as Solution-Focused Brief Therapy (SFBT), where clients and therapists work collaboratively to establish clear objectives, reflect on successful past experiences, and formulate actionable plans. Essential techniques include posing future-oriented inquiries, recognizing exceptions to existing problems, and underscoring progress. This approach empowers individuals to take charge of their circumstances, fostering hope, confidence, and resilience in overcoming challenges and realizing desired transformations.

Strengths-Based Interventions: Prioritize the identification and application of an individual's innate strengths, talents, and resources to facilitate positive transformation and enhance well-being. Rather than concentrating solely on deficits or challenges, these interventions aim to empower individuals by acknowledging their capabilities, resilience, and previous achievements. This methodology promotes self-efficacy, bolsters confidence, and assists individuals in formulating strategies to reach their objectives by harnessing their strengths. In practical terms, a strengths-based approach can be implemented in various fields such as counseling, education, social work, or rehabilitation, where professionals collaborate with clients to establish attainable goals and utilize their strengths. By redirecting attention from weaknesses to abilities, strengths-based interventions cultivate a more hopeful and proactive outlook, thereby increasing motivation and resilience in overcoming obstacles.

APPENDIX I: STUDY QUESTIONNAIRE

Table 3. Teachers' and parents' perspectives on the solutions to challenges in the career transition of students with ADHD questionnaire (TPPSCCTSAQ)

No.	Statements	SD	D	UD	A	SA
1	Teachers should receive adequate training to support students with ADHD in career transitions.					
2	Parents should be involved in planning career transition strategies for students with ADHD.					
3	Schools should provide sufficient resources for career counseling tailored to students with ADHD.					
4	Collaboration between teachers, parents and employers in supporting career transitions is one approach that will help resolve career transition challenges.					
5	Students with ADHD should be given adequate access to mentorship programs during career transition.					
6	Individualized Education Plans can help address career transition needs for students with ADHD.					
7	Teachers should be made aware of the specific career challenges faced by students with ADHD.					
8	Schools should offer workshops for parents on supporting career transitions for students with ADHD.					
9	Career transition programs should be tailored to the unique needs of students with ADHD.					
10	Students with ADHD should be given adequate support in developing job-related skills.					
11	Schools should have partnerships with local businesses for internships for students with ADHD.					
12	Teachers should use effective communication strategies with ADHD students to discuss about career options.					
13	Parents should be confident in supporting their child's career transition.					
14	Schools should provide information on career paths suitable for students with ADHD.					
15	Students with ADHD should be encouraged to explore a variety of career options.					
16	Teachers should seek feedback from parents regarding career transition strategies they consider appropriate for students with ADHD.					
17	Schools should periodically evaluate the effectiveness of career transition programs for students with ADHD.					
18	Parents should identify with the school's support team for input concerning their child's career transition.					
19	Students with ADHD should be exposed to career assessments that consider their unique strengths.					
20	Schools should provide follow-up support after students with ADHD transition to careers.					
21	Teachers should be proactive in identifying the career interests of students with ADHD.					
22	Parents and teachers should collaborate on setting realistic career goals for students with ADHD.					
23	Schools should provide technology aids to support students with ADHD in their career transitions.					

No.	Statements	SD	D	UD	A	SA
24	Students with ADHD should be prepared for the social aspects of the workplace.					
25	Teachers and parents should be given more access to career development resources for supporting the career transitions of students with ADHD.					

SD=Strongly Disagree, D=Disagree, UD=Undecided, A=Agree, SA=Strongly Agree

APPENDIX II: ADDITIONAL STATISTICS

Table 4. Item-total statistics

No.	Statements	Cronbach's Alpha if Item Deleted
1	Teachers should receive adequate training to support students with ADHD in career transitions.	.581
2	Parents should be involved in planning career transition strategies for students with ADHD.	.598
3	Schools should provide sufficient resources for career counseling tailored to students with ADHD.	.581
4	Collaboration between teachers, parents and employers in supporting career transitions is one approach that will help resolve career transition challenges.	.598
5	Students with ADHD should be given adequate access to mentorship programs during career transition.	.665
6	Individualized Education Plans can help address career transition needs for students with ADHD.	.601
7	Teachers should be made aware of the specific career challenges faced by students with ADHD.	.581
8	Schools should offer workshops for parents on supporting career transitions for students with ADHD.	.598
9	Career transition programs should be tailored to the unique needs of students with ADHD.	.625
10	Students with ADHD should be given adequate support in developing job-related skills.	.647
11	Schools should have partnerships with local businesses for internships for students with ADHD.	.635
12	Teachers should use effective communication strategies with ADHD students to discuss about career options.	.639
13	Parents should be confident in supporting their child's career transition.	.636
14	Schools should provide information on career paths suitable for students with ADHD.	.656
15	Students with ADHD should be encouraged to explore a variety of career options.	.629
16	Teachers should seek feedback from parents regarding career transition strategies they consider appropriate for students with ADHD.	.653
17	Schools should periodically evaluate the effectiveness of career transition programs for students with ADHD.	.641
18	Parents should identify with the school's support team for input concerning their child's career transition.	.662
19	Students with ADHD should be exposed to career assessments that consider their unique strengths.	.641
20	Schools should provide follow-up support after students with ADHD transition to careers.	.620

continued on following page

Table 4. Continued

No.	Statements	Cronbach's Alpha if Item Deleted
21	Teachers should be proactive in identifying the career interests of students with ADHD.	.659
22	Parents and teachers should collaborate on setting realistic career goals for students with ADHD.	.658
23	Schools should provide technology aids to support students with ADHD in their career transitions.	.663
24	Students with ADHD should be prepared for the social aspects of the workplace.	.642
25	Teachers and parents should be given more access to career development resources for supporting the career transitions of students with ADHD.	.668

Table 5. Communalities (extraction method: principal component analysis)

No.	Statements	Extraction
1	Teachers should receive adequate training to support students with ADHD in career transitions.	.938
2	Parents should be involved in planning career transition strategies for students with ADHD.	.964
3	Schools should provide sufficient resources for career counseling tailored to students with ADHD.	.938
4	Collaboration between teachers, parents and employers in supporting career transitions is one approach that will help resolve career transition challenges.	.964
5	Students with ADHD should be given adequate access to mentorship programs during career transition.	.688
6	Individualized Education Plans can help address career transition needs for students with ADHD.	.721
7	Teachers should be made aware of the specific career challenges faced by students with ADHD.	.938
8	Schools should offer workshops for parents on supporting career transitions for students with ADHD.	.964
9	Career transition programs should be tailored to the unique needs of students with ADHD.	.755
10	Students with ADHD should be given adequate support in developing job-related skills.	.746
11	Schools should have partnerships with local businesses for internships for students with ADHD.	.909
12	Teachers should use effective communication strategies with ADHD students to discuss about career options.	.848
13	Parents should be confident in supporting their child's career transition.	.825
14	Schools should provide information on career paths suitable for students with ADHD.	.892
15	Students with ADHD should be encouraged to explore a variety of career options.	.830
16	Teachers should seek feedback from parents regarding career transition strategies they consider appropriate for students with ADHD.	.745
17	Schools should periodically evaluate the effectiveness of career transition programs for students with ADHD.	.841
18	Parents should identify with the school's support team for input concerning their child's career transition.	.885

continued on following page

Table 5. Continued

No.	Statements	Extraction
19	Students with ADHD should be exposed to career assessments that consider their unique strengths.	.756
20	Schools should provide follow-up support after students with ADHD transition to careers.	.779
21	Teachers should be proactive in identifying the career interests of students with ADHD.	.610
22	Parents and teachers should collaborate on setting realistic career goals for students with ADHD.	.871
23	Schools should provide technology aids to support students with ADHD in their career transitions.	.729
24	Students with ADHD should be prepared for the social aspects of the workplace.	.804
25	Teachers and parents should be given more access to career development resources for supporting the career transitions of students with ADHD.	.795

About the Authors

Boitumelo Molebogeng Diale is a Professor of Educational Psychology and the current Dean of the Faculty of Education at Sol Plaatje University, Kimberley, Northern Cape, South Africa. Her enthusiasm for career transitions particularly extends to youth, with a specific focus on those with neurodiversity. She holds the position of Visiting Professor at the University of Nigeria, Nsukka. Previously, she co-coordinated the Centre for Neurodiversity at the University of Johannesburg, located at the Soweto Campus, where she concentrated on facilitating career transitions for individuals with neurodiversity within the community.

Chiedu Eseadi serves as a Senior Lecturer in the Department of Educational Psychology at the University of Johannesburg, South Africa. His research focuses on career transition and disabilities, mental health and career counselling. Dr Eseadi was a Postdoctoral Research Fellow at the University of Johannesburg during the period of the project which led to this book. Dr Eseadi is currently an NRF-rated researcher.

Index

A

Abia State 8, 80, 81, 85, 96, 98, 200, 204, 208, 216, 218

ADHD 1, 2, 3, 4, 5, 6, 8, 9, 10, 11, 12, 13, 14, 15, 16, 17, 18, 19, 20, 21, 22, 23, 24, 25, 26, 27, 28, 29, 30, 32, 36, 37, 38, 39, 40, 41, 42, 43, 44, 45, 46, 47, 48, 49, 51, 52, 53, 54, 55, 56, 57, 58, 59, 60, 62, 63, 64, 65, 66, 70, 73, 74, 75, 77, 78, 79, 80, 81, 82, 83, 84, 86, 87, 88, 89, 90, 91, 92, 93, 94, 96, 97, 99, 100, 101, 102, 103, 108, 109, 110, 111, 113, 114, 115, 116, 117, 118, 119, 122, 123, 124, 125, 126, 127, 128, 129, 130, 131, 132, 133, 134, 135, 136, 137, 138, 139, 140, 141, 142, 143, 144, 145, 146, 147, 148, 149, 150, 151, 155, 157, 158, 159, 161, 162, 163, 164, 165, 166, 168, 169, 170, 172, 173, 174, 175, 176, 177, 178, 179, 180, 181, 182, 183, 184, 185, 186, 187, 188, 190, 192, 194, 195, 196, 197, 198, 199, 200, 201, 202, 204, 206, 207, 208, 209, 210, 211, 212, 213, 214, 215, 216, 217, 218, 219, 220, 221, 222, 223, 224, 225, 226, 227, 228, 229, 230, 231, 232, 239, 240, 241, 243, 244, 245, 246, 247, 248, 250, 251, 252, 253, 254, 255, 256, 257, 258, 259, 260, 261, 262, 263, 264, 265, 266, 267, 268, 269, 270, 271, 272, 273, 274, 275, 276, 278, 280, 281, 282, 283, 284, 285, 286, 287, 288, 289, 291, 292, 293, 295, 296, 297, 299, 300, 301, 304, 306, 307, 308, 309, 310, 311, 312, 313, 314, 315, 316, 323, 324, 325, 327, 328, 329, 330, 331, 332, 333, 335, 336, 337, 338, 339, 340, 341, 342, 343, 344, 345, 346, 347, 348, 349, 350, 351, 352, 353, 354, 360, 361, 362, 363, 364, 365, 366, 367, 368, 371, 372, 374, 375, 376, 377, 378, 379, 380, 381, 382, 383, 384, 385, 386, 387, 388, 389, 390, 391, 392, 393, 395, 399, 400, 401, 402, 403

assessment tools 243, 244, 245, 246, 247, 248, 249, 250, 251, 252, 253, 254, 255, 256, 257, 258, 267, 268, 272, 273, 274, 275, 280, 281

C

career 1, 2, 3, 4, 5, 6, 8, 9, 10, 11, 12, 13, 14, 15, 16, 17, 18, 19, 20, 21, 23, 24, 27, 30, 31, 36, 37, 38, 39, 40, 41, 42, 43, 44, 45, 46, 47, 48, 49, 51, 52, 53, 54, 55, 56, 58, 61, 62, 63, 67, 68, 71, 72, 73, 74, 75, 77, 78, 80, 81, 82, 83, 84, 86, 87, 88, 89, 90, 91, 92, 93, 94, 96, 100, 101, 102, 103, 105, 109, 110, 111, 113, 117, 118, 119, 122, 123, 124, 125, 126, 127, 128, 132, 135, 143, 155, 156, 157, 158, 159, 161, 162, 163, 164, 165, 169, 170, 172, 173, 174, 175, 177, 186, 187, 188, 189, 194, 195, 196, 197, 199, 200, 201, 204, 205, 206, 207, 208, 210, 212, 214, 218, 233, 235, 239, 240, 241, 243, 245, 246, 247, 248, 249, 250, 251, 252, 253, 254, 255, 256, 258, 260, 262, 280, 281, 282, 283, 284, 285, 286, 287, 288, 289, 290, 291, 292, 293, 294, 295, 296, 297, 298, 299, 300, 301, 302, 303, 304, 305, 306, 307, 308, 309, 310, 311, 312, 313, 314, 315, 316, 317, 318, 319, 320, 321, 322, 323, 324, 325, 327, 328, 329, 330, 331, 332, 333, 335, 336, 337, 338, 339, 340, 341, 342, 343, 344, 345, 346, 347, 348, 349, 351, 352, 355, 356, 358, 360, 361, 362, 363, 364, 365, 366, 367, 368, 371, 372, 373, 374, 375, 376, 377, 378, 379, 381, 382, 384, 385, 386, 387, 393, 399, 400, 401, 402, 403

counseling models 41, 283, 285, 286, 287, 288, 289, 291, 292, 293, 294, 295, 296,

297, 319, 320, 323, 324, 325
counseling theories 39, 40, 43, 44, 45, 47, 48, 49, 51, 52, 53, 55, 57, 73, 74, 75, 299
counselors 18, 28, 30, 36, 37, 38, 39, 40, 41, 42, 43, 44, 45, 46, 47, 48, 49, 51, 52, 53, 54, 55, 56, 57, 58, 59, 60, 61, 62, 63, 64, 67, 68, 69, 70, 72, 73, 97, 113, 116, 117, 118, 119, 121, 122, 123, 124, 125, 126, 127, 128, 129, 131, 132, 140, 154, 155, 157, 158, 159, 193, 201, 219, 237, 239, 240, 241, 246, 256, 280, 281, 282, 283, 285, 286, 287, 288, 289, 290, 291, 292, 293, 294, 295, 296, 297, 298, 299, 300, 301, 303, 304, 305, 306, 309, 312, 313, 316, 317, 318, 319, 321, 322, 323, 328, 346

E

educational psychologists 161, 162, 163, 164, 165, 166, 168, 170, 171, 172, 173, 174, 175, 176, 177, 178, 179, 181, 186, 191, 193, 194

I

inclusive schoolteachers 1, 2, 4, 5, 6, 8, 10, 11, 13, 14, 16, 17, 85, 92, 96, 121

P

perceived effectiveness 94, 117, 118, 122, 124, 125, 126, 132, 197, 200, 204, 207, 208, 210, 224, 243, 246, 247, 251, 253, 254, 255, 256, 257, 258, 280
practice guidelines 131, 161, 162, 163, 164, 165, 166, 168, 169, 170, 172, 173, 174, 175, 177, 180, 181, 183, 185, 189, 194, 195, 196
psychological interventions 113, 114, 115, 116, 117, 118, 119, 122, 123, 124, 125, 126, 127, 128, 130, 131, 132, 135, 139, 157, 158, 159, 173

S

school 1, 2, 3, 4, 6, 9, 11, 12, 15, 16, 17, 18, 20, 21, 22, 23, 24, 25, 26, 27, 28, 29, 30, 32, 35, 36, 37, 38, 39, 40, 41, 42, 43, 44, 45, 46, 47, 48, 49, 51, 52, 53, 54, 55, 56, 57, 58, 59, 60, 61, 62, 63, 64, 65, 66, 69, 70, 71, 72, 73, 77, 78, 81, 82, 90, 91, 92, 93, 94, 95, 98, 101, 102, 104, 109, 110, 111, 113, 114, 115, 116, 117, 118, 119, 121, 123, 124, 125, 126, 127, 128, 130, 131, 132, 133, 134, 135, 136, 137, 138, 139, 140, 141, 142, 143, 144, 146, 148, 149, 150, 151, 152, 154, 155, 161, 162, 163, 164, 170, 172, 173, 174, 175, 176, 177, 178, 179, 180, 181, 182, 183, 184, 185, 186, 188, 191, 193, 197, 198, 199, 200, 201, 204, 205, 206, 207, 208, 209, 210, 211, 212, 213, 214, 215, 216, 217, 218, 219, 221, 222, 223, 224, 225, 227, 228, 229, 231, 232, 233, 234, 235, 239, 240, 241, 243, 244, 245, 246, 247, 249, 251, 253, 254, 256, 258, 259, 261, 262, 263, 264, 266, 269, 270, 283, 284, 285, 286, 287, 288, 290, 292, 293, 294, 295, 296, 297, 298, 299, 301, 302, 303, 304, 306, 308, 312, 313, 314, 315, 316, 317, 321, 322, 327, 328, 330, 335, 341, 342, 343, 344, 345, 346, 347, 348, 349, 352, 360, 361, 362, 363, 366, 367, 371, 372, 376, 380, 381, 382, 384, 385, 386, 387, 389, 390, 391, 396, 399, 401, 402
social cognitive 5, 19, 20, 23, 25, 27, 40, 58, 73, 74, 75, 180, 248, 259, 287, 300, 302
South Africa 7, 45, 84, 120, 163, 167, 177, 178, 202, 250, 289, 334, 347, 349, 369
special needs 14, 25, 28, 40, 54, 57, 59, 79, 80, 96, 97, 99, 130, 191, 225, 227, 274, 312
students 1, 2, 3, 4, 5, 6, 8, 9, 10, 11, 12, 13, 14, 15, 16, 17, 18, 19, 20, 21, 22, 23, 24, 26, 28, 29, 30, 32, 33, 34, 35, 36,

37, 38, 39, 40, 41, 42, 43, 44, 45, 46, 47, 48, 49, 51, 52, 53, 54, 55, 56, 57, 58, 59, 61, 62, 63, 64, 65, 66, 69, 70, 71, 72, 73, 74, 75, 77, 78, 79, 80, 81, 82, 83, 84, 86, 87, 88, 89, 90, 91, 92, 93, 94, 95, 96, 97, 98, 99, 100, 101, 102, 104, 105, 106, 108, 109, 110, 111, 113, 114, 115, 116, 117, 118, 119, 122, 123, 124, 125, 126, 127, 128, 129, 130, 131, 132, 133, 135, 136, 137, 138, 139, 140, 141, 143, 147, 150, 152, 153, 154, 155, 157, 158, 159, 161, 162, 163, 164, 165, 166, 168, 169, 170, 172, 173, 174, 175, 177, 180, 181, 182, 184, 185, 188, 189, 191, 193, 194, 195, 196, 197, 198, 199, 200, 201, 202, 204, 206, 207, 208, 209, 210, 211, 212, 213, 214, 215, 217, 218, 220, 222, 223, 224, 225, 226, 227, 228, 230, 231, 232, 233, 235, 236, 239, 240, 241, 243, 244, 245, 246, 247, 248, 249, 250, 251, 252, 253, 254, 255, 256, 257, 258, 260, 261, 262, 263, 264, 265, 266, 268, 269, 270, 272, 274, 277, 280, 281, 282, 283, 284, 285, 286, 287, 288, 289, 291, 292, 293, 294, 295, 296, 297, 298, 299, 300, 301, 302, 303, 304, 305, 307, 308, 309, 310, 312, 313, 314, 316, 317, 319, 321, 322, 323, 324, 325, 327, 328, 329, 330, 331, 332, 333, 335, 336, 337, 338, 339, 340, 341, 342, 343, 344, 345, 346, 347, 349, 351, 353, 360, 361, 362, 363, 364, 365, 366, 367, 368, 371, 372, 374, 375, 376, 377, 378, 379, 381, 383, 384, 385, 386, 387, 388, 397, 399, 400, 401, 402, 403

support services 32, 70, 80, 155, 164, 174, 197, 198, 199, 200, 201, 202, 204, 206, 207, 208, 209, 210, 211, 212, 214, 217, 223, 239, 360, 361, 362, 396

T

teachers 1, 2, 3, 4, 5, 6, 8, 9, 10, 11, 12, 13, 14, 15, 16, 17, 19, 20, 21, 22, 23, 24, 25, 26, 27, 33, 34, 35, 36, 40, 52, 53, 56, 61, 64, 65, 66, 72, 73, 74, 75, 77, 78, 79, 81, 82, 83, 84, 86, 87, 88, 89, 90, 91, 92, 93, 94, 95, 96, 97, 98, 99, 100, 109, 110, 111, 113, 114, 116, 117, 118, 119, 122, 123, 124, 125, 126, 127, 128, 129, 130, 131, 132, 134, 136, 137, 138, 139, 141, 142, 143, 145, 152, 157, 158, 159, 163, 177, 179, 189, 191, 193, 209, 211, 216, 223, 233, 234, 239, 240, 241, 246, 257, 260, 270, 303, 309, 312, 316, 327, 328, 329, 330, 331, 332, 333, 335, 336, 337, 338, 339, 340, 341, 342, 344, 345, 346, 349, 352, 360, 361, 362, 363, 365, 366, 367, 368, 371, 372, 373, 374, 375, 376, 377, 378, 379, 381, 382, 383, 384, 385, 387, 388, 399, 400, 401, 402, 403

teachers' perspectives 1, 2, 4, 5, 9, 10, 11, 12, 13, 16, 17, 25, 36, 77, 81, 83, 84, 86, 88, 89, 90, 91, 109, 113, 117, 118, 122, 125, 132, 141, 157

t-test analysis 51, 124, 125, 126